LONGSTREET HIGHROAD MOUNTAIN GUIDES

LONGSTREET HIGHROAD GUIDE
——— TO THE ———

WASHINGTON
CASCADES

BY ALLAN MAY

LONGSTREET
ATLANTA, GEORGIA

Published by
LONGSTREET PRESS, INC.
a subsidiary of Cox Newspapers,
a subsidiary of Cox Enterprises, Inc.
2140 Newmarket Parkway
Suite 122
Marietta, Georgia 30067

Great efforts have been made to make the information in this book as accurate as possible.
However, over time trails are rerouted and signs and landmarks may change. If you find a
change has occurred to a trail in the book, please let us know so we can correct future editions.
A word of caution: Outdoor recreation by its nature is potentially hazardous. All participants in
such activities must assume all responsibility for their own actions and safety. The scope of this
book does not cover all potential hazards and risks involved in outdoor recreation activities.

Printed by RR Donnelley & Sons, Harrisonburg, VA

1st printing 1999

Library of Congress Catalog Number 99-61768

ISBN: 1-56352-536-4

Book editing, design, and cartography by Lenz Design & Communications, Inc., Decatur, Georgia

Cover illustration by Harry Fenn, *Picturesque America*, 1872

Cover design by Richard J. Lenz, Decatur, Georgia

Illustrations by Danny Woodard, Loganville, Georgia

Photographs: Pages 27, 45, 77, 80, 189, and 227 by Allan May. Pages 1, 9, and 293 courtesy of
Mount St. Helens National Volcanic Monument. Pages ix, 22, 123, 129, 170, and 179 by John
Pawley, USFS. Pages 257 (photo by Dan Miller), 282 top (photo by Richard P. Hoblitt), 282
bottom (photo by Michael P. Doukas), and 285 (photo by Phil Carpenter) courtesy of the
United States Department of the Interior, U.S. Geological Survey, David A. Johnston Cascades
Volcano Observatory, Vancouver, Washington.

…Our camp was pitched on a high knoll crowned by a grove of balsam firs, near a turbulent glacial torrent. About nine o'clock, after we had laid down for the night, the firs round our camp took fire and suddenly burst out in a vivid conflagration. The night was dark and windy, and the scene—the vast dim outlines of Takhoma (Mount Rainier), the white snow fields, the roaring torrent, the crackling blaze of the burning trees—was strikingly wild and picturesque…

…Hastening forward in this way along the dizzy, narrow, and precarious ledge, we reached at length the highest point. Sheltered behind a pinnacle of ice we rested a moment, took out our flags and fastened them upon the Alpine staffs, and then, standing erect in the furious blast, waved them in triumph with three cheers.

—Hazard Stevens, who, in 1870, with Philemon Beecher Van Trump, was the first to reach the peak of Mount Rainier, highest of Washington's Cascades. From *The Ascent of Takhoma*, Hazard Stevens. *Atlantic Monthly*, November, 1876.

Contents

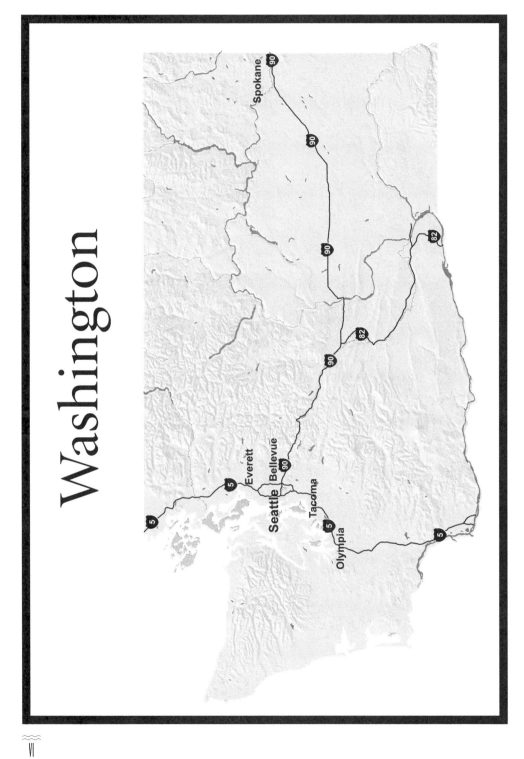

Washington

How Your Highroad Guide is Organized

How To Use Your Highroad Guide

T he *Longstreet Highroad Guide to the Cascade Mountains of Washington* includes a broad array of details about the range's best attractions, including
physical descriptions of the mountains and forests and a scientific overview of
how they got that way. It also is a guide to hiking, camping, fishing, hunting, mountain biking; all-terrain vehicle and horse trails; and other attractions, as well as
factual descriptions of the flora and fauna of the wild places of the Cascades. It is
designed to give the reader the basis for becoming more acquainted with the mountains and all they offer.

The mountains are managed primarily by four national forests and two national
parks, with smaller areas under the jurisdiction of the State Department of Natural
Resources and State Parks Commission. There are chapters on each of the federal
jurisdictions and the land they manage as well as references to nearby state facilities
that complement them. The book begins with a chapter on the natural history of the
mountains and then describes each of
the jurisdictions, beginning at the
northern extreme of the state adjacent to
the Canadian border and working
southward to the Oregon border at the
Columbia River. It ends with descriptions of some of the best specific long
hikes, including the 500-mile Washington portion of the Cascade Crest National
Scenic Trail that covers the entire width
of the United States from Canada to
Mexico.

Maps in the book are intended to
orient casual and expert visitors. Below
is a legend explaining the symbols on the
maps. Before venturing into the backcountry, visitors should obtain supple-
mental maps from the national forest or
national park they intend to visit. It also
is advisable to obtain a Green Trails Map
and a U.S. Geological Survey topographical

Stevens Pass.

Boulder River Falls.

map of the appropriate area. They are sold at the national park and national forest offices and at numerous stores specializing in outdoor merchandise.

The season when a trail or an area in the mountains opens or closes depends entirely on the weather and that can differ greatly from year to year. Any given trail may open in mid-spring one year and not until summer the next. Or snow may close it in the summer one year and not until mid-fall the next. In some cases a given trail may not open at all during a year. Trails that are listed in the book as being open in summer may actually be open before or after that season. The seasonal listings in the book should always be checked with a ranger.

In the mid-1990s, the Forest Service began experimenting with fees as a means for raising funds to maintain trails, campgrounds, and other amenities in Washington and Oregon. The experiment included requiring visitors to pay a fee for permits to park at trailheads. The permits were sold at Forest Service offices. If the experiment succeeds, the fees are to be made permanent. If it fails, the agency plans to find some other way to pay for public facilities. The decision was to be made during the year 2000 or later. For that reason, the notations at the end of trail descriptions in this book that say, "Trailhead fees may be charged" may no longer be valid when the experiment is concluded. In that case, there probably will be another set of fees. Check with a ranger for the latest information.

A major characteristic of the mountains is constant change, ranging from cataclysmic eruptions such as the one that removed the top quarter mile of Mount St. Helens in brief seconds in the spring of 1980, to the subtleties of a seldom-used trail being lost under the encroaching plants of a meadow. Then, too, the land managers may close old roads and trails and open new ones. It is always advisable to contact the agency in charge before visiting the mountains and forests.

Keep in mind, also, that mountains can be dangerous. Weather can change from sunny and warm to stormy and frigid in a matter of hours. Blizzards can occur at any time of the year. It is important that anyone venturing into the backcountry be equipped with what is widely known as the 10 essentials:

1. Extra clothing for bad weather.

2. Extra food.

3. Sunglasses suitable for the glare of snow.

4. Knife.

5. Fire starter such as candles or chemicals for igniting wet fuel.

6. First aid kit and knowledge of how to use it.

7. Matches in waterproof container.

8. Flashlight with extra batteries and bulbs.

9. Maps of area being visited.

10. Compass and the ability to understand it.

Streams in the mountains can be deceptive when they run high. Visitors should keep in mind that even a small one can have the force to sweep people, especially children, off their feet and carry them away. If in doubt turn back rather than risk a crossing.

The ethics of the mountains are fairly simple—leave no trace that you have been here. Camp and travel on durable surfaces. Carry out what you carried in. Properly dispose of what you can't carry out. Avoid damaging the natural setting. That is true throughout the mountains, but it is especially true in the wildernesses. Contact a ranger for specific instructions.

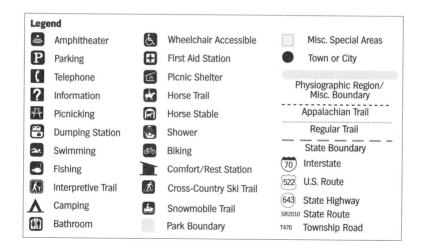

Legend		
Amphitheater	Wheelchair Accessible	Misc. Special Areas
Parking	First Aid Station	Town or City
Telephone	Picnic Shelter	
Information	Horse Trail	Physiographic Region/ Misc. Boundary
Picnicking	Horse Stable	Appalachian Trail
Dumping Station	Shower	Regular Trail
Swimming	Biking	State Boundary
Fishing	Comfort/Rest Station	70 Interstate
Interpretive Trail	Cross-Country Ski Trail	522 U.S. Route
Camping	Snowmobile Trail	643 State Highway
Bathroom	Park Boundary	SR2010 State Route
		T470 Township Road

Preface

I was raised in Illinois and New York, but when I was 23 years old I married an extremely delightful young redhead from Washington State. That was the best thing I ever did. More than a little dubiously, I let her persuade me we should live in her locale rather than mine. That was the next best.

It didn't take long for me to learn that the long spine of the Cascade Mountains that runs without interruption between the state's northern and southern borders was within a short drive of my new home and was both beautiful and awe inspiring.

We spent a great deal of time exploring the mountains, hiking, camping, climbing, skiing, biking, and taking the kids to places of raw, unspoiled beauty where they could experience nature much as it was in the beginning. They grew up knowing the trees of the forests, the flowers of the meadows, the rock and ice of the high country. And I learned and enjoyed with them.

Since I am a writer by both vocation and avocation, the mountains soon became one of my major subjects. My research brought me in contact with others who frequent the mountains, people who live and work there, people who play there, and people who spend their lives studying geology, botany, zoology, and other aspects of the mountains. They are, for the most part, as fascinating as the mountains themselves. They pile up sometimes conflicting information about their subjects that is as interesting and awesome as the mountains. They work hard to assimilate the information they acquire. Then they go back to collect more information in an ever-continuing quest to understand the mountains and their nature.

Their ultimate goal is to learn all there is to know about the Cascades. They'll never achieve that, of course, but the more they try, the more fascinating the game becomes. And the business of writing about them, the mountains they know and love, and the information they amass is a better, more satisfying existence than a mere mortal should expect. It is a job that I would be glad to do even if I didn't get paid.

I hope the publisher doesn't find out.

And profound thanks to the extremely delightful redhead.

—Allan May

Acknowledgments

So many people gave their valuable time and energy to this project that it is not possible to make a list without missing at least a few. But it would also be wrong to overlook entirely the debt they are owed so here is the incomplete list, with apologies to those who are not included.

My wife, Eleanor May, whose strong right arm and keen eye sustained and supported the book from beginning to end. Editors Pam Holliday and Richard Lenz, who kept us on the right track without losing patience. Marge McDonald, the Longstreet Press project director, who got us started. And Dave Workman, editor, friend, and hiking companion, who steered Marge in my direction. Then there is the vast horde of people who provided much of the information poured into the book: People like Mark Nesse, Dave Dilgard, Margaret Riddle, Vickie Grassl, Mary Allen, Marlin Olson, Cameron Johnson, Marge Bodre, Sue Selmer, Scott Condon, Ellen Chou, and Eileen Simmons, all of the Everett library staff, provided valuable help from the inner recesses of the library. Ron DeHart, Penny Custer, and Lorette Ray, of the Mount Baker-Snoqualmie National Forest, went out of their way to be helpful. Allan Gibbs of the Forest Service Northwest Regional office provided not only information about the region but hints on where to locate others who could help. Others who cheerfully helped with information and advice included Kim Mann and Dan Allen of the North Cascades National Park; Donna Carriker and Kristy Longanecker of the Okanogan National Forest Public Affairs Office and Dave Yenko, that forest's expert on snowmobiling and snowmobile trails; Powys Gadd of the Okanogan and Wenatchee national forests; John Robinson and Pam Young of the Skykomish Ranger District. Terry Skorheim, Rick Worthen, and Diane Holz of the Darrington Ranger District; Curtis Edwards and Jim Archambeault of the Methow Valley Ranger District; Shannon O'Brien of the Tonasket Ranger District; Paul Hart, Marty Ames, and Robin Demario, of the Wenatchee National Forest public affairs office; Debbie Kelly of the Cle Elum Ranger District; Randy McLandress of the Entiat Ranger District; Jim Bannister of the Cle Elum Ranger District; Greg Thayer of the Leavenworth Ranger District; Ken Frederick of the Chelan Ranger District; Terstin Burlingame, Ted Stout, Carol Spurling, Sheri Forbes, and Ralph Bell of the Mount Rainier National Park; Tom Knappenberger, Roger Peterson, and Linda Peterson of the Gifford Pinchot National Forest Public Affairs Office; and Mary Bean of the Mount Adams Ranger District.

—Allan May

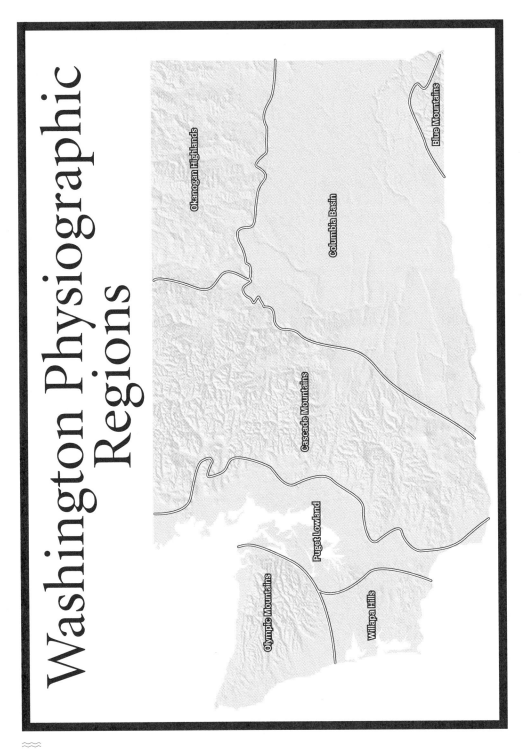

Washington Physiographic Regions

Okanogan Highlands

Blue Mountains

Columbia Basin

Cascade Mountains

Puget Lowland

Olympic Mountains

Willapa Hills

Natural History of Washington's Cascades

Washington's Cascade Mountains are a long, high, rocky spine that stretches from the state's northern Canadian border to Oregon in the south. It divides the state for its full length, separating it into two distinctive parts. The state west of the mountains has a mild, wet climate with a very different environment from the dry east side, where there is a wide swing from summer to winter temperatures.

From the beginning that has resulted in major differences in vegetation, wildlife, and even human cultures. Abundant resources from thick forests as well as salmon and other seafood made the original native peoples on the west side of the summit among the wealthiest hunter-gatherers of American prehistory. They lived much of their lives in permanent, split cedar homes and had the leisure to develop complex arts and crafts. Those on the east side fared less well. Resources were more difficult to come by in their parched land and they spent more time gathering basic food and materials as they

[*Above:* Big Creek Falls in the Mount St. Helens National Volcanic Monument]

Geologic Time Scale

Era	System & Period	Series & Epoch	Some Distinctive Features	Years Before Present
CENOZOIC	Quaternary	Recent	Modern man.	11,000
		Pleistocene	Early man; northern glaciation.	1/2 to 2 million
	Tertiary	Pliocene	Large carnivores.	13 ± 1 million
		Miocene	First abundant grazing mammals.	25 ± 1 million
		Oligocene	Large running mammals.	36 ± 2 million
		Eocene	Many modern types of mammals.	58 ± 2 million
		Paleocene	First placental mammals.	63 ± 2 million
MESOZOIC	Cretaceous		First flowering plants; climax of dinosaurs and ammonites, followed by Cretaceous-Tertiary extinction.	135 ± 5 million
	Jurassic		First birds, first mammals; dinosaurs and ammonites abundant.	181 ± 5 million
	Triassic		First dinosaurs. Abundant cycads and conifers.	230 ± 10 million
PALEOZOIC	Permian		Extinction of most kinds of marine animals, including trilobites. Southern glaciation.	280 ± 10 million
	Carboniferous	Pennsylvanian	Great coal forests, conifers. First reptiles.	310 ± 10 million
		Mississippian	Sharks and amphibians abundant. Large and numerous scale trees and seed ferns.	345 ± 10 million
	Devonian		First amphibians; ammonites; Fishes abundant.	405 ± 10 million
	Silurian		First terrestrial plants and animals.	425 ± 10 million
	Ordovician		First fishes; invertebrates dominant.	500 ± 10 million
	Cambrian		First abundant record of marine life; trilobites dominant.	600 ± 50 million
	Precambrian		Fossils extremely rare, consisting of primitive aquatic plants. Evidence of glaciation. Oldest dated algae, over 2,600 million years; oldest dated meteorites 4,500 million years.	

migrated in annual circuits, searching for seasonal food sources. They lived in relatively flimsy, temporary structures which they could carry from place to place.

Archeologists have found evidence that people occupied sites in what is now the North Cascades National Park during at least the past 8,400 years, with larger numbers coming in three distinct time periods. Most of the sites were temporary camps used by small groups of people who stopped in places ranging from the low valleys to above tree line. They have not found signs of large permanent villages but there may have been some.

The mountains separate different cultures in modern times, too. The gifted west side, with ample natural resources and transportation hubs, has developed heavily populated, industrial centers, while the east side depends heavily on agriculture such as orchards on the mountains' lower slopes and wheat and vegetables in the reclaimed desert of the lowlands.

Those different weather conditions are created by the mountains themselves. The prevailing winds come from the Pacific Ocean, bearing huge amounts of moisture they absorb from the sea. When they reach the mountains they are forced up over the slopes. As they rise they cool, and their moisture condenses and precipitates, providing the rain that has given Washington its nickname of the Evergreen State. When they reach the summit they start downward, become warm, and dry out, leaving half the Evergreen State ironically dry. In Everett, near the western foothills, for instance, precipitation during 1997 totaled 40.00 inches while just 100 miles to the east, in Wenatchee, the precipitation was only 9.46 inches.

An ancient Native American myth tells that the Ocean Spirit became angry at the selfish acts of a group of Indians so he built the Cascades to separate them from himself. Modern geologists' explanation for the mountains is also highly imaginative. They believe a process they call Plate Tectonics causes the land masses and ocean bottoms to float on the hot, plastic interior of the earth. During the course of millions of years, the sea bottom west of North America has, like a carrier belt, brought pieces of land from far away places to the continent, depositing many kinds of rock and adding to the continent's land mass. That left a vast mixture of different kinds of rock on the West Coast that make up today's mountains. They consist of the three basic types of rock — igneous that pushes up from the molten interior of the earth and hardens as it cools; sedimentary, made up of the sediments of silt, sand, and shells of sea creatures that once littered the bottoms of oceans and lakes and were pressed into hard stone by the weight of layers of other material that formed above them; and metamorphic, which is the other two rock types after they have been changed by heat and pressure far below the earth's surface. Thus, the crust where the Cascades are now consists of many layers of many kinds of rock from various parts of the world.

All of those ancient rocks laid in layers with the oldest at the bottom until the earth's forces raised them into mountains, which were eroded until they became flat plains called peneplains. Then they were raised and flattened several more times until what remained was a jumbled confusion of rock.

During the Tertiary Period, the forces of nature came into play again as the tectonic plates came together near the northwestern edge of the continent. One of them, the Juan de Fuca plate beneath the Pacific Ocean, is relatively small. It moves in a southeasterly direction, and where it meets the continent, it sinks under the land mass. All of this movement is measured in a few inches a year, rather slow, but over thousands of millennia a great deal of the Juan de Fuca plate is swallowed under the western edge of the continental plate. That creates unimaginable underground forces that during the past million years or so pushed upward hard enough to raise the rock layers above. The layers folded, bent, and broke, often at an angle that can still be seen in layered rock exposed in bare cliffs throughout the Cascades. Those geological faults guided glaciers that gouged out valleys that now are the lowlands of the mountains.

The result of the uplift process is the majority of the mountains that became Washington's Cascades. The higher ones, averaging 8,000 feet elevation, are in the north part of the state. Those in the south average about 3,500 feet.

But the uplifted mountains are only part of the story of the state's tectonic activities. Even today the pressures they create force molten rock up through fissures in the earth's mantle. Sometimes it hits an impervious layer below the surface and fills the void with intrusions of lava that hardens into new rock, a process that contributes to uplifting. But in the five places where Washington's volcanos have relatively recently formed, the forces have erupted onto the surface and spewed out lava and ash that, over time, formed layers. That happened again and again over the millennia, gradually building Washington's five volcanos, four of which — Baker, Glacier Peak, Adams, and Rainier, the highest at 14,411 feet — tower over their uplifted brothers. The fifth, Mount St. Helens, lost 1,313 feet of its peak in an eruption, shrinking it from 9,677 feet high, the fifth highest in the Washington Cascades, to 8,364 feet, less than some of its uplifted neighbors.

All that happened in brief moments on the balmy Sunday morning in 1980 when the peak crashed into the valley below in one of the most violent volcanic eruptions in this country's history. Despite its lost eminence, St. Helens still is an impressive mountain and it may eventually regain its position of dominance; later, small eruptions have built a lava dome in the crater that by 1998 had already reached more than 3,500 feet in diameter and 925 feet high. If that process continues, the mountain may, over time, again reach the heights of glory it once knew. In addition to St. Helens, all of Washington's volcanos still show signs of life, such as hot springs and steam vents, a situation that is brought to Washington residents' minds occasionally by earthquakes that shake their homes and work places to remind them that tectonic forces far beneath the surface are still active.

All of that is the fire part of the Cascades story. Ice is another part. It came in a series of ice ages that engulfed much of the earth repeatedly over a period of many millions of years. Geologists aren't sure how many there have been because each of them wiped out much of the evidence for those that came before. What is certain is that they had a major effect on the surface of the earth. They are a result of the earth's climate becoming cooler, possibly because of variations in the earth's orbit. During cold periods, summer heat isn't enough to melt all of the snow that falls in the winter, so it piles ever higher. The weight of new snow transforms the old snow beneath into ice and squishes it outward and downward into what we call glaciers. The most recent of those eras began at the beginning of the Quaternary Period, about 2.5 million years ago when ice ages were interspersed with warmer periods and huge ice caps advanced over much of the world, then retreated, then advanced again. There is some evidence that one of those periods occurred about 100,000 years ago, followed by the usual warmer period when the ice melted back for a time then returned in the most recent episode, which ended about 16,000 years ago. The ice sheet advanced down from the mountains in what is now Canada's province of British Columbia through the Straits of Georgia and the Fraser River valley. As it moved it gouged huge amounts of rock before it, bulldozing, for instance, the immense bowl which eventually became Puget Sound, the central element in the lives of the people who have lived in Western Washington ever since.

That major ice sheet carried rock composed of material found only in Canada far into Washington, depositing it there on mountains as much as 1 mile above sea level. That provides a clue as to how thick the ice was. The ice cap engulfed the northern Cascades, rounding off the tops of lower mountains and making other physical changes.

The Ice Age also saw smaller glaciers move down from the high peaks. The valleys originally had been left in a V shape when they were washed out by rivers, but the tremendous power of the glaciers concentrated on the bottom under the weight of the ice and carved out the lower sides of the valleys, leaving them in a broad, flat, U shape that is an earmark of glaciated valleys. One sign of this is what scientists call hanging waterfalls that may fall as much as hundreds of feet into glaciated valleys from the high ground above that escaped the icy bulldozer. Another sign is cirques, the circular, amphitheater-like rock formations at the heads of valleys near the mountain crest. They mark the high spot where glaciers began, carving out troughs in the rock as they pushed their way down the mountainside. Sometimes cirques formed opposite each other on both sides of mountain ridges. There the glaciers cut away both the sides of the mountains leaving depressions in the ridge called cols.

The glaciers also dammed rivers, forcing them to change course into another valley or to form lakes that left deep layers of sediment in the valley floor when they receded. Perhaps more significantly, when the glaciers reached their peak and began to retreat they sometimes left immense deposits of the rocks and sand they had been pushing before them in mounds and hills on the valley floors. Even today those deposits, called terminal moraines, can be a conspicuous part of the valley floor. Similarly, as the climate warmed, the rock walls of the valley collected heat and melted the ice beside it, providing another place for large deposits of debris, called lateral moraines. In some cases huge isolated remnants of ice remained after most of the glaciers had melted back. They were surrounded by sediment deposited by the melted water of the retreating ice flow and when they too melted away, they left large holes that became lakes.

Elk (*Cervus elaphus*)

These large, cloven-hoofed animals grow to 7 or 8 feet long with a tail that may make them about 6 inches longer. In the Cascades they are tan with a lighter patch on the rump. Fawns are spotted and adult males have antlers. They travel in herds much of the year, with male herds separated from the female groups. In the late summer, the bulls separate with the stronger ones forming harems of females and defending them from other bulls. Elk in the vicinity of Mount St. Helens have made a remarkable recovery from the disastrous eruption of 1980. That probably is the best place to see them in the Washington Cascades.

There is more to erosion than ice, of course. Wind blows sand and dust off high places and deposits them in low places. Rivers cut constantly at their edges and bottoms; sometimes the current of a fast stream rolls large rocks that thump and bang as they are pushed down the stream by the force of the water. Each thump and bang marks a crash of two or more rocks and the collisions result in small pieces of the rocks being broken off, especially on the corners, which have more exposure to the wearing process. That results in the bottom of the river being lined with what gardeners call river-rounded rocks that continue to roll and diminish in size as they roll toward the ocean.

The erosion means that the mountains are slowly wearing away, being washed out to sea by the many erosional forces. At the same time the earth forces that created them are continuing to operate, pushing them upward. It is a race, perhaps, but no one alive today will be here to see who wins.

Life Develops

The most recent continental ice flow receded from Washington about 16,000 years ago, leaving an empty landscape with very little vegetation or animal life. But new ecosystems moved into the void, providing the plant and animal communities with many life forms, including humans. Some of those life forms are now extinct, including the huge, elephant-like mastodon, which occupied the western Washington lowlands until it died out some 8,000 years ago. Other life forms flourished and expanded into the entire area from the sea-level coast to the mountain peaks in what became complex life systems. Ecologists have established distinct life zones designating specific elevations on the mountain slopes where the environment allows certain species to exist. The zones vary so much that they are of little use in a general description of a specific mountain or range, but they are based on the scientific fact that the environmental conditions change so much at different elevations that each has its own ecology of plants and wildlife.

Then, too, while today forests have become the most obvious vegetation on both the east and west sides of the Cascades, the climatic variations between the east and west sides make them so different from each other that scientists put them in different geographical zones, designating those on the east side as part of the Rocky Mountain Forest while they call those on the west side the West Coast Forest.

The most obvious species on the west side is the Douglas fir (*Pseudotsuga menziesii*), named after David Archibald Menzies, the first scientist to explore Washington. An evergreen, it grows wide, straight, and some 250 feet tall. It is abundant below 4,000 feet elevation. Its bark is up to 12 inches thick, a good defense against the fires that damage or kill other species. That gives it an immense advantage and makes it the dominant tree in the forest.

It is an interesting anomaly that the Douglas fir is not truly a fir tree. Its cones hang down from the branch. Cones on other trees that bear the name fir, such as grand fir, subalpine fir, Pacific silver fir, and noble fir, point upwards from the branch. Scientifically, they are considered members of the Abies family and are collectively known as true firs.

ELK

(*Cervus elaphus*)
Also called "wapiti" — the Indian word for "white" — referring to the light color of the animal's rump, elk herds are distributed through mountain forests and valleys in the West.

Botanists have long been baffled about what to call the Douglas fir. One of the early botanists called it a Douglas spruce, but the literature of the 1800s classified it as a true fir, and as a hemlock. It also has been classified as an Oregon pine, and as a *Pseudotsuga douglasii* in honor of botanist David Douglas. That was changed to *Pseudotsuga taxifolia*, meaning false hemlock with leaves like the yew tree.

Finally, at least for now, the tree was renamed *Pseudotsuga menziesii*, after Dr. Archibald Menzies, the Scottish naturalist who recorded the earliest discovery of the species when he found it growing on the coast of British Columbia's Vancouver Island in 1791.

Whatever it is called, Douglas fir is a magnificent, tall, vigorous evergreen, with thick, corklike bark and a dense crown. It is beautiful whether growing individually or in the forest. It provides excellent structural lumber and is popular as a yard decoration and as a Christmas tree.

The Douglas fir, however, is only the next to last in the forest succession that begins after an old forest has been destroyed by fire, disease, insect infestation, wind storm, or logging. The first step in that succession often is the ubiquitous plant called, appropriately, fireweed (*Epilobium angustifolium*). It may be accompanied by plants such as lupine (*Lupinus latifolius*), beargrass (*Xerophyllum tenax*), and snow-brush (*Ceanothus velutinus*) but the fireweed is often first and thickest. The fireweed plant produces numerous seeds equipped with long soft hairs that catch the wind and travel great distances. It may subsist in the dark forest floor in a weakened condition until the fire clears the overstory, allowing the sun to bring it to robust life. Sometimes for years, after the forest is gone fireweed will cover vast areas each year, its flowers painting the entire field a light purple. Other early plants in the succession include bracken fern (*Pteridium aquilinum*) and small woody plants such as thimble-berry (*Rubus spectabilis*), Pacific wild blackberry (*rubus ursinus*), or one of a variety of blueberries (*Vaccinium* spp.), which often are called huckleberry after the similar East Coast berry with that common name (*Gaylussacia* spp.). The blueberries not only provide a delicious snack for hungry bears and weary hikers, but also when its leaves turn in the fall, the blueberry colors vast slopes a brilliant, spectacular russet.

The short woody plants are eventually replaced in the forest succession by low deciduous trees such as the red alder (*Alnus rubra*), which has a relatively short life span and grows only about 100 feet high, but it is similar to legumes which take nitrogen from the air and store it in nodules on the roots. That fertilizes the soil for later plants. The wood of a freshly cut red alder turns a bright red color and Native Americans used it for red dye.

Eventually the early plants in the succession give way to forest giants such as the Douglas fir, which dominates the forest in vast numbers so thickly that the sun rarely seeps through to the forest floor. That in the long run spells the Douglas fir's own demise. Unable to thrive without bright sun, the Douglas fir's seeds sprout but the saplings soon wither and die. Meantime western hemlock (*Tsuga heterophylla*), which is tolerant of shade, sprouts from seeds possibly carried in by birds or animals. It grows slowly but in good health in the shade until storm, disease, or some other calamity kills out part of the fir forest. Then the hemlock saplings, already well established, shoot up, growing faster than the firs. Soon they have established themselves as the climax of the succession. Their thin bark gives them little protection from fire so they maintain that position only until the next major blaze fells them and the succession begins anew.

The western redcedar (*Thuja plicata*) is another giant of the forest, sometimes living as much as 1,000 years and growing to as much as 60 feet in circumference. Scattered individuals grow throughout the forest up to 4,200 feet elevation, but in places that are too moist for other species they may grow in pure stands. They formed a fundamental part of the Native American economy.

In the high country above 4,000 feet, the Douglas fir forest gives way to a zone where spruce and fir forests are mixed. In addition to the Douglas fir, the higher zone contains several varieties such as Pacific silver fir (*Abies amabilis*), which grows at about 3,000 to 5,000 feet elevation and reaches a diameter of about 40 inches and some 165 feet high. Noble fir (*Abies procera*), found from about 3,100 to 4,800 feet elevation, reaches 50 inches in diameter and 210 feet tall.

High on the mountain slopes, above the continuous, closed forest, is the subalpine zone, where wicked winters and short growing seasons make conditions so harsh that trees are unable to grow as large as those in the lowlands. There groves of trees are interspersed with meadows. The trees often are subalpine fir (*Abies lasiocarpa*), which can grow to a 24-inch diameter and 100 feet high, mountain hemlock (*Tsuga mertensiana*), with a 36-inch diameter and 110-foot height, and whitebark pine (*Pinus albicaulis*), which grows at the highest elevation of any Cascade tree, up to 5,000 to 8,200 feet. It can have a diameter of 20 inches and grow up to 65 feet high. At the highest levels the winter cold is so severe that it kills any part of the trees above the snow, forcing them to grow laterally and assume a strange, bushlike appearance.

In the lower elevations the forests on the west side of the Cascades are often so

The 1980 eruptions of Mount St. Helens created pumice plain, a difficult place for vegetation to gain a foothold.

thick and crowded with vegetation that it is difficult to walk except on a developed trail. In the sparser, shorter forest on the east side, there usually are large spaces between the trees and the forest understory is so thin and grassy that there is little difficulty in traveling in any direction. That makes the forests very different in general appearance, often changing within the space of less than 1 mile from one side of the crest to the other. But in addition to general appearance, the forests on the two sides of the mountains are very different in types of vegetation. Perhaps the most notable of the trees on the lower elevations of the slopes on the eastern side of the Cascades is the ponderosa pine (*Pinus ponderosa*), which reaches a diameter of 44 inches and a height of 175 feet. Like the Douglas fir, its bark is so thick that moderately hot fires don't damage it. But unlike the Douglas fir, which grows its roots in masses near the surface, the ponderosa pine has a deep tap root that burrows far into the ground to find moisture. That makes it possible for the trees to grow and prosper even in the dry east side climate. Even so, the pines compete heavily for nourishment and tend to be spaced much farther apart than the west side trees. That gives the east side forest environment an appearance of a charming, grassy park.

The Douglas fir, which is so widespread and huge on the west side of the mountains, also prospers on the east side when it can find adequate nourishment. It is smaller and less dominant on the east, perhaps losing its prevalence to species such as the Engelmann spruce (*Picea engelmannii*), which grows to 40 inches in diameter and 160 feet tall. The spruce is found from 3,000 feet elevation to 8,000 feet, especially in cold and swampy locations.

Above 3,500 feet, the lodgepole pine (*Pinus contorta latifolia*) is common on the east side of the mountains. A tough species, they reproduce prolifically in poor soil and grow fast, reaching as much as 20 inches in diameter and 100 feet tall, although they usually live less than 200 years. The name comes from the straight, thin trunk which, when young, provided support poles of Native American lodges. When fire attacks a stand of lodgepole it may damage the trees, but some of the cones on the trees are sealed shut by a resin that melts at 113 degrees Fahrenheit. After the fire has passed through, the cones slowly open and release seeds to grow where the fire has reduced competition. That process is even more common among lodgepoles that grow in the Rockies. Everywhere the species tends to be relatively short and not shade-tolerant, so larger conifers crowd them out where the microclimate or other conditions allow them to.

Rocky mountain juniper (*Juniperus scopulorum*) in the Sierra Nevada Mountains of California have been known to grow as large as 14 inches in diameter and 87 feet tall and as old as an estimated 3,000 years. They are lesser trees in the Eastern Washington Cascades but they can be found in rocky ground and clearings induced by drought. Its cousin, the stunted common juniper (*J. communis*), is found in many parts of the world including the cold, windy slopes of the Cascades.

Another of the high species on the east side is the subalpine larch (*Larix lyallii*) which can grow to a 32-inch diameter and 70 feet tall. A deciduous conifer, it is found at elevations from 5,800 to 7,500 feet. They are tough and hardy, living in an environment where there is no liquid water for their roots for months on end during the winter and dropping their needles after they are sucked dry and killed by the winter wind.

The subalpine larch's larger cousin, western larch (*Larix occidentalis*), grows a little lower on the slopes, from 2,500 to 5,000 feet elevation. They reach 52 inches in diameter and 170 feet tall. The larches are the only conifers in the Cascades that lose their needles in the winter.

Lesser Trees

While the forests on both sides of the Cascades are obviously ruled by evergreens the flowering, leafed trees appear at many elevations. Examples include the big leaf maple (*Acer macrophyllum*), which grows on the east side from 2,000 to 4,600 feet elevation and on the west side under 2,000 feet. The smaller, bushier vine maple (*A. circinatum*) grows as far up the slope as timberline. Its leaves turn a brilliant red in midsummer, providing the Cascades with their major tree colors. The bark of the cascara (*Rhamnus purshiana*) which grows below 2,500 feet and reaches a height of 35 feet, produces a strong laxative and was used so

Blueberry/huckleberry (*Vaccinium* spp.)

Technically, American huckleberries grow only on the East Coast and bear the Latin name *Gaylussacia*, while their numerous cousins on the West Coast are really blueberries, including the red ones that grow at lower elevations. Despite that, blueberries are generally called huckleberries and are delicious under any name. About a dozen species grow in the Pacific Northwest. One of them, the Cascades blueberry (*V. deliciosum*), turns color in the fall, painting subalpine slopes a bright russet color.

heavily in the early days that the tree became scarce. It has since been superseded by other medicines and is making a comeback. Pacific dogwood (*Cornus nuttalli*), scattered through the west side forest as either trees or shrubs, has showy bracts surrounding its tiny flower, which makes it a colorful addition to the lower forest. They produce a bitter berry that is considered delicious by band-tailed pigeons (*Columba fasciata*).

The defiant sitka alder (*Alnus sinuata*) is also called slide alder because it grows on avalanche slopes where few other plants can survive. The supple, short trunk leans toward the lower slope and bends under the tremendous power of a mountain avalanche so the thundering snow pack simply rides over it.

Another notable leafed tree in the forest is the black cottonwood (*Populus trichocarpa*), which releases seeds covered with fluff that floats on the breeze and looks like a blizzard of raw cotton. It grows on stream sides as high as the midelevations, reaches a height of 150 feet, and is a favored nesting tree for fisher birds such as the bald eagle (*Haliaeetus leucocephalus*) and great blue heron (*Ardea herodias*). A similar tree on the east side is the quaking aspen (*Populus tremuloides*), which provides an easy browse for wildlife.

Shrubs

Numerous species of shrub grow in the mountains. Some have berries that can be eaten and enjoyed by both humans and wildlife. Some have berries that are poisonous when eaten. Some are poisonous even to the touch. Among those with poison berries are the baneberry (*Actaea rubra*), possibly the most poisonous. A handful of its glossy red or white berries can make one violently ill, but fortunately they taste so bad that it's unlikely anyone would eat that many. The western yew (*Taxus brevifolia*), which can grow as either a shrub or a tree, tastes better and its juicy red cup-shaped fruit is less poisonous. Neither is usually deadly.

Shrubs that should not be touched are the poison ivy (*Rhus radicans*) and poison oak (*Rhus diversiloba*). Highly susceptible people can be affected by a simple touch, which can cause intense itching if the irritant, urushiol, which is contained in the sap, is not washed away within 10 minutes. Inhaling smoke from these plants can be fatal.

Another nasty plant, although it does not cause illness, is the devil's club (*Oplopanax horridum*), an attractive, innocent-appearing plant as much as 10 feet tall with leaves from 6 to 15 inches across. Both its stalk and the underside of the leaves are thickly covered with very sharp spines that are mildly toxic and sting like the devil, which may explain the name. They grow in wet black earth that is often steep and slippery. It is not a good idea to grab one to help climb up the bank of a creek. Native Americans used the bark as medicine for a variety of afflictions and the ash for cosmetics and tattooing ink.

One of the most tasty, and healthful, berries in the Cascades is the huckleberry/blueberry. Another that is popular with both people and bears is the wild blackberry. The blackberry bush has sharp thorns, but like the huckleberry/blueberry it is delicious when raw, or in pies, jams, jellies, and other forms.

Other shrubs with edible but less tasty berries are the Oregon grape, (*Berberis nervosa*), choke cherry (*Prunus virginiana*), serviceberry (*Amelanchier alnifolia*), salmonberry (*Rubus spectabilis*), thimbleberry (*Rubus parviflorus*), as well as gooseberries, and currants (*Ribes sanguineum, R. lacustre, and R. howellii, and R. cereum*). Salal (*Gaultheria shalon*) is another edible low mountain shrub but it is probably more often used as garden greenery than as food. Native Americans and early explorers considered it a delicacy, either raw or pressed into cakes for storage.

The showy Pacific rhododendron (*Rhododendron macrophyllum*), Washington's state flower, grows in dry midelevation forests in the southern portions of the state. The native version grows in masses on shady slopes, which it paints an amazingly beautiful pink when it flowers. The native plant has been combined with those from Asia and elsewhere to become a popular garden shrub with innumerable variations.

Flowers

Trees and shrubs are awesomely handsome from the lowest elevations of the mountain slopes and valleys to above timberline, where winter is so severe that it takes special adaptations of nature for them to grow. But smaller plants huddled in shade or open clearings and meadows bring infinite variations of color that rival anything their bigger cousins offer. Scientists divide the plants into categories such as flowering herbs, grasses, sedges, and rushes, and the study of that can take a lifetime. Most people are content with learning the names of a few of the infinite numbers of plants and enjoying their colorful, ever-changing show.

The mountain wildflowers belong to literally dozens of families with many different plants in each family. Some are outstanding because of their color, others because of their habits, which sometimes can be bizarre.

Among the most unusual, perhaps, are the glacier lily (*Erythronium grandiflorum*) and its cousin, the avalanche lily (*E. montanum*). They generate enough heat that they actually grow through the last, inches-thick layer of snow in the spring. As the snow melt progresses they appear abundantly near timberline or scattered at lower elevations near the edge of a snow field. They melt a small hole in the snow and poke their leaves and flowers through it. The most noticeable difference in the two species is that the deceptively dainty flowers on the glacier lily are yellow, while on the avalanche lily they are white with a yellow center and sometimes pink when they dry. They pop out only near the edge of the snow where it has melted to a few inches deep, but they follow the snow bank as it melts back through the field, covering it with masses of white or yellow.

Another strange but attractive little plant is the Indian pipe (*Monotropa uniflora*), a saprophyte with no roots and no chlorophyll to produce nourishment from sunlight. It apparently obtains its nutrients directly through fungi, which obtain it from conifers, especially Douglas fir. With no need for sunlight it grows sparsely in the dark, low-level forest. It is a strange pinkish-white color with translucent leaves and turns black with age or when picked.

Thistles (*Cirsium edule*) are a bright pink or purple beauty with a nasty bite. The leaves, on low stems, have multiple spines that make it unwise to brush against them and even worse to grasp. They grow mainly in sunny, west side places.

The spreading phlox (*Phlox diffusa*) is one of the few plants that has evolved a way to survive in the extreme cold, dry winters of the high country ridges, where ferocious winds sweep away both nutritious soil and sheltering snow. What's left is precious little ground for a plant to take root in and nothing to protect it from the high country's repeated freezing and thawing cycles and the wind's drying action. The phlox retaliates by growing in close-to-the-ground masses that trap a little of the earth's warmth while the smooth, convex surface deflects the wind over the top with minimum effect. The plant often grows behind rocks or in crevices that protect it from the wind, which eddies and drops nourishing soil in the protected places. A similar but unrelated plant is the moss-campion (*Silene acaulis*).

Hundreds of varieties of flowering plants have adapted to most of the conditions of most of the Cascades' environments. Indian paintbrush (*Castilleja*) and mountain daisy (*Erigeron peregrinus*) are widespread through the mountains, for instance. Miner's lettuce (*Montia sibirica*); trillium (*Trillium* spp.), the small, spring beauty with three leaves and three petals; and vanillaleaf (*Achlys triphylla*), which smells like vanilla when dried, are among the forest dwellers. The startlingly colorful high country meadows are carpeted with magnificent beauties such as rock slide larkspurs (*Delphinium glareosum*); shooting stars (*Dodecatheon spp.*); subalpine buttercups (*Ranunculus eschscholtzii*); cow parsnip (*Heracleum lanatum*), which unfortunately is sometimes mistaken for the poisonous water hemlock (*Cicuta douglasii*); poison hemlock (*Conium maculatum*); and many others waving their colored bright plumes in the wind.

Some flowering plants, such as the iris (*Iris* spp.) and anemones (*Anemone* spp.), have varieties on both sides of the crest, and lucky hikers may find dwarf raspberries (*Rubus pedatus* or *R. lasiococcus*) or wild strawberries (*Fragaria vesca or F. virginiana*) and have a

Western Gray Squirrel (*Sciurus griseus*)

This 12-inch-long squirrel has a bushy tail that is nearly as long as its body. It is mostly a frosted gray color with white tips on its hair. The belly is white and the ears are somewhat reddish. It is found in pine forests on the east side of the Washington Cascades and in the lowlands on the west side.

feast. There is food for the body as well as the soul among the magnificent beauty of wildflowers.

Many other plants, vascular and nonvascular, are found in the mountains. Perhaps the most unusual are the many kinds of lichens that consist of fungi specialized to obtain the carbohydrates they need from algae that are enclosed within the fungi. Clearly the fungi benefit from this symbiotic relationship, but scientists argue that it may not be an advantage to the alga. It gets its moisture and minerals from the fungi, but it is also slowly killed by it. Scientists have counted 38 algae and bacteria that participate in more than 400 kinds of lichen fungi. The lichens form as thin crusts on rocks or bark, as sheets or heaps on their base, or as attractive light green, stringlike masses that hang from tree branches. Rock growing lichen are equipped with tiny gripping cups that expand and contract as they moisten and dry. That action is powerful enough to crumble bits of the rock they cling to. The bits of rock may, over a period of many years and many generations, mix with the decomposed lichen plants to produce enough soil to support other organisms.

Perhaps the most bizarre alga is the red variety that occurs in snow fields at very high elevations. It often grows in masses that stain large patches of the snow a deep red, which may leave neophyte climbers wondering if the altitude has done something to their eyesight. The moist soils of the forest also support many types of vascular cryptogams, plants that have tubes which carry moisture and nourishment to their upper parts. Among these are at least seven varieties of ferns such as sword fern (*Polystichum munitum*) and deer fern (*Blechnum spicant*), as well as many kinds of clubmosses (*Lycopodium* spp.), spikemosses, (*Selaginella* spp.), and horsetails (*Equisetum* spp.). Beneath the vascular cryptogams are the nonvascular plants that are limited to a few inches in height because they lack the tubes to bring nourishment any higher. They include at least 16 kinds of the deep green moss that can appear on the ground, on trees, or on rocks where their slight acidity helps break down the stone into soil. They include the haircap mosses (*Polytrichum* spp.), bearded moss (*Pogonatum alpinum*), and curly leaf moss (*Hypnum circinale*).

All of the plants in the mountains, both those with names and descriptions and those that have not yet been discovered by scientists, play a role in the ecology of their own environment and, in turn, that of the mountains themselves. When one plant appears or disappears from a site the whole site is affected.

Fauna

As plant life established itself in the barren mountains left by the glaciers, some animals, from the biggest to the smallest, wandered in from places the ice had not reached. They were looking for something to eat amidst the rich variety of plants. Other animals came looking for something to eat amidst the rich variety of animals that eat plants.

There may be 100 or more kinds of mammals in the Cascades, ranging from several kinds of bats (*Chiroptra*) that weigh less than an ounce to black bears (*Ursus americanus*) which can weigh up to 500 pounds and are seen occasionally at elevations ranging from the lowlands to the subalpine zone. It is well known that some grizzly bears (*Ursus arctos horribilis*) also have existed in the northern Cascades, and government officials say there have been a few recent sightings there. They have discussed plans to introduce more, which they would take from Montana and other places, but so far, that project has not been carried out. The grizzly is larger than the black bear, which usually tries to avoid contact with humans unless it is injured, guarding a cub, or domesticated to the extent that it associates people with a handout of food. Both varieties of bear go into semihibernation in the winter, which means they have to eat enough in the warm months to carry them through the cold months. To keep up, they eat enormous amounts of almost anything that grows, animal or vegetable. Grizzlies are less predictable than their smaller cousins. They can be very dangerous, but hikers and campers who take simple steps greatly reduce the risk. Prudent hikers and campers take care to avoid bears if they can. They also take precautions, such as hanging their food in a tree where an enterprising bear can't get at it, avoiding having the smell of food on equipment or clothing, avoiding getting between a sow and her cubs, and avoiding startling a bear.

While black bears and, perhaps, grizzlies are not completely shy of humans and, fortunately or unfortunately, may be seen from time to time, cougars (*Felis concolor*), another large Cascades animal with a mildly poor reputation, are only rarely seen. Also known as mountain lion or puma, cougars are furtive, secretive, elusive, large cats that

WESTERN GRAY SQUIRREL
(*Sciurus griseus*)
Active all year, this squirrel buries food
and steals birdseed to eat in the winter.

lurk where they can't be seen. Measured at 4 to 5 feet long plus 2.5 feet of tail, cougars in the Cascades are all one, hard-to-see gray color. They hunt alone for game ranging from grasshoppers to elk, but their primary prey is deer. The larger male eats up to 20 pounds at a time, hiding the remainder and returning for up to a week to finish it. Cougars locate their prey by hearing or smelling it, then slowly stalk it within 30 feet or so and pounce it in a rush that gives the victim little chance to escape. There have been rare reports of cougars stalking people, sometimes for long distances, and even rarer reports of them attacking children both in Canada and the United States.

The cougar's somewhat smaller cousins, the bobcat (*Lynx rufus*) and lynx (*Lynx canadensis*), are just as shy as the cougar. People often spend their lifetimes hiking and camping in the mountains without seeing any of the cats. When they do, it usually is just for the brief moment it takes for the animal to disappear in the nearest cover. The tawny to gray bobcat lives on rodents and hares in the warm months and on carrion and deer, usually young, in the winter. If it is to be seen by humans it probably will be in broken, brushy, or logged terrain.

The lynx in the Cascades looks larger than the bobcat because its fur and legs are longer and its feet are larger, but the two cats actually are about the same size. The lynx specializes in preying on snowshoe hares (*Lepus americanus*), so much so that the lynx population tends to rise and fall in harmony with the hare population.

Perhaps the large animal most likely to be seen in the mountains is the deer, the blacktail deer (*Odocoileus columbianus*) on the west side of the mountains and the mule deer (*Odocoileus hemionus*) on the east side. On rare occasions an overly friendly deer will approach very close to humans, even venturing into their camps. But more often they ignore people at a distance. When a person gets too close they simply disappear with a bound into what appears to humans to be a solid wall of vegetation but to a deer looks like an open road to safety.

When mule deer are startled by an enemy they may break into a long, leaping, graceful gait called stotting through rough terrain. They can change direction from leap to leap, choosing the obstacles they want the pursuer to stumble over. On more open terrain they may simply sprint, hoping to outdistance their hungry pursuer. In the winter deer tend to find shelter on south-facing, wooded, lowland slopes. The forest canopy and southern exposure provide a little warmth and the understory provides shrubs to browse on. In the summer they may migrate to open country such as farmland and clear-cut or second-growth forests where the browsing

WESTERN TOAD
(Bufo boreas)
A common toad found from Alaska to Baja California, it is recognized by its light-colored stripe down the middle of its back.

is good. Civilization has decreased the number of wolves and cougars that prey on deer and increased the number of clear-cuts, resulting in improved conditions for deer. The Washington State Department of Fish and Wildlife compensates by allowing hunters to take more or fewer deer as the need arises.

Elk (*Cervus elaphus*), like deer, tend to ignore humans at a distance, but there is less chance to see them because there are fewer of them and there are only a few, isolated groups in the Cascades. They travel in segregated herds, mature males in one group and females and young bulls in the other. In rutting season the males compete with each other for the females.

Gray wolves (*Canis lupus*) have largely been hunted out of the lower 48 states. A few packs may have wandered down from Canada into the northern fringe of Washington's Cascades, but they are very rare and seldom seen. Their smaller cousin, the coyote (*Canis latrans*), however, has fared better in modern civilization and appears to have moved in where the wolf was forced out. Coyotes may live almost anywhere but apparently prefer brush over forest. They avoid being seen by humans but their distinctive howl may occasionally be heard at night. They hunt mainly insects, rodents, and hares but in an emergency will hunt down a weakened deer, working as a pack. Their running speed is the fastest of all American predators.

Mountain goats (*Oreamnos americanus*) sometimes are seen, usually at a distance, high on an inaccessible cliff. Hunters consider them a valuable trophy. Nonhunters consider getting a photograph equally valuable.

Some smaller animals are less shy than the larger mountain dwellers. The Douglas squirrel (*Tamiasciurus douglasii*), in summer and late fall, drops green cones from trees then scurries around the ground gathering them to be stored for the winter. When a hiker, or an animal comes by, the Douglas squirrel sits in its tree scolding the intruder in a loud voice.

Among the most likely to be seen of the four-footed wildlife are the golden mantled ground squirrel (*Spermophilus saturatus*), Townsend's chipmunk (*Eutamias townsendii*), and yellow pine chipmunk (*Eutamias amoenus*). All frequent campgrounds and other places people gather. They are looking for handouts and for crumbs fallen from the table. Naturalists warn, however, that feeding wildlife can be dangerous for both the animals and the person feeding them. Even small animals can inflict painful bites that can cause diseases in humans. From the animals' standpoint, the food they get from people is rarely good for them. It also may lead to their dependence on people, and then the loss of their ability to survive in the wild.

Hoary marmots (*Marmota caligata*) can be seen often but only by those willing to hike to the high country. The handsome, 20-inch creature with a 9-inch tail might be innocently sunning itself above its burrow in a rock pile that was left by winter snow slides. When it sees a human it will emit a shrill whistling sound, which sends all the other marmots on the rock pile scurrying for cover in a kind of slow motion, hopping gait that is the best the marmot can do. If it turns out there is no danger, the creatures

BALD EAGLE
(Haliaeetus leucocephalus)
It is believed that bald eagles mate for life. The 40-inch-long bird, which can have a 7½-foot wingspan, builds a large nest in trees, cliffs, or on the ground that can weigh up to 1,000 pounds. Eagles eat carrion, fish, and waterfowl.

will, one by one, peek out of their burrows, then gradually ease their way back out into the open, occasionally standing up on their back legs, using their tail as a prop.

Once they are used to a human's presence, marmots may on rare occasions become bolder than the humans like, prying into possessions to find whatever is interesting to marmots. They can tear open a tent or backpack with one quick swipe. They leave when the humans approach but return to their dirty work as soon as they are alone. On the other hand, they may just put on a show of scuffling and tumbling for the humans' benefit, whistling, grunting, and growling to accompany the fisticuffs.

Pikas (*Ochotona princeps*) are another of the rock dwellers, often in the subalpine regions, sometimes in the lowlands, but always in the rocks where they can be secure from predators. They leave the rocks only to make fast foraging trips and carry big mouthfuls of the vegetation back to safety. Unlike the marmot, which hibernates through the winter, pikas remain active all year and store large amounts of food under dry rocks for winter use.

Birds

Some kinds of birds may be seen relatively easily by people who happen to be in the right place. And watching them can be a fascinating occupation. The common merganser (*Mergus merganser*), a carnivore, may be spotted sometimes. They may be seen near streams, diving into the water in search of prey, mostly fish but also insects and amphibians.

Bald eagles (*Haliaeetus leucocephalus*) are the white-headed symbol of the United States. They congregate in season near salmon streams where they eat the carcasses of the fish that die after they spawn, but they sometimes also are seen near high lakes and even in deep-forest areas. They may be soaring gracefully far overhead or perching in high trees. They usually don't mind humans at a distance but leave the premises when someone gets too close.

Bald Eagle (*Haliaeetus leucocephalus*)

This symbol of the United States has an immense wingspread of 80 or more inches and, in the Cascades, is most often found on streams where salmon spawn and die, leaving their carcasses as free dinner. During the salmons' spawning season, large numbers of bald eagles may be seen roosting in trees along the stream banks, but the birds also venture into the mountains, especially near water but also in forest.

When they are about six years old, they breed in the winter. Chicks incubate in the nest for about 6 weeks with both parents taking turns keeping the eggs warm. After hatching, the young stay in the nest 10 to 12 weeks before flying.

Indians considered eagles and eagle feathers to be important in rituals to heal the sick.

Golden eagles (*Aquila chrysaetos*), distinguished by the golden coloration around the head or neck, are even more wary of humans but sometimes can be seen in open hilly country where there are small wildlife for prey. Red-tailed hawks (*Buteo jamaicensis*) are less shy and may be seen many places, especially in grassy areas with a few trees such as the ponderosa pine timberline areas on the east side of the mountains. They soar above a potential small-animal prey, patiently awaiting a chance to swoop in for dinner. Or they may simply land between a rodent and its place of refuge, trapping the little creature. Several kinds of owls (order Strigiformes) inhabit the forests. Perhaps the most famous (though seldom seen) is the spotted owl (*Strix occidentalis*), which received widespread attention when the government eliminated much of the logging in the forests of the western Cascades to preserve this owl's habitat after it was declared a threatened species.

One of the odd birds in the mountains is the tiny rufous hummingbird (*Selasphorus rufus*), which darts from flower to flower collecting huge amounts of nectar to provide the energy to keep its wings whirling so fast that they make a humming sound. It, of course, performs a major bit of pollination while it flits from flower to flower. The little creatures' flight is so maneuverable that they can hover or even fly backwards. They consume as much as half their body weight of the nectar's sugar each day to provide the energy to keep those wings whirring.

Perhaps even more strange is the American dipper or water ouzel (*Cinclus mexicanus*), which stays near cold mountain streams where it performs an odd, dipping dance on the bank. It has the ability to swim underwater even in a fast-moving stream. There, it searches for a meal of aquatic insects. It usually is seen where the air is moist from rushing water and it likes to nest behind a waterfall.

Hikers may not often see members of the woodpecker family (family Picidae) but sometimes they may hear one of the several varieties that frequent the Cascades. They use their strong, sharp claws to hold themselves onto a tree trunk, then use their sharp, chisel-like beaks to cut into the tree either in search of insects for food or, in the case of the white-headed woodpecker (*Picoides abbolarvatus*), to dig its nest out of the tree.

The American crow (*Corvus brachyrhynchos*) frequents the lowland stream meadows and partly deciduous forests scavenging carrion, snails, insects, frogs, and the eggs and nestlings from other birds' nests. The similar, but larger, long-tailed common raven (*Corvus corax*) is more likely seen in the subalpine regions of the east side of the mountains, but is fairly common in all habitats of Washington's Cascades. It eats what its smaller cousin does, plus it sometimes gangs up with others to take larger prey such as hares. Its courtship flight in the spring includes awesome maneuvers, such as barrel rolls, plummeting tumbles, swoops, and motionless hanging, all accompanied by loud calls designed to attract a raven of the opposite sex.

Perhaps the bird most likely to be seen at higher elevations is the gray jay (*Perisoreus canadensis*). It is more commonly known as the camp robber because of its insistence on sharing a hiker's lunch. Stingy hikers who refuse to share are likely to find the fluffy pale gray bird with dark, brownish wings will invite itself, even to the extent of taking a morsel out of the host's hand while the hand is on the way to his mouth.

Ground Crawlers

There are many cold-blooded creatures in the mountains. Slimy banana slugs (*Ariolimax columbianus*) can often be seen crawling out from under the forest-floor debris onto a damp trail after a rain, but they look like short, fat worms, and few people consider them terribly attractive.

There are northwestern garter snakes (*Thamnophis ordinoides*), racers (*Coluber constrictor mormon)*, and gopher snakes (*Pituophis melanoleucus*) in the mountains, but only the western rattlesnake (*Crotalus viridis oreganus*) is dangerous. Its venom is highly painful and debilitating to adults and can be fatal to children. It is native only to east side lowlands. Rattlers avoid humans when they can, but if a rattler thinks it is cornered, it sounds the rattles on the end of its tail and strikes. They may crawl under a low, overhanging rock or log and attack when someone steps over the rock or log. Hikers should always be sure there's nothing behind whatever they step over.

Fish

Salmon (*Oncorhyncus*) are anadromous fish that are hatched in cold, running streams as tiny alevin. After a period in the stream's fresh water they migrate to the ocean where they stay for a number of years. When they mature they instinctively return to the stream where they were hatched to spawn a new generation. Then they die. The headwaters of some of the streams where they begin and end their lives are in the foothills of the mountains. And, if salmon are trapped behind a natural or man-made dam, they seem to be able to adopt a freshwater life cycle. But people who are interested in catching a delicious salmon are better off trying in waters closer to the sea.

Like salmon, rainbow trout or steelhead (*Salmo gairdneri*) are hatched in freshwater streams, go to sea to mature then return to the stream where they lay eggs for a new generation. But unlike the salmon, they do not die after spawning but go back to sea. They, too, are more likely to be caught in relatively lowland areas.

Cutthroat trout (*Salmo clarki*), Dolly Varden *(Salvelinus malma)*, and brook trout (*Salvelinus fontinalis*) are found in higher lakes and streams, often because they were planted there. They may migrate to saltwater if they can get to it but they don't stay very long. They are what anglers in the mountains are often after. Rainbow, cutthroat, and Dolly Varden are native to the Northwest while brook trout are imported from Eastern North America.

Insects

There are uncounted numbers of different insects in the mountains. Those most likely to be noticed by human visitors include mosquitoes (family Culicade) and several distinct types of biting flies (Dipterra), all of which can make an otherwise pleasant visit definitely unpleasant. Some of the insects attack in vast swarms so thick that a clap of hands can kill a half dozen or so. Insect repellent helps during the day and mosquito netting during the night.

People

Native Americans on the east side of the mountains occupied the land even as the glaciers receded, developing a prairie economy based on hunting and gathering and migrating from place to place to where the seasons provided food and materials. Their economy was based on what they could carry or safely stash until they returned to the same location the next year. Their leisure and their opportunity to acquire large numbers of possessions were severely limited by their lifestyle, but they knew their territory well and what time of year the materials they wanted would be in a certain vicinity. Because the climate they lived in was severe, they became expert at making clothing which they adorned with decorations and which became a major part of their trade with people on the west side of the mountains.

During the Ice Age the huge glacier that moved down from Canada bulldozed the immense trench that became Puget Sound. An arm of that glacier turned west to the sea and gouged out the Strait of Juan de Fuca. When the ice receded, the trenches filled with sea water and became an extension of the Pacific Ocean. People moved onto islands and along the mainland shore soon after the ice receded. Apparently, at least some of the

Picture Lake in the Mount Baker-Snoqualmie National Forest is reputedly one of the most photographed mountain scenes in North America.

earliest arrivals were hunters who depended on killing land animals for their subsistence. But that soon changed to an increasing dependence on the abundant wealth of the sea, primarily but not entirely dominated by salmon, an anadromous fish that is hatched in cold, fast freshwater streams then migrate far out to sea. They return to the same place they were hatched to lay and fertilize the eggs of the next generation. Then they die, providing a feast for wildlife such as the bald eagle that gather along the riverbanks. The earliest Native Americans quickly learned they could catch vast numbers of the adult salmon as they concentrated in the streams. The fish that weren't immediately consumed were dried and kept for later use.

The abundance of fish and other resources in the Puget Sound area gave the people the leisure to develop an advanced technology, highlighted by wooden houses built of boards made by splitting the straight-grained cedar that grows abundantly in the forest. The cedar also provided cloth from its inner bark, medicines, carved tools and icons, and the material for large dugout canoes built by using fire and stone tools to shape and carve a tree. The canoes were nearly ubiquitous and, since the thick forest was not well suited for horses, were the main means of transportation. Eventually some of the people moved away from the saltwater shores and far up the rivers, stopping somewhere short of the country where bitter cold, severe winter winds, and snow far over peoples' heads made permanent residence nearly impossible.

Villages consisting of several houses developed, with each house sheltering 20 to 40 people. The residents lived in the houses through the winter, engaging in activities such as ceremonies, dances, story telling, and arts and crafts. In the summer months they traveled over the water or on trails to hunt, fish, gather vegetation for food and other uses and to trade. Permanent trails were established across the Cascade passes, leading to marketplaces where people from many places gathered to trade their goods. Much of the trade was by gambling in what they called the bone game. Participants would form lines facing each other and put their wagers on the ground between them. One person from one of the sides would hold a piece of carved bone in his hands, passing it from hand to hand while he and his teammates shouted and gesticulated to distract the other team. In the end the person with the bone would hold out his hands and invite the opposing team to choose which hand it was in. If they guessed right they won. If they guessed wrong they lost. The trade extended from area to area and items that could originate only from hundreds of miles away are occasionally found by archeologists who dig into the site of a village.

Even though they came from widely different cultures and their languages were so dissimilar that neighboring villages had difficulty communicating with each other, the people within Washington's Cascade areas were generally peaceful, although they were subject to raids for goods and slaves by people from more warlike areas on Vancouver Island to the north. In rare cases of local violence, custom required that the victim's family revenge his death in a system very similar to the revenge system of justice in ancient Europe. An ancient legend tells of families of the Skagit and Thompson tribes that traditionally had their summer camps near each other on the upper Skagit River near where the North Cascades National Park's Goodell Creek Campground is now. Someone from one group killed a member of the other. When the victim's relatives responded by killing the killer, it was necessary to take revenge on them. A feud developed that lasted for three summers and ended only when no one survived except one young boy. A nearby valley in the park is still called Stetattle, meaning something like "place of death."

The Spanish navy had an early base at Nootka Sound on the western shore of Vancouver Island, and it is likely that some of their excursions took them to places where they could see the Washington portion of the Cascades. But the first European to leave a meticulous record was Capt. George Vancouver of the British Royal Navy. He sailed into Puget Sound in the summer of 1792 to explore and to lay claim to new lands. He put on the map many of the geographic names still in use. He named Mount Rainier, for instance, after a Royal Navy official. Mount Baker was named after one of the officers of Vancouver's crew. The name not only stuck but was extended later to the Baker River, which was not discovered until decades after Vancouver left. When in the twentieth-century Baker River was dammed, it created a lake that also took the Baker name.

Probably the first European to cross the mountains was Alexander Ross who, in 1811, was part of John Jacob Astor's Pacific Fur Company. His group went up the Columbia River past the gorge that cut through the Cascades and established a fur-trading post near the confluence of the Okanogan River. Three years later, after the fort became the property of the Northwest Company, Ross set out to find a way to cross the mountains on foot as a means of avoiding tolls that natives on the Columbia collected. He may have gone up the Stehekin Valley and across Cascade Pass, which was a main trail of the Native Americans who crossed between the eastern and western sides of the mountain. It is still a major corridor for modern hikers who cross the mountains on the North Cascades National Park's Cascade Pass Trail. If Ross did not follow the Stehekin Valley he may have gone up Granite Creek, now the right-of-way of State Route 20, the so-called North Cascades Scenic Highway which leads through the Okanogan National Forest to the park.

Ross was followed for the next three quarters of a century by a host of explorers. Some were soldiers, including George McClellan who went on to twice command the Union Army of the Potomac during the Civil War and who ran for president against Abraham Lincoln in 1864. The soldiers were looking for places to locate roads across the mountains. Other early explorers were engineers looking for rights-of-way to build the railroads that spread modern civilization across the West. One individual was Henry Custer, a topographer who was assigned to accompany the commission that established the border between Canada and the United States. He left in the archives a fascinating report of his travels through what is now the North Cascades National Park.

Probably the widest early knowledge of the Cascades was gained by the hordes of gold-seeking miners who from time to time swarmed through the mountains, especially in the North Cascades where most of the mineral deposits are. They came and went in waves, rushing from one gold field to another as new "strikes" were found. In some cases they rushed from the Cascades so suddenly that they left dishes on the tables in their cabins. They also left in the archives numerous maps, reports, and records that added to the knowledge of the mountains.

In the earliest colonial times, land was America's cheapest commodity, but as the population grew it became obvious that situation would not last forever. An early attempt to conserve some of the land for noncommercial uses occurred in 1891 when Congress adopted the Forest Reserves Act, which allowed the president to set aside lands he deemed worthy of being kept under federal jurisdiction. In 1893 some areas of the Cascades were made part of The Pacific Forest Reserve. In 1905 Congress created the U.S. Forest Service, which eventually became part of the Department of Agriculture. The national forests were created and made the Forest Service's responsibility in 1907.

In the early days, work in the forests was pretty rudimentary. Rangers spent their entire summers living in the forests, fighting fires, rescuing lost hikers, enforcing the law, building trails, bridges, and shelters, and performing whatever other functions were called for.

That expanded and now the Forest Service has divided the Washington Cascades into four national forests and employs hundreds of people educated in forest and related sciences as well as managers who plan and execute management programs. In the past the management programs had largely to do with logging and replanting the forest but that has changed over the past generation to an emphasis on the environment and ecology.

Meantime the national park system was born in 1872 when Congress established under the Department of Interior the Yellowstone National Park in what were then the territories of Montana and Wyoming. That was the world's first national park, but the idea caught on both in the United States and much of the rest of the world. In 1899 Congress established Mount Rainier in the middle of the Washington Cascades as a National Park. The North Cascades National Park at the Canadian border was added to the park system in 1968. The parks devote themselves to conserving nature and educating visitors.

Over the decades both the Forest Service and the Park Service have developed hundreds of trails to the interior of the mountains. Many of them originally were built primarily to provide access to forest fires and fire lookouts. They still are used for those reasons to a certain extent. Modern technology has made it possible, however, to use aircraft both to spot fires and to parachute firefighters to the scene as well as to spray fire retardant on the blaze, so the focus of the trails now has shifted to providing a way for people who love mountains and the outdoors to reach isolated places of rare, awe-inspiring beauty. The trails range from short byways less than 1 mile long and suitable for wheelchairs to the Pacific Crest National Scenic Trail that follows the rugged crest of the Cascades some 450 miles between the borders with Canada and Oregon. It passes through the parks and the national forests, tying Washington's Cascades into a single unit for people with the desire and the strength to follow it.

Many other trails are scattered throughout the mountains. Some are long, some are short, some are difficult, some are easy. All lead to places city people seldom experience.

The five highways that traverse Washington's Cascade high country in an east-west direction all cross magnificent country that can be experienced from a comfortable car seat. Four of them, U.S. Highway 2, Interstate Highway 90, State Highway 410, and U.S. Highway 12 are more or less developed into National Forest Scenic Byways. The fifth, State Route 20, was built with scenery in mind and may be the most awesomely beautiful of them all. It crosses two national forests, Mount Baker-Snoqualmie and Okanogan, as well as the North Cascades National Park, tying them together in an east-west direction for motorists. State Routes 20 and 410 are closed through the winter months by heavy snow. At the extreme southern end of Washington, the Columbia River has washed through the mountains. There is a sixth east-west road, State Route 14, that follows the twists and turns of the river without getting much higher than sea level.

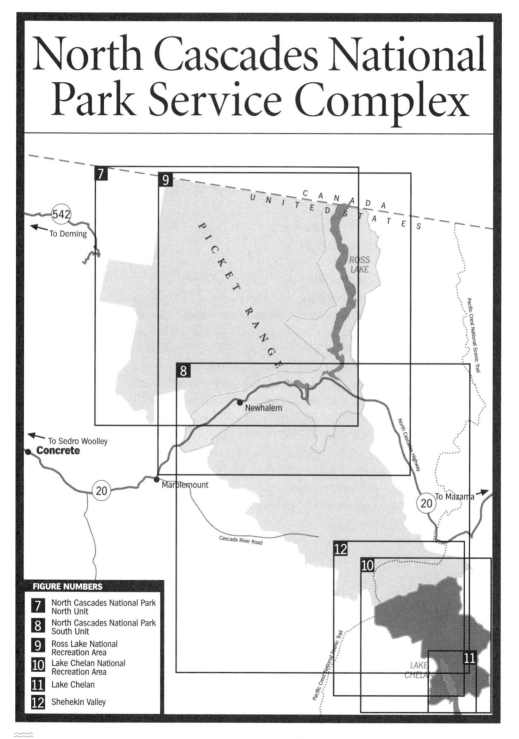

North Cascades National Park Service Complex

FIGURE NUMBERS

7	North Cascades National Park North Unit
8	North Cascades National Park South Unit
9	Ross Lake National Recreation Area
10	Lake Chelan National Recreation Area
11	Lake Chelan
12	Shehekin Valley

North Cascades
National Park Service Complex

The North Cascades National Park Service Complex [Fig. 6] was created by Congress in 1968. It consists of three units, the North Cascades National Park which Congress designated as the Stephen Mather Wilderness in 1988, the Ross Lake National Recreation Area which divides the two sections of the park, and the Lake Chelan National Recreation Area at the southeastern end of the complex. Together, they encompass some 684,000 acres of rugged, awe-inspiring beauty that attracts about 400,000 visitors a year. They span the sweep of experience from modern highway, to backcountry trail, to high peaks and glaring glaciers. There are lakes large and small, high and low. Crashing streams thunder as they wash down from melting glaciers, pausing in quiet lakes before flowing down toward the Pacific Ocean. Thick forests compare with open meadows and the panoramic views from mile-high peaks.

Visitors can challenge the hardships of mountain climbing or view majestic scenery

[*Above:* Magic Glacier from above Cascade Pass in the North Cascades National Park Complex]

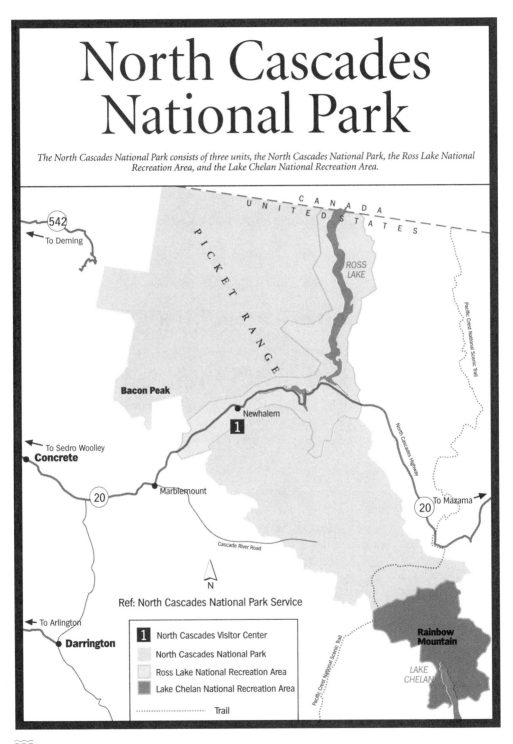

North Cascades National Park

The North Cascades National Park consists of three units, the North Cascades National Park, the Ross Lake National Recreation Area, and the Lake Chelan National Recreation Area.

Ref: North Cascades National Park Service

1	North Cascades Visitor Center
	North Cascades National Park
	Ross Lake National Recreation Area
	Lake Chelan National Recreation Area
··········	Trail

OSPREY
(Pandion haliaetus)
Also known as the fish hawk, the osprey hovers over water before plunging in feetfirst to grasp the fish with its talons.

from the comfort of their cars. There are more than 300 miles of trails and three drive-in campgrounds on State Route 20, also known as the North Cascades Highway. The campgrounds on the highway have a total of 300 campsites. Many other more primitive campgrounds scattered throughout the complex can be reached by foot or boat. Permits required for all backcountry camping are available from any park office.

There are tiny villages within the complex. Two are company towns that house employees of Seattle City Light, which has a series of power dams beside State Route 20 that follows the Skagit River. Another, Stehekin Landing, is so isolated it cannot be reached by road.

When Congress created the park in 1968 it ended one era and began another. Miners began the first one. The earliest miners were small parties of prospectors. It is possible some may have worked their way up the Nooksack and Skagit rivers after the Fraser River gold rush in Canada died out in the late 1850s. If so, they left no record.

But in 1877—three men John Rowley, John Sutter, and George Sanger—did leave a record. They went up the Skagit River in a canoe to where Newhalem is now, then hiked and rafted to a creek where Ross Dam is now. There, Sutter found a red stone that gave a name to Ruby Creek and Ruby Mountain.

That started successive floods of gold seekers. At first they were placer miners, the prospectors of Wild West tales. They panned for the loose gold that had been eroded out of the mountains' hard rock by wind, rain, and ice. More and more of them came as word leaked that pay dirt had been found. By 1879 nearly 80 men were prospecting in the

Ruby Creek area. They formed the Ruby Creek Mining District and platted Ruby City. Perhaps some made a little money, but they soon washed off all of the easy gold, and by the end of the year most of them left to seek their fortunes somewhere else.

Ten years later there was a new influx. The easy gold had been panned from the sand of the valley bottoms, the newcomers reasoned, but it had originated in the hard rock of the mountains and there was more still there. That left them with the necessity to dig into the solid rock to find the riches they were hunting. For that they needed to punch tunnels into the rock, and that required heavy machinery, expensive blasting powder, crews of men, and, of course, large amounts of capital.

They worked hard to peel wealth out of the North Cascades' rock but there are more stories of failure than success among the miners. When word spread up the valleys in 1898 of a strike in northern Canada's Yukon Territory the gold seekers lost interest in the Cascades, abandoned everything, and rushed to the far north, leaving their mines, shelters, and equipment where it sat. Another round of gold excitement in the Cascades had ended as suddenly as it began.

The pendulum swung back to the Cascades in the new century with just as little success as in the previous rushes. The Ruby Creek Mining Company was one of the losers. It spent $300,000 to build structures for a large crew and shops for heavy machinery. It brought in a saw mill over the rough trails and built a 4-mile wooden flume up the side of the mountain. The plan was to bring water down the flume and use it in a hydraulic system to wash pay dirt from the hillside. After two years of work they turned on the water and discovered it wasn't sufficient to wash out the rock. They turned off the water and went back to civilization, leaving a watchman who, it is said, panned out $3,000 worth of gold from their debris.

Old timers in the mountains believe the only people who made any money in the mines were those who sold their claims for more than they put into them. But that didn't stop the hopeful from coming even into modern times.

Sometimes hikers who have spent days struggling up a trail will find a hole in a rocky cliff that is all that remains of a mine someone blasted out of the solid rock. Mules and strong men brought up on their strong backs the material to build structures. They also carried up unbelievably heavy equipment as well as the food and supplies the crews needed. The weary hiker can only wonder how they did it and how they felt when they realized the rocks would not yield enough wealth to pay expenses.

Others in the old days came to stay. Lucinda Davis went to Goodell Creek in 1893 with her sons, Glee and Frank, and her daughter Ides. They built a store catering to miners that they operated during the summers. Later they moved a few miles up the river to Cedar Bar where the village of Diablo is now. They opened an inn there and operated it for many years. The 7,000-foot-high Davis Peak still towers where their cabins once were. John McMillan came down the Skagit River from his Canadian homeland in 1894. He lived in a cabin near where McMillan Creek empties into Big Beaver Creek until he died in 1922.

Tommy Rowland lived beside the Skagit River for years on a high spot whose name now is misspelled as Roland Point on Ross Lake. His troubled mind resulted in names like Devil's Dome, Devil's Creek, Hidden Hand Pass, and Hells' Basin on landmarks near his cabin.

After President Cleveland created the immense Washington Forest Reserve in 1897, government rangers moved in to patrol and protect the mountains and forests. That function evolved and expanded through the creation of the Forest Service in 1907.

Proposals to designate the land for a national park began as early as 1892 when people of the town of Chelan in eastern Washington sought to end the hunting of mountain goats and grizzly bears. The proposals were repeated several times over the years but little came of them until the 1960s. Despite their years of hard work and ingenuity, the miners and settlers had left only very small marks on the thousands of acres of land. But by the 1960s, loggers were working their way up the valleys. Their effects on the land were less permanent than the gouged out rock of the miners, but logging left huge swaths of denuded forest that glared at even the casual observer. The trees would come back whether planted or left to natural seeding, but that would take years and the offense would continue.

In 1963 the secretaries of agriculture and interior persuaded President Kennedy to authorize a formal study of more than 6 million acres of federal lands in the North Cascades. A special study team issued its report two years later and recommended that Congress create a national park of 700,000 acres. Congress reduced it to 675,000 acres in 1968 and carved the park complex out of portions of the Mount Baker, Okanogan, and Wenatchee national forests.

Congress had to do some juggling to come up with its plan. Some of the land of the North Cascades was already being used for purposes that were not in the character of the wild, untrammeled land that is typical of national parks. Seattle City Light had three dams that formed three man-made lakes in the center of the land. There were two villages there for City Light employees. And the state was working toward completing State Route 20, the North Cascades Highway. To the southeast the isolated village of Stehekin Landing stood at the head of the Stehekin Valley, which had been roaded, mined, farmed, and logged for generations. Congress resolved the inconsistency by dividing the land into categories. The largest section is the 505,000-acre park proper which the National Park Service administers as separate north and south units. Two smaller sections, the 107,000-acre Ross Lake National Recreation Area and the 62,000-acre Lake Chelan National Recreation Area were established as parts of the complex the park service would administer with less rigid regulations. Some small parcels of land have been acquired since.

The bill to create the park was sponsored by two members of Congress from western Washington, Senator Henry M. Jackson and Representative Lloyd Meeds. Both had lived near the wild Cascades and knew them very well. The law was adopted on October 2, 1968. The Park Service established its headquarters in Sedro-Woolley and began the business of keeping the land as it has always been and showing it to the people.

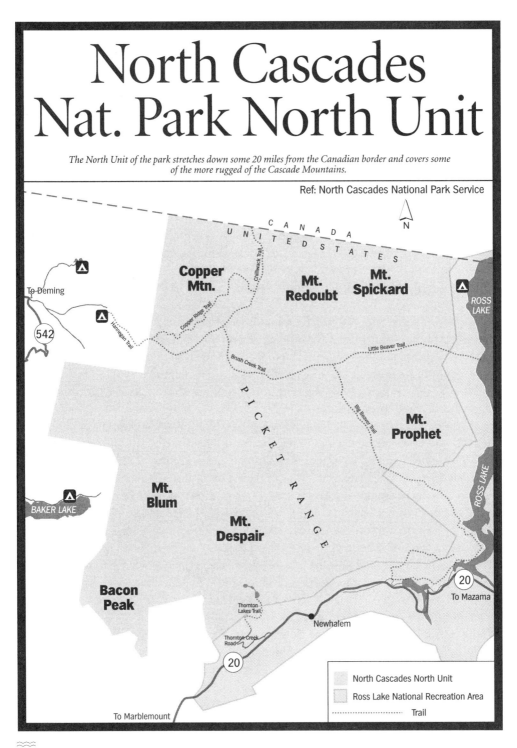

North Cascades Nat. Park North Unit

The North Unit of the park stretches down some 20 miles from the Canadian border and covers some of the more rugged of the Cascade Mountains.

Ref: North Cascades National Park Service

N

CANADA

UNITED STATES

To Deming

Copper Mtn.

Chilliwack Trail

Mt. Redoubt

Mt. Spickard

ROSS LAKE

542

Copper Ridge Trail

Hannegan Trail

Brush Creek Trail

Little Beaver Trail

P I C K E T   R A N G E

Big Beaver Trail

Mt. Prophet

ROSS LAKE

BAKER LAKE

Mt. Blum

Mt. Despair

Bacon Peak

Thornton Lakes Trail

20

To Mazama

Newhalem

Thornton Creek Road

20

To Marblemount

North Cascades North Unit

Ross Lake National Recreation Area

Trail

The Park Service lost no time. Logging was banned within the park and tightly controlled in the recreation areas. Old mining claims and homesteads were acquired quickly as they became available. Hunting was banned in the park but allowed in the recreation areas. Fishing is permitted throughout the complex. Valid state fishing licenses are required for both fishing and hunting.

Existing drive-in campgrounds were spruced up and added to. Guided nature walks and evening programs were begun for visitors who want to understand the magnificent natural places they see.

Rangers established campgrounds along backcountry trails and abolished camping in other places where vegetation might be worn thin. To reduce wear on the natural environment, a permit system limits to 12 the number of people allowed in an overnight hiking party.

A new dedication to protection and education became the approach to management of the land.

The landscape is diverse and all-encompassing. The forests vary from the Douglas fir that carpets much of the west side of the mountains to the pines of the east side. Vegetation and wildlife change from the lowland species to the rugged varieties that withstand the onslaughts of high country winters. The large lowland lakes contrast with the small natural lakes of the highlands and the tarns that nestle in the hollowed out bottom of cirques. There are more than 300 mountain glaciers, half of all those in the lower 48 states. The interior has places that have only rarely been visited, if ever.

The park proper attracts much fewer visitors than the adjacent Ross Lake National Recreation Area, which is only 20 percent as large. That is deliberate. The park proper is a place where nature is supreme and people enter it only on nature's terms. The national recreation areas are just what the name implies, places where people are welcome to visit and to learn and nature is modified a little to make that possible.

North Unit

[Fig. 7] The North Unit of the park stretches down some 20 miles from the Canadian border and covers some of the more rugged of the Cascade Mountains. It is, as it has been from time immemorial, a place of tremendous hardship blessed by incredible beauty. When Henry Custer, the topographer for the party that surveyed the border with Canada in 1859, worked his laborious way up the Ensawkwatch Valley he complained of his party's struggles, "winding our way along the steep slopes of the mountains...or breaking our way through dense tissues of bush vegetation always found in the bottoms of these streams." Then he found a place to camp on the side of the mountain which he called, "a most lovely spot, sunny and free of snow. The grass has grown luxuriously, rare flowers...everywhere..." So it was in Custer's day and so it is in ours.

The essence of the North Unit is its mountains. Many of them were named by

Henry Custer

The earliest formal explorer of the far northern section of the Washington Cascades was Henry Custer, the topographer of the commission that surveyed the border between the United States and Canada in 1859. His assignment was to explore and describe the territory 10 miles on each side of the border, but his enthusiasm for climbing unknown mountains and seeing unknown land enticed him to lead his party of two white men and nine Indian guides far beyond those limits. His report contains the first description of numerous mountains, valleys, rivers, and glaciers that still are seldom visited.

modern climbers who tagged them with the name they felt most nearly matched the climbers' experience, names like Mount Redoubt, Mount Challenger, Mount Fury, Mount Terror, and Mount Despair. Permits are required for mountain climbing and overnight stays. Pets and firearms are not permitted in the park except dogs on a leash are allowed on the Pacific Crest Trail that stretches from Canada to Mexico along the crest of the mountains.

Directions: The North Unit is adjacent to the north side of the Ross Lake National Recreation area which is bisected by State Route 20 north of Marblemount.

Activities: Hiking, camping, mountain climbing, scenic viewing.

Facilities: None.

Dates: Seasonal, summer.

Fees: None, but a free permit is required for an overnight stay.

Closest town: Marblemount, 5 miles from the southern edge of the national park.

For more information: North Cascades Visitor Center, near the Newhalem Creek Campground in Newhalem. The mailing address is 502 Newhalem Street, Rockport WA 98283. Phone (206) 386-4495. Or Wilderness Information Center, 7280 Ranger Station Road, Marblemount, WA 98267. Phone (360) 873-4500.

PICKET RANGE

[Fig. 7] Perhaps the most rugged of the North Unit's rocky bulk is the Picket Range, a long subsection of the North Cascades that runs in a northwest-southeast direction through the middle of the North Unit. The mountains consist of biotite gneiss rock and run in a forbiddingly steep, rocky ridge for 7 miles.

There are well over 20 craggy peaks ranging from 7,500 to 8,200 feet elevation. From a distance the sharp peaks resemble a picket fence. Some authorities believe that gave the range its name. Others believe it was named after Captain George Pickett who was the commanding officer of Fort Bellingham on Puget Sound in the mid-1800s. During the Civil War he became a general in the Confederate Army and gained fame as the commander of the last charge on Cemetery Hill during the Battle of Gettysburg.

The northernmost peak, Mount Challenger, has a tremendous glacier, one of many above timberline throughout the Pickets. The Pickets are obscured by the other mountains of the North Unit but rare views are possible from a few places.

Directions: There are two viewpoints: 1) just off State Route 20 near the exit for the Goodell Creek Campground 12 miles north of Marblemount and 2) at the end of the Sterling Munro Trail behind the North Cascades Visitor Center in Newhalem.

Activities: Viewing mountain scenery, mountain climbing. **Warning:** climbing mountains such as those in the Picket Range is extremely hazardous and should not be attempted without the proper training and equipment.

BLUEGILL
(Lepomis macrochirus)
Juveniles of most species of the sunfish family usually exhibit a similar color pattern on their sides.

Closest town: Newhalem, 12 miles.

Fees: None, but a free permit is required for an overnight stay.

Facilities: None.

Dates: Year-round.

For more information: North Cascades Visitor Center, near the Newhalem Creek Campground in Newhalem. The mailing address is 502 Newhalem Street, Rockport WA 98283. Phone (206) 386-4495. Or Wilderness Information Center, 7280 Ranger Station Road, Marblemount, WA 98267. Phone (360) 873-4500.

THORNTON LAKES TRAIL

[Fig. 7] One of the few day hikes in the park's North Unit, the Thornton Lakes Trail was not built but just developed as a miners' or fishermen's trail, which means it is as straight as possible. Thus, it is steep and in places muddy. The reward at the end is three lakes nestled in rocks that long ago were gouged out by glaciers. The beginning of the trail is an abandoned logging road in an area that was logged as recently as the late 1960s.

Once beyond the logging road most of the trail passes though typical west side forests and subalpine forests except where it crosses a small creek in an open area about 1 mile from the trailhead. There are nice views across the Skagit Valley, at least until the trees in the replanted clear-cuts cut them off. Past the old road, the trail switchbacks through the largely fir and hemlock forest, which gives way to mountain hemlock (*Tsuga mertensiana*)

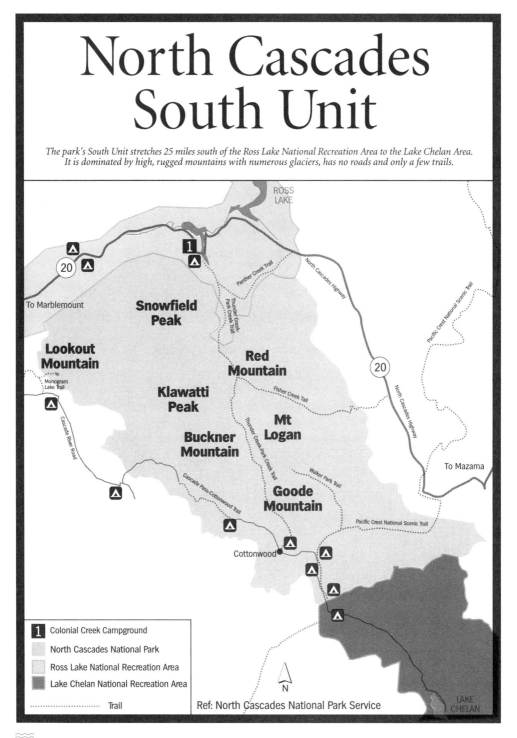

North Cascades South Unit

The park's South Unit stretches 25 miles south of the Ross Lake National Recreation Area to the Lake Chelan Area. It is dominated by high, rugged mountains with numerous glaciers, has no roads and only a few trails.

ROSS LAKE

To Marblemount

Snowfield Peak

Panther Creek Trail

North Cascades Highway

Thunder Creek Park Creek Trail

Pacific Crest National Scenic Trail

Lookout Mountain

Red Mountain

20

Monogram Lake Trail

Klawatti Peak

Fisher Creek Tall

North Cascades Highway

Cascade River Road

Mt Logan

Thunder Creek-Park Creek Trail

Buckner Mountain

To Mazama

Walker Park Trail

Cascade Pass-Cottonwood Trail

Goode Mountain

Pacific Crest National Scenic Trail

Cottonwood

1 Colonial Creek Campground

North Cascades National Park

Ross Lake National Recreation Area

Lake Chelan National Recreation Area

N

Trail

Ref: North Cascades National Park Service

LAKE CHELAN

and Alaska yellow cedar (*Chamaecyparis nootkatensis*) in the higher elevations. It becomes progressively steeper until it reaches a level bench at 3.5 miles from the trailhead and 4,100 feet elevation. Past the bench the trail goes upward again to the crest of a rock ridge smoothed by an ancient glacier at 5,100 feet elevation. There are a multitude of blueberry bushes in the later part of the trail. The view at the crest is dominated by Mount Triumph in the Picket Range.

Below, down a rough, 0.5-mile trail that loses 500 feet of elevation, is the first and lowest of the three lakes. There are a few campsites here, fires not allowed and overnight permits required. There may be some trout in the lake, but it is very deep, and fishing in the early season is said to be best for those who bring a rubber raft. Trappers Peak rises sharply to the northeast waiting to be explored and admired.

To reach the other two lakes it is necessary to find the way by a faint-to-nonexistent trail to the west. The middle lake may still be partly iced over in July and the upper one, deep in a steep cirque, often doesn't thaw until mid-August.

A difficult side trip from the ridge above the first lake follows a faint, steep, and rough trail with nearly 1,000 feet elevation gain to the summit of Trappers Peak. The view below is the Skagit Valley with the village of Newhalem nestled in the bottom. Looking up, the view is an awesome vista of the Picket Range. The route can be treacherous, especially when there are snow patches on it.

Directions: From Marblemount the drive is 11 miles north on State Route 20, North Cascades Highway, to the Thornton Creek Road past milepost 117. From there the route goes west up a steep road that was built long ago for logging trucks. The trailhead is at mile 5 and 2,500 feet elevation.

Dates: Seasonal, summer.

Fees: None, but a free permit is required for an overnight stay.

Closest town: Marblemount on State Route 20, 11 miles.

For more information: Wilderness Information Center, 7280 Ranger Station Road, Marblemount, WA 98267. Phone (360) 873-4500 or Park Headquarters, 2105 State Route 20, Sedro-Woolley, WA, 98284, (360) 856-5700 or North Cascades Visitor Center, 502 Newhalem Street, Rockport, WA 98283. Phone (206) 386-4495.

Trail: One-way hike to first lake is 4.75 miles.

Elevation: The elevation gain is approximately 2,600 feet.

Degree of difficulty: Moderate.

South Unit

[Fig. 8] The park's South Unit stretches some 25 miles south of the Ross Lake National Recreation Area to the Lake Chelan Recreation Area. The North and South units are both part of the park proper and have similar characteristics of being dominated by high, rugged mountains with numerous glaciers. Like the North Unit, the South Unit has no

Mountain Hemlock (*Tsuga mertensiana*)

This dweller of the high country seldom is found below 4,500 feet in elevation where it may reach some 110 feet tall and 36 inches in diameter. Its upper limit is about 5,500 feet in elevation, and it may grow as a prostrate shrub at the upper limit of its range. It is able to accept winter snowfalls that would break lesser trees. Smaller trees are bent over at the top by the weight of a snowfall then buried during successive storms. In the spring as the snow cover melts away, the bent portion may suddenly be released from the snow cover, popping several feet into the air and startling people who happen to be in the vicinity.

roads and only a few trails. Most of the land is as it has been for uncounted centuries, seldom visited by humans. Hiking, fishing, mountain climbing, and admiring the awesome beauty of the mountains are the primary pursuits of people who come here. Permits are required for overnight stays and mountain climbing. Pets and firearms are not permitted in the park with the exception of leashed dogs on the Pacific Crest Trail.

THUNDER CREEK-PARK CREEK TRAIL

[Fig. 8] The Thunder Creek-Park Creek Trail crosses between the west side and east side of the Cascades. Beginning on the west side in Colonial Creek Campground [Fig. 8(1)] at 1,200 feet elevation, it passes though some magnificent old-growth firs, cedars, and hemlock. The trail crosses level ground past the Thunder Arm cove of Seattle City Light's Diablo Lake for 1 mile to a bridge. After another mile it passes the junction with the Fisher Creek Trail and beyond to two meadows that resulted from lightning fires in the early 1970s. There are views there of Snowfield and Colonial peaks. At 6 miles the trail leaves the Ross Lake Recreation Area and enters the park's South Unit. And there it starts seriously upward, traversing the side of Red Mountain to avoid a nearly impenetrable swamp. Beyond are views of the huge Boston Glacier and several mountains. The trail loses elevation then climbs back to the junction with Skagit Queen Creek at 13 miles from the trailhead. Once there was a miners' village here. They were working The Skagit Queen mines a short distance up Skagit Queen Creek. Among their facilities was an electrical powerhouse with hydropowered generators that provided their quarters with light and the mines with power for machinery. They managed all that in the midst of a wilderness with nothing more than intelligence and muscle to get it there.

Approximately 2.5 uphill miles later is Thunder Basin Camp, the last one before Park Creek Pass. Fires are not allowed. Beyond that there are 2.5 uphill miles to the pass at 6,100 feet elevation.

The pass is a narrow divide between Buckner Mountain and Mount Logan. Beyond it is the 8-mile-long Park Creek Trail that leads to the Stehekin Valley and an 18-mile ride on the Park Service Stehekin Shuttle Bus (Reservations are recommended. Contact the Wilderness Information Center, 7280 Ranger Station Road, Marblemount, WA 98267.

Phone (360) 873-4500. Or Golden West Visitor Center, Stehekin, WA 98852. Phone (360) 856-5700, extension 340, then extension 14.) to Stehekin Landing in the Lake Chelan National Recreation Area.

There is no camping at the pass and the first campground is 3 miles and a 2,000-foot elevation loss beyond it. The Park Creek Trail passes through magnificent meadows with fine mountain views. It crosses many small creeks and ends in a series of switchbacks at the Park Creek Campground in the Stehekin Valley.

Directions: Trailhead at Colonial Creek Campground on SR 20 about 10 miles east of Diablo Dam.

Activities: Hiking, backcountry camping.

Dates: Seasonal, summer.

Fees: None, but a free permit is required for an overnight stay.

Closest town: Newhalem, about 10 miles south on State Route 20 from the western trailhead. Stehekin, about 18.5 miles from the eastern trailhead.

For more information: The Wilderness Information Center, 7280 Ranger Station Road, Marblemount, WA 98267. Phone (360) 873-4500. Or Golden West Visitor Center, Stehekin, WA 98852. Phone (360) 856-5700 extension 340 then extension 14.

Trail: Approximately 35 miles.

Elevation: The elevation at the pass is 6,040 feet. That is a 4,840-foot elevation gain from the Thunder Creek Trailhead and 3,740-foot elevation gain from the Park Creek Trailhead.

Degree of difficulty: Strenuous.

CASCADE PASS-COTTONWOOD TRAIL

[Fig. 8] A preferred route between the east and west sides of the North Cascades since long before Europeans first became aware of the range, Cascade Pass was a major trade route for Native Americans and probably was the route Alexander Ross took in 1814 when he became the first white man to cross the range. Ross followed his guide, Red Fox, and two other natives from his headquarters at Fort Okanogan on the Columbia

MOUNTAIN HEMLOCK
(Tsuga mertensiana)
Growing in the shade of other trees, hemlocks reach maturity producing a dense shade that few other species can survive under.

River. Soon after they started Ross became puzzled because he could not see the trail on the ground they were crossing. He was a little disturbed when Red Fox told him the trail was in his head, not on the ground. But they reached a pass where Ross saw the water in a creek running in the opposite direction, and he knew he had crossed the divide. His journal of the trip makes it likely that Cascade Pass was where he crossed. He got only a little farther, though, before a violent windstorm forced him to turn back.

The hike is much shorter, easier, and more pleasant now. And popular. On a warm summer day there are likely to be a fair number of people going to, from, or across the pass. Some avoid the trail for that reason. Others simply enjoy the company.

The trail begins at 3,600 feet elevation in a parking lot at the end of the Cascade River Road near the headwaters of the river. It goes into forest for 33 switchbacks up moderately steep trail. At the top of the switchbacks it levels off and enters open meadow with a wide variety of wildflowers that change as the season moves from early to late. The pass is at 5,400 feet elevation, a little more than 3 miles from the trailhead. There are magnificent views of 8,200-foot Johannesburg Mountain and its glacier and the masses of ice that break off from time to time in showy display.

A side trail from the pass goes steeply up to the north, leading to Sahale Arm, a long ridge that goes to Sahale Glacier where the view stretches many miles to the perpetual snows of 10,000-foot Glacier Peak. About 1 mile above Cascade Pass a fork to the right in the Sahale Arm Trail leads down to Doubtful Lake.

The Cascade Pass Trail continues past the pass and downward for 4 miles, past the blueberry bushes of Pelton Basin to the Stehekin Road. There hikers can catch the Park Service shuttle bus through the Stehekin Valley to Stehekin Landing and Lake Chelan. (Reservations for the bus are highly recommended. Contact the Wilderness Information Center, 7280 Ranger Station Road, Marblemount, WA 98267. Phone (360) 873-4500. Or Golden West Visitor Center, Stehekin, WA 98852. Phone (360) 856-5700, extension 340, then extension 14.)

A side trip that begins 3 miles from the pass with a fork to the north of the main trail leads up the rocky remnants of a mining road that once brought supplies from Stehekin Landing. After a short uphill hike the trail enters Horseshoe Basin. High cliffs rise steeply on three sides of the basin and waterfalls crash down their sides in all directions. Depending on the season, there may be 10 or more waterfalls. Despite the rocky floor of the basin, flowers that, like the falls, change with the season, make a scene of awesome beauty. At the end of the basin, near one of the larger falls, is the long abandoned Black Warrior mine. The mine was discovered in 1891 by Albert Pershall and M.M. Kingman who sold their claim for $30,000. It was worked by a series of new owners on and off until the 1940s. Usually the miners left for civilization in the winter, but one year when some stayed on, they moved from their cabin to the mine through a 50-foot tunnel in the snow.

There is no camping at Cascade Pass but there is a walk-in campground where campers carry their camping equipment a short distance from the car to an isolated campsite at the Cascade Road trailhead. Another campground is in Pelton Basin, a short distance east from the pass. Camping is also allowed at the end of the Sahale Arm route near Sahale Glacier and there is a campground at Cottonwood near where the Stehekin Valley bus stops.

The main trail goes over the old miners' road for a short distance from Horseshoe Basin to Cottonwood Camp and on to the shuttle-bus stop.

Directions: From Marblemount and State Route 20 drive east 23 miles on the gravel Cascade River Road to the trailhead.

Activities: Hiking, camping.

Dates: Seasonal, summer.

Fees: None, but a free permit is required for an overnight stay.

Closest town: Marblemount, 23 miles.

For more information: The Wilderness Information Center, 7280 Ranger Station Road, Marblemount, WA 98267. Phone (360) 873-4500. Or Golden West Visitor Center, Stehekin, WA 98852. Phone (360) 856-5700, extension 340, then extension 14. Or Park Headquarters, 2105 State Route 20, Sedro-Woolley, WA 98284. Phone (360) 856-5700.

Trail: 8.5 miles over Cascade Pass between Cascade River and Cottonwood in the Stehekin Valley.

Elevation: Cascade River trailhead is at 3,600 feet. Pass is 5,400 feet. Cottonwood Camp is 2,800 feet.

Degree of difficulty: Moderate.

MONOGRAM LAKE TRAIL

[Fig. 8] This is a pleasant lake in a rocky cirque with campsites and scenery. The Monogram Lake Trail is actually a less developed fork on the trail to the old Forest Service fire lookout on Lookout Mountain. The trailhead is in the Mount Baker-Snoqualmie National Forest on the Cascade River Road. The route switchbacks steeply up a ridge between Monogram and Lookout creeks and past a rocky outcrop with a good view. There is a campsite at 2.5 miles and about 0.25 mile beyond that is the fork. To the left is the ever upward, 4 mile trail to the peak and the site of the lookout. To the right is the shorter trail that leads into the national park and over a 5,400-foot ridge then down 600 feet to the lake. Both trails pass through forests to meadows. The view from Lookout Peak is long and beautiful. Camping is permitted at the lake but fires are not. Strenuous side trips from the lake can provide good views for experienced hikers.

Directions: East from Marblemount about 7 miles on the Cascade River Road. The trailhead is on the left side of the road a few feet beyond where it passes Lookout Creek.

Activities: Hiking, camping.

Dates: Seasonal, summer.

Fees: A parking permit fee may be charged.

Closest town: Marblemount, about 7 miles.

For more information: Wilderness Information Center, 7280 Ranger Station Road,

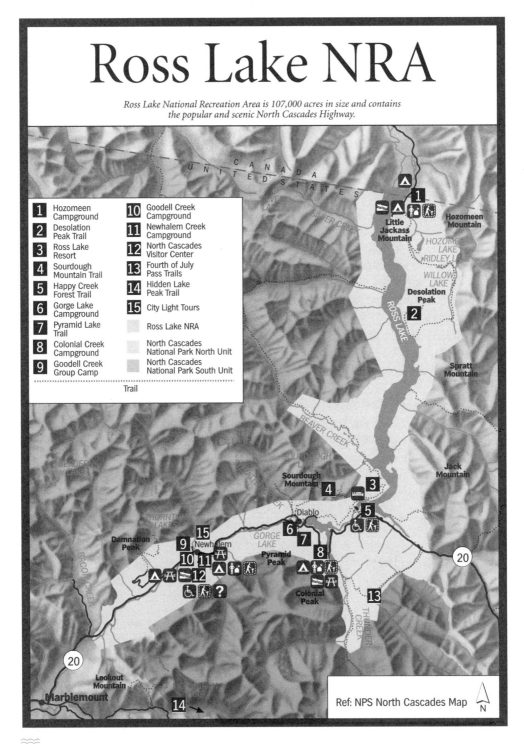

Ross Lake NRA

Ross Lake National Recreation Area is 107,000 acres in size and contains the popular and scenic North Cascades Highway.

1. Hozomeen Campground
2. Desolation Peak Trail
3. Ross Lake Resort
4. Sourdough Mountain Trail
5. Happy Creek Forest Trail
6. Gorge Lake Campground
7. Pyramid Lake Trail
8. Colonial Creek Campground
9. Goodell Creek Group Camp
10. Goodell Creek Campground
11. Newhalem Creek Campground
12. North Cascades Visitor Center
13. Fourth of July Pass Trails
14. Hidden Lake Peak Trail
15. City Light Tours

Ross Lake NRA

North Cascades National Park North Unit

North Cascades National Park South Unit

Trail

Ref: NPS North Cascades Map

Marblemount, WA 98267. Phone (360) 873-4500. Or Park Headquarters, 2105 State
Route 20, Sedro-Woolley, WA 98284. Phone (360) 856-5700.

Trail: 3.5 miles one-way.

Elevation: The elevation gain is approximately 4,200 feet.

Degree of difficulty: Moderate.

Ross Lake National Recreation Area

[Fig. 9] The Ross Lake Recreation area is by far the most heavily visited part of the
park complex, attracting about 40 percent of the 400,000 or so annual visitors. In large
part that is because the recreation area is the corridor through which State Route 20, the
North Cascades Highway, bisects the park's North and South units. Work on the highway
was well along when Congress was deciding what to do with the North Cascades in the
1960s, and that was one of the reasons it used the corridor to split the isolated park
proper into two sections and to accommodate people in the corridor.

But there is more to it than that. The recreation area also is the location of innumerable
attractions, ranging from short nature walks to large campgrounds to three lakes, two of
which are among the state's major recreation sites. There are many organized attractions
but there are also places where the individual can be alone to admire the vast panorama of
mountains, forests, lakes and waterfalls. There is much to see and do here whether the
visitor stays for an extended camping trip or just drives through to see the sights.

Directions: On the west side of the Cascades, go north on State Route 20 from
Marblemount about 4 miles to the west entrance to the recreation area. On the east side
of the Cascades, go west about 38 miles from Mazama on State Route 20 to the east
entrance. In Canada, drive 40 miles on the gravel Skagit River Road from Hope, B.C.

Activities: Camping, hiking, fishing, boating.

Dates: State Route 20 is closed east of Colonial Creek during the winter and most
other facilities except Colonial Creek Campground are also closed.

Fees: There are fees for camping at Goodell Creek, Newhalem Creek and Colonial
Creek campgrounds and for lodging and services at Ross Lake Resort.

Closest town: Marblemount, 4 miles.

For more information: Wilderness Information Center, 7280 Ranger Station Road,
Marblemount, WA 98267. Phone (360) 873-4500. Or Park Headquarters, 2105 State
Route 20, Sedro-Woolley, WA 98284. Phone (360) 856-5700.

STATE ROUTE 20, NORTH CASCADES HIGHWAY

[Fig. 8, Fig. 9] The highway connects with I-5 at exit 230 near Burlington. It passes the
park headquarters at 2105 State Route 20 in Sedro-Woolley about 6 miles from the
freeway. Maps, books, posters, and information about nearby public lands are available at
the headquarters along with displays of recreation facilities in the area. It is open seven

days a week during the summer and on weekdays throughout the year. About 30 miles farther, between Rockport and Marblemount, the highway passes through the Skagit River Bald Eagle Natural Area. Many of the majestic birds that have long been the symbol of the United States can be seen during the winter months when salmon come up the Skagit River to spawn before they die. Their carcasses provide nutrition to get the birds through the winter.

A short distance beyond the eagle sanctuary, just west of Marblemount, a road on the north side of the highway leads 1 mile to the park's Wilderness Information Center, where backcountry information and permits are available during business hours in the summer. Information and permits also are available during the summer at the North Cascades Visitor Center near Newhalem Creek Campground, just southeast of Newhalem.

The highway within the park boundaries and beyond to near Early Winters has been designated by Congress as the North Cascades Highway Scenic Byway in recognition of its magnificent beauty. Within the park the road passes the drive-in campgrounds and overlooks that provide spectacular views of Diablo and Ross lakes along with their surrounding scenery. A popular scene on the road is the spectacular Gorge Creek falls that sends cascades of whitewater toward Gorge Lake near where the lake is formed by Gorge Dam. The highway closes in the winter when snow and avalanches become unmanageable. It remains closed until the spring. Many of the park facilities close at the same time.

PARK SITES ON STATE ROUTE 20

The several sites on the highway within the park offer a wide range of attractions. They often are crowded on warm summer weekends and especially on holidays. Fishing is available at nearby lakes and streams. Hunting is allowed in the recreation area but not in the park proper.

GOODELL CREEK CAMPGROUND. [Fig. 9(10)] Site of camping both before and after Europeans found the Upper Skagit River. Twenty-two rustic sites along Skagit River. Suitable for tents and small trailers. Pit toilets. Launching area for river rafters. Open year-round. Fee required. The campground is about 12 miles northeast of Marblemount on the south side of State Route 20.

GOODELL CREEK GROUP CAMP. [Fig. 9(9)] Three sites for large groups. By reservation only. Available through Marblemount Wilderness Information Station. Phone (360) 873-4590, extension 16. Pit toilets. Open year-round. No potable water during the winter. Fee required. The campground is about 12 miles northeast of Marblemount on the north side of State Route 20.

NEWHALEM CREEK CAMPGROUND. [Fig. 9(11)] One hundred and twenty-nine sites. Near the Seattle City Light employees' village of Newhalem at the confluence of the Skagit River and Newhalem Creek. There are sites for tents, trailers, and walk-in camp-sites where campers carry their equipment a short distance to isolated camping. The campground has flush toilets and a trailer dump station but no hookups. Ranger-led walks, talks, and evening campfire programs are provided on an irregular schedule. The To Know A Tree Nature Trail is a feature. Some groceries are available at the General Store in Newhalem. Closed in winter. Fee required. The campground is about a mile south of State Route 20 on the Newhalem Creek Road that meets State Route 20 about 13 miles northeast of Marblemount.

NORTH CASCADES VISITOR CENTER. [Fig. 9(12)] On the road to the Newhalem Creek Campground off State Route 20. Contains an exhibit room, theater for visual presentations, information desk, and interpretative programs. Short interpretive trails are nearby. Some are wheelchair accessible. A rock shelter used by ancient Native Americans 8,400 years ago is nearby with archeological interpretations. The visitor center is just beyond the Newhalem Creek Campground about a mile south of State Route 20 on the Newhalem Creek Road that meets State Route 20 about 13 miles northeast of Marblemount.

*In Cascades forests a variety of blueberries (*Vaccinium *spp.) provide nourishment to wildlife as well as hungry human visitors.*

COLONIAL CREEK CAMPGROUND. [Fig. 9(8)] One hundred and sixty four units on Diablo Lake's Thunder Arm. Campsites on both sides of the highway. Sites for tents, trailers, and walk-ins where campers carry their camping equipment a short distance to isolated camping. Flush toilets, piped water, trailer dump station but no hookups, boat-launching ramps, fishing, ranger-led walks, talks, and campfire programs. There is a self guided Thunderwoods Nature Trail nearby and the trailhead of the Thunder Creek Trail (*see* Thunder Creek-Park Creek Trail, page 38) is within the campground. Summer only. Fee required. The campground is on both sides of State Route 20 about 25 miles northeast of Marblemount.

GORGE LAKE CAMPGROUND. [Fig. 9(6)] Six sites. Pit toilets. Boat launch. Open all year. No potable water. No fee. On State Route 20, go 6 miles east of Newhalem and turn northeast onto the road to Diablo Villlage and go about a mile.

MARBLEMOUNT. [Fig. 9] Town at the junction of State Route 20, which goes through the park, and the Cascade River Road, which winds through Mount Baker-Snoqualmie National Forest land past some magnificent country, old-growth forests, and several rustic campgrounds to the Cascade Pass Trail trailhead. In addition to the park's

Wilderness Information Station, Marblemount has limited lodging, stores, restaurants, and gas stations. The next service going east is many miles away at Mazama on the east side of the mountains.

🌸 MAJOR LAKES IN THE NATIONAL RECREATION AREA

The three major lakes in the recreation area are all in the upper Skagit Valley and accessible from State Route 20. They are within a few miles of each other and were formed by a series of dams on the Skagit River. Seattle City Light built them before the National Recreation Area was created. Their primary purpose is to generate electricity for Seattle some 100 miles away, but they also create recreation opportunities that make them one of Washington's primary places for summer outdoor activities.

Gorge Lake was the first of the three lakes Seattle City Light created to provide electricity for Seattle. It also is the smallest. The long, narrow lake was originally formed in 1924 by the small Gorge Dam which was replaced with the present 300-foot dam in 1960. The inviting banks of the Skagit River below the dam as far as Newhalem are hazardous because of severe fluctuations in the stream flow when the dam releases water unexpectedly. There are campsites (*see* Gorge Lake Campground, page 45) and a boat launch. Major activities are boating and fishing, and some canoeing.

The second of the three lakes in terms of both age and size, Diablo Lake is impounded behind Diablo Dam, which was completed in 1930. The dam is 389 feet high and the lake is 354 feet deep at the deepest point. It is popular for camping, boating, canoeing, and fishing for rainbow, brook, Dolly Varden, and cutthroat trout, some of them native fish rather than planted. The lake is closed to fishing at the mouths of tributary streams to protect fish spawning areas. Access is at boat ramps in Colonial Creek Campground (*see* Colonial Creek Campground, page 45).

Ross Lake is the newest and by far the largest of the lakes created by City Light's engineers. Ross Dam was built at the confluence of the Skagit River and Ruby Creek where generations of miners had fought a losing battle to wrench wealth out of the hard rock of the Cascades. The dam is a 540-foot giant that impounds a 1.5-mile-wide by 23-mile long lake. It reaches northward to the Canadian border. The lake is a major recreation site for both Americans and Canadians. It has 19 backcountry campgrounds with 67 sites accessible by foot, horse, or boat. Free overnight permits may be obtained at park offices. By far the largest of these campgrounds is the Hozomeen Campground which is accessible only over a 40-mile road from Hope, British Columbia in Canada (*see* Hozomeen Campground, page 47).

The campgrounds have fire rings, picnic tables, and vault toilets. Water from the lake should be boiled for at least 10 minutes or otherwise treated. Access is by a steep, downhill, 1-mile trail from State Route 20 south of the Ross Lake Overlook then over the top of the dam, or by a longer 5-mile trail that begins near the Diablo Lake Boat Launch. Access is also available by City Light boats on Diablo Lake and a walk up a steep, old construction road to Ross Dam. By prior arrangements, a truck from the Ross Lake

Resort can carry small boats up the steep incline from Diablo Lake to Ross Lake. Boats can be rented at the Ross Lake Resort, or ferry service to campgrounds and trailheads can be arranged at the resort. Phone (206) 386-4437.

Directions: The lakes all are accessible from State Route 20 within the Ross Lake National Recreation Area. Gorge Lake is 3 miles northeast of Newhalem. Diablo Lake is 6 mile northeast of Newhalem. Ross Lake is 10 miles northeast of Newhalem.

Activities: Camping, boating, fishing, hunting, swimming, and hiking.

Facilities: Campgrounds, boat launching, and, on Ross Lake, lodging and boat rentals.

Fees: Fees are required at most drive-in campgrounds and for services at Ross Lake Resort.

Closest town: Newhalem, 3 miles from Gorge Lake.

For more information: Wilderness Information Center, 7280 Ranger Station Road, Marblemount, WA 98267. Phone (360) 873-4500. Or Park Headquarters, 2105 State Route 20, Sedro-Woolley, WA 98284. Phone (360) 856-5700. Or North Cascades Visitor Center near Newhalem Campground. Phone (206) 386- 4495.

▒ HOZOMEEN CAMPGROUND AT ROSS LAKE

[Fig. 9(1)] On the far northern tip, Hozomeen is the only Ross Lake campground accessible by car. The route is by a 40-mile gravel road from Hope, British Columbia, Canada. The campground can also be reached by trail and by boat from Ross Dam. It has 122 sites. There is no garbage service. Naturalist-led walks, hikes, and evening campfire programs are conducted on an irregular basis. There is a self-guided nature trail along the international border. Three miles from Hozomeen on the Lightning Creek Trail a fork to the left goes up a short side trail to Hozomeen Lake and a pleasant campground with trout fishing and scenery. Two miles past the Hozomeen Lake fork the Lightning Creek Trail passes Willow Lake and another campground, where there is also trout fishing and scenery. There are no fees at any Hozomeen facilities but permits are required for overnight stays in the backcountry. The permits are available from rangers in the campground on Ross Lake.

Directions: By boat on Ross Lake from Ross Dam or take the East Bank Trail beside Ross Lake about 20 miles to Lightning Creek Campground, then take the Lightning Creek Trail about 6 miles to the junction with Hozomeen Creek Trail. Follow The Hozomeen Trail about 5 miles to the Hozomeen Campground. The East Bank Trailhead is 8 miles east of Colonial Creek Campground on State Route 20 near the Panther Creek Bridge. The Hozomeen Campground is also accessible by car over a 40 mile gravel road from near Hope, British Columbia, Canada. Take the Silver Skagit Road from the Trans-Canada Highway 1 near Hope, B.C. and go through the Skagit Valley Provincial Recreation Area to Hozomeen Campground at the end of the road.

Facilities: 122 camp sites, piped water, vault toilets, fire rings, boat docks.

Dates: Seasonal, summer.

Fees: None, but a free permit is required for an overnight stay.

Closest town: Hope, British Columbia, Canada, 40 miles.

For more information: Wilderness Information Center, 7280 Ranger Station Road, Marblemount, WA 98267. Phone (360) 873-4500. Or Park Headquarters, 2105 State Route 20, Sedro-Woolley, WA 98284. Phone (360) 856-5700. Or North Cascades Visitor Center near Newhalem Campground. Phone (206) 386- 4495.

▓ ROSS LAKE RESORT

[Fig. 9(3)] Ross Lake Resort has 13 cabins ranging from rustic to modern and accommodating from four to nine persons. They have varying types of cooking facilities. Some have private showers and some have shared showers. The cabins float on rafts on the lake.

The resort is the primary means of access to the lake from the south. It has 40 rental boats and also offers ferry service to campgrounds and trailheads on the lake. In addition to the motorboats, there are canoes and kayaks for rent.

Trailheads for many trails are located on both sides of the lake. The East Side Ross Lake Trail follows the shore for nearly the entire length of the lake.

The view from the cabins covers a broad expanse of the lake and the mountains that border it.

Directions: There are two trails to the resort: one begins at State Route 20 south of the Ross Lake Overlook and goes down very steeply for 1 mile, then over the top of Ross Dam and a short distance along the bank of the lake to the resort. The second is a longer, 5-mile, route. To find the trailhead, go 6 miles northeast of Newhalem on State Route 20, then go north on the Diablo Lake Road. Cross over the dam and go 1 mile. The trailhead is on the left side of the road. The trail goes inland through forest then back to the shore where it crosses a bridge over a narrow neck of the lake at the bottom of Ross Dam. Then it goes up the steep road that leads over the dam and on to the resort.

Access is also available by City Light boats on Diablo Lake and a walk up a steep, old construction road to Ross Dam. By prior arrangements, a truck from the resort can carry small boats and equipment up the steep incline from Diablo Lake to Ross Lake.

Activities: Hiking, fishing, hunting, boating, swimming.

Dates: Seasonal, summer.

Fees: There are fees for most resort services, and a free permit is required for an overnight stay in the backcountry.

Closest town: Newhalem, 10 miles.

For more information: Write or call Ross Lake Resort, Rockport, WA, 98283. Phone (206) 386-4437.

▓ CITY LIGHT TOURS

[Fig. 9(15)] A four-hour, fully guided tour of Seattle City Light facilities in the North Cascades begins with a program on the project's history in the theater at the tour center of the company town at Diablo. The tour includes a 560-foot ride up the incline railway on the side of Sourdough Mountain and a 25-minute boat cruise through the scenery of

Cougar (*Felis concolor*)

Also called mountain lion and puma, the cougar grows to 4 or 5 feet long with a 2.5-foot tail. In the Washington Cascades cougars are a sort of ruddy brown but elsewhere they can range from gray to a sandy color. They are uncommon, elusive, and secretive, preferring to see but not be seen. They hunt alone, taking anything from insects and mice to coyotes and even elk, but their preferred prey is deer. A large male may eat 20 pounds at a time. Cougars usually bury what they don't eat immediately after a kill and return for more when they become hungry again.

They locate large animals by sound or smell and stalk them slowly, stopping from time to time in a still crouch. They don't pounce until they are within about 30 feet when they can reach the prey in a few bounds. The males and females travel in twos for a few weeks after she comes in heat, then separate and go their solitary ways. There are stories of one stalking a human for days, or even weeks, then disappearing. On very rare occasions they have attacked children.

Diablo Lake to Ross Power House, where the water impounded behind Ross Dam is directed to generators that produce electricity to light Seattle 100 miles away. The tour ends with an all-you-can-eat dinner of chicken or vegetarian spaghetti. A shorter, 90-minute tour includes a historical video, a ride up the incline railway, and a walk across Diablo Dam. City Light also provides picnic sites, landscaped grounds, a rock garden, and the short Trail to the Cedars. The spectacular Ladder Creek Waterfall behind the Gorge Power House near Newhalem is on a half-mile-long trail that also passes beautiful pools and flower gardens. It is beautifully lighted at night but the trail includes some steps and handrails. Flashlights are advisable in the dark.

Directions: For tour hours and reservations contact the Skagit Tour Desk, 500 Newhalem Street, Rockport, WA 98283. Phone (206) 684-3030. The tours begin at the City Light Tour Center, which can be reached by taking State Route 20 to Newhalem then following the signs to the Tour Center.

Activities: Guided tours and developed park-like facilities.

Dates: Summer only.

Fees: There is a charge for the tour.

Closest town: Tours begin at Newhalem.

For more information: Contact Seattle City Light. Phone (206) 684-3030, or write Skagit Tours Desk at 500 Newhalem Street, Rockport, WA 98283.

TRAILS IN THE ROSS LAKE AREA

HAPPY CREEK FOREST TRAIL. [Fig. 9(5)] A short, 0.3-mile, pleasant, wheelchair-accessible boardwalk through an ancient forest grove.

Directions: The trailhead is about 10 miles northeast of Newhalem at milepost 134.5

Coyote (*Canis latrans*)

Coyotes are doglike animals about 32 inches long with a 14-inch tail. They are gray and have pointed faces and erect ears. They may be found nearly anyplace, even in towns, but they are more often in brushy rather than forested areas. They are adaptable and intelligent and have prospered where their larger cousins, the wolves, have largely disappeared. They are wary and not often seen but sometimes can be heard howling at night. The howling may help members of a family locate each other.

Like other members of the dog family, coyotes have a well-developed sense of smell and can detect other animals more than a mile away. They commonly feed on small mammals and birds, but if necessary they eat small creatures such as grasshoppers or even fruit. They hunt by stalking, pointing, pouncing, and chasing. Rarely, they hunt large prey such as deer by forming packs.

The same couple often mates year after year. Coyotes tend to increase mating and litters tend to be larger when their population is depleted. Young coyotes may stay with their families for a second year, helping to raise the next litter.

on State Route 20 and just east of the Ross Dam trailhead.

Activities: Short walk through old growth forest.

Dates: Year-round, weather permitting.

Fees: None, but a free permit is required for an overnight stay.

Closest town: Newhalem, 0.5 mile.

For more information: Wilderness Information Center, 7280 Ranger Station Road, Marblemount, WA 98267. Phone (360) 873-4500. Or Park Headquarters, 2105 State Route 20, Sedro-Woolley, WA 98284. Phone (360) 856-5700. Or North Cascades Visitor Center, phone (206) 386- 4495.

Trail: The Happy Creek Trail is 0.3 miles long, and level.

Degree of difficulty: Easy.

Surface: A boardwalk.

DESOLATION PEAK TRAIL. [Fig. 9(2)] Separate campgrounds for horse riders and hikers at the foot of Desolation Peak Mountain can be reached over the 12-mile Lightning Creek Trail from Hozomeen Campground (*see* page 47) or on the 16-mile East Bank Trail which follows the east bank of Ross Lake from Panther Creek on State Route 20 about 8 miles east of Colonial Creek Campground (*see* page 45). An easier way is by boat from Ross Dam to the campground (*see* Ross Lake Resort, page 48). At the campground the East Bank Trail forks, with one route skirting inland along Lightning Creek and the other continuing along the bank of the lake for 2 miles where it begins going steeply up Desolation Mountain. The trail up the mountain is closed to livestock, so horse riders must leave their animals at the horse camp and hike to the top.

The mountain gets its name from the desolation left by a catastrophic fire that destroyed the forest in 1926. The forest is recovering but the name has stuck. The trail goes 5 miles and gains 4,000 feet elevation up the side of the mountain. There is little water along the trail and hikers should carry a good supply. Ross Lake is deep within the Cascades and the forests here are a mixture of the west side's fir and the east side's pine.

Much of the trail is within the stands that are replacing those devastated by the fire but there are occasional rock outcroppings that provide long views of the lake and mountains, dominated by the perpetual ice of the huge 10,000-foot-high Mount Baker volcano to the west. Blacktail deer, bear, and coyotes may be seen briefly. Cougars, if they are present, probably will not allow a visitor to see them.

Like the trees, the meadows near the top are likely to grow flowers from both the east and west side as the species succeed each other during the short growing season. Below are the blue waters of the long, narrow Ross Lake flecked here and there by boats. The trail passes a campground about 0.5 mile from the peak. Fires are banned and there may not be much water late in the season. At the peak is one of the three lookouts in the park complex that are still manned throughout the summer, partly to watch for telltale smoke, partly to perform environmental tasks in the vicinity, and partly to maintain contact with visitors. All three of the lookouts (Desolation Peak, Sourdough Mountain, and Copper Peak) are on the National Register of Historic Places, and the one on Desolation Peak is also famous because the author and poet Jack Kerouac spent the summer here in 1956. He described his experience in his book *Desolation Angels*. He went on to become well known for his poetry and his novels on the "beat generation" of the 1950s.

Directions: Go by boat on Ross Lake from Ross Dam approximately 10 miles to Lightning Creek Campground. Or hike the East Bank Trail beside Ross Lake approximately 15 miles to Lightning Creek Campground. From Lightning Creek Campground follow the trail that goes north beside Ross Lake for 2 miles then veers eastward to go up

COYOTE
(Canis latrans)
Easily adapting to the presence of man, the coyote often preys on rodents, small animals, and livestock. It is a member of the dog family and has been known to mate with domestic dogs.

Desolation Peak. The East Bank Trailhead is 8 miles east of Colonial Creek Campground on State Route 20, near the Panther Creek Bridge.

Activities: Hiking, camping.

Dates: Seasonal, summer.

Fees: None, but a free permit is required for an overnight stay.

Closest town: Newhalem, 10 miles to Ross Dam.

For more information: Wilderness Information Center, 7280 Ranger Station Road, Marblemount, WA 98267. Phone (360) 873-4500. Or Park Headquarters, 2105 State Route 20, Sedro-Woolley, WA 98284 Phone (360) 856-5700. Or North Cascades Visitor Center near Newhalem Campground, phone (206) 386- 4495.

Trail: Approximately 7 steep miles one-way from Lightning Creek Campground.

Elevation: The elevation gain is approximately 4,400 feet.

Degree of difficulty: Strenuous.

SOURDOUGH MOUNTAIN TRAIL. [Fig. 9(4)] The trail to the Sourdough lookout is a steep climb that takes a long day. The route begins at the Seattle City Light employee village of Diablo and goes up steep switchbacks, gaining 3,000 feet elevation in a little more than 2 miles. The rest of the hike is 4 miles with a 2,000-foot elevation gain. Much of the early part of the trail is in mixed fir-pine forest that obscures the view, but there is an open section about 1.5 miles from the trailhead that provides good views, and at 3 miles a fork to the left goes up about 0.5 mile to the site of a satellite dish that provides television reception to Diablo. That, too, provides a good view. The satellite dish site, at 4,800 feet elevation, is a good place to turn around for those who don't wish to make the hike all the way to the top. For those who want to see the top, the trail is less steep beyond the satellite dish. At 4 miles from the trailhead, the trail passes Sourdough Creek and a no-fires campsite. It makes a sharp right turn beyond the creek and remains compara-tively level, despite a switchback or two, for 1.5 miles to the lookout, which is near the end of a long ridge with a view of City Light's lakes and mountain peaks for many miles. The route continues from here and makes a long loop down the Pierce Mountain Trail to Ross Lake and past the Ross Lake Resort, then either back to Diablo or across Ross Dam and up the steep, 1-mile trail to State Route 20, where hikers can either be met or have a car stashed at the Ross Lake trailhead. The Pierce Mountain Trail is not well used or maintained and portions are indistinct enough that it is easy to miss them. It is tempting from the top where it can be easily distinguished, but it is not a good trail. The better choice is to turn around and return on the trail to Diablo.

Directions: About 6 miles north of Newhalem on State Route 20 take a left fork to the City Light employee village of Diablo. The trailhead is at the far end of the village.

Dates: Seasonal, summer.

Fees: None, but a free permit is required for an overnight stay.

Closest town: Diablo.

For more information: Wilderness Information Center, 7280 Ranger Station Road, Marblemount, WA 98267. Phone (360) 873-4500. Or Park Headquarters, 2105 State

Route 20, Sedro-Woolley, WA 98284. Phone (360) 856-5700. Or North Cascades Visitor Center near Newhalem Campground. Phone (206) 386- 4495.

Trail: 6 miles one-way.

Elevation: The elevation gain is approximately 5,100 feet.

Degree of difficulty: Strenuous.

PYRAMID LAKE TRAIL. [Fig. 9(7)] This is a short, pleasant hike to a small, pleasant lake that has few attractions other than it is just there. There are no fish in the lake and no campsites. This is mainly a day hike except for the occasional climbers who use it as a route to ascents of Pyramid Peak and its neighbors, Pinnacle Peak and the strangely named Paul Bunyon's Stump. Pyramid Peak, which looks like a pyramid except that the top has been rounded by glaciers, is visible from the lake.

The trail begins at about 1,100 feet elevation and goes above a small cliff then upward for about 1 mile through a young forest with salal distributed on the forest floor. Eventually the trail enters a gully where old-growth hemlock and fir giants dominate over the younger trees.

The route leads over a high spot at 2,600 feet elevation then goes downward to 2,450 feet and ends in the rocks and cliffs at the lake a little more than 2 miles from the trailhead. There may be some deer, bear, or coyotes along the way and marmot and pika could be among the rocks at the lake.

Directions: The trailhead is on the south side of State Route 20 about 6 miles east of Newhalem.

Dates: Seasonal, summer.

Fees: None, but a free permit is required for an overnight stay.

Closest town: Newhalem about 6 miles

For more information: Wilderness Information Center, Marblemount, (360) 873-4500 or North Cascades Visitor Center near Newhalem Campground (206) 386-4495 or park Headquarters, 2105 State Route 20, Sedro-Woolley, WA 98284, (360) 856-5700.

Trail: 2 miles one-way.

Elevation: The elevation gain is approximately 1,550 feet.

Degree of difficulty: Easy.

FOURTH OF JULY PASS TRAILS. [Fig. 9(13)] Two trails meet at Fourth of July Pass on the slopes of Ruby Peak so it is possible to make an 11-mile through hike with the pass in the middle if transportation can be arranged at either end. Some of the trail is in the park's South Unit where pets and firearms are not permitted. There are three campgrounds along the way. Fires are permitted and overnight permits are required at all three.

Starting at 1,200 feet elevation in the Colonial Creek Campground on the Thunder Creek Trail (*see* Thunder Creek-Park Creek Trail, page 38), the route begins nearly level and passes through old-growth forests of gigantic firs, hemlock, and cedar. At about 2 miles, a little past a wooded backcountry campground, there is a junction with the Fourth of July Pass Trail, which climbs fairly gently 2.5 miles to the Fourth of July Camp, where there are views of the Snowfield Creek, Colonial Peak, and Neve Glacier.

Another 0.25 mile reaches the pass which, at 3,500 feet elevation has typical high country hemlock and silver fir forests and views of the Panther Potholes, two deep-green little lakes to the right.

The pass was bulldozed by an ancient glacier and is fairly level for 0.33 of a mile. That made it a good staging area for miners of years past. The mining was far up the side of Ruby Peak and the miners' trail leads off to the left from the pass. The farther it goes from the pass the thinner it becomes until it disappears entirely. Beyond where the trail is lost is the 7,408-foot peak of Ruby Mountain, about 4.5 miles from the pass. The view from there is of mountains, glaciers, and Ross Lake and is magnificent, but the climb is not for the inexperienced.

Hikers can turn around at the pass and return to Colonial Creek Campground or they can continue down the Panther Creek Side which ends at State Route 20 about 10 miles from the campground.

For those who continue, the trail wanders past some small swamps, then at about a mile from the pass, joins Panther Creek, a noisy, cascading, whitewater stream that parallels most of the rest of the trail. There are some avalanche slopes along that part of the trail where there may be marmots or pikas, and about 2 miles from the pass is a campsite beside the creek. Near the end the trail passes open stands of the lodgepole pine that is typical of the forests on the east side of the mountains. There also are Douglas firs, western hemlock, lush ferns, moss, and large cedars typical of the wet west side. The latter part of the trail goes painfully upward for 600 feet then back down for 700 after leaving the creek. Then it continues for less than 1 mile to State Route 20. The parking lot is at the East Bank Trailhead, about 0.33 mile to the west.

Directions: Trailhead is in the Colonial Creek Campground about 4 miles south of Diablo Dam on State Route 20.

Activities: Hiking, camping.

Dates: Seasonal, summer.

Fees: None, but a free permit is required for an overnight stay.

Closest town: Newhalem, about 10 miles south on State Route 20.

For more information: Wilderness Information Center, 7280 Ranger Station Road, Marblemount, WA 98267. Phone (360) 873-4500. Or North Cascades Visitor Center near Newhalem Campground. Phone (206) 386-4495. Or park headquarters, 2105 State Route 20, Sedro-Woolley, WA 98284. Phone (360) 856-5700.

Trail: 10 miles.

Elevation: The Thunder Creek trailhead is at 1,240 feet. The Panther Creek trailhead is at 1,850 feet. Fourth of July Pass is 3,500 feet.

Degree of difficulty: Strenuous.

HIDDEN LAKE PEAK TRAIL. [Fig. 9(14)] The trail is almost entirely within the Mount Baker-Snoqualmie National Forest, but it ends just inside the park border after a steep 1,000- foot descent from a saddle above to the lake. The lake usually is frozen over until late in the summer, but there are campsites (fires prohibited) near the lake and, possibly, trout in it. The view from the lake looks up the Cascade River valley to Boston Peak, and Sahale Peak, and their glaciers. The view is even better from the saddle above the lake.

The trail begins in a clear-cut at the end of a logging road. After a short upward hike it enters a stand of old growth then emerges in a beautiful meadow with high country plants like Indian paintbrush and monkey flowers (*Mimulus* spp.) It crosses Sibley Creek, courses through the meadow and past stands of alder trees, then turns and crosses the creek again after 2.5 miles. It levels off a little here and crosses some heather fields to a basin that leads to the saddle above the lake. Much of the trail is covered by snow fields that make it dangerous for inexperienced climbers until late in the season. An old fire lookout a short distance from the saddle is just barely on the national forest side of the park forest border. It was abandoned as a fire lookout in the 1960s and has been maintained by volunteers since. The trail from the saddle to the lookout is short but so hazardous that horses in the pack trains that supplied it stopped at the saddle and people carried supplies on their backs from here.

Directions: The trailhead is at the end of Forest Road 1540, which connects with the Cascade River Road about 2 miles southeast of the Marble Creek Campground.

Activities: Hiking, camping, fishing.

Dates: Seasonal, summer.

Fees: A parking permit fee may be charged.

Closest town: Marblemount, 10 miles.

For more information: Wilderness Information Center, 7280 Ranger Station Road, Marblemount, WA 98267. Phone (360) 873-4500. Or park headquarters, 2105 State Route 20, Sedro-Woolley, WA 98284. Phone (360) 856-5700.

Trail: 4 miles, one-way.

Elevation: The elevation gain is approximately 3,300 feet.

Degree of difficulty: Strenuous.

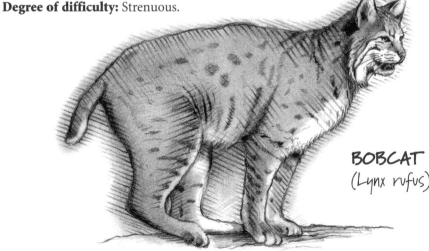

BOBCAT
(*Lynx rufus*)

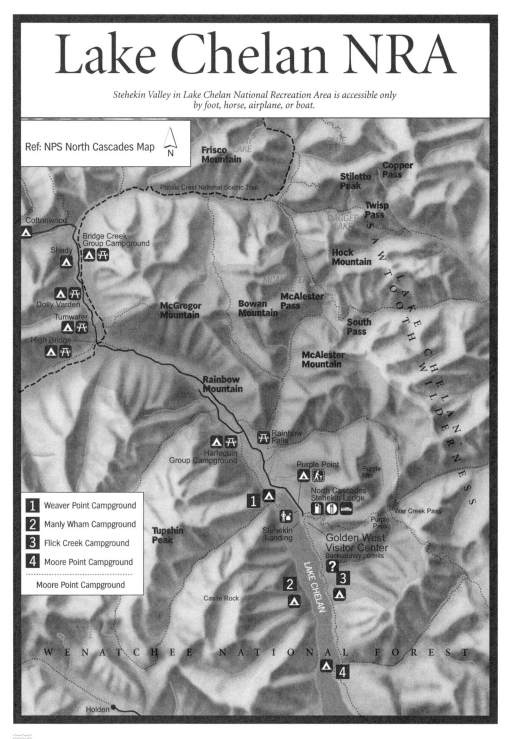

Lake Chelan NRA

Stehekin Valley in Lake Chelan National Recreation Area is accessible only by foot, horse, airplane, or boat.

Ref: NPS North Cascades Map N

Frisco Mountain

Copper Pass

Stiletto Peak

Twisp Pass

Pacific Crest National Scenic Trail

Cottonwood

Bridge Creek Group Campground

Shady

Dolly Varden

Tumwater

High Bridge

McGregor Mountain

Bowan Mountain

Hock Mountain

McAlester Pass

South Pass

McAlester Mountain

Rainbow Mountain

Rainbow Falls

Harlequin Group Campground

Purple Point

Purple Mtn

North Cascades Stehekin Lodge

War Creek Pass

Purple Pass

1 Weaver Point Campground

2 Manly Wham Campground

3 Flick Creek Campground

4 Moore Point Campground

Moore Point Campground

Tupshin Peak

Stehekin Landing

Golden West Visitor Center
Backcountry permits

LAKE CHELAN

Castle Rock

W E N A T C H E E   N A T I O N A L   F O R E S T

Holden

Lake Chelan National Recreation Area

[Fig. 10] The Lake Chelan National Recreation Area consists largely of the Stehekin Valley, a 25-mile-long glaciated valley that goes up from Lake Chelan to Cascade Pass. It is so isolated that the Park Service and Forest Service jointly maintain a ranger station (428 W. Woodin Avenue, Route 2, Box 680, Chelan, WA 98816, phone (509) 664-2576) in Chelan 50 miles away to provide information about the valley and Lake Chelan, which is its principal means of access.

Stehekin Valley has been lived in, logged, farmed, and mined for more than a century but no road leads to it and people cannot drive to it. The only access is by foot, horse, airplane, or boat, with boat being by far the most popular and airplane being by far the fastest, making the trip in half an hour. The Chelan Airways Co. is based in Chelan. It has been operating charter float planes since 1945. It offers daily, year-round service to Stehekin Landing and other destinations. For more information call (509) 682-5555.

The boat trip to Stehekin is on Lake Chelan. Some private boats start from one of several boat launches along the lake shore between Chelan and the dock at Twenty-Five Mile Creek State Park in the Wenatchee National Forest. But other private boats and the commercial passenger-freight boats start at the city of Chelan and cover the entire length of the lake, which is 50 miles long and averages about 1 mile wide. There are also self-propelled freight barges that carry heavy materials from Chelan to the Stehekin Landing as well as to the few residents above Twenty-Five Mile Creek. The commercial passenger boats make regular stops to pick up passengers and freight at Fields Point Landing, which was developed jointly by the Park Service and the Forest Service to provide for boaters. Facilities here include a parking lot for people traveling on the lake, restrooms, snacks, and pay phones.

The passenger boats are the *Lady of the Lake II*, the *Lady Express*, and since the summer of 1998, a high speed catamaran. They are part of a line of "Lady" boats that began when the original was launched in 1900. At that time there were several boats making the trip from Chelan to Stehekin under power of wood-fed steam engines. They were slow, taking days to make a one-way trip, and were fitted with cabins, galleys, and separate lounges for men and women.

The first "Lady" was 113 feet long, the largest of the boats that have sailed on the lake. Her owners added a second deck in 1903 to accommodate up to 125 passengers. She burned up to 10 cords of wood on a trip from one end of the lake to the other. She was retired in 1915 and replaced by boats that used petroleum power.

The second *Lady of the Lake* was moved from her original home on Lake Roosevelt to the Lake Chelan run in the mid-1940s and made regular, one-day runs to Stehekin. In the 1970s the owners began building a new, larger boat. Working when time and money allowed, they took five years to complete the new vessel, which they dubbed the *Lady of the Lake II*. In 1990 that vessel was joined by the *Lady Express* and eight years later by the catamaran.

Lake Chelan

Lake Chelan was originally formed when the glacier in the Columbia Valley created a 400-foot moraine across the mouth of the Chelan Valley, damming the valley's streams.

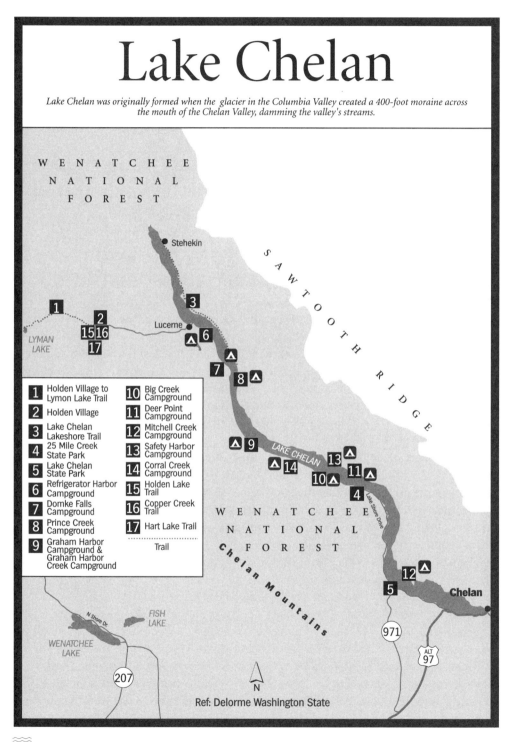

WENATCHEE
NATIONAL
FOREST

SAWTOOTH RIDGE

Stehekin

LYMAN LAKE

Lucerne

1 Holden Village to Lymon Lake Trail
2 Holden Village
3 Lake Chelan Lakeshore Trail
4 25 Mile Creek State Park
5 Lake Chelan State Park
6 Refrigerator Harbor Campground
7 Domke Falls Campground
8 Prince Creek Campground
9 Graham Harbor Campground & Graham Harbor Creek Campground
10 Big Creek Campground
11 Deer Point Campground
12 Mitchell Creek Campground
13 Safety Harbor Campground
14 Corral Creek Campground
15 Holden Lake Trail
16 Copper Creek Trail
17 Hart Lake Trail

········· Trail

LAKE CHELAN

WENATCHEE
NATIONAL
FOREST

Chelan Mountains

Lake Shore Drive

Chelan

FISH LAKE

N Shore Dr.

WENATCHEE LAKE

207

971

ALT 97

N

Ref: Delorme Washington State

All three vessels now make the run. *The Lady Express* maintains a year-round schedule, daily in the summer, and on varying days of the week the rest of the year. It makes the run in 2 hours and 15 minutes with a maximum 100 passengers and a 1-hour layover in Stehekin. During the summer the *Lady of the Lake II* makes the one-way trip in 4 hours, carrying up to 350 passengers, and takes a 90-minute layover at Stehekin Landing. The catamaran makes the one-way trip in 1 hour and 15 minutes, makes a 1-hour layover and carries as many as 49 passengers. The catamaran is scheduled to make two trips a day. The old *Lady of the Lake* still is used for odd jobs by her owners.

The vessels travel through a valley that was carved out by two glaciers. One came down from the Stehekin valley and another came up from the Columbia River valley. They met about a third of the way up the valley from the Columbia and churned out a deep gouge called the Lucerne Basin. The bottom of the lake at the basin is 1,529 feet below the surface of the lake and 429 feet below sea level, making it the seventh deepest lake in the world.

The lake was originally formed when the glacier in the Columbia Valley created a 400-foot moraine across the mouth of the Chelan Valley, damming the valley's streams. A hydroelectric dam built in 1926 raised the level of the lake by 21 feet. The dam is 40 feet high and 490 feet long. A 14-foot-diameter tunnel carries the water 2 miles to a generating station near the town of Chelan Falls on the banks of the Columbia River.

The boats start their trips in Chelan in the foothills of the Cascades and move ever farther into the range until at Stehekin Landing they are in the heart of the mostly igneous rock mountains. After they leave Fields Point, the *Lady II* and the *Lady Express* make regular stops at Lucerne to pick up and discharge passengers, freight, and mail. The catamaran is scheduled to make all the stops, except that it will stop at Lucerne only on the return trip. The vessels also make flag stops at trailheads and campgrounds along the way. They stop when they see a signal from the shore but it is advisable to make prior arrangements. All of the stops along the way are dependent on whether the lake level is high enough so the boats can reach the docks.

For more information: Contact the Lake Chelan Boat Company, PO Box 186, Chelan, WA 98816. Phone (509) 682-2224, or (509) 682-4584.

FOREST SERVICE, PARK SERVICE CAMPGROUNDS ON LAKE CHELAN

The boats stop at four campgrounds that have side trails leading to the high country trails in the Lake Chelan Sawtooth Wilderness in the mountains above the east bank and the Glacier Peak Wilderness above the west bank. Hikers can camp here until they are picked up by either a private or a commercial boat. Fee permits may be required for docking private boats. The permits and information are available at the ranger station in Chelan, 428 Woodin Avenue, Route Two, Box 680, Chelan, WA 98816, phone (509) 682-2549 or at the Golden West Visitor Center in Stehekin, phone (360) 856-5700 extension 340 then extension 14. Below is a list of the campgrounds:

LUCERNE CAMPGROUND. [Fig. 12(9)] On the west bank. Two tables, two toilets, one dock, and a boat basin with capacity of about 11 boats. A Forest Service guard station is nearby. Railroad Creek Road leads 11 miles to Holden Village (*see* Holden Village page 63). Lucerne also is the trailhead for a two mile-trail to Domke Mountain, 4,067 feet elevation above the lake. A branch of that trail goes 2 miles to Domke Lake where there are three campgrounds.

PRINCE CREEK CAMPGROUND. [Fig. 11(8)] On the east bank. Six tent sites, tables, fire rings, toilets, a floating dock for about three boats.

FLICK CREEK. [Fig. 10(3)] On the east bank with access from the Lake Shore Trail that follows the bank between Prince Creek and Stehekin Landing. Two tent sites and a shelter. Fire rings, tables. Can accommodate 12 boats.

WEAVER POINT CAMPGROUND. [Fig. 10(1)] On the west bank. Sixteen tent sites, tables, fire rings, toilets. Can accommodate 20 boats.

MOORE POINT CAMPGROUND. [Fig. 10(4)] On the east bank. One shelter, tables, fire rings, toilets, dock for about three boats.

There is also a series of boat-only campgrounds on the lake beyond Fields Point Landing, which is on the west shore of the lake approximately 16 miles above Chelan.

MITCHELL CREEK CAMPGROUND. [Fig. 11(12)] On the east bank. Popular picnic area. One shelter, tables, fire rings, toilets, dock with capacity of about 17 boats.

DEER POINT CAMPGROUND. [Fig. 11(11)] On the east bank. Good protection from downlake wind but not from uplake wind. Five tent sites, fire rings, toilets, floating dock with capacity of about eight boats.

SAFETY HARBOR CAMPGROUND. [Fig. 11(13)] On the east bank. Good shelter from wind. Four tent spaces, tables, fire rings, toilet. Floating dock with capacity of about six boats is accessible year-round.

BIG CREEK CAMPGROUND. [Fig. 11(10)] On the west bank. One shelter, four tent sites, tables, fire rings, toilets, fixed dock with capacity of about four boats.

CORRAL CREEK CAMPGROUND. [Fig. 11(14)] On the west bank. Good shelter from wind. Four tent sites, fire rings, tables, toilet, floating dock with capacity of about four boats.

GRAHAM HARBOR CAMPGROUND. [Fig. 11(9)] On the west bank. Good shelter from downlake wind but not uplake. Five tent sites, tables, fire rings, toilets, floating dock with capacity of about 10 boats.

GRAHAM HARBOR CREEK CAMPGROUND. [Fig. 11(9)] On the west bank. One shelter, five tent sites, tables, fire rings, toilets, fixed dock with capacity of about six boats.

DOMKE FALLS CAMPGROUND. [Fig. 11(7)] On the west bank. Four tent sites, fire rings, tables, toilet, floating dock with capacity of about six boats.

REFRIGERATOR HARBOR CAMPGROUND. [Fig. 11(6)] Good shelter from downlake wind but not from uplake wind. Four tent sites, fire rings, toilets, capacity of about four boats. Accessible year-round.

MANLY WHAM CAMPGROUND. [Fig. 10(2)] Two tent sites, fire rings, toilets. Limited boat capacity.

Boat fuel is available at Chelan, Twenty-five Mile Creek, and Stehekin Landing. There are boat dump stations at Chelan and the Old Mill and Old Mill Park on the east bank about 6 miles uplake from Chelan. Boat launch facilities are available at Chelan, Old Mill Park, Lake Chelan State Park, and Twenty-five Mile Creek State Park. The North Cascades Stehekin Lodge operates a Marina at Stehekin Landing with moorage for 30 or more boats.

STATE PARKS ON LAKE CHELAN

The Washington State Parks and Recreation Commission maintains two drive-in campgrounds on the lower portion of Lake Chelan. They are convenient places to launch private boats for a few hours of pleasant boating on the lake, or for access to one of the uplake campgrounds, or to travel to Stehekin Landing.

LAKE CHELAN STATE PARK. [Fig. 11(5)] With well over 1 mile of shoreline and 127 acres, the Lake Chelan State Park is the largest and most popular public campground in the area. It has a boat launch, docks, and many water activities as well as numerous campsites and facilities for recreation, including 2.1 miles of paved trail. During winter months it is heavily used for sledding and as a base for cross-country skiing and snow-mobiling. The lake nearby has salmon, trout, and burbot (*Lota lota*).

A grassy picnic area is shaded by ponderosa pine, elm, black walnut sycamore, and maple trees. Some campsites are secluded by dense brush and require that camping gear be carried a short distance. A few have views of the lake. There is an old homesteader's cabin in the park and rangers give campfire programs on the wildlife and history of the area.

Directions: The park is 7 miles northwest of Chelan on the South Lakeshore Road.

Activities: Camping, swimming, boating, sailing, paddling, picnicking, fishing, water skiing, sledding, cross-country skiing, snowmobiling, and scuba diving.

Facilities: Boat launch, boat docks, water ski floats, bath house, swimming beach, 127 tent sites, 17 RV sites, 52 picnic sites, picnic shelter, restrooms, trailer dump stations, and playground.

Dates: Summer and from the end of October through March, on weekends and holidays only.

Fees: Fees are required for overnight camping, includes boat launch. A fee also is required for launch only.

Closest town: Chelan, 7 miles.

For more information: Washington State Park Information Office, 7150 Cleanwater Lane, Olympia, WA 98504-2650, Phone 1-800-233-0321. For camping reservations phone 1-800-452-5687.

TWENTY-FIVE MILE CREEK STATE PARK. [Fig. 11(4)] At one time this was the uplake station where the boats picked up and discharged passengers who did not make the entire trip to or from Stehekin Landing. The boat trips became so popular that there was not room in the cramped space on the lake shore for boat passengers to park, so the Park Service and the Forest Service developed Fields Point on the lake to accommodate the Lady boats and private vessels. Facilities at Fields Point include a parking lot for people traveling on the lake, restrooms, snacks, and pay phones.

The park has 1,500 feet of shoreline and 235 acres on what was once the Chelan Valley's oldest resort. The State Parks and Recreation Commission purchased it in 1975 and maintains the amenities. There is a marina with a gas float and moorage for about 35 boats and a two-lane boat launch with a boarding float. The campsites are rustic with dirt or grass bases and gravel pull-outs. Sites are in a second-growth ponderosa pine, cottonwood, and birch forest. There is good fishing for rainbow trout in the adjacent Twenty-five Mile Creek. Lake fishing also is a feature.

The park is bordered by the Wenatchee National Forest, and in the fall it is a base for hunters. In the winter there is cross-country skiing and snowmobiling in the forest.

Directions: Seventeen miles northwest from Chelan on the South Lakeshore Drive.

Activities: Boating, swimming, fishing, snowmobiling, cross-country skiing, picnicking.

Facilities: Boat launch, 52 tent sites, 23 RV sites, group camp for 88 persons, restrooms, marina with docks and fuel, grocery store, volleyball court, picnic sites.

Dates: Summer, May through Oct.

Fees: Fees are required for overnight camping, includes boat launch. A fee also is required for launch only.

Closest town: Chelan, 17 miles.

For more information: Washington State Park Information Office, 7150 Cleanwater Lane, Olympia, WA 98504-2650. Phone (800) 233-0321. For camping reservations, phone (800) 452-5687.

FISHING ON LAKE CHELAN AND WILDLIFE IN THE LAKE CHELAN BASIN

Few native fish remain, having been decimated by overfishing and other natural and manmade problems. The lake, however, has been successfully stocked with rainbow (*Oncorhynchus mykiss*), and cutthroat (*Salmo clarki*) trout, and sockeye (*oncorhyncus nerka*) salmon, as well as others. That has created at least a temporary balance between fish and fishing.

Deer often are numerous in the area around Deer Point and Safety Harbor campgrounds and can be seen from the lake. The Forest Service and Chelan County Public Utility District enhance the browsing conditions in the area by intentionally starting fires under carefully controlled conditions. The fires clear the ground and many nutritious plants such as bitterroot (*Lewisia rediviva*) quickly replace the burned plants. Equipped with large, oval-shaped hooves with a hard outer shell surrounding a soft pad, the mountain goat (*Oreamus americanus*) can easily climb among the sheer rock faces of cliffs above the lake, finding both food and safety from predators. The goats are completely covered by shaggy woolly hair and have beards. Both sexes have four inch black horns with sharp points. Black bears can sometimes be seen along the lake shore. Sometimes more likely to be heard than seen, bird species in the area include the blue grouse (*Dendragapus obscurus*), which is distinguished by the males' series of low humming sounds. There also are numerous songbirds.

For more information: In Chelan, Chelan Ranger Station, 428 W. Woodin Avenue, Route 2, Box 680, Chelan, WA 98816. Phone (509) 682-2549. At Stehekin Landing, Golden West Visitor Center, phone (360) 856-5700 extension 340 then extension 14.

▨ HOLDEN VILLAGE

[Fig. 11(2)] In 1896 J. H. Holden, a prospector who had had little luck searching for wealth near the banks of Lake Chelan, ventured 11 miles up Railroad Creek and found what eventually became the largest copper mine in Washington. The first shipment of ore concentrate down the lake was not made until 1938, 20 years after Holden died, but from then until the mine closed in 1957, it shipped more than $66 million worth of concentrated ore over the lake.

The mine contained 50 miles of railroad track and numerous caverns, some as big as a football field. Since the mine was many miles deep in the wilderness, the company built one town, called Holden, at the mine and another, called Lucerne, at the foot of Railroad Creek where barges brought in supplies and took out ore. Holden Village had a population as large as 600 and provided housing, meals, stores, and recreation for the people.

After the miners left, the Howe Sound Mining Company donated the property and buildings to the Lutheran Bible Institute which developed the original buildings into a year-round, non-denominational, backcountry educational and recreational retreat, open to all people of all faiths. It consists of 12 houses, called chalets, for guests, crew, and teaching staff and a large building, called the hotel, which houses guest rooms, the dining hall, a recreation hall, and shops including a bookstore, and post office. There are no telephones.

The village is at the end of a long finger of land that juts up Railroad Creek into the midst of the Glacier Peak Wilderness. It is near many majestic mountains including nearby Buckskin, Copper, and Dumbell, all more than 8,000 feet high. It is wild land and wildlife including bear, deer, marmots, and rabbits roam in the village. There is a trail beside the Railroad Creek Road for people who would rather hike than ride between Holden and the lake, and there are trailheads of trails that go far into the wilderness in all directions. There also are a number of short, day hikes, including the following:

HOLDEN LAKE TRAIL. [Fig. 11(15)] 4 miles one-way.

COPPER CREEK TRAIL. [Fig. 11(16)] 2 miles one-way.

HART LAKE TRAIL. [Fig. 11(17)] 4 miles one-way.

People staying at the village can use the trails for day hikes and many people either stay at the hotel or in a nearby campground as a jumping-off place for overnight hikes into the wilderness.

Holden operates throughout the year and conducts seminars during the winter. Visitors also use it as a base for cross-country skiing, sledding, and snowshoeing. There are classes, including studies of literature, the environment, crafts, the Bible, and theology.

Directions: Take a boat on Lake Chelan from Chelan or Fields Point Landing to the site of the abandoned village of Lucerne, then catch the Holden Village shuttle bus up the Railroad Creek Road.

Activities: Hiking, camping, educational classes, wilderness shelter, spiritual retreat.

Dates: Open year-round.

Fees: There are daily or weekly rates for accommodations at the village.

Closest town: Chelan, 55 miles.

For more information: Write to Registrar, Holden Village, HCOO Stop 2, Chelan, WA 98816-9769. There are no phones or e-mail at Holden.

HOLDEN VILLAGE TO LYMAN LAKE TRAIL

[Fig. 11(1)] This is an overnight, 18-mile hike from Holden Village to a rugged, beautiful wilderness basin with a large lake just below the crest of the Cascades. The trailhead is about 1 mile above the village on the Railroad Creek Road. After 1 mile it passes the junction with the Holden Lake Trail then continues up the glaciated valley into the Wenatchee National Forest and the Glacier Peak Wilderness. It goes past stands of cottonwood, willows, and mixed conifer with a varied understory including red-osier dogwood (*Cornus stolonifera*), Douglas maple (*Acer glabrum douglasii*), salmonberry (*Rubus spectabilis*), and serviceberry (*Rubus parviflorus*). To the west are the Bonanza Peak crags. At Hart Lake, Railroad Creek veers to the left and the trail goes with it above the lake. The trail wends above Crown Point Falls and passes a mine shaft and a grassy meadow where blueberry fields begin to appear. The route goes on to a bench to Lake Lyman near a fork. The right fork goes over the crest and into the Mount Baker-Snoqualmie National Forest portion of the Glacier Peak Wilderness toward the Suiattle River valley. There are awesome views from there across the valley to the perpetual snows and glaciers of the Glacier Peak Volcano. The left fork passes the smaller Upper Lyman Lakes, Lyman Glacier, and 8,459-foot Chiwawa Mountain. Camping and fires are banned within 200 feet of Lyman Lake.

Directions: The access is by boat on Lake Chelan to Lucerne, then the shuttle bus on the Railroad Creek Road to Holden.

Activities: Hiking, camping, fishing.

Dates: Seasonal, summer.

Fees: Fees are charged for riding the commercial boats and for those people who stay at Holden Village.

Closest town: Chelan, 55 miles.

For more information: Chelan Ranger Station, 428 W. Woodin Avenue, Route 2, Box 680, Chelan, WA 98816. Phone (509) 682-2576.

Trail: 9 miles one-way.

Elevation: The elevation gain from Holden Village to Lyman Lake is approximately 2,400 feet.

Degree of difficulty: Strenuous.

LAKE CHELAN LAKESHORE TRAIL

[Fig. 11(3)] The lake portion of the trail begins at Prince Creek where the Prince Creek Trail wends down from the high country. The campground at Prince Creek can be reached by boat. From there the trail follows the east shore of the lake, undulating from the water's edge to high bluffs above the lake. The views of the lake and the mountains are magnificent. The trail passes groves of old-growth Douglas fir and ponderosa pine and quaking aspen (*Populus tremuloides*). In the spring there are flowers such as trillium (*Trillium* spp.), and glacier lily. Later they are replaced by beauties such as balsamroot (*Balsamorhiza sagittatsa*) and Miner's lettuce (*Montia sibirica*).

There are several campsites along the way at Cascade Creek, Meadow Creek, Moore Point and Flick Creek. The hike can be shortened by disembarking from the boat at Moore Point at the bottom of the Fish Creek Trail from the backcountry or at Flick Creek. The Moore Point Campground was once the site of a resort. Its wide level spaces still have the orchards and New England-style rock fences of that long-gone development.

The trail ends at Stehekin about 6 miles from Moore Point. There are campsites nearby or a room can be rented from one of the facilities at the landing or farther up the Stehekin Road.

Directions: By boat from Chelan or Fields Point to one of the campgrounds where boats can land along the trail.

Activities: Hiking, camping.

Facilities: Campsites have tent spaces, fire rings, toilets, and other facilities.

Dates: Seasonal, spring through fall.

Fees: Fees are charged on the commercial boats.

Closest town: Stehekin, 17 miles from Prince Creek.

For more information: Chelan Ranger Station, 428, W. Woodin Avenue, Route 2, Box 680, Chelan, WA 98816. (509) 682-2576.

Trail: The trail to Stehekin Landing from Prince Creek is 17.5 miles one-way. From Moore's Point to Stehekin Landing, the trail is 6.5 miles. From Flick Creek to Stehekin Landing, it is 4 miles.

Elevation: The elevation gain between the low point and the high point is approximately 600 feet but the trail undulates and the total climb is more than that.

Degree of difficulty: Moderate.

SNOWSHOE HARE
(Lepus americanus)
A shy boreal species that is more active at night. Dark brown in summer, white in winter.

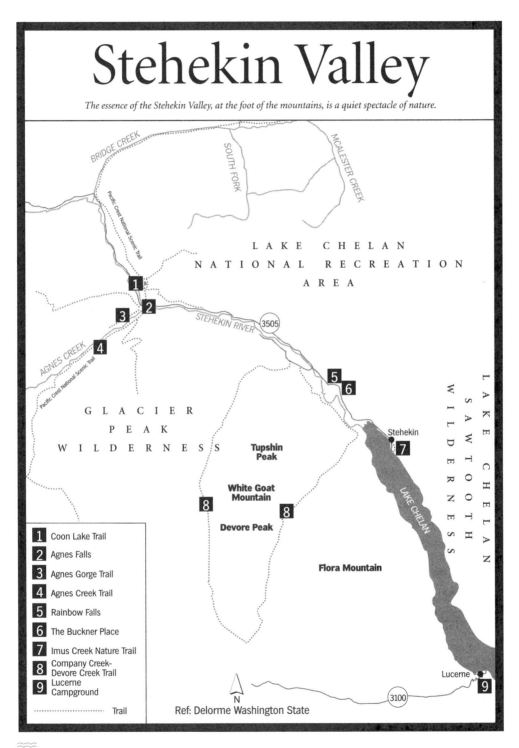

Stehekin Valley

The essence of the Stehekin Valley, at the foot of the mountains, is a quiet spectacle of nature.

BRIDGE CREEK

SOUTH FORK

MCALESTER CREEK

Pacific Crest National Scenic Trail

LAKE CHELAN
NATIONAL RECREATION
AREA

STEHEKIN RIVER 3505

AGNES CREEK

Pacific Crest National Scenic Trail

GLACIER
PEAK
WILDERNESS

Tupshin
Peak

White Goat
Mountain

Devore Peak

Flora Mountain

Stehekin

LAKE CHELAN

LAKE CHELAN SAWTOOTH WILDERNESS

LAKE CHELAN

Lucerne

1 Coon Lake Trail
2 Agnes Falls
3 Agnes Gorge Trail
4 Agnes Creek Trail
5 Rainbow Falls
6 The Buckner Place
7 Imus Creek Nature Trail
8 Company Creek-
Devore Creek Trail
9 Lucerne
Campground

·············· Trail

N

Ref: Delorme Washington State

3100

Stehekin Valley

[Fig. 12] Whether visitors travel on foot, on horseback, by airplane, by private boat, or on one of the Lady commercial vessels, when they reach what Stehekin Valley dwellers call simply "The Landing" they are entering an isolated community that must be unlike any other in the United States. Passengers alight to a charming community that has little relationship with the rest of the world, which valley dwellers refer to as "down lake."

The only road has no inlet and no outlet. It once led some 25 miles up the valley to the mines in Horseshoe Basin. But after the mines closed, a flood washed out the automobile bridge at Cottonwood and it was never replaced. The Park Service bus usually goes to the end of the road at Cottonwood but from time to time floods wash out portions of the road, making it impossible for the bus to reach Cottonwood until the road is repaired, sometimes years later. When that happens the bus goes only to wherever the road is impassable. Beyond that it is a matter of walking, or riding a horse.

Something like 70 to 100 people live year-round in the nine inhabited miles of the valley, most of them in the vicinity of the landing. A few of them are retired or make their living at independent occupations such as art or writing, but most either work for the Park Service or in the tourist business.

The community came into existence in the late nineteenth century as part of the local mining industry, but even before the mines petered out tourists discovered the community and entrepreneurs began catering to visitors. In 1892 M.E. Field purchased a two-story boarding house called the Argonaut in the valley and converted it into an elegant hotel for both miners and tourists. By 1905 it had become a luxury hotel attracting guests from many parts of the country. The local services were limited so the hotel had its own barn, wood shed, ice house, fruit trees, and laundry. During the 1920s a power dam near Chelan raised the level of the lake and flooded the site of the hotel. The building was dismantled and the material used to construct the Golden West Lodge, which now is used as a visitor center by the Park Service. Field's hotel was an early step in the tourist business that is a mainstay of the valley's economy to this day, providing jobs for many of the residents.

Of necessity, the residents are self-reliant individuals who enjoy an isolated, self-sufficient life without some of the amenities that most Americans take for granted. There is no physician's office or hospital in the valley. Some people have gardens to produce some of their food. When someone decides to build a new shed, he likely calls on some neighbors and they all work together to build it. The food and supplies they don't produce themselves they get by sending a note and a blank check to a store in Chelan. The store fills the order and puts it on a Lady boat to be delivered to the landing.

Children in the valley attend a tiny school with one classroom. There is one full-time and several part-time teachers from kindergarten through eighth grade. When the pupils graduate from the eighth grade, they go to high school down lake in Chelan. Usually one or both parents go with them to live in Chelan. During weekends, holidays, and vacations they may go home to Stehekin. When the new school building opened in 1988, it was the last one-room school in the state. Enrollment varies from year to year, ranging from 1 to 18 pupils. The school has one classroom, a library, and a gymnasium. The building it replaced was a log cabin built in 1921 by volunteers from the community with logs they felled and peeled on the site. That building now is a museum.

Until recently there were no telephones in the valley. Now the Park Service offices have a satellite phone system which includes a pay phone for residents and visitors. Some residents and businesses also have radio phones. Indeed some old-timers can remember when there was no electricity, except what a few residents concocted by channeling a hillside stream to a private hydroelectric generator or by installing a gas-powered generator. For the rest, candles and lanterns provided all the light they needed.

Cars are brought up the lake on barges and most residents do their own repair and maintenance work. Shoveling snow from the driveway to the road takes a good deal of time in the winter when 20 feet may fall. Television is limited to those families that have installed satellite dishes, and radio reception is spotty in many locations.

The community is close knit, with family helping family whenever help is needed. There are frequent community parties and celebrations. "We work together and we play together and it's a little like one big family," a resident once said.

The present residents are not the first people attracted to the valley. Stehekin is an Indian word meaning something like "the way we came" or "the way through." The name refers to the routes Indians traditionally traveled to cross the mountains through Stehekin Valley and over Cascade Pass. Some residents believe there was a trade center at a pleasant place in the valley now called Bridge Creek. Natural routes lead there over passes and through tributary valleys from several directions, and the Stehekin Valley there is flat and level with room for many people. That still is a hub for trails from many directions, including the popular Cascade Pass Trail (*see* Cascade Pass-Cottonwood Trail, page 39).

The reward for residents is living in a beautiful valley that is something like the frontier of early America, when humans still had made only a slight mark on the natural world around them. Obviously the mines, farms, and structures have had an effect on the Stehekin valley but the harvested forests have largely regrown, and it is a lovely place that still retains a flavor of the America of long ago.

Scientists have counted 138 species of wildlife in the lower valley, including 5 amphibians, 8 reptiles, 25 mammals, and 104 varieties of birds. Deer browse in the fields. Black bear conduct their frantic search for food. Coyotes feed on insects, mice, and other small mammals. An occasional cougar travels secretly through the mixed pine and fir forest. There are squirrels, chipmunks, raccoons, and, in the high, rocky places, mountain goat. Dusk and dawn sometimes provide a symphony of birdsongs. Rocks, brush, and fallen logs give rattlesnakes shelter in secret places from heat or cold. They flee from intruders if they can. They strike if they think they must.

The valleys of Lake Chelan and Stehekin are hemmed in by mountains. Inland from the lake is the Lake Chelan Sawtooth Wilderness on the east side and the Glacier Peak

Wilderness on the west side. The Lake Chelan National Recreation Area, dominated by the Stehekin Valley, borders on both the Glacier Peak Wilderness and the North Cascades National Park. The land is primeval and the mountains are both rugged and high. Among the giants of the lower lake are South Navarre Peak, 7,870 feet high and its neighbor North Navarre Peak, 7,963 feet. Farther up the lake the

Giardia (*Giardia duodenalis*)

This is a single-celled intestinal parasite that causes intense diarrhea and very unpleasant related symptoms. It is carried by animals that defecate in or near water where the cyst remains dormant until an unsuspecting mammal drinks the water. The symptoms usually begin within three weeks. So drinking the seemingly pure, cold water of a mountain stream or lake may have very disagreeable consequences. One method for avoiding the parasite is to bring water to a full boil before consuming it. Another is to use disinfectant tablets available at outdoor stores and drug stores. Another is to use one of the better filtering devices on the market.

gneissic rock of White Goat Mountain stretches some 7,484 feet high. At the head of the lake, Purple Mountain looms over the landing at 7,161 feet, and upriver McGregor Mountain cradles its glaciers 8,122 feet above sea level. Scores of other rocky peaks stretch out in every direction.

For people whose families have lived here for generations and for casual visitors who stay for a few brief minutes between the boat's arrival and departure, the essence of the Stehekin Valley at the foot of the mountains is a quiet spectacle of nature. There is much to do and much to see and something to learn.

LODGING IN STEHEKIN VALLEY

Many visitors, those who hike or ride horses to the valley and some of those who arrive by boat or airplane, stay in one of the 11 campgrounds near the landing and along the road. They are all primitive, with tent sites, toilets, and little else. The water supply in campgrounds away from the landing comes from streams and like that in other backcountry places it must be purified. Boiling for at least 10 minutes is one recommended method.

The campgrounds can be reached by hiking; on a private bus equipped to carry backpacks and bicycles (phone 509-682-4677 or 800-536-0745) but that goes only 9 miles up the valley (reservations not required); or on the Park Service shuttle bus which can carry packs but not bicycles. Reservations are recommended on the Park Service bus and can be made from the Golden West Visitor Center in Stehekin Landing, phone (360) 856-5700, extension 340, then extension 14.

Bicycles can be brought in on the boat or rented at Stehekin Landing. Cascade Corrals conducts horse rides during the day on the road and on nearby trails and a wagon ride on the road. There are several places in the Valley where indoor lodging is available:

THE NORTH CASCADES STEHEKIN LODGE. [Fig. 10] A short distance above the boat dock, behind the restaurant, is the North Cascades Stehekin Lodge. It has year-round accommodations in 28 lodging units with accommodations for parties of from one to eight persons. Some units have kitchens. There are lake views, decks, handicap facilities, and a sitting room that overlooks the lake and mountains. There is a restaurant that can seat 50 guests, and the lodge has a convenience store, gasoline sales, bike and boat rentals, and makes arrangements for tours of the valley. Phone (509) 682-4494.

SILVER BAY LODGING. Bed and breakfast or rental cabins at the head of Lake Chelan. Has views, a swimming beach, croquet, bicycles, and canoes. Phone (509) 682-2221.

STEHEKIN VALLEY RANCH. Nine miles up the valley. Rustic accommodations in tent cabins with framed walls and canvas roofs. Meals, showers, laundry, and toilets are provided in a nearby cookhouse. Transportation provided to guests. Phone (800) 536-0745.

FISHING IN STEHEKIN VALLEY

The Stehekin drainage measures 250 square miles and has more than 150 miles of streams as well as many lakes. Streams are high and muddy in the spring and early summer and require special skills. Good fishing has been reported in many streams, including Bridge Creek, Agnes Creek, Company Creek, and the upper Stehekin River. Dry flies, spinners, and weighted nymphs are often successful, and the catch is likely to be rainbow and cutthroat trout. The lakes often contain cutthroat from 10 to 20 inches that take flies and lures. Coon Lake, up the Coon Creek Trail from the Stehekin Road near High Bridge (*see* Coon Lake Trail, page 75) is easy to get to. Trapper Lake, 1 mile west of Cottonwood Camp at the end of the Stehekin Road (a 1-mile, very steep, very rough hike from the camp) is said to have produced cutthroat more than 20 inches long.

VISITOR FACILITIES AT STEHEKIN LANDING

[Fig. 10] Visitor facilities at the landing begin with the Park Service's Golden West Visitor Center, which offers exhibits and information about the valley and its cultural and natural histories. Visitors can obtain maps and publications, as well as backcountry and climbing permits. Rangers provide scheduled nature talks, walks and evening programs. The Imus Creek Nature Trail begins behind the visitor center and circles around behind the buildings of the landing (*see* Imus Creek Nature Trail), page 74. When the visitor center is closed, many of its services may be obtained at the nearby ranger station. A small building a short distance up the road from the ranger station has public telephones and shower and laundry facilities. The landing also has a post office, picnic areas, public docks, and trailheads to the backcountry.

The Courtney Log Office arranges for rafting on the Stehekin River, bicycle rentals, ranch dinners, horse and wagon tours, horseback rides, and horse-supported guided trips into the backcountry. They can be contacted at Box 67, Stehekin, WA 98852. Phone (509) 682-4677.

The McGregor Mountain Outdoor Supply Shop sells outdoor equipment and fishing and hunting licenses. Locally made crafts are available at the House that Jack Built shop.

There is also a wide range of activities available for visitors in the Stehekin Valley, ranging from the short period between the arrival and departure of the Lady boats, to day hikes, to major climbing and hiking excursion into the wilderness. The stay can last for days or weeks, or a one-day trip can be extended to several hours by arriving on one boat and leaving on another.

RAINBOW FALLS EXCURSION

[Fig. 12(5)] When the Lady boats arrive at Stehekin Landing, they are met by a tour bus that takes visitors on a 45-minute, narrated excursion 3.5 miles up the valley to the thundering Rainbow Falls, which cascades 312 feet from the cliff above the valley floor. The 90-minute layover of the *Lady of the Lake II* allows time for lunch in the restaurant at the landing. The other boats have only a one-hour layover, requiring passengers to eat either on the bus or during the boat's downlake trip.

THE BUCKNER PLACE

[Fig. 12(6)] In 1889 Bill Buzzard, a prospector who wore a black hat with a conspicuous bullet hole, came to the valley. He looked for gold, and he did a little carpentry work, but he also took out a 160-acre homestead 3 miles up the valley from the landing. Some time later he sold it to William Van Buckner whose son, Harry, arrived at the place in 1911. Harry left briefly for military service during World War I then returned to live there until he died in 1953. Like the people before him, he spent his time building, improving, and adding until the place became a prime example of the ingenuity and strength of pioneers who settled the land throughout the New World.

In the early days, the homestead was largely self-sufficient, its inhabitants living off what they produced. Later they found a market for their crops among the other residents and the hotels that became part of the valley's economy.

Even a short visit to the Buckner Place makes it obvious that carving a home out of the wilderness wasn't easy. The tools they used and the home they built attest to that. They used cross-cut saws and axes to clear the trees off the land. Then they used the leverage of a clever stump puller to pull out the stumps and convert the fields into meadows for livestock, gardens for vegetables, and an orchard for fruit. They used materials from the downed trees to erect a house out of logs and rough-sawn lumber. The ingenuity becomes obvious even on the trail through the woods that leads to the fields. It parallels an irrigation ditch that carried the water the Buckners needed for their home and fields. When the builders reached a low spot in the ground, they erected a pile of rocks to hold the wooden flume. Building a homestead out of the

RED FOX
(Vulpes vulpes)
Notorious for preying on chickens, the red fox feeds mainly on small mammals and birds.

wilderness took hard work and an understanding of nature and of the rudiments of science and engineering, and the homestead is still there to be admired by visitors.

The Park Service has preserved the homestead deep in a Cascade Mountain Valley as a chronicle of the past, leaving it much as it was when Harry Buckner left, including the fields, the tools, some of the buildings, furniture, and an orchard that grows a species of apples no longer available on the commercial market. During the summer the Park Service provides a brochure for a self-guided walking tour of the homestead.

Directions: 3 miles up the Stehekin Valley Road from Stehekin Landing.

Facilities: An open-air museum.

Dates: Open year-round depending on weather.

Fees: None.

Closest town: Stehekin Landing.

CAMPING IN STEHEKIN VALLEY

A series of primitive campgrounds are dotted along the Stehekin Valley. They can be reached on foot, by bicycle, by horse, or by the Park Service bus. The free Park Service backcountry camping permit is required.

HIKING IN THE LAKE CHELAN NATIONAL RECREATION AREA

For many people the essence of the national recreation area and the Stehekin Valley is the many trails which, as during the thousands of years before Europeans arrived, give access to places in the high country as well as to the flat lands where most people live to the east and west of the mountains.

Today the trails lead to and from places of primeval beauty where it is possible to be alone with natural elements that are very little different from the time before recorded history began. As in much of Washington's Cascades, people who venture deep into these lands depend on what they carry on their backs or the backs of animals and their ability to use that material to provide shelter and food until they return to civilization with, perhaps, a new outlook on life.

Among the longer hikes that begin in the valley are the following:

COMPANY CREEK-DEVORE CREEK TRAIL. [Fig. 12(8)] This is a major hike deep into the Cascades that loops 28 miles around 8,380-foot-high Devore Peak and ends near where it started. Dogs must be leashed and mountain bikes are banned. The hike begins and ends at about 1,200 feet elevation, but it gains, then loses, nearly 1 mile in between. Early in the season much of it is covered by snow fields, and there are treacherously fast creeks to cross, but conditions tend to improve late in the summer when the high country snowmelt decreases.

The first segment of the trail is over sandy, rocky tread on a relatively level portion of the Pacific Crest National Scenic Trail that passes through a thick pine and fir forest. After about 2 miles it leaves the North Cascade National Recreation Area and enters the Wenatchee National Forest portion of the Glacier Peak Wilderness. It goes upward, closely following Company Creek to its headwaters near 6,638-foot Hilgard Pass, passing campsites at 3.5 and 10 miles along the way. The trail leads to a Company Creek ford at about 5 miles, and that is a good place to turn around if the water is too high or if people are only interested in a long day hike.

After Hilgard Pass the way parallels Tenmile Creek to Tenmile Pass then heads down Devore Creek. The Tenmile portion is only 2 miles from Holden Village (see Holden Village, page 63) but Martin Ridge is a formidable barrier to reaching it. There is camping along Tenmile Creek and on Tenmile Pass. From there the trail goes downhill along Devore Creek past Bird Creek Camp about halfway down. Beyond that it goes down to a short side trail that leads to the Weaver Point campground on Lake Chelan. Past that it goes 3.5 miles up the Stehekin River past the Stehekin Airport to the side road of the Stehekin Road less than 1

AMERICAN GOLDFINCH (Carduelis tristis)

mile from the trailhead where the hike began. Lower portions of the trail pass typical east Cascades lodgepole pine forest, which blends in the high places into typical subalpine forest. There are nice views of Tupshin Peak and Devore Peak along the way. Wildlife may include deer, bear, marmot, and rattlesnakes.

Directions: About 4 miles from Stehekin Landing at the Harlequin Campground, a side road to the left called Company Creek Road goes about 1 mile to the trailhead.

Activities: Hiking, camping.

Dates: Seasonal, summer.

Fees: None, but a free permit is required for an overnight stay.

Closest town: Stehekin Landing, 5 miles.

For more information: Golden West Visitor Center, phone (360) 856-5700, extension 340, then extension 14. Or Chelan Ranger Station, 428 Woodin Avenue, Route 2, Box 680, Chelan, WA 98816. Phone (509) 682-2576.

Trail: 28 miles long and steep.

Elevation: The elevation gain is approximately 5,300 feet.

Degree of difficulty: Strenuous.

AGNES CREEK TRAIL. [Fig. 12(4)] This is a hike to a high country junction that leads to several places. The trailhead is at about 1,600 feet elevation at the Stehekin River. The route leads upward beside Agnes Creek for 5 miles where it crosses Pass Creek near Five Mile Camp and a junction to the deadend hike up the West Fork of Agnes Peak. There are views of Agnes Mountain, McGregor Mountain, and glacier-laden Dome Peak. The forest has stands of large cedar, hemlock, and fir.

The route rises gently for 17 miles to the 4,000-foot level where it enters meadow country and meets a trail to the left that goes up 1,000 feet in 1 mile and over Cloudy Pass and down Railroad Creek to Holden Village (see Holden Village, page 63) From there hikers can walk the Railroad Creek Trail, or take the Holden Village Bus down the Railroad Creek Road to Lucerne and the Lady boats on Lake Chelan. Another route from the top of the Agnes Creek Trail is a right turn to the Suiattle Pass Trail, which goes over that pass then down the Suiattle River across the valley from the awesome, 10,000-foot, glacier-clad Glacier Peak, a truly magnificent sight. Marmots, pikas, bear, and deer may show themselves along the way.

A side trip from Suiattle Pass goes several miles in a loop to Image Lake and a classic view of Glacier Peak reflected in the quiet waters of the lake. Photographs of that scene are suitable for framing.

Directions: The trailhead is near High Bridge about 11 miles from Stehekin Landing on the Stehekin Road.

Activities: Hiking, camping.

Dates: Seasonal, summer.

Closest town: Stehekin Landing, 11 miles.

For more information: Golden West Visitor Center, phone (360) 856-5700, extension 340, then extension 14. Or Chelan Ranger Station, 428 Woodin Avenue, Route 2, Box 680, Chelan, WA 98816. Phone (509) 682-2576.

Trail: 17 miles one-way.

Elevation: The elevation gain is approximately 2,800 feet.

Degree of difficulty: Strenuous.

SHORT HIKES IN THE STEHEKIN VALLEY

Many, possibly most, visitors to the Stehekin Valley are content with short day hikes that take them a short distance to where they can admire the backcountry while they eat lunch then go back to their camp or rooms for the night. The longer trails offer that option to hikers who turn around after a few miles but there also are many shorter trails designed just for day use:

IMUS CREEK NATURE TRAIL. [Fig. 12(7)] The shortest of the short trails, the Imus Creek Trail begins in Stehekin Landing, wanders for 0.5 mile through forest and over some alluvial fans, then back to the Stehekin Road, 0.3 of a mile from where it started.

The trail is designed as a self-guided nature trail and pamphlets describing the points of interest are available from the Golden West Visitor Center near the trailhead. It goes up a short distance from the trailhead to a waterfall that exposes its metamorphic bedrock and feeds a lush stand of hardwood trees, including big leaf maple and black cottonwood. It goes on from there to an opening where there are long views of Lake Chelan and its mountains. From there the way goes down through typical east side forest to the Purple Point Campground.

Directions: Trailhead is a few feet behind the Golden West Visitor Center.

Dates: Open year round.

Fees: None.

Closest town: Stehekin Landing.

For more information: Golden West Visitor Center, dial (360) 856-5700 extension 340, then extension 14. Or Chelan Ranger Station, 428 Woodin Avenue, Route 2, Box 680, Chelan, WA 98816, (509) 682-2576.

Trail: 0.3 mile.

Degree of difficulty: Easy.

COON LAKE TRAIL. [Fig. 12(1)] A little more than 2 miles round-trip, the Coon Lake Trail gains only about 600 feet elevation but goes to a backcountry wetland and a lake that has a reputation for containing cutthroat trout. The trail goes up a series of benches through typical east side forests of Douglas fir and ponderosa pine. There are open places that provide nice views of Agnes Creek and Agnes Mountain looming 8,115 feet above. A side trail forks off to the right and goes to a bluff above the southeastern corner of the lake. Near the northwestern end of the lake another fork separates trails to McGregor Mountain or to Bridge Creek.

Directions: The trailhead is behind the High Bridge Guard Station on the Stehekin Road.

Activities: Hiking, fishing.

Dates: Spring, summer, and fall.

Fees: None, but a free permit is required for an overnight stay.

Closest town: Stehekin Landing, 12 miles by Park Service bus.

For more information: Golden West Visitor Center, dial (360) 856-5700, extension 340, then extension 14. Or Chelan Ranger Station, 428 Woodin Avenue, Route 2, Box 680, Chelan, WA 98816 (509) 682-2576.

Trail: Approximately 2 miles round trip.

Elevation: Gain of approximately 600 feet.

Degree of difficulty: Easy.

AGNES GORGE TRAIL. [Fig. 12(3)] Across the stream from the Agnes Creek Trail (*see* page 73) the trail goes about 2.5 miles up a narrow gorge past numerous waterfalls, gaining only about 425 feet elevation. It begins with a mild climb in open forest of pine and Douglas fir. After 1 mile or so it leaves the recreation area and enters the Glacier Peak Wilderness. Near the end, the forest opens to reveal towering Agnes Peak. The trail ends at a steep cliff above Agnes Creek where there are views of the stream as it tumbles down to join the Stehekin River. A nearby side trail goes upstream a short distance and ends at the water's edge near a small waterfall.

Directions: Trailhead is on the Stehekin Road between High Bridge and High Bridge Campground.

Activities: Hiking.

Dates: Seasonal, summer.

Fees: None.

Closest town: Stehekin Landing, 12 miles by Park Service bus.

For more information: Golden West Visitor Center, phone (360) 856-5700, extension 340, then extension 14. Or Chelan Ranger Station, 428 Woodin Avenue, Route 2, Box 680, Chelan, WA 98816. Phone (509) 682-2576.

Trail: Approximately 2.5 mile one-way.

Elevation: The elevation gain is approximately 425 feet.

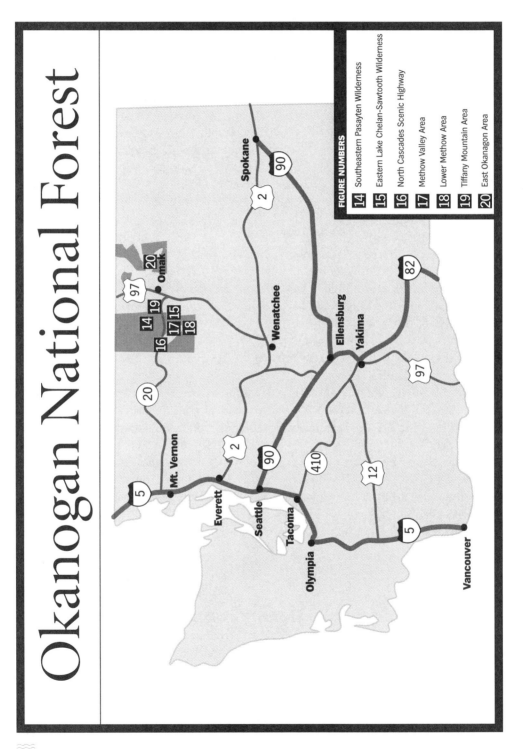

Okanogan National Forest

FIGURE NUMBERS

14 Southeastern Pasayten Wilderness
15 Eastern Lake Chelan–Sawtooth Wilderness
16 North Cascades Scenic Highway
17 Methow Valley Area
18 Lower Methow Area
19 Tiffany Mountain Area
20 East Okanagon Area

Okanogan
National Forest

The Okanogan National Forest encompasses 1,706,000 acres in the northeast corner of Washington's Cascade Mountains. The only major road through it is Washington State Route 20, which also is called the North Cascades Highway. Some 87,000 acres beside the highway in the Okanogan Forest and in the adjacent Ross Lake National Recreation Area have been designated as one of the country's National Scenic Byways because of the magnificent scenery the road passes through. It enters the western border of the forest deep in the mountains, travels east, then veers south to follow the Methow Valley.

Some 1,600 miles of trails crisscross the backcountry, which includes two wilderness areas. The Pasayten Wilderness covers nearly a third of the national forest on the northern edge, bordering the Canadian province of British Columbia and the large Manning and Cathedral provincial parks. The Lake Chelan-Sawtooth Wilderness covers 146,000

[*Above:* Lake Ann near Rainy Pass in the Okanogan National Forest]

Rainbow Trout/Steelhead (*Oncorhynchus mykiss*)

Rainbow trout are freshwater creatures. Some of them that are not landlocked migrate to sea before returning to spawn in the river they came from. Those are called steelhead. The steelhead grow faster and larger than the stay-at-home rainbow trout and are more sought after by sport fishermen both for their size and because they have a reputation for fighting. Both native and stocked rainbow trout are found in many waters in the Washington Cascades.

acres in the Okanogan and Wenatchee national forests and is administered by both.

The national forest is part of a rural area with a small population and little industry. But in addition to State Route 20, the forest has hundreds of miles of forest roads, ranging from paved, two-lane roads to rough dirt tracks. Some of the roads are converted to cross-country skiing and snowmobiling during the winter, and the Methow Valley in the forest has become famous for its winter recreation.

It is also possible to enter the forest using trails from neighboring jurisdictions. In addition to the two Canadian parks, the forest is next to both federal and state lands, interconnected by trails. The 50-mile-long Lake Chelan borders the forest's Lake Chelan-Sawtooth Wilderness, and visitors may enter the wilderness at several points by either private or commercial boats (*see* Lake Chelan, page 57).

The Okanogan is one of the oldest national forests in the country, and was one solution of the nation's early struggle to decide what to do with its diminished, unsettled land. It was included in the original Forest Reserve, created on February 22, 1891, Washington's birthday. Then President Grover Cleveland signed a proclamation called the Washington's Birthday Reserves, creating 13 forest reserves. That proclamation set aside land and made it clear that the federal government, not the states, had control of 21 million acres of public land in the West, but did not establish a system of administration. In 1897 Congress took responsibility for both administrating and protecting the land.

One of the reserves extended over land that now includes the Okanogan, Wenatchee, and Mount Baker-Snoqualmie National Forests and was called the Washington Forest Reserve. In 1905, Congress created the Forest Service under the Department of Agriculture, and transferred the reserves from the Department of Interior to the new agency. In 1907 the name of the forest reserves was changed to the National Forests.

What is now the Okanogan National Forest went through a series of changes in size, organization, and name. In 1921, it became the Chelan National Forest. Finally, in 1955, it was redesignated the Okanogan National Forest.

The forest headquarters is the supervisor's office, 1240 S. Second Avenue, Okanogan, WA 98840, (509) 826-3275. The forest is divided into two ranger districts; the Methow Valley Ranger District, 502 Glover, Twisp, WA, 98856, (509) 997-2131, and the Tonasket Ranger District, One West Winesap, Tonasket, WA 98855, (509) 486-2186.

When Congress created the North Cascades National Park in 1968, the new park divided into two sections what was then the Mount Baker National Forest, leaving about 200,000 acres of the Mount Baker National Forest separated from its parent agency. The separated territory is administered by the Okanogan Forest even though it technically still is part of what has become the Mount Baker-Snoqualmie National Forest.

The land is typical of the dry Eastern Washington Cascades. Much of the lower elevation is covered

FISHER
(Martes pennanti)
A boreal species, the shy fisher is an adept climber and swimmer that eats porcupines and snowshoe hares.

by grass and shrubs at the lowest elevations. Mid-elevation slopes bear open forests of predominantly ponderosa pine, as well as other trees suited to dry conditions. Above that, Douglas fir becomes more prominent, and in the high country above 6,000 feet there are subalpine and alpine species. North Gardner Mountain just north of the Lake Chelan-Sawtooth Wilderness is the highest mountain in the national forest at 8,974 feet elevation. Many other peaks measure from 7,000 to 8,000 feet high.

The word Okanogan means rendezvous in the language of the Okanogan Indian Tribe, and refers to the Osoyoos Lake area where, in ancient times, the Okanogan people and Native Americans from what are now Washington State and British Columbia met in the summer to hunt, fish and trade.

The national forest is well known for its herds of mule deer, and it recently worked with the state Department of Fish and Wildlife and the National Fish and Wildlife Foundation to conduct a five-year survey of carnivores within the forest borders. By using baited cameras to identify animals and by tracking them in the snow, scientists documented the presence of lynx (*Felis lynx*), wolverine (*Gulo gulo*), and martin (*Martes Americana*). They believe there may also be fishers (*Martes pennanti*), which would make the Okanogan forest one of the few places where all four are present. Fish species in the forest include rainbow, brown, bull, cutthroat, and brook trout, as well as chinook salmon, steelhead, smallmouth bass, and whitefish.

Like other national forests on the east side of the Cascades, the Okanogan Forest has begun a practice of starting relatively small and harmless forest fires under rigid controls. The practice is called "prescribed natural fire," and is conducted because the controlled fires replace the natural fires of ancient times. Those ancient fires reduced the buildup of fuel on the forest floor, thus limiting the damage caused by later fires which, with more fuel, can become extremely hot and destroy even mature trees. The fires also return nutrients to the soil, and provide more sun to help trees replanted after an area has been cleared by storm, disease, or logging.

The fires are carefully planned to burn cleanly, and carefully controlled so they can be extinguished at the right time, and when the winds are such that smoke does not blow to inhabited areas. Foresters admit, however, that neither the weather nor the wind is completely predictable and sometimes mistakes can occur.

The result of prescribed burning is what foresters call a naturally open, ponderosa pine forest with trees of all ages. The trees are widely spaced and grass covers the forest floor, which in the Okanogan climate means a healthy forest.

The essence of the Okanogan Forest is the great outdoors, combined with a wide variety of the recreational opportunities offered by an immense area of uncrowded land. The list of opportunities is long, and includes exploring on foot or horse, camping, mountain climbing, rock climbing, biking, whitewater rafting, boating, fishing, hunting, skiing, snowmobiling, and just plain admiring the beauty of the landscape. The Okanogan National Forest to a large extent is a place where few people stay but many go to enjoy themselves for a time before they go back home.

Like other national forests in the Pacific Northwest Region, the forest is experimenting with a program of charging for use of forest land. There may be fees charged for parking and for other uses. To learn what the current fees are, contact the forest supervisor's office or ranger district office in the area you plan to visit.

Directions: From Marblemount take State Highway 20 about 70 miles through the North Cascades National Park to Mazama, the first community in the Okanogan National Forest, and the first service station after Marblemount.

Activities: Hiking, horseback riding, camping, fishing, hunting, cross-country and downhill snow skiing, snowmobiling, picnicking, river rafting, boating.

Facilities: Trails, campgrounds, downhill ski areas, cross-country skiing, and snowmobiling.

Dates: Open year-round.

Fees: There are fees for skiing, river rafting, and a trailhead fee may be charged.

Closest towns: Mazama, Winthrop, and Twisp.

For more information: Okanogan National Forest Supervisor, 1240, S. Second Avenue, Okanogan, WA 98840. Phone, (509) 826-3275.

Wilderness Areas in the Okanogan National Forest

When Congress adopted the Wilderness Act in 1964, it defined wilderness as "an area where the earth and its community of life are untrammeled by man, where man himself is a visitor who does not remain." The Forest Service took those words quite literally. It manages the wilderness so that people are simply visitors who pass through, using only their own muscle or that of animals for transportation. There are no roads in the wilderness, nor are there machines of any kind. Except for emergencies, landing a helicopter or dropping supplies from an airplane are outlawed. Bicycles and chain saws are banned. Storing supplies, equipment, or other personal property for more than 48 hours, a practice called caching, is prohibited.

If so many people visit a wilderness that they leave signs they have been there, the forest administration reduces the number allowed to visit, or what they may do there. One strict rule is that parties are limited to 12 persons and 18 head of stock. In some cases the administrators make recommendations rather than regulations. They suggest, for instance, that pack animals be used in certain, prescribed ways to avoid having an effect on the land, hobbled rather than tied, as an example, and except when animals are being loaded and unloaded, people are asked to keep them at least 200 feet from meadows, lakes, and streams.

Wilderness is managed to look and feel like it did in the days of Columbus. Wilderness rangers roam the area during the summer, maintaining trails, removing trash, and replanting places that have been trampled.

Those who venture into a wilderness are expected to respect it as "an area where the earth and its community of life are untrammeled by man, where man himself is a visitor who does not remain."

The Pasayten and Lake Chelan-Sawtooth wildernesses are two such places.

BLACK FLY
(Simulium spp.)
Found near running water, these biting flies are the curse of human visitors to the mountains and forests.

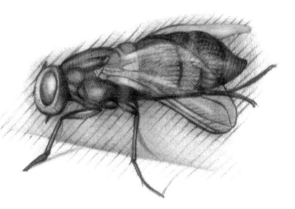

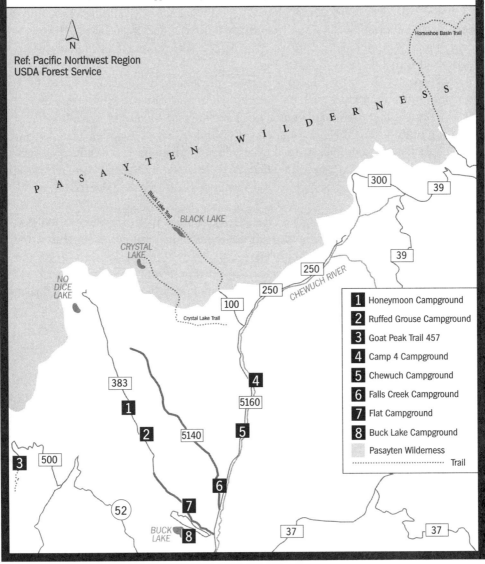

Southeast Pasayten Wilderness

The 530,000 acre wilderness extends to about 53 miles east from the Ross Lake Recreation Area and approximately 23 miles south from the Canadian border.

N

Ref: Pacific Northwest Region
USDA Forest Service

PASAYTEN WILDERNESS

Horseshoe Basin Trail

Black Lake Trail

BLACK LAKE

CRYSTAL LAKE

NO DICE LAKE

Crystal Lake Trail

CHEWUCH RIVER

300
39
39
250
250
100

383
5160
5140
500
52

BUCK LAKE

37
37

1 Honeymoon Campground
2 Ruffed Grouse Campground
3 Goat Peak Trail 457
4 Camp 4 Campground
5 Chewuch Campground
6 Falls Creek Campground
7 Flat Campground
8 Buck Lake Campground
Pasayten Wilderness
.... Trail

THE PASAYTEN WILDERNESS

[Fig. 14] This 530,000-acre wilderness extends to about 53 miles east from the Ross Lake Recreation Area of the North Cascades National Park and approximately 23 miles south from the Canadian border. The far western part of the wilderness is technically in the Mount Baker-Snoqualmie National Forest but, like the rest of the wilderness, it is administered by the Okanogan National Forest.

Congress designated it as a wilderness area in 1968 when it created the national park. Until then it had been a primitive area that was used by trappers, hunters, miners, and for livestock grazing as well as recreation. The act that created it specifically allows stock grazing in areas that had been traditionally used for that purpose, some since early in the twentieth century, so now the land is devoted exclusively to grazing, recreation, and the processes of nature.

The wilderness is east of the central portion of the Cascades so the mountains within it are higher in the west and generally smaller in the east, where the Cascades end. The highest peak is 9,066-foot Jack Mountain, near the southwest corner of the wilderness. The average elevation of the land is 5,500 feet. The west end of the wilderness tends to have more precipitation than the east because the mountains are higher there but, as anywhere in the mountains, the weather can be treacherous and sudden. It is possible to experience sunshine, rain, sleet, and snow within a few hours. The high country is usually covered by snow from October to late June, although the higher trails, such as the Pacific Crest National Scenic Trail, may not be free of snow until late July. Trails in the eastern and central areas may not be open until early July.

Wildlife in the wilderness ranges from the tiny deer mouse (*Peromyscus maniculatus*) to black bear, deer, and an occasional moose (*Alces alces*). Hunting is permitted in the proper season, and regulations are enforced by state game agents.

Some 500 miles of maintained trails, plus numerous primitive routes, crisscross the wilderness. They range from easy strolls to strenuous climbs in high places. The environment is difficult for high-country plants. In the freezing weather of fall, winter and spring there is little moisture on the surface or in the ground, and in the summer the warm winds tend to dry the plants. Some of the vegetation in the high country mimics desert plants by growing hairy surfaces to hold moisture. They also tend to be low to the ground and have only a few small leaves to escape the wind. Most of the Pasayten trails lead eventually to high country, but there are comparatively level hikes too.

Directions: The Pasayten Wilderness measures 50 miles by 20 miles, so the way to get there depends on what part of the wilderness a visitor wants to see. The shortest way to the eastern edge of the wilderness is to drive north from Loomis toward Palmer Lake. At 1.5 miles turn left, cross Sinlahekin Valley, and drive on Forest Road 39 up the long, steep climb for 16 miles (passing the North Fork Campground at 11 miles) to a fork with Forest Road 500 which is called Iron Gate Road. Turn right onto the rough, steep route, and go 6 miles to the trailhead at the end of the road.

To reach the west boundary of the wilderness, drive about 17 miles north and east from Newhalem on State Route 20 to the East Bank Trailhead at the trailhead, which serves both the Panther Creek Trail and the Ruby Creek Trail. Cross the bridge over Ruby Creek and go to the right and follow the Ruby Creek Trail about 3 miles to the southwest corner of the Pasayten Wilderness.

To reach the southern border of the wilderness, go west on State Route 20 about 7 miles from Winthrop, and turn right onto Forest Road 1163 and go about 4 miles to the village of Mazama. Then follow the Harts Pass Road, Forest Road 5400, for 7.2 miles and turn right on a side road that goes 0.3 mile to the Lost River Trailhead. Hike up the trail about 3.5 miles to the Pasayten Wilderness border.

Activities: Hiking, camping.

Facilities: None.

Dates: Seasonal, summer.

Closest town: East boundary, Loomis 23.5 miles. West boundary, Newhalem, 20 miles. South boundary, Winthrop, 22 miles.

For more information: Methow Valley Ranger District, 502 Glover, Twisp, WA 98856. Phone (509) 997- 2131.

THE BLACK LAKE TRAIL 50

[Fig. 14] Black Lake is about 4 miles from the trailhead, and the trail gains only about 800 feet. The lake is a little more than 1 mile long, and nestles in a valley surrounded by forested peaks that reach 7,000 feet in elevation. The lake itself is less than 4,000 feet in elevation, which means it is open longer than some others, usually about mid-May through October.

The hike is beside Lake Creek on a forest-duff trail that is a soft pleasure to walk on, and late summer adds the pleasure of fields of wild blueberries and raspberries (*Rubus* spp.). A point of interest is a huge, 10-by-20 foot boulder at about the 1.5 mile point. It crashed down from the mountainside during the winter of 1984-85 and came to rest against some trees beside the trail.

The short, easy, round-trip hike can easily be made in one day, but there are comfortable campsites on either end of the lake that make for more leisurely fishing and a good base for exploring farther up the trail, which goes deep into the wilderness to a multitude of destinations.

On the way to Black Lake the

BLACK BEAR
(Ursus americanus)

Black Bear (*Ursus americanus*)

Black bears in the Cascades can be gray or brown, but usually they are black. They are one species, regardless of color. Indeed, it is possible that a litter will have members of different colors. They grow 4 to 6 feet long, and 3 to 3.5 feet high at the shoulder. They have tremendous strength and will eat almost anything in their effort to gain enough fat to last them through the long winter of semi-hibernation. They seem especially fond of berries that become available in the fall.

Often in the spring, when they emerge from their dens, they attack young trees, stripping the trunk of the outer layer of bark to get at the inner, cambium layer, which contains some nutrients. Frequently they destroy the tree by girdling it, leaving a line of dead trees on the side of a hill. In the fall, black bears prepare dens, perhaps lining them with something soft and resilient, such as cedar bark. They sleep the winter away, curled in a ball, maintaining a body temperature of about 88 degrees Fahrenheit, compared with the approximately 40 degrees of hibernating animals. The bears' heart beat may slow to as few as eight beats per minute.

Bears will eat food that humans bring to the woods for themselves, unless the humans take the precaution of hanging it in a tree or other standard, where bears can't reach it. It is also a good idea to establish an eating camp at least 150 feet from the sleeping camp since bears are attracted to the smell of cooking utensils.

trail passes through a forest which consists of Douglas and subalpine fir, spruce, and lodgepole, ponderosa, and white pine, all towering high overhead. Along the edge of the lake there are black cottonwood, birch, aspen, and sitka alder. The understory includes thimbleberry (*Rubus parvivflorus*), serviceberry (*Amelanchier alnifolia*), and spiraea (*Spiraea spp.*). Deer, marmots, black bear, squirrels, coyotes, and water ouzels are among the local residents. Black Lake is an easy hike through nice country and, sometimes, to good fishing, all of which probably accounts for it being one of the most popular hikes in the Pasayten Wilderness.

Directions: Take Forest Road 9137 from Winthrop about 6 miles on the east side of the Chewuch River. Cross the bridge to the west side and Forest Road 51, which becomes Forest Road 5160. Go about 15 miles on roads 51 and 5160 then turn left for 2 miles on Forest Road 100. Go about 2 miles to the trailhead at the end of that road.

Dates: Seasonal, summer.

Fees: A trailhead fee may be charged.

For more information: Methow Valley Ranger District, 502 Glover, Twisp, WA 98856. Phone, (509) 997- 2131.

Trail: 4 miles.

Elevation: 800 feet elevation gain.

Degree of difficulty: Easy.

Lodgepole Pine (*Pinus contorta*)

This is the most prolific of the Washington pines. Common on the dry east side of the Cascades above 3,500 feet, it produces large numbers of seeds each year, and releases some of them year-round. The young trees grow faster than other pines and begin fruiting at a younger age. The seeds are contained inside cones that open after a forest fire heats them. The open cones release the seed into an open field where older trees have been eliminated by the fire and the competition is minimal. The downside is that so many seeds may have been released at the same time that the new trees become overcrowded and are stunted by the competition of their own species. Because they don't grow much over 100 feet tall and they need a great deal of sun, even healthy stands are likely to be crowded out by their taller neighbors.

CRYSTAL LAKE TRAIL 517

[Fig. 14] Crystal Lake and its neighbors are only a short distance from Black Lake (*see* Black Lake Trail, page 84). One of its neighbors, Half Moon Lake, for instance, is less than 2 miles to the west of Black Lake as the crow flies. But it also is 3,000 feet higher than Black Lake and there is no trail between them. The trailhead is near the mouth of Farewell Creek, and the route goes relentlessly upward, paralleling the creek, for about 4 miles, completely exposed to the hot sun. It then makes a sharp right turn to go over the divide into the Disaster Creek Valley. It follows Disaster Creek, still relentlessly upward, for about 6 miles to Crystal Lake.

The early part of the hike is through ponderosa, lodgepole, and white pine that merges into Engelmann spruce and subalpine fir.

Fishing, camping, and admiring the magnificent scenery are the main occupations at Crystal Lake, and that is where the trail ends as far as the forest map is concerned. But there is a faint, rocky, rough trace of a fisherman's trail that goes about a 0.5 mile over the next ridge to the larger Kidney Lake, and another mile of ridge hopping to the still larger Halfmoon Lake.

Fishing, hunting and scenery are the attractions at those lakes. From a high point at Halfmoon Lake it is possible to see Black Lake 3,000 feet below, but it is not advisable to attempt to go directly to Black Lake from there.

Directions: Take Forest Road 9137 from Winthrop, about 6 miles on the east side of the Chewuch River. Cross the bridge to the west side and Forest Road 51, which becomes Forest Road 5160. Go about 13 miles on roads 51 and 5160 to the Farewell Creek Trailhead near the fork with Forest Road 100.

Dates: Seasonal, summer.

Fees: A trailhead fee may be charged.

For more information: Okanogan National Forest Supervisor, 1240, South Second Avenue, Okanogan, WA 98840, (509) 826-3275.

Trail: 8 miles, one-way.
Elevation: 3,000 feet elevation gain.
Degree of Difficulty: Strenuous.

HORSESHOE BASIN TRAIL

[Fig. 14] Horseshoe Basin is a broad park-like meadow that stretches for many miles through grasses, flowers, and subalpine forests. There is a view of mountain peaks that extend into the 8,000-foot elevation level. Yet it is a relatively short, 9-mile round trip with moderate elevation gain.

The hike follows Trail Number 533, which begins at the Iron Gate Trailhead. There is a short downhill walk on an abandoned road that led to an old tungsten mine many miles into what is now the wilderness. The route is level to moderately uphill for a time, passing through lodgepole pine stands that have

LODGEPOLE PINE
(Pinus contorta)
Growing up to 80 feet tall, this pine has needles growing in twisted pairs and cones that are closed and prickly, pointing away from the branch.

regenerated after a series of major forest fires in the 1920s. The meadows begin at a little more than 3 miles from the trailhead and the trail becomes steeper briefly, then enters Sunny Basin and goes up to Sunny Pass, at about 7,200 feet elevation, and on to Horseshoe Basin. The numerous peaks in the basin can be climbed fairly easily from a base camp for hikers who stay overnight or longer. They afford magnificent views of the surroundings in all directions. The summit of Armstrong Peak is on the border between Canada and the United States, which is marked by a series of monuments. Side trails lead in several directions from the basin, making it possible to extend the hike for many days and end up many miles away in the Ross Lake Recreation Area.

Directions: Drive north from Loomis toward Palmer Lake. At 1.5 miles turn left, cross Sinlahekin Valley, and drive on Forest Road 39 up the long, steep climb for 16 miles (passing the North Fork Campground at 11 miles) to a fork with Forest Road 500 which is called Iron Gate Road. Turn right onto the rough, steep route, and go 6 miles to the trailhead at the end of the road.

Dates: Seasonal, summer.

Fees: A trailhead fee may be charged.

For more information: Tonasket Ranger District, 1 West Winesap, Tonasket, WA 98855. Phone (509) 486-2186.

Trail: 4.5 miles, one-way.
Elevation: 1,200 feet elevation gain.
Degree of difficulty: Moderate.

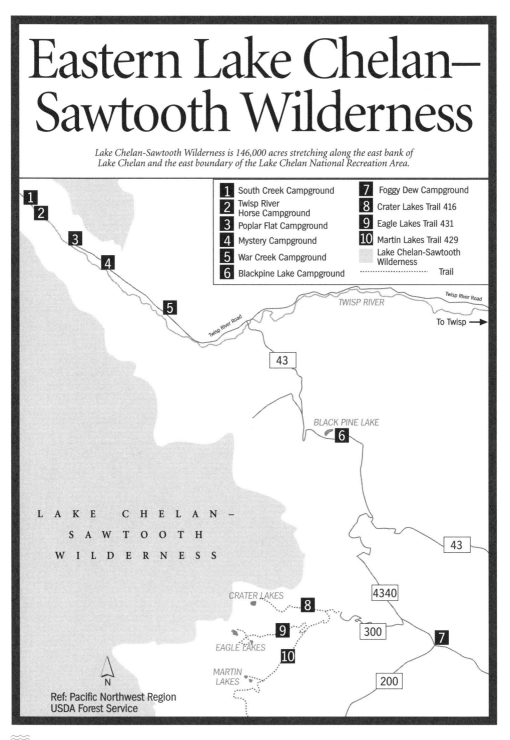

Eastern Lake Chelan– Sawtooth Wilderness

Lake Chelan-Sawtooth Wilderness is 146,000 acres stretching along the east bank of Lake Chelan and the east boundary of the Lake Chelan National Recreation Area.

1. South Creek Campground
2. Twisp River Horse Campground
3. Poplar Flat Campground
4. Mystery Campground
5. War Creek Campground
6. Blackpine Lake Campground
7. Foggy Dew Campground
8. Crater Lakes Trail 416
9. Eagle Lakes Trail 431
10. Martin Lakes Trail 429

Lake Chelan-Sawtooth Wilderness

·············· Trail

TWISP RIVER

Twisp River Road

To Twisp →

43

BLACK PINE LAKE

LAKE   CHELAN –
SAWTOOTH
WILDERNESS

43

CRATER LAKES

4340

300

EAGLE LAKES

200

MARTIN LAKES

N

Ref: Pacific Northwest Region
USDA Forest Service

LAKE CHELAN-SAWTOOTH WILDERNESS

[Fig. 15] Smaller than the Pasayten Wilderness, the Lake Chelan-Sawtooth Wilderness is 146,000 acres that stretch along the east bank of Lake Chelan and the east boundary of the Lake Chelan National Recreation Area (*see* Lake Chelan National Recreation Area, page 57). The southern third borders the lake and is in the Wenatchee National Forest. The northern section is in the Okanogan National Forest.

Congress designated the land as wilderness in 1984 and like all wilderness areas, the Forest Service policy is to keep it as pristine as possible with strict rules on its use. Mechanical transportation of all kinds is banned and it is used primarily by hikers, horsemen, fishermen and hunters.

It is reached primarily by taking the River Valley Road from Twisp, the South Navarre Road from Chelan or by private or commercial boat on Lake Chelan. Boats on Lake Chelan are a popular method of travel to the wilderness. All the trailheads lead to magnificent country, which has remained much the same for thousands of years.

Directions: The Lady of the Lake boats on Lake Chelan stop at several campgrounds and trailheads in the wilderness.

Activities: Hiking, camping, fishing, hunting.

Facilities: None.

Dates: Seasonal, summer.

Fees: Fee required for overnight-visit permit.

Closest town: Twisp, 20 miles.

For more information: Okanogan National Forest Supervisor, 1240 South Second Avenue, Okanogan, WA 98840. Phone (509) 826-3275. Wenatchee National Forest Supervisor, 215 Melody Lane, Wenatchee, WA 98801-5933. Phone (509) 662-4335.

TWISP PASS TRAIL NUMBER 432

[Fig. 16] Some historians believe Twisp Pass was the route that Alexander Ross took in 1814 when he became the first European to cross over the Cascade Range. He was guided by Red Fox and several other Indians. After a few days he mentioned to Red Fox that he could not see the trail they were following. He was chagrined to hear Red Fox answer that the trail was simply the way his people went to cross the mountains, but there were no visible markings.

If this is the way they went, they crossed over the pass to Bridge Creek, then either turned right to State Creek where State Route 20 is now, or turned left toward the Stehekin Valley and crossed Cascade Pass. (*see* Cascade Pass-Cottonwood Trail, page 39). Either way took him to the west side of the mountains, although he failed to reach the Pacific Ocean he was trying to find.

The route is as much an exposition of primeval beauty today as it was in Ross's time. The trail begins at 3,650 feet elevation, with a moderate climb through typical east Cascades mixed forest for 1 mile or so, to a junction with the Copper Pass Trail, another of Ross's possible routes but less likely, because it is a longer climb and Indians rarely took any but the quickest way. The trail from Copper Pass down the other side to Bridge

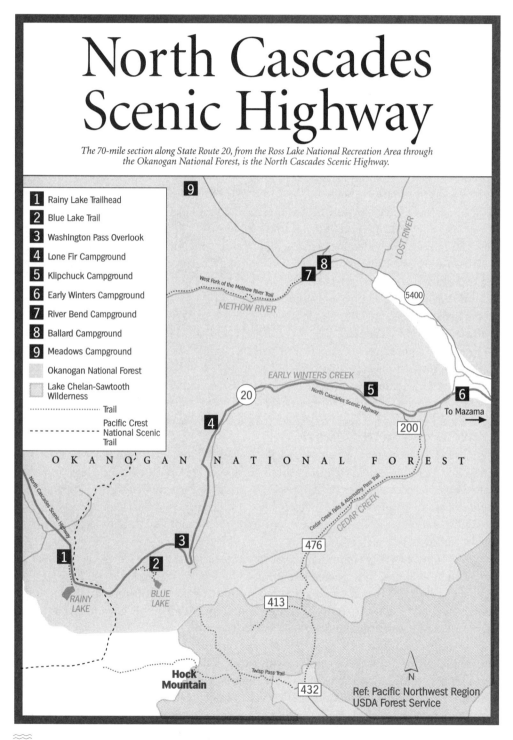

North Cascades Scenic Highway

The 70-mile section along State Route 20, from the Ross Lake National Recreation Area through the Okanogan National Forest, is the North Cascades Scenic Highway.

1 Rainy Lake Trailhead
2 Blue Lake Trail
3 Washington Pass Overlook
4 Lone Fir Campground
5 Klipchuck Campground
6 Early Winters Campground
7 River Bend Campground
8 Ballard Campground
9 Meadows Campground
▨ Okanogan National Forest
▨ Lake Chelan-Sawtooth Wilderness
········· Trail
------ Pacific Crest National Scenic Trail

Ref: Pacific Northwest Region
USDA Forest Service

Creek has been closed. There is a campsite at the junction of the Twisp and Copper Pass trails. The Twisp River is said to contain trout.

The trail crosses the North Fork of the Twisp River on a foot log and continues 3 fairly steep miles past outcroppings of glacier-polished rock, where there are long views over the forest top to the valley bottom and Hock Mountain. Beyond that, the tread changes from soft forest duff to rocky and rough, with switchbacks. At about 5 miles it passes meadows of heather and flowers that vary through the season. A short hike farther reaches the pass, at 6,064 feet elevation, and the boundary between the wilderness and the Lake Chelan Recreation Area of the North Cascades National Park. The view from the pass includes Dagger Lake, with its thick forest in the foreground and the rocky peaks above. There are unofficial side trails to explore from the pass including one over a very faint, hard-to-follow tread to the site of an old fire lookout at the 7,225-foot level of Stiletto Peak. It was built in 1931 and removed in 1953, but the magnificent, long views that its crews enjoyed generations ago are still there.

On the other side of the pass, the trail goes about 1 mile to Dagger Lake, losing about 600 feet elevation in the process. There are campsites at the lake but they are on the national park side of the border and a backcountry permit is required to camp there.

Beyond the lake, the trail goes back into the short views of old-growth pine for 4 miles to the Bridge Creek section of the Pacific Crest Trail, which leads to either Highway 20 or the Stehekin Valley. The junction was called Fireweed because a long ago fire cleared out the forest. It was replaced by a vast sea of purple fireweed plants that marked the first phase of the forest's regeneration.

Directions: The trailhead is at the end of the Twisp River Road, Forest Service Road 44, 25 miles west of Twisp.

Dates: Seasonal, summer.

Fees: A trailhead fee may be charged. A free overnight permit is required in the National Park.

For more information: Methow Valley Ranger District, 502 Glover, Twisp, WA 98856. Phone (509) 997- 2131.

Trail: 8.5 miles, one-way.

Elevation: 1,400 feet elevation gain.

Degree of difficulty: Moderate.

North Cascades Scenic Highway

WASHINGTON PASS OVERLOOK

[Fig. 16(3)] For those who drive to the Okanogan National Forest from the Ross Lake National Recreation Area, the only route is over State Route 20, and that 70-mile drive will give ample demonstration of why Congress designated that section of the highway as the North Cascades Scenic Highway. The magnificence begins in the recreation area, as the highway crosses land where the transition from west side Douglas fir forests to east-side pine begins to become obvious. It passes Ross Lake and Ruby Arm, where gold mining history in the North Cascades began. Then it follows Granite Creek through country where once large numbers of miners dug deep holes into the hard granite sides of the mountains that, in those days, were scores of miles from the nearest civilization.

The name of Granite Creek derives from the rock of the mountains beside it. A road cut along Ruby Arm shows a deposit of migmatite, but the mountain's base is a pale granite near the entrance to Granite Creek, and becomes Golden Horn Granite toward the pass. Traces of the old Forest Service road the miners once used can still be seen on the bank across the creek from the highway. That road has been abandoned since the highway was built.

After 15 miles on Granite Creek the road reaches Rainy Pass (*see* Rainy Lake Trail, page 99), dips down to the heads of, first, Bridge Creek, then State Creek, and up to the 5,477-foot elevation summit of Washington Pass and the Washington Pass Overlook.

The overlook consists of a short, easy, broad, paved, wheelchair-accessible trail that leads from the parking area at the summit to a platform that overlooks Washington Pass and all the awesome world around it. Among the more majestic sights are Silver Star Peak, Early Winter Spires, and the dominating, high, bare-granite walls of Liberty Bell Peak.

The view to the east is of the long, straight, wide valley that was gouged by a large glacier in the last Ice Age. Looking back to the west, visitors see the valley of State Creek, also the result of a long-ago glacier. The eastern view is of the east side's dry pine forests. The western view is mountain sides covered with the lush Douglas fir, and the western redcedar of the west side.

There are benches on the overlook platform, and room to walk to see the view from various angles.

Directions: On the north side of State Route 20, 16 miles west of Mazama, or 40 miles east of Newhalem.

Activities: Sight-seeing, picnicking.

Facilities: Short, paved trail, restrooms, picnic sites.

Dates: Seasonal, summer.

Fees: None.

Closest town: Mazama, approximately 16 miles.

For more information: Methow Valley Ranger District, 502 Glover, Twisp, WA 98856. Phone (509) 997-2131.

WINTHROP

[Fig. 17] When the North Cascades Highway leaves Washington Pass, it goes down Early Winters Creek to join the Methow River, which flows into the Columbia River, and, eventually, into the Pacific Ocean. The Methow Valley has cretaceous sandstone and shale in the west wall and volcanics on the east. It was carved partly by glaciers fed by ice that came down from nearby mountains, but also by a glacier from British Columbia that flowed over the summit of Harts Pass at 7,000 feet elevation.

A visitor's dominant impression of that vast country is the rugged beauty of the dry, east side mountains and valleys and their pine forests and broad meadows. The second impression is that, despite its beauty, the land seems empty. The entire Methow Valley has only about 3,600 permanent residents, about one fourth the number of deer. The residents like it that way, but they also like visitors and have provided many facilities to accommodate and entertain them.

One of the most striking examples of that is the town of Winthrop, population 350, at the confluence of the Methow and Chewuch rivers. The main street of the town is a colorful line of wooden buildings with false fronts, wooden sidewalks and old-fashioned street lamps. It looks much like the small western towns of the late nineteenth century when Owen Wister spent his honeymoon in Winthrop. He included descriptions of the town and its people in his classic novel *The Virginian*. Wister had been the Harvard University roommate of Guy Waring, the founder of Winthrop, but the town was named after a Yale University man, Theodore Winthrop, a nineteenth-century author.

Among the attractions are lodging facilities that range from a luxury resort hotel with a good restaurant, to bed and breakfasts, and rustic forest campgrounds. Attractions in the summer include many trails and campgrounds in the valley. There are places for mountain biking, horseback riding, river rafting, fly fishing, and mountain climbing. The Shafer Museum, at Guy Waring's home, adds to the frontier character of the community with displays of an old fashioned physician's office, general store, log cabin, and print shop, as well as outdoor displays of mining relics.

During the winter the valley has more than 150 kilometers of groomed cross-country ski trails, and 300 miles of groomed snowmobile tracks on the forest roads. With more than 300 days of sunshine annually, the valley has gained a reputation as a major winter sports center.

Directions: On State Highway 20, The North Cascades Highway, go about 80 miles east of Marblemount.

Activities: Hiking, camping, fishing, hunting, river rafting, horseback riding, horse pack trips, and mountain biking.

Facilities: Shops, lodging, restaurants, service stations.

Dates: Year round, depending on the activity.

Fees: Fees are charged for most facilities and services.

For more information: Methow Valley Information Center, PO Box 39, Winthrop, WA 98062. Phone (888) 463-8469 or (509) 996-2125.

Methow Valley Area

The Methow Valley was carved partly by glaciers fed by ice that came down from nearby mountains, but also by a glacier from British Columbia that flowed over the summit of Harts Pass.

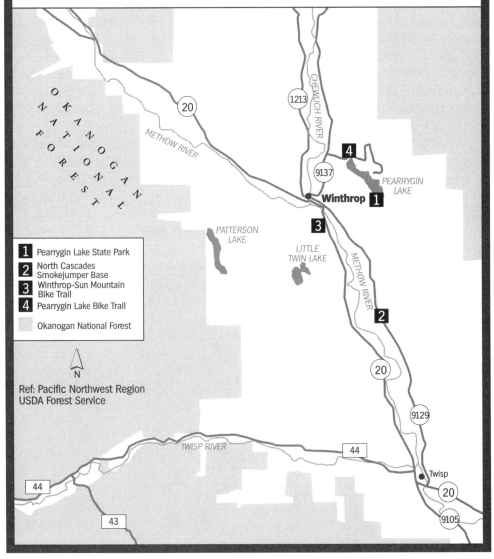

OKANOGAN NATIONAL FOREST

20

METHOW RIVER

1213

CHEWUCH RIVER

4

9137

PEARRYGIN LAKE

Winthrop 1

3

PATTERSON LAKE

LITTLE TWIN LAKE

METHOW RIVER

2

1 Pearrygin Lake State Park
2 North Cascades Smokejumper Base
3 Winthrop-Sun Mountain Bike Trail
4 Pearrygin Lake Bike Trail

Okanogan National Forest

N

Ref: Pacific Northwest Region
USDA Forest Service

20

9129

TWISP RIVER

44

44

43

Twisp

20

9105

Methow Valley and Methow River

🚵 MOUNTAIN BIKING IN THE METHOW VALLEY

Bicycles are banned in the wildernesses, but when the snow melts in the spring many of the nonwilderness roads and ski trails automatically become mountain bike trails. The routes include paved roads, dirt roads and trails. They range from the 6-mile Winthrop to Sun Mountain route to trails of 15 to 30 miles, and more than 4,000 feet of elevation gain.

Some of the trails provide long, high country views and heavy exertion through mostly open country with scattered pine trees typical of the east side of the Cascades. Others roll easily along a scenic and comparatively level valley bottom or backcountry roads. There are routes and challenges for many kinds of biking adventure.

Bicyclists are cautioned to be watchful on curves for bicycles coming from the other direction around curves, and to avoid spooking horses on the trail. The proper procedure when horses approach is to dismount from the bike, take it to the downhill side of the trail, and wait quietly for the horses to pass.

There are bike shops in several of the towns in the Methow Valley. The Methow Valley Sports Trails Association sponsors bike events and races during the season.

WINTHROP-SUN MOUNTAIN BIKE TRAIL. [Fig. 17(3)] This 6-mile, 1,000-foot elevation gain route begins across from the Cascade Inn Motel south of Winthrop on State Route 20. It meets the Twin Lakes Road that goes south about 100 yards to an old jeep road, which climbs past Patterson Lake to Sun Mountain Lodge, where there are other trails nearby.

PEARRYGIN LAKE BIKE TRAIL. [Fig. 17(4)] A 12-mile loop route with just 800 feet of elevation gain. It affords magnificent views of the Methow Valley and its mountains. Beginning at Winthrop, it goes 4 miles to Pearrygin Lake State Park, then onto a dirt road that goes 2 miles to a T-intersection at the Methow Wildlife Area, then turns right to a downhill ride past the Bear Creek Golf Course. From there it is a paved road that goes 3 miles to the starting point in Winthrop.

BEAVER CREEK-STARVATION MOUNTAIN BIKE TRAIL. An ambitious 30-mile ride for skilled mountain bikers. It is called "tough and demanding," and goes 30 miles, gaining 4,000 feet in elevation. It should not be attempted by persons who are not experienced mountain bikers or who are not familiar with the terrain. The route goes 5 miles south of Twisp, towards the Loup Loup Ski Area, on State Route 20, then 6 miles up the Beaver Creek Road to the junction with Forest Road 4225 (the South Fork Beaver Creek Road) then up Beaver Creek and Blue Buck Creek to Beaver Meadows, back to Starvation Mountain, then another mile along a ridge to where it begins a long descent with obstacles such as rocks, roots, bars, side hills and streams.

Directions: Numerous trails begin in and near Winthrop and Twisp.

Activities: Mountain biking.

Dates: Seasonal, summer.

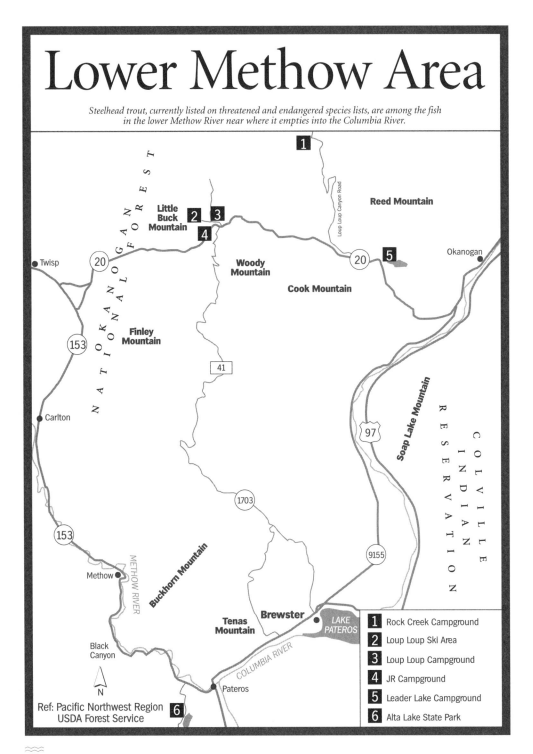

Lower Methow Area

Steelhead trout, currently listed on threatened and endangered species lists, are among the fish in the lower Methow River near where it empties into the Columbia River.

1 Rock Creek Campground
2 Loup Loup Ski Area
3 Loup Loup Campground
4 JR Campground
5 Leader Lake Campground
6 Alta Lake State Park

Ref: Pacific Northwest Region
USDA Forest Service

Fees: Trailhead fees may be charged in the national forest.

Closest towns: Winthrop and Twisp are close to most of the trails.

For more information: Methow Valley Sport Trails Association, PO Box 147, Winthrop, WA 98862, (509) 996-3287. Maps and other publications are available from the Methow Valley Visitor Center, PO Box 579, Winthrop, WA, 98862, (509) 996-4000.

FLOATING ON THE METHOW RIVER

Different seasons and sections of the river offer different kinds of rafting and kayaking on the Methow River. During the spring and early summer when the snow melt in the mountains is at its peak, the river between the towns of Methow and Carlton offers exciting white water . The portion of the river called Black Canyon, below the town of Methow, churns with furious rapids and huge waves during the early season. There is excitement, too, at places with names like Hurricane Rapids and Cinder Block Drop.

After midsummer, the snow melt decreases, the river becomes tamer and rafting is milder. On quiet stretches, the river is suitable for families and children.

The river runs through a wide, glaciated valley of open ponderosa pine forests and dark basalt cliffs. A 20-mile four-hour run may begin in high-altitude alpine forest and end in semiarid surroundings near the Columbia River. A rafting trip may pass wildlife such as deer, beaver, eagle, blue heron, and songbirds.

There also are nearby campgrounds, motels, and other places to stay. Instruction, equipment and guides are available in the valley. Guide companies handle parties with as many as 100 persons. They can supply rafts, equipment, food and shelter as needed, as well as designate places along the bank for swimming, picnicking, or camping.

Directions: Near Winthrop, Twisp and other Methow Valley communities on State Route 20.

Activities: River rafting, kayaking.

Facilities: Both sides of the river are private property and there are no public facilities. The river parallels State Route 20 and there are shops, restaurants, and lodging at several towns along the highway. To find a guide service, contact the Methow Valley Information Center.

Dates: Seasonal, spring, summer, fall.

Fees: Guide, instruction, and outfitting fees are charged.

Closest towns: Twisp, Methow, and Carlton, are near the banks of the Methow River.

For more information: Methow Valley Information Center, PO Box 39, Winthrop, WA 98062. Phone, 1-888-463-8469 or (509) 996-2125.

FISHING IN THE METHOW VALLEY

Streams in the Methow Valley are in the Methow, Chewuch, and Twisp watersheds. They and the lakes they form offer fishing opportunities for rainbow, brown, brook, and cutthroat trout as well as smallmouth bass, and whitefish, both native and stocked. As in other parts of the Cascades, fishing is regulated by the state.

Some of the lakes, such as Black Lake and Crystal Lake (*see* Black Lake and Crystal Lake Trails, pages 84 and 86) are high in the Pasayten Wilderness backcountry and may be reached only by muscle power, whether human or horse. Others, such as the lakes at Pearrygin State Park and Alta Lake State Park are in the lowlands where the angler can drive to a boat launch, put a boat in the water, and start fishing. There are scores of other lakes and streams scattered through the mountains and valleys, both in the national forest and in the State Department of Natural Resources lands adjacent to the forest. The valley is especially popular for fly-fishing.

Among the many places recommended by local fishermen are:

BLACK LAKE. (*see* Black Lake Trail, page 84.) [Fig. 14] Best for anglers who get away from the bank on float tubes.

PATTERSON LAKE. [Fig. 17] A 1.5-mile long lake, 7 miles from Winthrop, with a state-operated, public boat launch on the north side. It is also the site of the private Patterson Lake Resort which is operated by the nearby Sun Mountain Lodge.

NO DICE LAKE. [Fig. 14] About 2 miles southwest of the end of the Eightmile Creek Road, Forest Road 383 and some 21 miles northwest of Winthrop, the lake is accessible only by a tough, cross-country hike. It is good for cutthroat trout. A trailhead fee may be charged.

FISHING IN THE METHOW RIVER. Steelhead trout are among the fish in the lower Methow River, especially near the place it empties into the Columbia River, but they are listed under the threatened and endangered species laws and fishing for them is banned. Fishing is permitted for other species but special rules for the Methow River require equipment like barbless hooks and unscented lures.

There are several state fishing spots off State Route 20 in the vicinity of the towns of Carlton and Methow.

LITTLE TWIN LAKE. [Fig. 17] Approximately 4 miles north of Winthrop on County Road 9120, it is used for ice fishing during the winter cross-country skiing season.

BLACK PINE LAKE. [Fig. 15] On the Buttermilk Creek Road, Forest Road Number 43. (Take the Twisp River Road, Forest Road 44, from Twisp about 10 miles to Forest Road 43, and go south about 7 miles.) The Forest Service Blackpine Lake Campground

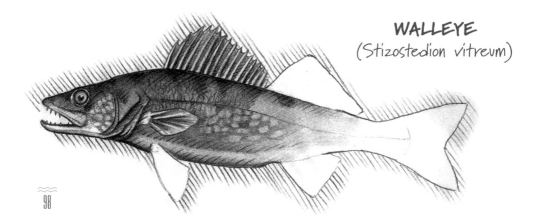

WALLEYE
(*Stizostedion vitreum*)

has a wheelchair-accessible boat dock (*see* Blackpine Lake Horse Campground, page 207). The spectacular view from the lake includes the Sawtooth Peaks. For availability of guides and pack horses contact the Methow Valley Information Center, PO Box 39, Winthrop, WA 98062. Phone (888) 463-8469, or (509) 996-2125.

Directions: Along State Route 20, south of the North Cacades National Recreation Area, and along State Route 153, from the junction with State Route 20 to Pateros.

Dates: State fishing-season regulations change from year to year but, generally, fishing may be legal through the spring-to-fall season. Little Twin Lake is open during the winter for ice fishing.

Activities: Lake and river fishing.

Facilities: Varies from none in the wilderness to extensive in the state park and forest campgrounds.

Fees: A fee may be charged for parking.

Closest towns: Many Methow Valley towns such as Winthrop and Twisp are nearby.

For more information: Methow Valley Information Center, PO Box 39, Winthrop, WA 98062. Phone, (888) 463-8469 or (509) 996-2125.

Hiking Trails in the Okanogan National Forest

Both the wilderness and nonwilderness sections of the Okanogan National Forest are crisscrossed by trails that intersect with each other, and lead to hikes ranging from a few hours to as many weeks as the hiker's provisions hold out.

The trails in the wildernesses tend to be long (*see* Pasayten and Lake Chelan-Sawtooth Wilderness sections, pages 83 and 89), but it is always possible to go as far as time or muscles permit then turn around. Other trails go only relatively short distances, requiring the hiker to either camp, go cross-country, or return to the trailhead. It is all a matter of opportunity and taste, but whatever one chooses the hike is likely to be a memorable time in unique, primitive, and beautiful territory.

▒ RAINY LAKE TRAIL

[Fig. 16(1)] This is an easy, one-hour, two-mile, round-trip hike from the high spot on the North Cascades Highway. The pass, at 4,860 feet, has access to the Pacific Crest Scenic Trail both to the north and the south. The Rainy Lake Trailhead is in the Rainy Pass Picnic Area and is on the south side of the highway at the pass. The broad, paved, level, wheelchair-accessible route begins as a very short segment of the Pacific Crest Trail in a forest stand then crosses a meadow. It gently undulates along the crest trail then turns right at a junction and goes to the north end of the lake. The lake is a good spot for a sandwich and for views of alpine cirques. There is a waterfall at the south end of the lake. Rainy Lake makes an ideal break in the 70-mile drive between the gas stations at Marblemount and Mazama.

Directions: South side of State Route 20 at the summit of Rainy Pass.

Dates: Seasonal, summer.

Fees: A trailhead fee may be charged.

Closest town: Mazama, 20 miles.

For more information: Methow Valley Visitor Center, PO Box 579, Winthrop, WA, 98862, (509) 996-4000.

Trail: 1 mile, one-way, wheelchair-accessible.

Degree of difficulty: Easy.

BLUE LAKE TRAIL

[Fig. 16(2)] This is a moderately easy, high-country hike that begins on the North Cascades Highway between Rainy and Washington passes. The trailhead is at 5,200 foot elevation and the lake is a little more than 2 miles from there at 6,300 feet. From beginning to end the scenery is fabulous.

The first steps are in high-country silver fir forest, and meadow, then the route goes into higher ground where the forest thins and the view becomes wider. The hard, granite cliffs of nearby Liberty Bell Peak and Early Winters Spires loom directly above the trail. The scene across State Creek is dominated by Cutthroat Peak and Whistler Mountain. After a little more than 1.5 miles, the trail crosses a field of boulders, then skirts a cirque covered with mountain heather and blueberry bushes. Stands of mountain hemlock and subalpine larch (*Larix lyallii)* replace the silver fir. Beyond the meadows is the lake shore at a little more than 2 miles from the trailhead.

The long, narrow, tree-lined lake is at timberline and has a reputation for containing large cutthroat trout. The deep-blue lake is below steep banks at the foot of the cliffs and a large avalanche chute marks part of its shoreline. It reflects the nearby rock buttresses and peaks, and it makes a pretty picture for anglers and nonanglers alike.

Directions: The trailhead is on the south side of State Route 20 between Rainy and Washington passes.

Dates: Seasonal, summer.

Fees: A trailhead fee may be charged.

For more information: Methow Valley Visitor Center, PO Box 579, Winthrop, WA, 98862, (509) 996-4000.

Trail: 2 miles, one-way.

Elevation: 1,100 feet elevation gain.

Degree of difficulty: Moderate.

CEDAR CREEK FALLS AND ABERNATHY PASS TRAIL 476

[Fig. 16] This trail begins with 2 easy miles to a spectacular mountain waterfall that plunges over two 30-foot granite cliffs. Then, the trail continues on a more-rigorous 7 miles to the pass. The route to the falls, 4 miles round-trip, follows Cedar Creek in the rocky valley below Gilbert, Silver Star and North Gardner mountains. It gains some 500 feet in 2 miles to the falls, where there is a tiny campsite next to the trail. Beyond the falls the gentle, uphill route slips past ponderosa pine and Douglas fir forest and gives good views across the Methow Valley to Goat Peak and its lookout. Subalpine larch on the ridges above shine in golden splendor during the fall. As the hike progresses Douglas fir becomes more dominant, interspersed with some western redcedar.

The waterfall can be heard long before it is seen and the song is a constant lullaby for those who camp overnight. The trailhead is at the 3,000-foot level and the highest point of the trip to the waterfall is 3,500 feet, making an easy hike. And the waterfall is where many hikers turn around.

Past the falls, the trail goes on 7 miles to Abernathy Pass, following Cedar Creek Valley all the way. The valley becomes steeper past the falls, changing about 4 miles above the trailhead from a narrow, eroded gulch to a wider, U-shaped valley, gouged out by long-dead glaciers. Then it becomes a little less steep.

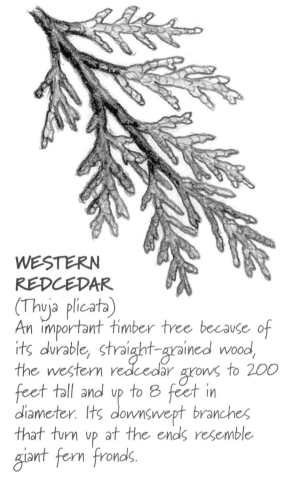

WESTERN REDCEDAR
(Thuja plicata)
An important timber tree because of its durable, straight-grained wood, the western redcedar grows to 200 feet tall and up to 8 feet in diameter. Its downswept branches that turn up at the ends resemble giant fern fronds.

Aspen punctuate some meadows below Gardner and Silver Star mountains, and several campsites mark the way. The last 2 miles leave Cedar Creek, and climb a long series of switchbacks on the side of Kangaroo Ridge to reach Abernathy Pass. The trail from there goes through a breach in the rock and down toward the Twisp Valley.

Directions: The trailhead is at the end of the 1 mile, one-lane, dirt Forest Road 200, which meets the south side of the North Cascades Highway about 13.5 miles east of Washington Pass.

Dates: Seasonal, summer.

Fees: A trailhead fee may be charged.

For more information: Methow Valley Visitor Center, PO Box 579, Winthrop, WA, 98862. Phone (509) 996-4000.

Trail: 2 miles one-way to Cedar Creek Falls; 9 miles one-way to Abernathy Pass.

Elevation: 500 feet elevation gain to Cedar Creek Falls, and 3,400 feet elevation gain to Abernathy Pass.

Degree of difficulty: To Cedar Creek Falls, easy, to Abernathy Pass, moderate.

GOAT PEAK TRAIL 457

[Fig. 14(3)] This is a relatively short, 2-mile trail with a 1,400-foot elevation gain from the trailhead, which is about 5,600 feet in elevation. The end of the trail is the site of a fire lookout that was built in 1932, rebuilt in 1948, and served double duty as an Aircraft Warning System station during World War II. The people who manned the lookout didn't see any enemy aircraft, but they had an immensely awesome view of the Methow Valley, and of spectacular Silver Star Mountain from its tree-shrouded slopes to the ice and rock of its peak. The aircraft spotters are gone but the view is still there.

The sometimes rough, rocky, and steep trail goes south along a mountain ridge through territory that begins in subalpine fir and Douglas fir, and changes to stands of Lyall larch amidst rock and meadows as it progresses from moderately to steeply uphill. Then it relents a little to less steep switchbacks through stunted whitebark pine, Lyall pine and subalpine fir. That leads to the lookout cabin on the peak at a little more than 7,000 feet in elevation.

There are open views along the way but the end reward is the vista from the lookout that includes not only Silver Star Mountain, but also North Gardner Mountain, at 8,956 feet the highest in that area. The view also looks up the Methow Valley toward the peaks near Washington Pass and north toward the Pasayten Wilderness. Once the snow melts, water is a problem.

Directions: Some 17 miles west of Winthrop turn off State Route 20 to Mazama, then go southeast on County Road Number 1163 about 2 miles and turn onto Forest Road Number 52. After about 3 miles on Road 52, turn onto Forest Road 5225. Take that road about 6 miles to Forest Road 200 on the right. After about 3 miles, turn right onto Forest Road 240 and go a short distance to the trailhead.

Dates: Seasonal, summer.

Fees: A trailhead fee may be charged.

For more information: Methow Valley Visitor Center, PO Box 579, Winthrop, WA, 98862, (509) 996-4000.

Trail: 2 miles, one-way.

Elevation: 1,400 feet elevation gain.

Degree of difficulty: Easy.

WEST FORK OF THE METHOW RIVER TRAIL 480

[Fig. 16] The trailhead is about 2,700 feet in elevation and the high point is about 3,600 feet, leaving about 900 feet to climb on the 6 miles of this trail before it starts uphill for 1 mile to the Pacific Crest Trail. Hikers who are not heading to the crest trail might as well turn around after 6 miles.

The trail follows the river it is named after past forests, meadows, and rock slides where marmot and pikas may live. Rattlesnakes may also be somewhere around. Much of the trail is in the valley bottom and forested, but occasionally there are holes in the forest that provide good views of the distance. Campsites are available at about 2 miles and 3 miles from the trailhead.

There are access points to the river along the way and the river is home to brown, cutthroat, and rainbow trout.

Directions: Some 17 miles west of Winthrop, turn off State Route 20 onto the short road to Mazama. Turn west at Mazama onto County Road 1163. Go about 9 miles and turn left onto Road 5400-060. Go about 1 mile, passing the River Bend Campground, to the trailhead.

Dates: Seasonal, summer.

Fees: A trailhead fee may be charged.

For more information: Methow Valley Visitor Center, PO Box 579, Winthrop, WA, 98862, (509) 996-4000.

Trail: 6 miles, one-way.

Elevation: 900 feet elevation gain.

Degree of difficulty: Easy.

TIFFANY MOUNTAIN TRAIL 345

[Fig. 19] This is a 3-mile, one-way hike to a mountain peak more than 8,200 feet above sea level. The trail begins at Freezeout Pass, elevation 6,500 feet, and follows Freezeout Ridge, going the first mile or so through typical high, east Cascades mixed

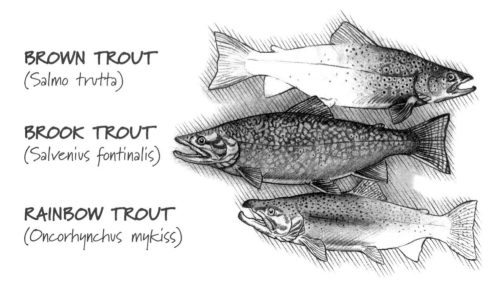

BROWN TROUT
(Salmo trutta)

BROOK TROUT
(Salvenius fontinalis)

RAINBOW TROUT
(Oncorhynchus mykiss)

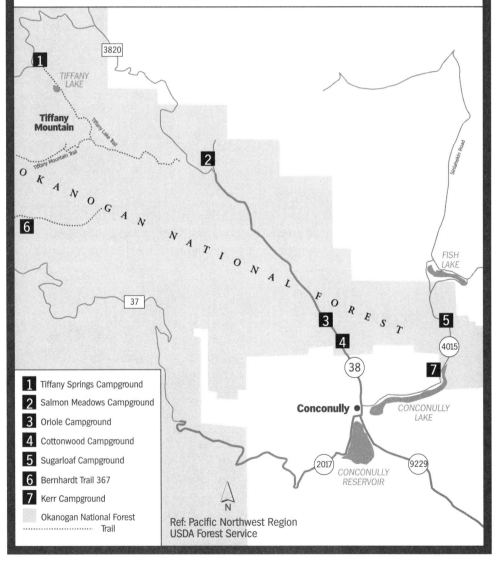

Tiffany Mountain Area

Tiffany Mountain is 8,200 feet above sea level and offers a view that covers a vast territory of mountains near and far, as well as farm fields in the Okanogan Valley.

1 Tiffany Springs Campground
2 Salmon Meadows Campground
3 Oriole Campground
4 Cottonwood Campground
5 Sugarloaf Campground
6 Bernhardt Trail 367
7 Kerr Campground

Okanogan National Forest
········· Trail

Ref: Pacific Northwest Region
USDA Forest Service

N

forest, including subalpine fir, Engelmann spruce, whitebark, and lodgepole pine, all of which become more stunted as the trail goes higher and sparse when it reaches timberline. Numerous flowers blossom as their seasons succeed each other, Indian paintbrush, lupine, and purple aster among them.

The trail becomes faint as it progresses, but experienced hikers can find the way by heading northeast up the mountainside. In the end the route forks off the main trail and becomes steep, running above Whistler Pass through open ground strewn with granite rocks to the top of the mountain.

The Forest Service built a fire lookout at the peak in 1932 but dismantled it in 1953. The view covers a vast territory of mountains near and far, as well as farm fields in the Okanogan Valley.

The trail goes on to intersect other trails going to various places, including Tiffany Lake on the other side of Tiffany Mountain. From the lake it is an easy 1-mile hike back to Forest Road Number 39, about 4 miles from the trailhead to the Tiffany Mountain Trail (*see* Tiffany Lake Trail, below).

Directions: Take County Road 9137 (the road toward Pearrygin Lake State Park), which follows the east side of the Chewuch River Road north from Winthrop, for about 8 miles and turn right on Forest Road 37. Follow Forest Road 37 past the end of the pavement for about 12 miles and turn left onto Forest Road 39. Then go about 3 miles to Freezeout Pass and the trailhead, elevation 6,500 feet.

Dates: Seasonal, summer.

Fees: A trailhead fee may be charged.

For more information: Tonasket Ranger District, 1 West Winesap, Tonasket, WA 98855. Phone (509) 486-2186.

Trail: 3 miles, one-way.

Elevation: 1,700 feet elevation gain.

Degree of difficulty: Moderate.

TIFFANY LAKE TRAIL 373

[Fig. 19] This is a short hike that goes slightly downhill 1 mile to Tiffany Lake. There is magnificent scenery and many trout. The trail passes high-country stands of spruce, fir, and pine as well as Lyall larch that turn glistening gold in the fall.

The lake is in a cirque with Tiffany Mountain on one side of the valley and Rock Mountain on the other side. It is possible for experienced hikers to scramble to the top of either mountain for wide views of the countryside.

There are campsites at the lake and the Tiffany Springs Campground, at the trailhead, has six campsites for trailers up to 16 feet long and for tents, and vault toilets.

Directions: Take County Road 9137 (the road that also goes toward Pearrygin Lake State Park) from Winthrop. Follow that road along the east side of the Chewuch River Road, north about 8 miles from Winthrop and turn right on Forest Road 37. Follow Forest Road 37 for about 12 miles, passing the end of the pavement, and turn left onto

Douglas fir (*Pseudotsuga menziesii*)

This tall, stately tree is not only the most abundant in the Washington Cascades, but also it is one of the most beautiful. It grows to 6 feet in diameter and some 250 feet tall. It owes its abundance, at least in part, to its thick bark that protects it from all but the worst forest fires. It was little valued by Native Americans because the wood is tough and difficult to work with stone. They preferred the soft, straight grain of the cedar. But white settlers brought steel tools that could be used to work the wood of Douglas fir.

Forest Road 39. Then go about 7 miles (4 miles past Freezeout Pass) to the trailhead at Tiffany Springs Campground.

Facilities: Vault toilets in the campground at the trailhead.

Dates: Seasonal, summer.

Fees: A trailhead fee may be charged.

For more information: Tonasket Ranger District, One West Winesap, Tonasket, WA 98855. Phone (509) 486-2186.

Trail: 1 mile, one-way.

Degree of difficulty: Easy.

BERNHARDT TRAIL 367

[Fig. 19(6)] This trail goes 3 miles to an old mine shaft sunk deeply into the hard granite of Clark Mountain, and to a finely crafted, privately owned cabin that was built by the miner whose name apparently was Bernhardt. The trail is steep, attesting to the notion that Indians, fishermen, and miners who blazed trails went as directly as possible to wherever they were going, regardless of topography. Switchbacks, apparently, came when foresters began to appear in the mountains and forests.

The trail crosses three streams and passes a boggy meadow in the first mile or so, but after that it is essentially a dry trail through a dry, pine-and-fir forest. Hikers carry whatever they drink, which can be a considerable amount when it's hot and the trail is steep. Game trails along the way can look deceptively like the main trail and lead people who aren't paying attention to a dead end.

The route to the cabin and mine forks a short distance to the right of the main trail about 2.5 miles from the trailhead. Both the cabin and the mine are old, neglected, and less than safe, but there is a lot to see and learn without actually entering them.

Day hikers may return to the trailhead from the mine but the main trail goes on from the fork and intersects with other routes.

Directions: Take County Road 9137 (the road that also goes toward Pearrygin Lake State Park) from Winthrop. Follow that road along the east side of the Chewuch River Road north about 6 miles from Winthrop and turn right on Forest Road 37. Follow that road for about 12 miles, passing the end of the pavement, and turn left onto Forest Road

39. Then go about 1.5 miles to the trailhead where the road widens to accommodate a hairpin turn at about 5,700 feet elevation.

Dates: Seasonal, summer.

Fees: A trailhead fee may be charged.

For more information: Tonasket Ranger District, One West Winesap, Tonasket, WA 98855. Phone (509) 486-2186.

Trail: 3 miles, one-way.

Elevation: 1,700 feet elevation gain.

Degree of difficulty: Easy.

DOUGLAS FIR
(*Pseudotsuga menziesii*)
Named after a 19th century explorer, David Douglas, this tall, straight tree is found from the coast to the mountains.

▒ CRATER LAKES TRAIL 416

[Fig. 15(8)] This is a trail to two lakes created long ago in topography that was produced when glaciers carved out the hard granite mountains, leaving the rocky spires of the rugged, granite Sawtooth Mountains, which are the most easterly peaks of the Washington Cascade subranges.

The hike is about 4 miles one-way. It begins at 4,750 feet elevation, and goes to the lakes, which, quite logically, are called Lower Crater Lake and Upper Crater Lake. Upper Crater Lake's elevation is 6,960 feet. That is more than 500 feet of elevation gain per mile of hiking.

The trailhead, which also serves Trail Number 431 to Eagle Lakes (*see* Eagle Lakes Trail, page 108), is well developed with vault toilets, campsites, horse ramps and watering facilities. From there the trail glides over an uphill grade through open forest with a grass surface, and soon passes an open spot with a view of the Crater Creek Valley where the trail is headed.

About 0.5 mile from the trailhead there is a bridge across Crater Creek, and a short distance beyond that the trail forks. The left fork goes 4 miles up to the Eagle Lakes and is open to motorcycles. The right fork follows Crater Creek to the Crater Lakes, and motorcycles are banned.

The forest of typical east Cascades, high-country spruce and fir continues to limit the view for 2 miles, then begins to open. In the evening and early morning, mottled gray-and-brown, great horned owls (*Bobo viginianus)* may sometimes be seen looking for something to eat. Gray jays, also known as camp robbers, may appear at any time, looking for a piece of a hiker's lunch. If it is not offered freely he may just take it when no one is looking. There may also be some deep-blue, crested Steller's jays (*Cyanocitta stelleri*) nearby, practicing their repertoire of noisy calls, including the one that sounds almost exactly like the scream of the red tailed hawk (*Buteo jamaicensis).*

The trail then goes up three steep switchbacks to views of the lower Methow Valley. From there, it goes over a series of benches to views of granite mountains. At 6,800 feet is a meadow with a campsite often used by people with horses. Some 40 feet higher, the official trail ends at the Lower Crater Lake, nestled beside a high-country forest of subalpine fir, Lyall larch, whitebark pine, and Engelmann spruce.

The view includes the rocky crags of peaks that have been savaged for thousands of years by glaciers and storms. To the southwest at 8,450 feet elevation is Mount Bigelow.

A faint fisherman's trail goes 0.3 mile southeast from the lower to the upper lake, which rests on a bench below high peaks. The timber is stunted here by the vicious winters but there is a variety of small plants including pink heather (*Phyllodoce empetriformis*), white heather (*Cassiope mertensiana*), and, late in the season, the deep indigo bloom of the mountain gentian (*Gentiana calycosa*) appears.

Both lakes produce pan-size trout, and there are campsites among the trees on the eastern shore of the lower lake.

Directions: On County Road Number 9105, which runs along the west side of the Methow River, go south about 15 miles from Twisp and turn right onto County Road Number 1034. After about 1 mile on that road turn right onto Forest Road 4340, which follows Gold Creek. About 5.5 miles farther turn left onto Forest Road 300 and go about 4.5 miles to the trailhead that is marked "Eagle Lakes Trail."

Activities: Hiking, horseback riding, camping, fishing.

Facilities: There are vault toilets, picnic tables, and horse ramps and watering facilities at the trailhead.

Dates: Seasonal, summer.

Fees: A trailhead fee may be charged.

For more information: Methow Valley Ranger District, 502 Glover, Twisp, WA 98856. Phone (509) 997-2131.

Trail: 4 miles, one-way.

Elevation: 2,200 feet elevation gain.

Degree of difficulty: Moderate.

EAGLE LAKES TRAIL 431

[Fig. 15(9)] This is the trail that shares its trailhead with the Crater Lakes Trail (*see* Crater Lakes Trail Number 416, page 107) About 0.5 mile from the trailhead there is a fork. The route to Eagle Lakes is on the left fork. Motorcycles are permitted. Indeed, it is a National Recreation Trail and the designers made it wide and smooth, with banked curves, especially for motorcycles.

The moderately easy trail goes 7 miles to the farthest of the two Eagle lakes, but hikers who choose to can go on to more lakes and more territory. The trail doesn't really begin going up until after the first mile, when it begins a steady elevation gain. It passes the side trails to the Crater Lakes and Martin Lakes (*see* Martin Lakes Trail Number 429, page 109) along the way as it heads upward through forest too thick to allow long views.

At approximately 4.5 miles, about 6,600 feet elevation, the trail goes between the two lakes with a side trail leading to each. The one on the left goes to Eagle Lake, the one on the right to Upper Eagle Lake. The left trail is closed to motorcycles. It loses more than 100 feet elevation in about 0.5 mile. There are good campsites at Lower Eagle Lake and near a small pool on the main trail. The lake offers trout fishing as well as views of Martin Peak, elevation 8,375, on the Lake Chelan Crest.

The upper Eagle Lake is some 600 feet higher than the Lower Eagle Lake. The trail to it is about 1 mile beyond the one to the lower lake and near the campsites. The way is short and climbs to about 100 feet higher than the trail. The blue of that lake reflects Mount Bigelow's 8,440 foot peak, but by midsummer, when its snow is gone, its reflection becomes a desolate scene of ragged, bare rocks.

About 1 mile past the lakes the trail goes across Horsehead Pass, at about 7,600 feet elevation, and then into the Wenatchee National Forest and down some switchbacks to Boiling Lake, which gets its name from bubbles that rise from underwater springs. Beyond that it intersects with a maze of trails, some of which go long distances along the ridge above Lake Chelan, or slightly shorter distances down to Lake Chelan itself.

Directions: On County Road Number 9105, which runs along the west side of the Methow River, go south about 15 miles from Twisp, and turn right onto County Road Number 1034. After 1 mile on that road, turn right onto Forest Road 4340, which follows Gold Creek. Approximately 5.5 miles farther, turn left onto Forest Road 300, and go about 4.5 miles to the trailhead that is marked "Eagle Lakes Trail."

Activities: Hiking, horse packing, camping, and fishing.

Facilities: There are vault toilets, picnic tables, and horse ramps and watering facilities at the trailhead.

Dates: Seasonal, summer.

Fees: A trailhead fee may be charged.

For more information: Methow Valley Ranger District, 502 Glover, Twisp, WA 98856. Phone (509) 997-2131.

Trail: 7 miles, one-way.

Elevation: 2,900 feet elevation gain.

Degree of difficulty: Moderate.

🏵 MARTIN LAKES TRAIL 429

[Fig. 15(10)] This trail is a branch of the Eagle Lakes Trail Number 431, and travels to the third of three pairs of lakes that share the same trailhead (see Crater Lakes Trail Number 416 and Eagle Lakes Trail Number 431, pages 107, and 108). The little Martin Lakes lie at the foot of 8,375-foot Martin Peak, one of the mountains on the Chelan Divide above Lake Chelan.

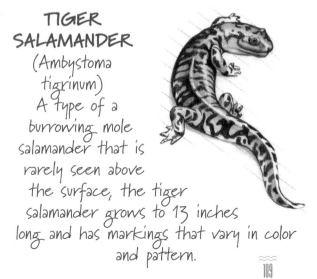

TIGER SALAMANDER (Ambystoma tigrinum) A type of a burrowing mole salamander that is rarely seen above the surface, the tiger salamander grows to 13 inches long and has markings that vary in color and pattern.

The Martin Lakes are rimmed with larch that display their golden radiance in the fall. Varieties of flowers change during the season, each adding colorful splendor to the scene.

The trail is 7 miles long and gains 2,400 feet to reach the highest point of about 6,800 feet. It begins at the Crater Creek Trailhead and follows the Crater Creek Trail for about 0.5 mile, then branches to the left onto the Eagle Lakes Trail, which is open to motorcycles.

It follows the Eagle Lakes Trail for about 1.5 miles, then takes another branch to the left. That puts the hiker onto the Martin Lakes Trail proper, which also is open to motorcycles. The trail loses about 400 feet elevation after the junction, but quickly gains it back. It follows Martin Creek, but far above it on the wall of the valley. Occasional openings in the forest allow glimpses of the creek.

A series of long switchbacks leads to 6,400 feet elevation and another branch in the trail about 6 miles from the trailhead. The route to the Martin Lakes is on the right fork, and motorcycles are banned from it. It goes about 1 mile to the first lake at about 6,700 feet elevation. A trail along the bank of that lake leads a short distance to the second lake. Sometimes the low, humming call of the male blue grouse can be heard nearby, but their mottled-gray plumage makes them difficult to see.

Directions: On County Road Number 9105, which runs along the west side of the Methow River, go south about 15 miles from Twisp and turn right onto County Road Number 1034. After 1 mile on Road 1034, turn right onto Forest Road 4340, which follows Gold Creek. Go about 5.5 miles farther and turn left onto Forest Road 300. Then go about 4.5 miles to the trailhead which is marked "Eagle Lakes Trail."

Activities: Hiking, horse-back riding, camping, fishing.

Facilities: There are vault toilets, picnic tables, and horse ramps and watering facilities at the trailhead.

Dates: Seasonal, summer.

Fees: A trailhead fee may be charged.

For more information: Methow Valley Ranger District, 502 Glover, Twisp, WA 98856. Phone (509) 997-2131.

Trail: 7 miles, one-way.

Elevation: 2,400 feet elevation gain.

Degree of difficulty: Moderate.

BIG TREE TRAIL 311

[Fig. 20(6)] This is a short, wheelchair-accessible trail to and through the Big Tree Botanical Area, and is a learning experience for both youngsters and their elders. The trail is a loop that wanders into the Okanogan National Forest's Big Tree Botanical Area where old-growth trees, typical of the eastern slopes of the Washington Cascades, have grown old and tall.

Among the trees are lodgepole, ponderosa, and whitebark pine, which are very impressive, but the major attraction of the botanical area are the two 600-year-old western larch trees, which provide a rare opportunity to see ancient larch up close.

Directions: The trailhead is inside the Lost Lake Campground, which is on Forest Road 33-050 about 10 miles from State Route 20.

Activities: Hiking, botanical information.

Facilities: Toilets in the campground, gravel trail suitable for wheelchairs, except for some steep sections where assistance may be needed.

Dates: Seasonal, summer.

Fees: A trailhead fee may be charged.

For more information: Tonasket Ranger District office. One West Winesap, Tonasket, WA 98855. Phone (509) 486-2186.

Trail: 1.5-mile, wheelchair-accessible loop.

Degree of difficulty: Easy.

Campgrounds in the Okanogan National Forest

There are many drive-in campgrounds in the national forest as well as those of other agencies. The forest camps have, between them, about 75 sites for tents only and 265 sites for either tents or trailers. Fees may be charged for overnight parking. There are campgrounds in all the major river drainages in the forest, including on State Route 20, which runs through much of the forest. Information about the campgrounds and a forest map may be obtained from Okanogan National Forest, 1240 South Second Avenue, Okanogan, WA 98840. Phone (509) 826-3275. Among the campgrounds are:

▨ METHOW VALLEY RANGER DISTRICT CAMPGROUNDS

BALLARD CAMPGROUND. [Fig. 16(8)] 22 miles northwest of Winthrop on Forest Road 5400 (the Methow River Road). 6 tent sites, 1 trailer site, fishing.

BUCK LAKE CAMPGROUND. [Fig. 14(8)] 12 miles north of Winthrop on Forest Road 51-100 (the Eightmile Creek Road). 4 tent sites, 5 tent-or-trailer sites, vault toilets, boat ramp, fishing.

CAMP 4 CAMPGROUND. [Fig. 14(4)] 18 miles northeast of Winthrop on Forest Road 5160 (the Chewuch River Road). 5 tent sites, vault toilets, fishing.

CHEWUCH CAMPGROUND. [Fig. 14(5)] 15 miles north of Winthrop on Forest Road 51, (the Chewuch River Road). 9 tent sites, vault toilets, fishing.

EARLY WINTERS CAMPGROUND. [Fig. 16(6)] 15 miles northwest of Winthrop on State Route 20. 7 tent sites, 5 trailer sites, drinking water, vault toilets, garbage facilities, fishing.

FALLS CREEK CAMPGROUND. [Fig. 14(6)] 11 miles north of Winthrop on Forest Road 51 (the Chewuch River Road), 4 tent sites, 3 tent-or-trailer sites, accessible by disabled persons, vault toilets, fishing.

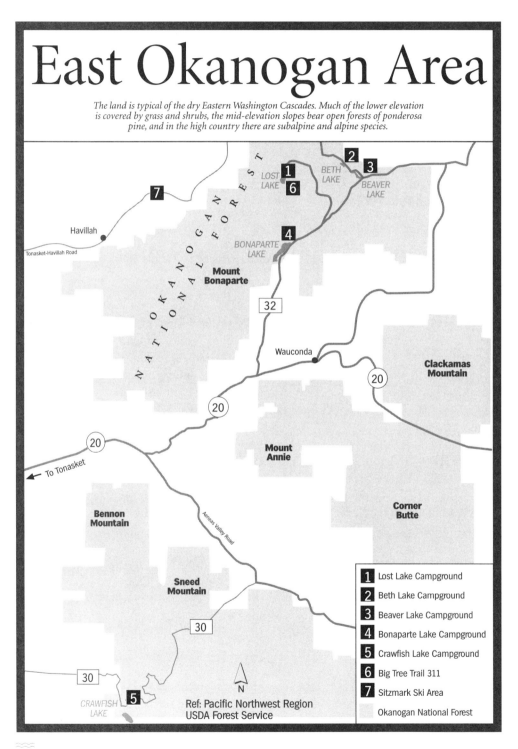

East Okanogan Area

The land is typical of the dry Eastern Washington Cascades. Much of the lower elevation is covered by grass and shrubs, the mid-elevation slopes bear open forests of ponderosa pine, and in the high country there are subalpine and alpine species.

7

Havillah

Tonasket-Havillah Road

1 LOST LAKE
6

BETH LAKE **2**
3 BEAVER LAKE

4

BONAPARTE LAKE

Mount Bonaparte

NATIONAL OKANOGAN FOREST

32

Wauconda

20

Clackamas Mountain

20

Mount Annie

← To Tonasket

20

Bennon Mountain

Aeneas Valley Road

Corner Butte

Sneed Mountain

30

30

N

5 CRAWFISH LAKE

Ref: Pacific Northwest Region USDA Forest Service

1 Lost Lake Campground
2 Beth Lake Campground
3 Beaver Lake Campground
4 Bonaparte Lake Campground
5 Crawfish Lake Campground
6 Big Tree Trail 311
7 Sitzmark Ski Area
Okanogan National Forest

FLAT CAMPGROUND. [Fig. 14(7)] 11 miles north of Winthrop on the Eightmile Creek Road. 9 tent sites, 3 tent-or-trailer sites, accessible by disabled persons, vault toilets, fishing.

HONEYMOON CAMPGROUND. [Fig. 14(1)] 18 miles northwest of Winthrop on Forest Road 5130 (the Eightmile Creek Road). Vault toilets, 6 tent sites, fishing.

KLIPCHUCK CAMPGROUND. [Fig. 16(5)] 19 miles northwest of Winthrop on State Route 20. 6 tent sites, 40 tent-or-trailer sites, accessible by handicapped persons, drinking water, flush toilets, vault toilets, garbage facilities, fishing.

LONE FIR CAMPGROUND. [Fig. 16(4)] 27 miles northwest of Winthrop on State Route 20. 21 tent sites, 6 tent-or-trailer sites, accessible by disabled persons, drinking water, flush toilets, vault toilets, garbage facilities, fishing.

MEADOWS CAMPGROUND. [Fig. 16(9)] 34 miles northwest of Winthrop on Forest Road 5400-500 (the Rattlesnake Creek Road). Vault toilets, 14 tent sites.

RIVER BEND CAMPGROUND. [Fig. 16(7)] 23 miles northwest of Winthrop on Forest Road 5400-060 (the Methow River Road). Vault toilets, 4 tent sites, 1 trailer site, fishing.

RUFFED GROUSE CAMPGROUND. [Fig. 14(2)] 17 miles northwest of Winthrop on Forest Road 5130-383 (the Eightmile Creek Road). Vault toilets, 4 tent sites, fishing.

BLACKPINE LAKE CAMPGROUND. [Fig. 15(6)] 19 miles southwest of Twisp on Forest Road 43 (the Buttermilk Creek Road). 3 tent sites, 21 tent-or-trailer sites, picnic site, drinking water, vault toilets, garbage facilities, boat ramp, fishing. There is a dock with facilities for handicapped persons.

FOGGY DEW CAMPGROUND. [Fig. 15(7)] 9 miles southwest of Carlton on Forest Road 4340 (the North Fork of Gold Creek Road). Vault toilets, 13 tent sites, fishing, motorcycle trails.

JR CAMPGROUND. [Fig. 18(4)] 12 miles east of Twisp on State Route 20 (near Loup Loup Ski Area). 6-tent-or-trailer sites, accessible by handicapped persons, drinking water, vault toilets, garbage facilities.

LOUP LOUP CAMPGROUND. [Fig. 18(3)] 13 miles east of Twisp on State Route 20 (near Loup Loup Ski Area), 21 tent-or-trailer sites, accessible by handicapped persons, drinking water, vault toilets, garbage facilities, designated sno-park, cross-country skiing, downhill skiing, snowmobiling.

MYSTERY CAMPGROUND. [Fig. 15(4)] 18 miles west of Twisp on Forest Road 4440, (the North Twisp River Road). 5 tent-or-trailer sites, picnic sites, vault toilets, fishing.

POPLAR FLAT CAMPGROUND. [Fig. 15(3)] 20 miles west of Twisp on Forest Road Number 4440, (the North Twisp River Road). 15 tent-or-trailer sites, accessible by handicapped persons, picnic sites, drinking water, vault toilets, garbage facilities, fishing, community kitchen.

SOUTH CREEK CAMPGROUND. [Fig. 15(1)] 22 miles west of Twisp on Forest Road Number 4440 (the Twisp River Road), vault toilets, fishing.

TWISP RIVER HORSE CAMPGROUND. [Fig. 15(2)] 22 miles west of Twisp on Forest Road Number 4440, (the Twisp River Road). Vault toilets, horse ramp, horse trail.

WAR CREEK CAMPGROUND. [Fig. 15(5)] 14 miles west of Twisp on Forest Road 44, (the north Twisp River Road). 11 tent-or-trailer sites, drinking water, vault toilets, garbage facilities, fishing.

For more information: Methow Valley Ranger District, 502 Glover, Twisp, WA 98856. Phone (509) 997-2131.

TONASKET RANGER DISTRICT CAMPGROUNDS

BEAVER LAKE CAMPGROUND. [Fig. 20(3)] 34 miles northeast of Tonasket on Forest Road 32 (the Bonaparte Creek Road). 9 tent-or-trailer sites, drinking water, vault toilets, garbage facilities, fishing, swimming.

BETH LAKE CAMPGROUND. [Fig. 20(2)] 34 miles northeast of Tonasket on County Road 9480. 14 tent-or-trailer sites, accessible by handicapped persons, picnic sites, drinking water, flush toilets, vault toilets, garbage facilities, boat ramp, fishing.

BONAPARTE LAKE CAMPGROUND. [Fig. 20(4)] 26 miles northeast of Tonasket on Forest Road Number 32 (the Bonaparte Creek Road). 26 tent-or-trailer sites, accessible by handicapped persons. Picnic sites, drinking water, flush toilets, vault toilets, garbage facilities, boat ramp, fishing, swimming.

COTTONWOOD CAMPGROUND. [Fig. 19(4)] 2 miles north of Conconully on Forest Road 38 (the Salmon Creek Road), 4 tent-or-trailer sites, drinking water, vault toilets, fishing.

CRAWFISH LAKE CAMPGROUND. [Fig. 20(5)] 20 miles east of Riverside on Forest Road 30. 22 tent-or-trailer sites, vault toilets, boat ramp, fishing, skiing, snowmobiling. This is a designated Sno-Park, which allows persons with special permits to park in places cleared of snow by the state Department of Transportation.

KERR CAMPGROUND. [Fig. 19(7)] 4 miles east of Conconully on Forest Road 38-055 (the Salmon Creek Road). 13 tent-or-trailer sites, vault toilets, boat ramp, fishing, skiing, snowmobiling, designated Sno-Park.

LOST LAKE CAMPGROUND. [Fig. 20(1)] 19 miles north of Wauconda on Forest Road 33-050. 22 tent-or-trailer sites, accessible by handicapped persons, drinking water, flush toilets, vault toilets, garbage facilities, snowmobiling, designated sno-park.

ORIOLE CAMPGROUND. [Fig. 19(3)] 3 miles northwest of Conconully on Forest Road 38 (the Salmon Creek Road). 13 tent-or-trailer sites, drinking water, vault toilets, fishing.

SALMON MEADOWS CAMPGROUND. [Fig. 19(2)] 9 miles northwest of Conconully on Forest Road 38 (the Salmon Creek Road). 14 tent-or-trailer sites, picnic sites, drinking water, vault toilets, community kitchen.

SUGARLOAF CAMPGROUND. [Fig. 19(5)] 5 miles northeast of Conconully on County Road 4015. 5-tent-or trailer sites, drinking water, vault toilets, garbage facilities, fishing, swimming.

TIFFANY SPRINGS CAMPGROUND. [Fig. 19(1)] 31 miles northwest of Conconully on Forest Road 39. 6-tent-or trailer sites, vault toilets.

For more information: Tonasket Ranger District, 1 West Winesap, Tonasket, WA 98855. Phone (509) 486-2186.

Winter Activities in the Okanogan National Forest

Everything changes in the Okanogan National Forest during the winter. The dry, dusty forests wear a white mantle that may be many feet deep by spring. The snow falls early, and after a few false starts becomes permanent for the winter. State Route 20 in the high mountains is almost always closed for the winter by midfall, when the snow piles so deep and the avalanches are so frequent that the state Department of Transportation's huge machines can no longer handle them. Visitors must arrive from the east until spring. Methow Valley residents like to say they are at the end of the road during the winter.

The snow falls throughout the winter, about 3 feet in the valleys, as much as 18 feet in the high country. As it accumulates through the winter, the grandeur of the valley changes to an airy, white wonderland. The temperature drops low, but the snow falls mostly at night and the sun shines an average of five days a week year round. The cold, dry weather creates a snow base as dry and powdery as the forest trails are dry and dusty in the summer. The area has the state's largest mule deer herd, and an occasional moose may be seen. The animals are driven off the mountains and into the lowlands by the snow. Herons and eagles dine on fish from the open pools of the Methow River.

The 3,600 residents of the Methow Valley have taken full advantage of their winter opportunities. They have created one of the nation's major winter recreation areas with many attractions in and near the valley. Among the attractions are two downhill ski areas, groomed snowmobile runs, heli-ski services, a hut-to-hut mountain skiing system that allows customers to ski for as much as three days and stay each night in a different, well equipped hut, and the second largest cross-country trail system in the United States.

There are scores of places to stay, ranging from bed and breakfasts to motels to cabins to the first class Sun Mountain Resort, which boasts an excellent restaurant. Ski clinics are available, and there is a series of indoor and outdoor events throughout the winter. Many parking lots at trailheads are plowed by the state Department of Transportation and require state Sno-Park passes for parking. The passes may be purchased at Forest Service offices and numerous retail and service outlets throughout the state.

Directions: Winter access to the Methow Valley is on U.S. Highway 97 north from Wenatchee to Pateros, then northwest on State Route 153 to the intersection with State Route 20, and north on State Route 20.

Activities: Downhill, cross-country, hut-to-hut, and heli-skiing, snowmobiling.

Facilities: Many groomed trails, food, lodging and equipment facilities.

Dates: Seasonal, winter.

Fees: Fees are charged for use of groomed cross-country ski trails and for services. Fees also are charged for state Sno-Park passes, which are required for parking in places cleared of snow by the State Department of Transportation.

Closest town: Winthrop and Twisp are within the area.

For more information: Methow Valley Information Center, (888) 463-8469 or (509) 996-2125 or Methow Valley Sport Trails Association, PO Box 147, Winthrop, WA 98862, (509) 996-3287.

DOWNHILL SKIING IN THE OKANOGAN NATIONAL FOREST
LOUP LOUP SKI BOWL

[Fig. 18(2)] The Loup Loup Ski Bowl contains some 550 skiable acres, and offers trails for downhill skiing and snowboarding, as well as 20 kilometers of groomed cross-country trails. The downhill area has 1,240 feet of vertical drop, and the ski area is proud of its beautiful slopes, dry powder snow, and machine-groomed runs for day or night skiing. The elevation at the base is 4,040 feet and the summit elevation is 5,240 feet. The average winter snowfall is 50 inches.

There are a quad lift, a rope tow, and 12 trails as much as 10,560 feet long. A lodge with a snack bar overlooks the ski runs. There also are a ski-rental shop and children's programs. Twenty percent of the trails are rated beginner, 40 percent intermediate, 30 percent advanced and 10 percent expert.

Directions: 12 miles east of Twisp on State Route 20.

Activities: Downhill, snowboard, and cross-country skiing.

Facilities: Groomed ski runs, lifts, lodge, ski rentals, snack bar and Ski Patrol.

Dates: Seasonal, winter.

Fees: Fees are charged for lifts, ski rentals and other services.

Closest town: Twisp, 12 miles.

For more Information: Loup Loup Ski Bowl, PO Box 1686, Omak, WA 98841. Phone, (509) 826-2720.

SITZMARK SKI AREA

[Fig. 20(7)] This smaller, family-oriented ski area has a 4,300-foot base elevation, and 4,950 at the summit. It has 650-foot vertical ski runs and is equipped with a double-chair lift and a tow rope. There are 80 skiable acres.

The uphill capacity of the chairlift is 1,700 persons an hour. Twenty percent of the 12 trails are rated easiest, 60 percent more difficult, and 20 percent most difficult. Snowboarding is allowed.

It has 3 kilometers of groomed cross-country trails at the ski area and operates another 12 kilometers 3 miles away at Highland Son Park. It is open on Thursdays, weekends, and holidays throughout the ski season.

There is a lodge with a restaurant and a ski-rental shop. A ski school operates through the season for both skiers and snowboarders.

Directions: On the Havillah Road 20 miles northeast of Tonasket.
Activities: Downhill and cross-country skiing.
Facilities: A ski lift, groomed trails, lodge, food, rentals, and ski school.
Dates: Seasonal, winter.
Fees: Fees required for skiing and services.
Closest town: Tonasket, 20 miles.
For more information: Phone (509) 486-2700. For snow conditions phone (509) 485-3323.

▓ CROSS-COUNTRY SKIING IN THE METHOW VALLEY

To a cross-country skier the Methow Valley in winter is like a candy store to a child, the place to be. And, as the sport has gained in popularity over the past few decades, the people of the valley have taken great pains to make it even more attractive.

Starting with the cold, dry, powder snow and a landscape that provides not only awesome beauty, but also the topography for all levels of skiing, they developed three separate trail systems with a total of 150 kilometers of groomed trail, plus a 25-kilometer Methow Valley Community Trail that connects the three systems. The trails are maintained and groomed by the Methow Valley Sport Trails Association, a private, nonprofit organization that creates and maintains trails on private and national forest land for year round, nonmotorized, trail-based recreation. They can be contacted for information, maps and trail passes at Methow Valley Sports Trails Association, PO Box 147, Winthrop, WA 98862, phone (509) 996-3287.

The longest of the three trail networks is the 70-kilometer Sun Mountain trail system of the Sun Mountain Resort, high on Sun Mountain near Winthrop. Billed as the oldest and largest cross-country ski resort in the Pacific Northwest, Sun Mountain has, in addition to its nice accommodations, cross-country trails ranging from family skiing to advanced. A pro shop and rentals, as well as individual or group instructions that cover all levels of skiing from beginner, to telemark, and skate skiing are available. For more information contact Sun Mountain Lodge, PO Box 1000, Winthrop, WA 98862, (800) 572-0493 or (509) 996-2211.

The 45 kilometers of the Rendevous Trail system are in the high elevations between 4,000 and 6,000 feet, overlooking the high-country hut system. Operated by Rendevous Outfitter, Inc., in the European mountain-skiing tradition, the system offers backcountry skiing on a variety of mountain trails. The company maintains fully equipped overnight huts along the trails. Guides and freight hauling for customers' equipment and supplies are available. For more information, persons within Washington State may phone (800) 422-3048 or phone (509) 996-2148 from throughout the United States.

The Mazama Trail system is operated close by the village of Mazama on State Route 20 near where the snowplows on the highway stop during the winter. With 35 kilometers of groomed trail, skiers can go from lodge to lodge among four cooperating lodges in the vicinity. There are machine-groomed trails over flat or hilly landscapes for day skiing.

Beyond that are the open slopes of the wilderness. Professional guides are available to take parties on overnight tours.

Heli-skiing may be the ultimate for skiing devotees. Intermediate and advanced skiers can make arrangements with the North Cascades Heli-Skiing Company in Winthrop for a helicopter ride to the high country. Working under a Forest Service permit, the company flies customers to any of 80 designated runs in some 300,000 acres of magnificent landscape. The runs begin at elevations as high as 9,000 feet. They range from 1,500 to 4,000 vertical feet, and cover a wide variety of terrain.

The company recommends that participants be at least strong intermediate skiers or snowboarders, and in good physical condition. Instructors and guides can be provided.

Directions: Winter access to the Methow Valley is on U.S Highway 97 north from Wenatchee to Pateros, then northwest on State Route 153 to the intersection with State Route 20, and north on State Route 20.

Activities: Cross-country skiing.

Facilities: Groomed trails, lodging, restaurants, ski schools.

Dates: Seasonal, winter.

Fees: Fees are charged for ski-trail passes, for use of ski huts, for guides and freight hauling, and for transportation in helicopters.

Closest towns: Winthrop and Mazama.

For more information: Methow Valley Sport Trails Association at PO Box 147, Winthrop, WA 98862, phone (509) 996-3287, or North Cascade Heli Skiing, PO Box 367 Winthrop, WA 98862, phone (800) 494-4354.

SNOWMOBILING IN THE METHOW VALLEY

Washington State grooms some 435 miles of snowmobile trails in the Okanogan National Forest under an agreement with the Forest Service. The grooming is funded through the state's snowmobile registration program on routes specified by the Forest Service on forest roads that are chosen to reduce as much as possible the exposure to avalanches, and to minimize disturbing wildlife. Many of those groomed trails are in the Methow Valley.

Directions: Winter access to the Methow Valley is on U.S Highway 97 north from Wenatchee to Pateros, then northwest on State Route 153 to the intersection with State Route 20, and north on State Route 20.

Activities: Snowmobiling on groomed trails.

Facilities: Groomed trails, lodging, restaurants.

Dates: Seasonal, fall, winter, and spring.

Fees: State snowmobile registration fee must be obtained. They are available from county court houses and private vendors throughout the state. A state Sno-Park Permit is required where parking areas are cleared of snow by the state Department of Transportation. They are available from Forest Service offices and private vendors throughout the state.

Closest town: Winthrop.

For more information: Okanogan National Forest Supervisor, 1240, S. Second Avenue, Okanogan, WA 98840. Phone (509) 826-3275.

▨ NORTH CASCADES SMOKEJUMPER BASE

[Fig. 17(2)] Fighting forest fires has become high-tech in many ways, using aircraft instead of mountaintop lookouts to spot fires and to get the firefighters to where the fire is burning. But the basic, hard work of fighting fires in the backcountry is still up to tough, well-trained people with hand tools. The North Cascades Smokejumper Base is one of nine places around the nation where such people are based and trained, and, indeed the Methow Valley is the birthplace of smoke jumping.

The national Smokejumper program began in 1939 when two Forest Service fire guards from the Okanogan National Forest (then called Chelan National Forest) and parachuters from a parachute company in Pennsylvania climbed into a Forest Service SR-10 Stinson aircraft and began an experiment to see whether parachuters could safely be dropped onto fires deep in the backcountry, before the blazes had a chance to grow so large they were difficult to fight.

After 58 experimental jumps the program was declared a success, and the first two operational smokejumper bases were established in Missoula, Montana and the Methow Valley. Since then the program has been expanded to nine bases around the country, with some 400 firefighters assigned to them.

The firefighters go through constant rigorous training to maintain their skills, both in jumping and in fighting fires. They work in teams that fly in planes or helicopters to fires so deep in the backcountry that ground crews cannot quickly reach them. At the fire, those in helicopters land, and those in fixed-wing planes parachute to the nearest safe place to the fire and go to work. Once the fire is out they retrieve their parachutes, sometimes by climbing high into the trees in which they landed, and walk to wherever they can be picked up and taken back to the base.

Many of the smokejumpers also are trained as emergency medical technicians, and can parachute to inaccessible places in the backcountry to give medical assistance to persons who are injured or ill.

During the summer fire season, smokejumpers at the North Cascades Base conduct daily, 45-minute tours of their base to talk about the facilities, their work, and their rigorous training. They demonstrate the use of their equipment, and talk about the history of the base and its program.

Directions: The base is on the Okanogan County Airport in the Methow Valley, approximately 4 miles south of Winthrop or 5 miles north of Twisp on County Road 9129.

Activities: Tours and displays at the North Cascades Smokejumper Base.

Facilities: None.

Dates: Daily during the forest fire season. Special arrangements may be made during the off-season.

Fees: None.
Closest town: Winthrop, 4 miles.
For more information: North Cascades Smokejumper Base, Route 1, Box 180, Winthrop, WA 98862 Phone (509) 997-2031.

State Campgrounds in the Okanogan National Forest Vicinity

The state Department of Natural Resources, and state Parks and Recreation Commission maintain several campgrounds on state land in the vicinity of the Okanogan National Forest. The Department of Natural Resources campgrounds typically are small and rustic. None have electric or sewage hookups, but they do have recreational-vehicle parking, tent pads, fire grills, and picnic tables. There are no fees on Department of Natural Resources sites. The state parks are larger and more elaborate, and often require fees.

LEADER LAKE CAMPGROUND
[Fig. 18(5)] Located 8.5 miles west of U.S. Highway 97 on State Route 20, then 0.25 mile north on Leader Lake Road, a one-lane paved byway. 16 campsites, 2 picnic sites, toilets, boat launch, fishing.

ROCK CREEK CAMPGROUND
[Fig. 18(1)] Located 10 miles west of U. S. Highway 97 on State Route 20, then 4 miles north on Loup Loup Canyon Road, a two-lane dirt byway. 6 campsites, 4 picnic sites, picnic shelter, drinking, toilets.

State Parks in the Methow Valley

PEARRYGIN LAKE STATE PARK
[Fig. 17(1)] This popular park has 578 acres of sagebrush-covered foothills, and a 0.75-mile-long lake. The glacial-till soil bears different kinds of flowers through the summer, including balsamroot, lupine, yellow bells, and sunflowers. Yellow-bellied marmots, deer, songbirds, and game birds may be seen in the park.

There are 53 standard campsites, 30 sites with utility hookups, and two primitive sites. There are campsites and restrooms for handicapped persons. The park has a boat launch, and a sewage pumpout station for boats, as well as a trailer dump. There is a sandy beach and a steep, moderately difficult, 0.5 mile trail to a plateau above the camping area. There is snowmobiling in the winter.

Directions: From Winthrop, go about 2 miles on County Road 9137, then turn right and go 2 miles on County Road 1631.

Activities: Camping, picnicking, boating, swimming, hiking.

Facilities: Campsites, picnic sites, restrooms, boat launch sewage pumpout and trailer dump stations.

Dates: Seasonal, summer.

Fees: Fees are required for camping and some services.

Closest town: Winthrop, 4 miles.

For more information: Pearrygin State Park, Route 1, Box 300, Winthrop, Washington 98862. Phone (509) 996-2370. The park accepts campsite reservations at least 14 days in advance. Contact Reservations Northwest, PO Box 500, Portland, OR 97207, phone (800) 452-5687.

ALTA LAKE STATE PARK

[Fig. 18(6)] When Alexander Ross set out in 1814 to become the first white man to cross the Cascade Mountains, he started his hike from Fort Okanogan at the confluence of the Methow and Columbia rivers, a few miles from where Alta Lake State Park is now. He, his guide, Red Fox, and the other Indians in the party certainly were well aquainted with the large lake that is the centerpiece of this water-oriented park in an otherwise dry country. Ross was the first factor of the fort built for John Jacob Astor's Fur Company, and lived there with an Okanogan Indian group that gathered the furs for his business. Astor's fur company was soon taken over by the Canadian Northwest Fur Company but not before the fort became the first place to fly the American flag in what now is Washington.

Some 86 years after Ross, in 1900, a miner named Heinz in the vicinity learned the lake had not been named so he took the necessary steps to have it officially named after his daughter, Alta Heinz.

The 182-acre park has 148 standard campsites, 32 utility campsites with hookups and 9 group campsites. There are special campsites and restrooms for handicapped persons. The park has 300 feet of beach, and is a popular place for small boats, as well as for camping, swimming, fishing, water skiing, and sunbathing.

Directions: From State Route 97, go about 2 miles west on State Route 153 and turn south on County Road 1517 for about 1.5 miles.

Facilities: Campsites, picnic sites, 3 restrooms, 2 boat-launch ramps, a boat-launch dock , a shop, trailer dump, and bath house.

Dates: Seasonal, summer.

Fees: Fees are required for camping and some services.

Closest town: Pateros, 4 miles.

For more information: Alta Lake State Park,40 Star Route, Pateros, WA 98846, phone (509) 923-2473.

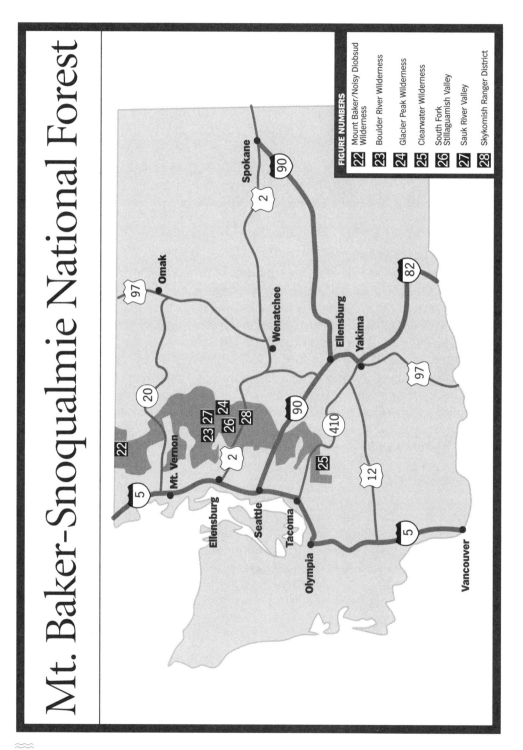

Mt. Baker–Snoqualmie National Forest

FIGURE NUMBERS

- **22** Mount Baker/Noisy Diobsud Wilderness
- **23** Boulder River Wilderness
- **24** Glacier Peak Wilderness
- **25** Clearwater Wilderness
- **26** South Fork Stillaguamish Valley
- **27** Sauk River Valley
- **28** Skykomish Ranger District

Mount Baker-Snoqualmie
National Forest

In many ways, the Mount Baker-Snoqualmie National Forest is the opposite of its brother, the Okanogan National Forest. The MBS, as it is known affectionately in the Forest Service, is on the west side of the North Cascades National Park and of the Cascades Range itself. That means that instead of the Okanogan's dry climate with the wide variations in temperature typical of the Cascades' eastern slopes, the MBS has the western slopes' wet climate with relatively minor variations in temperature. The hot, dry, dusty trails through open forests of predominantly lodgepole pine of the east side become the thick, moist, lush, predominantly Douglas fir forests of the west side. The trees grow higher and larger on the west side. It is not unusual, in an old-growth stand, for the trees' diameter to be greater than a man is tall. Most of the trees of that size have long since become houses, furniture, newspapers, and books, but thousands of acres of old-growth forest, where huge trees that were old when Columbus sailed, still are growing.

[*Above:* Massive, rugged, 6,135-foot Big Four Mountain]

The forest understory reflects the different climate as much as do the trees. The land between the trees in the Okanogan's east side forests is covered largely with grasses, sedges, and similar plants, but the thick brush of the MBS sometimes makes it difficult to walk off the developed trail.

The climatic variations bring about major differences in demographics as well. While the Okanogan has a small population scattered in tiny enclaves, the MBS is adjacent to five Puget Sound counties that contain about 3 million people, some 55 percent of the state's total, all living within 70 miles of the forest boundary. That, coupled with the inclination of Washington residents to be lovers of the outdoors, means heavy usage of the forests and mountains. On a warm, sunny, summer afternoon, trails and campgrounds are often full.

Information about the forest may be obtained from the forest's headquarters, Mount Baker-Snoqualmie National Forest, 21905 64th Avenue W., Mountlake Terrace, Washington 98043, phone (425) 775-9702, or (800) 627-0062. The Forest Service and Park Service also jointly operate a recreation information office that has information on specific trails, campgrounds, and other recreation-related features in the forests and parks of the Puget Sound area. That office, called the Outdoor Recreation Information Center, may be contacted at 222 Yale Avenue North, Seattle WA 98109-5429. Phone (206) 470-4060.

The national forest contains 1,712,049 acres that range in elevation from 184 feet above sea level in the Skagit River Valley to the 10,778 foot peak of Mount Baker, near the northwestern corner of the forest. Glacier Peak, at 10,541 feet, is the second highest in the MBS, but is less well-known because it is hidden near the eastern edge of the forest, out

MARTEN
(Martes americana)
Male martens are quarrelsome and associate with females only in the summer mating season.

of sight of most populated viewpoints. Mount Baker and Glacier Peak are two of the Washington Cascades' five active volcanoes. Many scores of other mountains range up to and over the 7,000 foot level, and there are numerous glaciers within the forest.

The forest's eastern edge runs along the Cascades summit for some 140 miles from the Canadian border to the northern boundary of the Mount Rainier National Park. It includes eight Congressionally designated wilderness areas, including four that are entirely within the MBS. The others are shared with the Wenatchee National Forest. The wildernesses cover 42 percent of the MBS acreage.

In addition to the wilderness areas is the protected Skagit River Wild and Scenic Area, which includes 19,521 acres along the Skagit River and some of its tributaries, such as the Cascade and Sauk rivers. There also are several small research areas where human activity is strictly limited.

The forest maintains more than 50 recreation features, including campgrounds, scenic viewpoints, and picnic spots. It supports water sports and winter activities, including four major downhill ski areas. The forest has more than 1,500 miles of trails, including parts of the Pacific Crest Trail, which wanders in and out of its borders.

Other summer activities in the forest are hiking, mountain climbing, hunting, fishing, river rafting, mountain biking, berry picking and sight-seeing. In addition to the down-hill skiing areas, winter activities include cross-country skiing, snowmobiling, snowshoe-ing, and snow-play areas. Hunting is a popular recreation in the autumn. Both fishing and hunting are managed by the state and state licenses are required. Snowmobiles must have state licenses.

Four of the five east-west highways in the state go through the MBS, including Interstate 90 and U.S. Highway 2, making access to its inner reaches quick and easy. Four roads in the forest have been designated as National Scenic Byways.

The forest was created in its present configuration after the North Cascades National Park was carved out of land that had been part of the Mount Baker National Forest in 1968. The park took so much of the Mount Baker National Forest's land that it could no longer be efficiently managed as an independent national forest, so it was combined with the adjacent Snoqualmie National Forest.

Like most other national forests, both the Mount Baker and MBS had been managed as major sources of forest products, as well as recreation and other uses, from the time they were created. Over the past several decades, however, logging has been drastically reduced from an output of 455 million board feet of lumber in 1972 to 12 million board feet in 1998. Management now emphasizes environmental and recreational concerns, and includes numerous programs to enhance and improve trees and other plants, soils, watersheds, fish, and wildlife habitat.

Much administrative energy goes toward managing the wildernesses under MBS jurisdiction. The basic policy is contained in the Wilderness Act of 1964, which estab-lished the nation's wilderness system. The act declares "…it is hereby declared to be in the policy of the Congress to secure for the American people of present and future

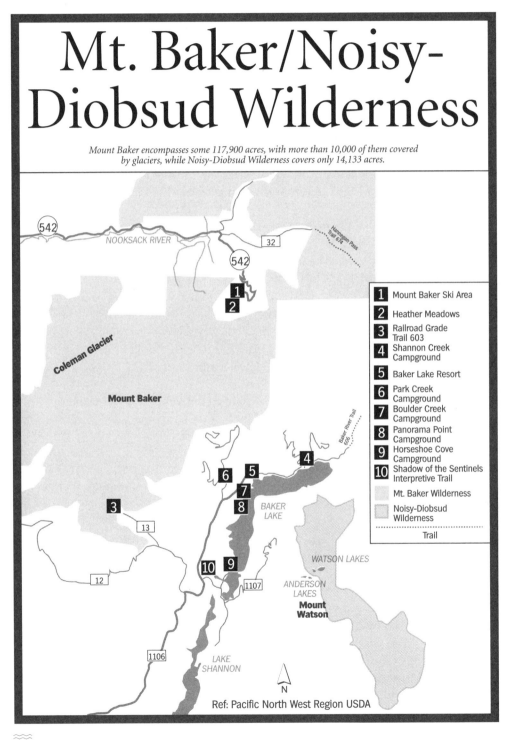

Mt. Baker/Noisy-Diobsud Wilderness

Mount Baker encompasses some 117,900 acres, with more than 10,000 of them covered by glaciers, while Noisy-Diobsud Wilderness covers only 14,133 acres.

542

NOOKSACK RIVER

32

Hannegan Pass Trail 674

542

1 Mount Baker Ski Area

2 Heather Meadows

3 Railroad Grade Trail 603

4 Shannon Creek Campground

5 Baker Lake Resort

6 Park Creek Campground

7 Boulder Creek Campground

8 Panorama Point Campground

9 Horseshoe Cove Campground

10 Shadow of the Sentinels Interpretive Trail

Mt. Baker Wilderness

Noisy-Diobsud Wilderness

Trail

Coleman Glacier

Mount Baker

Baker River Trail 606

1
2

4

6 5

7

8

BAKER LAKE

3

13

12

10 9

1107

WATSON LAKES

ANDERSON LAKES

Mount Watson

1106

LAKE SHANNON

N

Ref: Pacific North West Region USDA

generations the benefits of an enduring resource of wilderness...in contrast with those areas where man and his own works dominate the landscape." To carry out the policy, the MBS has established strict regulations on visits to wilderness lands. Among the regulations are a limit of 12 persons in a visiting party, and, except in emergencies, a ban on all motorized and mechanized equipment, including bicycles.

Below are some of the wildernesses administered entirely by the MBS or in cooperation with other agencies.

Mount Baker-Snoqualmie Wilderness Areas

▒ NOISY-DIOBSUD WILDERNESS

[Fig. 22] The smallest and most isolated of the MBS wildernesses, the Noisy-Diobsud is tucked away on the eastern edge of the national forest, adjacent to the North Cascades National Park's North Unit. It is named after two creeks that are its main waterways, Diobsud Creek, which drains southeast toward the Skagit River, and Noisy Creek, which drains northwest into Baker Lake.

There are only 14,133 acres within the wilderness, and they are almost inaccessible. The interior consists of rugged, avalanche-scarred peaks and thick forests of huge trees, including western hemlock, mountain hemlock, true fir, and Douglas fir.

The wilderness is isolated so deep in the forest that very few people visit it. The only trails are two short spurs from the steep Anderson Lakes Trail 611, which begins at the end of Forest Road 1107, east of the southern tip of Baker Lake. Neither spur goes much more than 1 mile into the wilderness. One of them goes up steeply past fields of blueberries and red heather to Anderson Butte Mountain, elevation 5,420 feet. The Forest Service built a fire lookout here in 1920, replaced it in 1936, then removed it in 1964. The view is magnificent, and includes the Sulphide and Crystal glaciers on Mount Shuksan, as well as the perpetual snows of Mount Baker.

The other spur goes to Watson Lakes, the only of any consequence in the wilderness. The Anderson Lakes Trail goes on past the spur to the two Watson Lakes, and leads to the Anderson Lakes, just outside of the wilderness, a little more than 2 miles from the trailhead.

Directions: From Sedro-Woolley, go east on State Route 20 for about 15 miles to the Grandy Creek Road which becomes Forest Road 11. Follow that for about 14 miles, turn onto Forest Road 1106, go about 1 mile, turn right to go over the power dam at the southern tip of Baker Lake, then take the left fork onto Forest Road 1107, and go about 10 miles to the trailhead.

Activities: Hiking, fishing, mountain climbing, rock climbing.

Dates: Seasonal, summer.

Fees: A trailhead fee may be charged.

Closest town: Concrete, about 13 miles.

For more information: North Cascades National Park/ Mount Baker Ranger District Information Center, 2105 Highway 20, Sedro-Woolley, WA 98284. Phone (360) 856-5700 Also, the Outdoor Recreation Information Center, 222 Yale Avenue North, Seattle, WA 98109-5429. Phone (206) 470-4060.

Trail: 2 miles, one-way.

Elevation: 1,700 feet elevation gain.

Degree of difficulty: Easy.

MOUNT BAKER WILDERNESS

[Fig. 22] With its northern lobe tucked up against the Canadian border, the Mount Baker Wilderness extends its ragged borders down some 25 miles to encompass Mount Baker, an active volcano that, at 10,778 feet elevation, is the third highest mountain in Washington, and the highest in the Mount Baker-Snoqualmie National Forest. The lowest valley floors in the wilderness are at about 2,000 feet elevation. There are hot springs on the slopes of Mount Baker, and periodically large clouds of steam vent from an ancient crater near the peak.

The wilderness extends from the border of the North Cascades National Park's North Unit on the east to the peaks of the Twin Sisters on the west. The Twin Sisters' unusual rock is weathered to a rough surface texture, making them popular with rock climbers.

Vegetation in the wilderness is typical western Cascades forest, with largely old-growth Douglas and true fir, western and mountain hemlock at the lower levels, and alpine meadows in the high country. The terrain throughout the wilderness is rugged, with many ridges and steep slopes.

There are 51 miles of trail in the wilderness, and many unmarked routes to its peaks and the backcountry.

The wilderness encompasses some 117,900 acres, with more than 10,000 of them covered by glaciers. Many of the glaciers are on the sides of Mount Baker, which may be seen from huge areas of both Washington and British Columbia. About 10,000 people attempt to climb Mount Baker each year. One of the popular routes begins at the Heliotrope Ridge Trailhead on the Glacier Creek Road, Forest Road 39. It follows Forest Trail 677 to the bottom of Coleman Glacier, then goes over the trailless glacier, past the Black Buttes, which are the remnants of an ancient andesite-rock cone that was formed before the volcanic pressures shifted toward the present peak. The climbers' route then turns left and goes to the summit crater, where the view is magnificent in all directions.

Another popular climbers' route begins at the Mount Baker National Recreation Area trailhead, at the end of Forest Road 13. It follows the Railroad Grade Trail 603 to the terminals of the glaciers then up the trailless snow to the peak (*see* Railroad Grade Trail 603, page 130).

There are many other routes but it must be noted that climbing mountains can be extremely dangerous, and no one should attempt it without the proper training, equipment, and experience.

Directions: Many roads approach the Mount Baker Wilderness from all directions. One of the many routes takes State Route 542 from the Interstate Highway 5 Exit 255 near Bellingham, east on State Route 542 to Glacier Creek Road near the town of Glacier, then south to Mount Baker Trail 677 trailhead. Another route takes State Route 542 past the Glacier Creek Road, to Artist Point, 1 mile beyond the Mount Baker Ski Area at the edge of the wilderness. A third route goes to the southeast section of the wilderness. From Sedro-Woolley go east on State Route 20 for about 15 miles to the Grandy Creek Road, which becomes Forest Road 11. Follow that for about 12 miles to just inside the national forest boundary, then turn west onto Forest Road 12 and go about 6 miles to the trailhead of Railroad Grade Trail 603. Hike that trail toward the wilderness.

Mount Baker, an active volcano, stands at 10,778 feet elevation and is the third highest mountain in Washington and the highest in the Mount Baker-Snoqualmie National Forest.

Activities: Hiking, climbing, hunting, fishing, camping, cross-country skiing.

Fees: A trailhead fee may be charged.

Closest town: South side, Sedro-Wooley, 35 miles. North side, Glacier, 7 miles.

For more information: North Cascades National Park/ Mount Baker Ranger District Information Center, 2105 Highway 20, Sedro-Woolley, WA 98284, (360) 856-5700, or, during the summer, the national forest's Glacier Public Service Center, 1094 Mount Baker Highway, Glacier, WA 98244, (360) 599-2714. Also, the Outdoor Recreation Information Center, 222 Yale Avenue North, Seattle, WA 98109-5429. Phone (206) 470-4060.

HANNEGAN PASS TRAIL 674

[Fig. 22] This is a 4 mile, one-way trail to a delightful pass, with an inviting side trail as well as access to the interior of the North Cascades National Park's North Unit. The trail begins at the Hannegan Trailhead at the end of the Ruth Creek Road, Forest Road Number 32, elevation 3,100 feet. A campground at the trailhead has been closed, but a few unmaintained sites still exist where hikers can stay overnight before starting out.

The Ruth Creek Road follows the valley wall on the north side of Ruth Creek, and the trail is simply an extension of the road. There are some shrubs and stands of mountain hemlock and silver fir, but much of the trail is open, and, after the first mile, the glistening, white, 7,100-foot high, hulk of snow-clad Ruth Mountain comes into view directly in front of the trail. Early in the season, the snow melt results in numerous waterfalls that enliven the scenery enormously, and demonstrate the depth of the glacier that carved the valley and left its shoulders high above the floor.

The trail becomes steeper as it travels farther up the hillside above the creek. At 4,600 feet elevation, a little more than 3 miles from the trailhead, it turns left and switches back fairly steeply toward Hannegan Pass. There is a nice campsite along the way, and a short distance beyond that is the pass at slightly more than 5,000 feet elevation.

There are good views from the pass, but they can be improved by climbing the side walls of the saddle that constitutes the pass. The side trip to the south works its laborious and treacherous way up toward the glaciers and snow fields of Ruth Mountain. The faint climbers' trail peters out after a while, and the route becomes a snare for those who are not trained and equipped for serious mountain climbing.

The side trip to the north follows Forest Trail 674.1, which goes less than 1 mile but is relentlessly uphill to the top of Hannegan Peak. That route goes through open forest and meadow, and along a ridge to the summit at just under 6,200 feet elevation, where there are views of valleys, slopes and dozens of peaks in all directions.

The pass is a good place to turn around and head back to the trailhead, but the main trail also continues northward from there. It goes steeply downhill into the North Cascades National Park and on to a fork. The left fork goes steeply up to a long walk on the ridge above the Chilliwack Valley, past two lakes and the Copper Mountain Fire Lookout, and then back down to the Chilliwack Valley. The fork to the right goes through the Chilliwack Valley, providing access to either Chilliwack Lake in British Columbia, or Ross Lake in the Ross Lake Recreation Area. Free backcountry permits are required for overnight stays in the park.

Directions: Take Exit 255 on Interstate 5 near Bellingham and go east on State Route 542, the Mount Baker Highway, for 31 miles to the town of Glacier. Proceed about 14 more miles and turn left onto Forest Road Number 32, and go 4 miles to the end of the road and the Hannegan Trailhead.

Dates: Seasonal, summer.

Fees: A trailhead fee may be charged.

Trail: 4 miles, one-way.

Elevation: 2,000 feet elevation gain.

Degree of difficulty: Moderate.

RAILROAD GRADE TRAIL 603

[Fig. 22(3)] From the trailhead, this trail enters the Mount Baker National Recreation Area, a small enclave of the Mount Baker Wilderness Area, which has fewer restrictions than the adjacent wilderness area. The recreation area, for instance, does not have the wilderness area's 12 person party limit, and some motorized equipment is permitted.

The trail leaves the trailhead and crosses Sulpher Creek into Schriebers Meadow, where there are blueberries for those who go in the right season. After 1 mile, it crosses a cable bridge over a creek, enters forest, and goes up steep switchbacks for 1 mile to the delightful Morovitz Meadow. It crosses the meadow, goes up a ridge and, at a little more than 3 miles from the trailhead, reaches the Park Butte Fire Lookout at about 4,500 feet elevation, near the border between the recreation area and the wilderness. The lookout is perched on a ridge opposite Mount Baker, providing close-up views of that massive volcano and its perpetual snow. Easton Glacier is directly in front of the lookout. In the other directions are the lesser but still impressive peaks of Hagen Mountain, Mount Blum, the Twin Sisters and Bacon Peak.

The lookout was built in the 1930s, and has been leased to a local hiking club after aircraft took over the fire-spotting duty. It is open to the public, on a first-come, first-served basis.

The Morovitz Meadow has views of Easton Glacier and the odd-looking Railroad Grade lateral moraine, a high wall of gravel left when the glacier receded. The name comes from the wall's striking resemblance to a railroad grade going up the side of the mountain. The meadow provides nice campsites in designated places outside the wilderness boundaries in the Mount Baker National Recreation area. These sites are beautiful places to camp overnight before climbing Mount Baker, which looms above the wilderness, but people without training and experience should resist the temptation to climb up the snow fields and glaciers toward the peak.

Directions: From I-5 Exit 230 at Mount Vernon, go east on State Route 20 about 23 miles, then turn north on the Baker Lake-Grandy Creek Road. Follow that road for about 12 miles, then take the Loomis-Nooksack Road, Forest Road 12, for about 3 miles and turn onto the Sulpher Creek Road, Forest Road 13, for about 5 miles to the trailhead that leads through the national recreation area to the wilderness.

Dates: Seasonal, summer.

Fees: A trailhead fee may be charged.

For more information: North Cascades National Park/Mount Baker Ranger District Information Center, 2105 Highway 20, Sedro-Woolley, WA 98284, (360) 856-5700

Trail: 4 miles, one-way.

Elevation: 2,250 feet elevation gain.

Degree of difficulty: Moderate.

BLACK RACER
(Coluber constrictor)
The racer holds its head up while gliding swiftly along the ground, and vibrates the tip of its tail against vegetation when threatened.

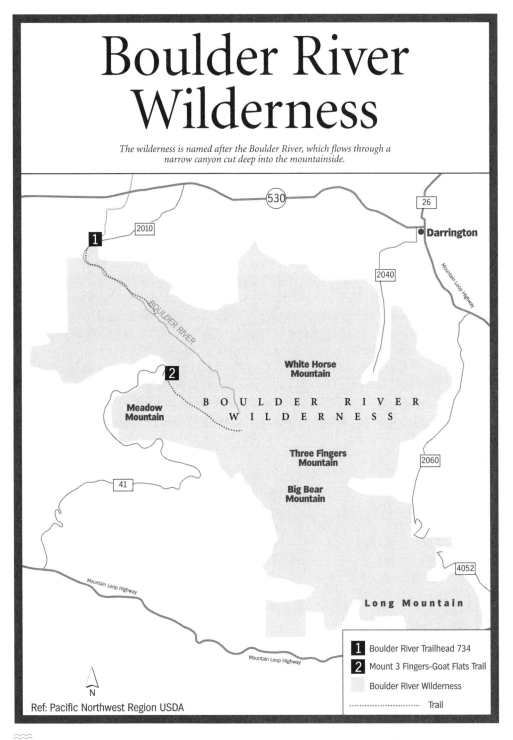

Boulder River Wilderness

The wilderness is named after the Boulder River, which flows through a narrow canyon cut deep into the mountainside.

530

26

2010

1

● **Darrington**

2040

BOULDER RIVER

Mountain Loop Highway

2

White Horse Mountain

B O U L D E R   R I V E R
W I L D E R N E S S

Meadow Mountain

Three Fingers Mountain

2060

41

Big Bear Mountain

4052

Mountain Loop Highway

Long Mountain

Mountain Loop Highway

N

Ref: Pacific Northwest Region USDA

1   Boulder River Trailhead 734
2   Mount 3 Fingers-Goat Flats Trail
     Boulder River Wilderness
·············   Trail

🏵 BOULDER RIVER WILDERNESS

[Fig. 23] The Mountain Loop Highway is a road rather than a highway, 14 miles of it gravel. It goes east from the city of Granite Falls for about 30 miles, then curls around in a loop 20 miles to the north and the west to the city of Darrington, completing the loop through lush forested valleys. Once there were railroads running where the road is now. They depended on mining, and on the logging of the forests on both sides of the tracks. When the mining business died and trucks replaced trains in the logging business, the tracks were replaced with roads, and both ends were pushed farther into the forest until they met at Barlow Pass.

That completed the large loop of clear-cut forest, which now is mostly second- and even third-growth forest. But much of the high country inside the circle was untouched old growth, or the meadows, rock and ice of the interior mountains. Congress in 1984 declared some 49,000 acres of that land to be wilderness.

The wilderness is named after the Boulder River, which flows through a narrow canyon cut deep into the mountainside (*see* Boulder River Trail 734, page 137). Another popular attraction in the wilderness is Three Fingers Mountain and the trail that goes partway to an old fire lookout on the rugged peak (*see* Three Fingers-Goat Flat Trail 641, below). The forests in the wilderness are typical west Cascades Mountain forest, consisting largely of Douglas and true fir, western redcedar, western hemlock and high-elevation alpine meadows.

The wilderness has nine small lakes, and numerous peaks, ranging from 5,000 to 6,000 feet in elevation. Two peaks stand out above them. They are Three Fingers Mountain at 6,854 feet and White Horse Mountain at 6,852 feet.

Directions: There are only a few routes to the interior of the wilderness. One is the Three Fingers Mountain-Goat Flats Trail 641. Another popular access is the Boulder River Trail. (*see* Boulder River Trail 734, page 137.)

Activities: Hiking, camping, mountain climbing, fishing, hunting.

Dates: Vary. Boulder River Trail is open much of the winter. Most other trails are open only in summer.

Fees: A trailhead fee may be charged.

Closest town: Granite Falls is 24 miles from the Mount Three Fingers-Goat Flats Trailhead and Darrington is 12 miles from the Boulder River Trailhead.

For more information: Darrington Ranger District, 1405 Emmens Street, Darrington, WA 98241. Phone (360) 436-1155. Also, the Outdoor Recreation Information Center, 222 Yale Avenue North, Seattle, WA 98109-5429. Phone (206) 470-4060.

MOUNT THREE FINGERS-GOAT FLATS TRAIL 641

[Fig. 23(2)] This is a 6-mile, one-way trail that half a century later still reveals that the construction crew struggled with a low budget. The route leads toward the old fire lookout on Three Fingers Peak, a structure with a long history that perches atop one of three rocky spires that give the mountain its name. In 1929 Darrington Ranger Harold Engel, of the Mount Baker National Forest's Darrington District, and Trail Foreman

Harry Bedal, made the first ascent of the mountain to look for a place to put a fire lookout. They made the climb through uncharted forests, meadows, snow fields and rock. They decided, despite the precarious slant of the peak at the highest finger, to put the lookout here, then made their way home to Darrington in the dark by another pioneering route. Both were men of tremendous strength, courage, and ability who knew and loved the forests where they worked.

The first step in establishing the lookout was to build a trail to the top of the mountain. It is much shorter now because roads have been built part of the way, but at the time they had to go 15 miles with some 4,000 feet of elevation gain. Much of it was through primeval forest, but the last several miles were in the meadows of Goat Flat and the ice and bare rock above that.

The trail crew went to work in 1930 under the supervision of Bedal and Engel. The problems of their low budget can still be seen at places like Cub Cove, where they tried to blast a tread horizontally across the face of a rock cliff. They blasted some 20 yards, then ran out of money to buy blasting powder so they backed off to a place where they could cut switchbacks down several hundred feet to the bottom of Cub Cove at the foot of the cliff. The trail wanders across the cove, past the bottom of the cliff for a few hundred feet, then climbs steeply up the other side to regain the lost elevation.

To this day hikers who aren't paying attention sometimes miss the fork that goes down to Cub Cove, and continue on the abandoned portion of the trail until they come to the dead end where the money ran out. They retrace their steps to find the fork, wondering about the trail that goes nowhere.

A mile or so beyond that, a huge rock outcrop blocks the trail, forcing hikers to climb over it, balancing the packs on their back as they go. The story is the same there, no money for powder to blast the outcrop away.

Just beyond the outcrop the landscape levels briefly at Saddle Lake, at about 3,700 feet elevation and 2.5 miles from Tupso Pass. People fish at Saddle Lake, and there are campsites here as well as hordes of mosquitoes and black flies when conditions are right for them, usually in midsummer. Some time after the trail from Tupso Pass was built, the Forest Service built alternate trails to Three Fingers Peak to avoid the problems on the original trail. One of them, Meadow Mountain Trail 715, still exists and meets the original trail near Saddle Lake. The other, the Boulder River Trail 734, has been a 4-mile-long, dead end since a bridge washed out many years ago.

From Saddle Lake, the Goat Flats Trail goes upward through the woods, becoming more open as it goes. Eventually it passes a series of benches that become more open until it reaches Goat Flats, about 2 miles from Saddle Lake and about 4,700 feet elevation.

There are blueberries and heather at Goat Flats, and, as the season wears on, varieties of wildflowers succeed each other, living for a few days, then dying back to make room for other varieties. The flats got their name from mountain goats that once browsed among the shrubbery, but are seldom seen now. Deer frequent the vicinity in the summer, and there have been reports of cougars that may have come looking for the deer. There may also be a black bear from time to time. Somewhere near the middle of Goat Flats are the remnants of a small log cabin that once was a storage-and-tool house for the lookout.

But perhaps the ultimate attraction of Goat Flats is the view. From the cliffs on either side of the trail, miles and miles of mountain landscape is visible and beyond that, to the west, Puget Sound and the Olympic Mountains, nearly 100 miles away. At night the lights of cities along Puget Sound sparkle in the distance.

For day hikers, Goat Flats is a good place to turn around. For backpackers it is a good place to make camp and explore the flats before turning around. The trail, however, does go on from here at least for a time. The route is up over another bench at the far end of the flats. Then it traverses a meadowed slope, and switches back up to a saddle called Tin Pan Gap, where the trail builders once had a camp. The places they leveled for their tents can still be seen. That is where a climate change has eliminated the trail.

The original route followed a ridge that went upward from Tin Pan Gap to bare rock near the top of the mountain. The trail is still there, but except for those rare years when the winter snowfall is light it remains covered by many feet of snow throughout the hiking season. A half century after he built the trail and the lookout, Harold Engel said they had never dreamed it would be buried year round. Since the 1940s or 1950s, however, it has been impassable except for a few summers.

That leaves a difficult route that is not safe for people without proper training and equipment. It goes a few feet over Tin Pan Gap, down onto a moderate-sized glacier with no track. The route goes straight up the glacier toward a gap in the cliff at the upper end. At the gap it is necessary to climb up the rock face onto the ledge above, and find the way over the unmarked, rocky surface to the pinnacle, where there are a series of three ladders perched precariously on the rock ledges. The top of the third ladder leads to a smooth rock ledge sloped at a steep angle, and at the top of the slope is the lookout.

The rock originally was a pinnacle, but the builders blasted off its top 15 feet to provide enough room for the lookout house, which they held down with cables. The cabin was completed in 1933. It still perches there with sheer drops of 1,000 foot on the north side and several hundred feet on the south side. There is a small ledge on the side opposite the door, which can be reached by climbing out a window. The door, of course, opens on the steep, smooth, sloping rock that leads about 10 feet to the ladders. That can be a difficult problem when an occasional summer storm leaves a few inches of snow on it.

The Three Fingers Lookout gained notoriety in 1937 when Catherine Eastwood wrote a story for *The Saturday Evening Post* about the 1936 summer when she and her new husband, Harland Eastwood, spent their honeymoon as lookouts here. Harland was a 6-foot-4-inch giant who had lost his right arm in an accident, but who, nevertheless, earned the respect of foresters throughout the Cascades for his mountaineering and mountain-rescue feats. His friend, Harold Engel, described him as a man who "had a handicap, but didn't know it."

Engel lived to be 90 years old and continued to climb mountains until the year before he died, including Mount Three Fingers. The cabin he built is no longer used as a fire lookout, but is maintained as a climbers' refuge by the Mountaineers Club.

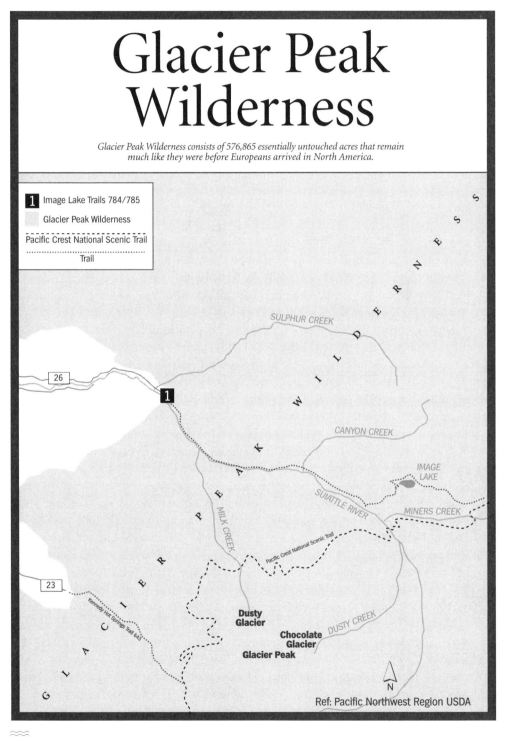

Glacier Peak Wilderness

Glacier Peak Wilderness consists of 576,865 essentially untouched acres that remain much like they were before Europeans arrived in North America.

1 Image Lake Trails 784/785

Glacier Peak Wilderness

Pacific Crest National Scenic Trail

Trail

SULPHUR CREEK

WILDERNESS

26

1

CANYON CREEK

IMAGE LAKE

GLACIER PEAK

MILK CREEK

SUIATTLE RIVER

MINERS CREEK

Pacific Crest National Scenic Trail

23

Kennedy Hot Springs Trail 643

Dusty Glacier

Chocolate Glacier

DUSTY CREEK

Glacier Peak

N

Ref: Pacific Northwest Region USDA

Directions: Take the Mountain Loop Highway and turn north on Forest Road 41. Stay to the left when Road 41 pavement ends at a fork, a little less than 1 mile from the Mountain Loop Highway. Stay on the main road past several minor branch roads, and pass the Meadow Mountain Trailhead at about 11 miles. The road number changes to 4100-025 at a little more than 17 miles from the highway. The trailhead is at Tupso Pass, about 7 miles from the Meadow Mountain Trailhead.

Dates: Seasonal, summer.

Fees: A trailhead fee may be charged.

Trail: 5 miles to Goat Flats. 8 miles to the peak.

Elevation: 1,800 feet elevation gain to Goat Flats, 3,950 feet elevation gain to Three Fingers Peak.

Degree of difficulty: Difficult.

BOULDER RIVER TRAIL 734

[Fig. 23(1)] A 4-mile, one-way hike that stops short where a bridge washed out many years ago. The entire trail is on the bottom of a deep ravine, carved out by glaciers in eons past, so the view is limited to the trees beside the trail, and the waterfalls that tumble from the cliffs above, but both are well worth seeing, and it is a gentle, pleasant trail in the cool shade of the ravine.

The trailhead is on a short spur of a logging road, and the trail follows an old road grade for less than 1 mile before it enters old-growth forest. In the first 2 miles, the route goes past two spectacular waterfalls. Although the river is hidden much of the way, there are side trails to the river and picnic spots during the early part of the hike.

The magnificent old-growth trees along the trail are of the typical west-side varieties, such as western hemlock, Douglas fir, and western redcedar.

There are a few rises, but generally the trail is fairly level and makes for easy walking. Once, years ago, the trail went to Saddle Lake and met with the trail to the Three Fingers Fire Lookout (*see* Mount Three Fingers-Goat Flats Trail 641, page 133), but a bridge across the river washed out many years ago and was never replaced. The trail beyond that spot has become heavily overgrown and makes for difficult walking. The dead end, however, is a fine place to eat a sandwich and listen to the river roar before heading back to the trailhead.

Directions: From Darrington go about 8 miles west on State Route 530 and turn south on the French Creek Road, Forest Road Number 2010. Go about 4 miles to the Trailhead.

Fees: A trailhead fee may be charged.

Trail: 4 miles, 1 way.

Elevation: 590 feet elevation gain.

Degree of difficulty: Easy.

GLACIER PEAK WILDERNESS

[Fig. 24] At the same time that Congress created the wilderness system in 1964, it also created the 464,258-acre Glacier Peak Wilderness. It later added 112,607 acres, making it a huge place of 576,865 essentially untouched acres that remain much like they were before Europeans arrived in North America. Like the other wildernesses, it is managed so it will stay that way; with no roads, no motorized vehicles, and, except for battery operated, hand-held equipment such as cameras and shavers, no mechanical devices. Even bicycles are banned. People who visit here go on foot, or with a saddle or pack animal, and only taking what they can carry.

This wilderness is a region of rugged, mountainous landscape that contains many streams and small, high-country lakes, as well as more active glaciers than any comparable area within the lower 48 states. It is dominated by Glacier Peak, a 10,541-foot active volcano which, despite being the fourth highest mountain in the Washington Cascades, is so deep inside the range that it can be seen from only a relatively few places outside the wilderness.

Glacier Peak is one of the five active volcanoes in Washington, and there still are hot springs nearby. It is a volcanic cone, consisting of pumice, ash, and basaltic rock, that sits over older mountain ridges. The rock welled up from the inner earth in a series of eruptions, including some that were as violent as the 1980 eruption of its sister volcano, Mount St. Helens. Ash from those early eruptions has been traced to as far away as Saskatchewan, Canada. The most recent eruption occurred about 12,000 years ago, and left an immense layer of ash as far away as eastern Idaho.

Geologists have learned that the oldest flows from Glacier Peak have normal magnetic polarity, indicating that they are less than 700,000 years old. The eruptions over the eons were largely debris of dacite lava, and had smaller amounts of pyroclastic debris, and basaltic or andesitic flows.

The mountain is named after the dozen or more glaciers that flow down all sides, giving much of it a permanent white coat, interspersed with dark rock striations. The glaciers are continually eroding the rock beneath them, as demonstrated by the Dusty Glacier and Chocolate Glacier, which are brownish colored

SPOTTED OWL

The spotted owl is identified by its large, dark eyes and white spots on the head, back, and underparts.

from the glacial dust that covers the glacial ice.

The wilderness is part of both the Mount Baker-Snoqualmie and the Wenatchee national forests, and is managed by those entities under the restrictions of the Wilderness Act. One major goal is ensuring the welfare of natural vegetation and wildlife. The huge wilderness extends into both the east and west sides of the Cascades, and has the moist climate of the west and the dry conditions of the east side. Thus, it has the vegetation of both climates within its borders. Dominant on the west side are dense forests of Douglas and true fir, spruce, and hemlock. Pine is predominant on the east side.

Bats

More than 200 years ago scientists learned that bats can navigate the black night with their eyes blocked but not with their ears blocked. Using a system similar to the modern radar, bats send out an ultrasonic signal and detect it when it rebounds from objects in their path. In 1938, scientists used specialized instruments to detect the high-frequency squeaks of bats' sonarlike systems. Bats use their radar to locate and capture prey as small as mosquitos which they take on the wing. The signal they send out begins focused, but it spreads out so they can detect objects at a wide range and direct their flight in the proper direction. They consume large numbers of insects, which they catch either in their mouths or in a membrane between their hind legs.

Wildlife is abundant and includes large mammals such as mountain goats, mule, and black-tailed deer, and black bear, as well as many smaller animals, including golden mantled ground squirrels, Douglas squirrels, pikas, hoary marmots, chipmunks, and marten. Birds such as gray jays, Clark's nutcrackers, ptarmigan, red-tailed hawks, and red shafted flickers (*Colaptes auratus*) also appear in the wilderness. Rarely, grizzly bear, gray wolf, peregrine falcon, wolverine, lynx, fisher, and spotted owl are reported.

Like the rest of the Cascades, the backcountry that is known as the Glacier Peak Wilderness was used by Native Americans as a source of raw material and a place for trade during the summer. They retreated in the winter to avoid the extreme cold, storms, and snow. Their frequently used routes now bear names such as White Pass and Indian Pass. Some of those routes are still in use. Like the people of today, the Native Americans held the imposing mass of Glacier Peak in awe. Some groups called it *Da Kobad*, which meant something like "Great White Mother."

A few fur trappers and traders were the first Europeans to travel in the Glacier Peak Wilderness, but the first recorded sighting of Glacier Peak was in 1870 when Daniel Linsley surveyed the area in search of a route for the Northern Pacific Railroad. The company eventually built its line south of the wilderness, at Stampede Pass. After the surveyors came prospectors, miners and shepherds with their flocks of sheep, but the mountains were so isolated that there were only a few such pioneers, and they made few lasting marks.

There are more than 450 miles of maintained trail in the wilderness, as well as ample opportunities for cross-country travel. Hunting for deer and other game is popular during the hunting season. Fishing is mostly for cutthroat trout.

Directions: There are no roads in the wilderness but there are several that go near it. On the west side of the Cascades is the popular White Chuck River Road, Forest Road Number 23, which meets the Sauk River Road (Forest Road 22) in a T intersection some 10 miles southeast of Darrington. A popular route on the east side of the mountains is by boat on Lake Chelan to Railroad Creek, then by bus to Holden Village, the isolated resort on the edge of the wilderness (*see* Holden Village page. 63).

Activities: Hiking, camping, hunting and fishing.

Dates: Seasonal, summer.

Fees: A trailhead fee may be charged.

Closest town: West side, Darrington, 17 miles. East side, Stehekin, 3 miles.

For more information: On the west side, Mount Baker-Snoqualmie National Forest Supervisor's Office, 219 64th Avenue W., Mountlake Terrace, WA 98043, (206) 744-3401, or, on the east side, Wenatchee National Forest, 215 Melody Lane, Wenatchee, WA 98801-5933, (509) 662-4335.

IMAGE LAKE TRAILS 784 AND 785

[Fig. 24(1)] This is a long, uphill hike to Image Lake, which gets its name because it lies across the Suiattle River Valley from the north side of Glacier Peak, and the mountain's reflection in its placid waters is a classic view of the Washington Cascades backcountry.

The route begins at 1,600 feet elevation, on the relatively level Miner's Cabin Trail 784, and passes through stands of magnificent western Cascades, old-growth forest. It skirts campgrounds at about 6 and 9 miles. Just beyond the second campground the route veers left onto the Miners Ridge Trail 785. That trail switches back steeply for about 2 miles into meadows with tremendous views of Glacier Peak and its neighboring country. At 13 miles from the trailhead, at 4,800 feet elevation, the trail meets Trail 795 on the right. Stay on Trail 785, which goes up another long series of switchbacks, through more trees, and into meadows where flowers bloom and there are blueberries late in the season, as well as ever-nicer views of Glacier Peak across the Suiattle Valley. At the top of the switchbacks there is a T-junction. About 0.25 mile to the left on Trail 785C is the Miners Ridge Fire Lookout, 16 miles from the trailhead and about 6,200 feet in elevation.

The site was used as an exposed fire lookout, with a tent for the crew in the 1920s. A small structure was built in 1930, and replaced in 1938 and again in 1953. It is listed on the historical Registry of Washington Lookouts and is still used as wilderness rangers' quarters. One of the rangers' duties is to make sure that the thousands of visitors each year do as little damage as possible to the environment. The T-junction at the end of Trail 785 also goes to the right on Trail 785A, and heads less than 1 mile to Image Lake at 6,050 feet elevation. The Image Lake image is so beautiful that it attracts too many people to camp there, so the Forest Service has provided an alternative campground for hikers about 0.25 mile below the lake.

Another alternative is Lady Camp horse camp, about 1 mile farther on Trail 785A. It was developed many years ago by sheepherders, who brought their flocks to the area to feed on the lush meadow plants. The name came from a woman's figure carved in a tree by a lonely shepherd, whose knowledge of the female anatomy was somewhat distorted.

For those who aren't ready to return to the trailhead there are a multitude of trails in the Image Lake area that go on to other places, including Holden Village and Lake Chelan, or the Cascade Crest Trail.

Directions: From Darrington go about 6 miles north on State Route 530, cross the Sauk River Bridge and go straight, onto the Suiattle River Road, Forest Road 26. Follow that road some 25 miles to the trailhead.

Dates: Seasonal, summer.

Fees: A trailhead fee may be charged.

Trail: 16 miles, one-way to Image Lake.

Elevation: 4,500 feet elevation gain.

Degree of difficulty: Strenuous.

KENNEDY HOT SPRINGS TRAIL 643

[Fig. 24] Kennedy Hot Springs is at the base of Glacier Peak and a result of that volcano's hot interior. The spring produces a constant supply of 90-degree water, which collects in a tublike pool nearby. The water is discolored and scummy, and high in coliform bacteria, which means some people use it for a toilet, but it still attracts bathers who rest and relax after hiking the trails that lead there. Some bathers don't bother about bathing suits, so a dip may include an anatomy lesson.

The Forest Service has counted as many as 6,000 visitors during the summer, and almost certainly missed many more. The trail, on a warm, summer weekend, is usually crowded. There is a wilderness guard station at the pool and camping nearby, as well as the junctions of several trails to other places, so people come here from many directions.

One of those other places is Kennedy Ridge. That trail, number 639, begins just before Trail 643 crosses the White Chuck River into the hot springs area. It goes 1 mile or so upwards, then joins the Pacific Crest Trail, which continues going upward past andesite cliffs for about 2 miles to Kennedy Ridge and Glacier Creek at 5,650 feet elevation.

At Kennedy Ridge, there are meadows and magnificent, close-up views of Glacier Peak, as well as campsites. The area is a base camp for climbers intent on reaching the top of Glacier Peak, which appears to be just a short hop away. The scale is deceptive. No one should attempt to go up the mountain without proper training and equipment.

Directions: From Darrington go about 8 miles southeast on the Sauk River Road, Forest Road 22, to the intersection with the White Chuck River Road 23. Go about 10 miles to the end of that road and the trailhead.

Dates: Seasonal, summer.

Fees: A trailhead fee may be charged.

Trail: 5.5 miles to Kennedy Hot Springs, 9 miles to Kennedy Ridge.

Elevation: 1,000 feet elevation gain to Kennedy Hot Springs, 2,950 feet elevation gain to Kennedy Ridge.

Degree of difficulty: Easy to Kennedy Hot Springs, difficult to Kennedy Ridge.

HENRY M. JACKSON WILDERNESS

[Fig. 26] Henry M. Jackson was a native of Everett, Washington, whose parents were poor immigrants in the mill town section of the city. As a boy, he camped, hiked and climbed in the wild lands of the Cascade Mountains near Everett. A star student, he worked his way through law school, went into politics and eventually became one of the most respected members of the U.S. Senate. He worked in both domestic and foreign programs in Congress, but perhaps those that most influenced the forests and mountains he had loved as a boy were the bills he sponsored to create the nation's wilderness system and to strengthen the national parks. In recognition of his contributions, Congress in 1984 created the 103,000-acre Henry M. Jackson Wilderness, encompassing the forests and mountains where he had wandered as a boy.

The wilderness is adjacent to the western border of the Glacier Peak Wilderness, and extends across the crest of the mountains into the Wenatchee National Forest. Much of it bears old-growth forest, including western redcedar, Douglas and true fir, spruce, western and mountain hemlock. There are many mountains within the wilderness that extend above the treeline, into meadows, and above meadows into places where there is little but rock and ice.

The wilderness was for many years a mining area, and even today there are some 900 acres of patented mining claims, although few are being worked regularly. The wilderness almost completely surrounds the mining ghost town of Monte Cristo, which once had a population of more than 1,000 people who worked a dozen mines.

There is a large deer population, but the wilderness also supports many other species of wildlife including hoary marmot, marten, mountain goat, lynx, cougar, black bear, and blue grouse.

There are some 30 lakes and numerous rivers in the wilderness, and fishing for cutthroat trout is popular. The same

BAND-TAILED PIGEON
(Columba fasciata)
This pigeon is identified by a purplish head and breast, yellow bill with a dark tip, yellow legs, and a gray band across the tail.

Band-tailed Pigeon (*Columbia fasciata*)

These large, gray pigeons have purple and white hues, yellow legs, a broad, gray, fan-shaped tail, and yellow bills with black tips. They rove through the forest in flocks through the summer then go south for the winter. Sometimes as many as 50 pairs may nest in a single tree. They eat many kinds of berries and are considered a delicacy by hunters.

natural forces that put gold and other metals in the rocks also left a legacy of natural arsenic, and that has left some of the lakes barren of fish.

The wilderness has 49 miles of trails, including a portion of the Pacific Crest National Scenic Trail that crosses the southern part.

Directions: There are several access trails to the wilderness. Possibly the most popular is the Pacific Crest National Scenic Trail, which crosses U.S. Highway 2 at Stevens Pass, 50 miles east of Everett. The wilderness border is about 2 miles north of the highway on that trail.

Activities: Hiking, camping, mountain climbing, hunting, fishing.

Dates: Seasonal, summer.

Fees: A trailhead fee may be charged.

Closest town: Index, 18 miles.

For more information: Mount Baker-Snoqualmie National Forest Headquarters, 21905 64th Avenue West, Mountlake Terrace, WA 98043. Phone (425) 744-3401, or Wenatchee National Forest, PO Box 811, Wenatchee, WA 98801. Phone (509) 622-4335,

GOAT LAKE TRAIL 647

[Fig. 26(15)] In the 1920s and 1930s, the Penn Mining Company dug into the hard rock at the head of Goat Lake, trying to find enough salable mineral to make ends meet. The mine was operated by two brothers and a sister from Pennsylvania, which explains the name. They worked the mine from the time the snow melted in the spring until it returned in the fall, then retreated to wait for another spring. That continued until the early 1930s, when, apparently, the Great Depression wiped out their dream, and they never returned.

They left a wagon road which now is simply a trail, a headquarters compound below the lake, and another large structure at the lake that was reportedly used as a dormitory for the crew and as a hotel for visitors who came to fish, climb or hunt. The structures collapsed, but the level place where the building at the lake once stood is still there, and makes a fine place for camping.

The trail parallels Elliott Creek and is about 5 miles long. It begins on an old logging road that passes through some lush, young, second-growth forests of mostly Douglas fir that the Forest Service replanted in clearcut areas. After some 3 miles it merges into the old Penn Mining Company Wagon Road, and shortly after that it enters the wilderness. At 4.5 miles there is a fork. To the right a short distance is the remains of the Penn

Mining Company headquarters compound. To the left is 0.5 mile or so of fairly steep switchbacks to the lake.

Once the trail continued along the east bank of the lake, to the mine in the cliffs at the far end. Part of the trail is still there for the benefit of anglers and picnickers, but it peters out before it reaches the mine. A rock outcrop over the lake next to that trail is a pleasant place to have a sandwich.

Directions: Take the Mountain Loop Highway 35 miles from Granite Falls, past Barlow Pass to the Elliott Creek Road, Forest Road 4080. Follow that road less than 1 mile to the trailhead.

Dates: Seasonal, summer.

Fees: A trailhead fee may be charged.

Trail: 5 miles, one-way.

Elevation: 1,275 feet elevation gain.

Degree of difficulty: Easy.

MONTE CRISTO GHOST TOWN TRAILS

[Fig. 26(18)] The Penn Mining Company dug its mine on the side of Foggy Peak Mountain. On the other side of the mountain is the site of the ghost town of Monte Cristo, where many mines once operated (*see* Monte Cristo Ghost Town, page 173).

The Monte Cristo mineral field was discovered in 1889 when Joseph Pearsall was prospecting in Silver Creek northwest of the town of Index. He climbed Hubbart Peak in search of minerals. When he got near the top of the 5,926-foot peak, he looked to the north and saw, in unexplored territory 5 miles away, a mountain streaked from its base to its summit with reddish rock that he knew indicated silver and other minerals. He made his way up Silver Creek, through forest so dense he could not see more than 100 feet in any direction. He climbed over the ridge at the headwaters of Silver Creek, and staked out claims.

With the backing of Eastern financiers, including John D. Rockefeller, the wilderness Pearsall discovered quickly became a full-fledged town of 2,000 people, boasting homes, stores, banks, hotels, saloons, and a newspaper, as well as the equipment for taking ore out of the ground and concentrating it for shipment. The Everett and Monte Cristo Railroad reached the town in 1892.

Wresting the ore from the hard rock and shipping it to the refinery in Everett proved to be too costly and the mines did not last long, although new companies tried to resurrect them from time to time until the 1920s. Then the town gradually decayed. The railroad right of way became a county road, then a trail. The Henry M. Jackson Wilderness was created on all sides of the town site, except the thin line that once was the railroad right of way. The huge turntable where the train engines turned around to return to Everett is about the only structure still left from the old days. A few summer cabins have been built since the original buildings disappeared. Only those few cabins, some collapsing mine openings, and the trails the miners used remain. The trails make interesting hikes.

POODLE DOG PASS TRAIL 708. [Fig. 26(17)] Joseph Pearsall, the prospector who discovered Monte Cristo, and the people who came immediately after him, reached Monte Cristo by hiking up Silver Creek from Mineral City, which no longer exists. They quickly wore a trail past Silver Lake on Poodle Dog Pass. They carried the supplies and equipment they needed on their backs for many months, until a wagon road was developed. Shortly after that, the railroad was completed.

The route begins at Barlow Pass and goes 4 miles on the closed-to-vehicles road to a campground at the entrance to the Monte Cristo townsite. The trailhead is just across the bridge from the campground. It goes steeply for 1.5 miles up the side of Silvertip Peak, past an abandoned mine site, into the wilderness, and on to Silver Lake, a pretty jewel but so full of arsenic that state game officials have never been able to stock it with fish. Despite that it is a beautiful mountain lake surrounded by meadows, cliffs, and waterfalls, at an elevation of 4,250 feet.

The trail goes on from the lake along the ridge between Silver Creek and 76 Gulch, where Pearsall located his earliest mining claims. It goes up and down for 2.5 miles, then drops steeply for 650 feet to camp sites at Twin Lakes, elevation 4,750 feet.

Directions: Take the Mountain Loop Scenic Byway about 30 miles from Granite Falls to Barlow Pass where the road forks. The fork to the right is closed to all motor vehicles except those of property owners, but is open to hikers and bicycle riders. Follow that road about 4 miles, cross the bridge to the Monte Cristo town site and find the trailhead on the right.

Dates: Seasonal, summer.

Fees: A trailhead fee may be charged.

Trail: From Monte Cristo town site to Silver Lake 5.5 miles, one-way; to Twin Lakes, 8.5 miles.

Elevations: 2,000 feet elevation gain to Poodle Dog Pass, 3,500 feet elevation gain to Twin Lakes.

Degree of difficulty: Strenuous.

GLACIER BASIN TRAIL 719. [Fig. 26(16)] A short but very rough and difficult trail that miners once used to get from their homes in Monte Cristo to the mines, where they worked in a basin that is wondrous for its raw, wild beauty as well as for its peek at history.

The route begins at Barlow Pass and continues down the closed-to-most-vehicles Monte Cristo Road, passes the campground at the edge of the townsite, and continues through the remnants of the town's main street, roughly paralleling Glacier Creek. A new forest of sitka alder and Alaska cedar has grown where the bustling town once was, but some of the old building sites are still visible. Beyond the town, the trail veers to the banks of Glacier Creek and a magnificent waterfall. For about 0.5 mile it is so well-worn that part of it is over bare rock, and so extremely steep that it is necessary for hikers to grasp tree branches to pull themselves up. Some of the branches have been grasped so often that they have a polished appearance.

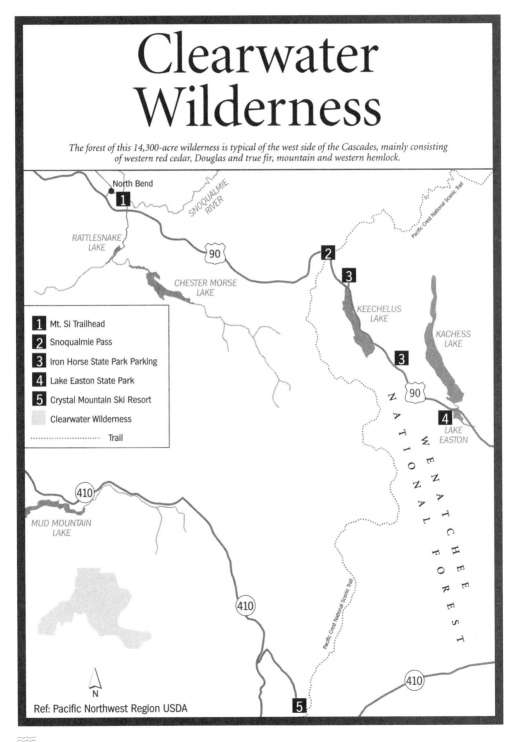

Clearwater Wilderness

The forest of this 14,300-acre wilderness is typical of the west side of the Cascades, mainly consisting of western red cedar, Douglas and true fir, mountain and western hemlock.

North Bend

1

SNOQUALMIE RIVER

Pacific Crest National Scenic Trail

RATTLESNAKE LAKE

90

2

3

CHESTER MORSE LAKE

KEECHELUS LAKE

KACHESS LAKE

3

1 Mt. Si Trailhead

2 Snoqualmie Pass

3 Iron Horse State Park Parking

4 Lake Easton State Park

5 Crystal Mountain Ski Resort

Clearwater Wilderness

.... Trail

90

4 LAKE EASTON

WENATCHEE NATIONAL FOREST

410

MUD MOUNTAIN LAKE

410

Pacific Crest National Scenic Trail

N

Ref: Pacific Northwest Region USDA

410

5

Eventually the trail crosses talus slopes at the approach to Glacier Basin, then makes a sharp right turn, and abruptly enters the basin itself. The remnants of mines are scattered throughout the basin which is about 1 mile long. It is not safe to enter the mines, but it is possible to get an idea of the places where the miners worked by shining a flashlight into the entrance.

Icy, white glaciers glisten in Glacier Basin, reaching all the way down to the grass and flower meadows. Camping is discouraged on the fragile meadows but spots may be found on Mystery Hill on the west side of the basin.

Directions: Take the Mountain Loop Highway about 30 miles from Granite Falls to Barlow Pass, where the road forks. The fork to the right is closed to all vehicles except those of property owners, but is open to hikers and bicycle riders. Follow that road about 4 miles, pass the campground at the edge of the city, cross the bridge to the Monte Cristo town site. Skirt around the Poodle Dog Pass Trailhead, and cross the creek to the site of what once was the town's main street, and follow that to the trail.

Dates: Seasonal, summer.
Trail: 7 miles, one-way.
Elevation: 2,200 feet elevation gain.
Degree of difficulty: Strenuous.

CLEARWATER WILDERNESS

[Fig. 25] A small area at the northern edge of the Mount Rainier National Park, the Clearwater Wilderness is, like all wildernesses, a place where there are no roads and very few other indications that humans have been here.

The 14,300-acre wilderness has only a moderate difference in elevation, with the low point being about 2,000 feet above sea level, and the high point being Mount Bearhead, at 6,089 feet. The forest is typical of the west side of the Cascades, mainly consisting of western redcedar, Douglas and true fir, mountain and western hemlock. There are alpine meadows in the upper elevations.

There are some steep rocky places, but the topography generally is moderate. The two major streams are the East Fork of Prairie Creek, and the Clearwater River, which has some stands of large old-growth trees in the lower elevations. There are eight lakes within the wilderness, and viewpoints on the trails provide rare views of the north side of towering Mount Rainier.

Directions: There are only two main roads to

AMERICAN KESTREL
(Falco sparverius)
This tiny bird can be seen hunting along parkways and fields, diving from above for other birds, insects or small mammals as prey.

the wilderness. For one, go to just west of the Carbon River Entrance to Mount Rainier National Park, at the extreme northwest corner of the park, turn north off the Carbon River Road onto the Cayada Creek Road, Forest Road 7810, and follow that about 7 miles to the end, where there is a trailhead into the wilderness area. (Note: Forest Road 7810 was closed in 1998 and no date for reopening had been announced). For the other access, drive east from Enumclaw on State Route 410 for 21.8 miles to Forest Service Road 47, then go south about 15 miles to the trailhead at the end of the road.

Activities: Hiking, hunting, fishing.

Dates: Seasonal, summer.

Fees: A trailhead fee may be charged.

Closest town: Enumclaw, about 36 miles.

For more information: White River Ranger District, 857 Roosevelt Avenue East, Enumclaw, WA 98022, (360) 825-6585.

Mount Baker Ranger District

With Mount Baker and the Mount Baker Wilderness as its centerpiece, the Mount Baker Ranger District shares a border with Canada at the northern edge of the Washington Cascades. Among its attractions are a summer resort and campgrounds on Baker Lake, which provide a base for fishing on the lake, as well as hunting and hiking in the nearby forests and the adjacent wilderness area.

There is also a National Forest Scenic Byway leading to Heather Meadows, a major downhill ski area, cross-country ski routes, and part of the Skagit Wild and Scenic River system. This system includes, just outside the border of the national forest, the Upper Skagit Bald Eagle Area, where as many as 600 of the birds that symbolize the United States perch in the cottonwood trees along the river bank during the fall and winter.

The eagles gather here from as far away as Alaska to feast on the carcasses of the multitude of chum and coho salmon that find their way from the Pacific Ocean to the Skagit River to spawn and die. Their carcasses make an easy meal for the eagles, which may be watched from viewpoints along State Route 20 or from boats and rafts on the river.

Directions: To the north part of the ranger district, take exit 255 from Interstate Highway 5 just north of Bellingham, and go east on State Route 542 for some 50 miles. For the Baker Lake area, take Interstate Highway 5 exit 230, and go east on State Route 20 through Sedro-Woolley. 15 miles beyond that city, turn left onto the Baker Lake-Grandy Road.

Activities: Hiking, camping, swimming, picnicking, boating, fishing, hunting, mountain climbing, snowshoeing, cross-country skiing, downhill skiing snowmobiling.

Facilities: Campgrounds, resort, boat launches, boat docks, downhill ski area, bald eagle viewing stations, restrooms.

Dates: Most activities are restricted to summer but cross-country skiing, snowshoeing, snowmobiling, and other snow-play activities are popular during the winter.

Fees: A trailhead fee may be charged.

Closest town: For the northern part, Glacier, 7 miles. For the Baker Lake area, Concrete, 7 miles.

For more information: North Cascades National Park/Mount Baker Ranger District Information Center, 2105 Highway 20, Sedro-Woolley, WA 98284, (360) 856-5700, or The Outdoor Recreation Information Center, 222 Yale Avenue North, Seattle, WA 98109-5429. Phone (206) 470-4060.

🌐 BAKER LAKE ATTRACTIONS

[Fig. 22] Baker Lake stretches about 10 miles along the base of Mount Baker, between the Noisy-Diobsud and Mount Baker Wildernesses. There is a trail along the eastern bank, and the rudimentary Maple Grove Campground about halfway along the trail. The campground is used by hikers and boaters.

Forest Road 11, which becomes Forest Road 1168 near the north end of the lake, parallels the western shore and provides access to a multitude of attractions. Among the attractions are the Puget Power and Light Company's viewpoints at the company's dam, which impounds Baker Lake. The company also maintains the Kulshan Campground nearby. Berry picking is a popular activity.

The Forest Service has numerous attractions along the road. Among them:

SHANNON CREEK CAMPGROUND. [Fig. 22(4)] Trailer sites, picnic area, restrooms, drinking water, swimming.

BAKER LAKE RESORT. [Fig. 22(5)] Cabins, campground, trailer sites, picnic area, restrooms, drinking water, campfires, boat launch, fishing.

PARK CREEK CAMPGROUND. [Fig. 22(6)] Trailer sites, restrooms, boat launch, fishing.

BOULDER CREEK CAMPGROUND. [Fig. 22(7)] Trailer sites, restrooms, fishing.

CHINOOK SALMON
(Oncorhynchus tshawytscha)
The chinook is the largest of the roughly 40 species in the salmon family.

PANORAMA POINT CAMPGROUND. [Fig. 22(8)] Restrooms, fishing, trailer sites, boat launch.

HORSESHOE COVE CAMPGROUND. [Fig. 22(9)] Trailer sites, restrooms, drinking water, boat launch, fishing, swimming.

SHADOW OF THE SENTINELS INTERPRETATIVE TRAIL

[Fig. 22(10)] A short, level, wheelchair-accessible, self-guided, loop trail through a magnificent stand of old growth Douglas fir. Much of the trail is paved with asphalt and the rest is a boardwalk. The route is level and looped, and the huge old Douglas firs make it a fascinating visit to an ancient forest that is rare in lowland areas. The trail is popular as a route for cross-country skiing and snowshoeing during the winter.

Directions: From I-5 Exit 230, go east on State Route 20 through Sedro-Woolley. Approximately 15 miles beyond that city, turn left onto the Baker Lake-Grandy Road, which becomes Forest Road 11 and leads to the side roads that go to visitor attractions.

Activities: Hiking, camping, boating, swimming, mountain climbing, fishing, hunting, snowshoeing, cross-country skiing.

Facilities: Campgrounds, picnic sites, restrooms, boat launches, cabins.

Dates: Open year-round.

Fees: Fees are charged at the Baker Lake area campgrounds. A trailhead fee may be charged.

Closest town: Concrete, about 10 miles from the Koma Kulshan Guard Station near the Forest Service boundary.

For more information: North Cascades National Park/Mount Baker Ranger District Information Center, 2105 Highway 20, Sedro-Woolley, WA 98284, (360) 856-5700, or The Outdoor Recreation Information Center, 222 Yale Avenue North, Seattle, WA 98109-5429. Phone (206) 470-4060.

BAKER RIVER TRAIL 606

[Fig. 22] This is an easy, 3-mile, one-way trail through ancient forests to the roaring Sulphide Creek in the North Cascades National Park. Sulphide Creek is fed by the melting ice of the Sulphide Glacier high on the slopes of Mount Shuksan. The rivulets that drip from the glacier merge just above tree line, and charge in white froth down the steep slope of the mountain in their rush to join the Baker River a short distance below the trail.

It is a wondrous place to stop for a sandwich or, for those who have obtained a National Park backcountry permit, to camp for the night. It also is a great place for water ouzels, also known as dippers. Visitors can watch as these birds of the Cinclidae family stand beside the rushing white water performing their strange, curtsylike dance, then suddenly plunge into the rushing stream in search of an unwary aquatic insect and somehow, swim under the rushing water.

The trail has only slight elevation gains and losses as it passes beside the Baker River. The thick forest allows only an occasional glimpse of the outside world, such as the glaciers on Mount Blum on the other side of the river. It stays in the forest until it reaches the open country, where Sulphide Creek empties into the Baker River about 3 miles from the trailhead, and about 1,000 feet beyond the border of the national forest and the North Cascades National Park.

The trail begins in young Douglas fir, but soon reaches a mixed forest of vine and big leaf maple, red alder, western hemlock, and some large western redcedar. About half way to Sulphide Creek, silver fir mixes into the forest. There are beaver ponds along the way.

Traces of the trail continue for 3 more miles to Bald Eagle Creek, but it is necessary to ford both Sulphide and Crystal creeks, and the trail becomes more and more overgrown until it disappears entirely. It may be used occasionally by hunters and anglers, but hikers can find more hospitable places.

Directions: From Sedro-Woolley go east on State Route 20 for about 15 miles, then turn north on the Grandy Creek Road, which becomes Forest Road 11. About 20 miles from State Route 20, Forest Road 11 meets Forest Road 1169. The trailhead is at the end of Forest Road 1169.

Activities: Hiking, camping, hunting, and fishing.

Dates: Seasonal, summer.

Fees: A trailhead fee may be charged.

Trail: 3 miles, one-way.

Elevation: 200 feet elevation gain.

Degree of difficulty: Easy.

MOUNT BAKER SKI AREA AND HEATHER MEADOWS

This is a major ski area in the winter, and a mountain wonderland in the summer. The Forest Service calls it a four-season recreation area. It is reached by driving to the end of State Route 542, one of the Forest Service's Scenic Byways, which has many natural splendors such as forests, streams, and mountain views.

The ski area is part of Heather Meadows, which lies on a shoulder at the edge of the Mount Baker Wilderness, between two glacier-clad giants — Mount Baker, a 10,788-foot glaciated volcano, and Mount Shuksan, a 9,127-foot monolith of jagged rock and glistening ice. Heather Meadows, whether in the winter or summer, provides a majestic foreground to the awesome beauty of the mountains.

The road to Heather Meadows, State Route 542, goes through the little town of Glacier where the Forest Service has a Public Service Center, at Mile Post 34, which operates seasonally from May to October, dispensing information and advice about Heather Meadows and the surrounding area. Glacier is also the beginning of the National Forest Scenic Byway that continues to the end of the road at Artist Point in the Meadows.

MOUNT BAKER SKI AREA

[Fig. 22(1)] This ski area receives a monumental annual average of about 600 inches of snowfall, some 50 feet. It has eight lifts and a rope-tow, servicing 8,000 passengers an hour. The elevation at the top is about 5,000 feet, and the vertical drop is about 1,500 feet. There are 38 major runs, including steep chutes and gullies, as well as groomed runs for beginners and intermediate skiers. Thirty percent of the runs are rated as beginner; 42

percent, intermediate, and 28 percent, advanced.

Mount Baker Ski Area traditionally is the first to open and the last to close during the season in the Washington Cascades. The snow is often powder. There is no lodging and no night skiing, but a new day lodge provides a pro shop, changing area, and limited rentals.

Directions: From Interstate Highway 5 take exit 255 just north of Bellingham, and go east on State Route 542 for 56 miles.

Activities: Downhill skiing, hiking, picnicking.

Facilities: Lifts, groomed trails, and a day lodge with a pro shop, changing area, and limited rentals.

Dates: Seasonal, summer.

Fees: There are fees for lift tickets, rentals, and services.

Closest town: Glacier, 24 miles.

For more information: For a snow report, phone (360) 671-0211. For information on the ski area, Mount Baker Ski Area, Inc., 1019 Iowa Street, Bellingham, WA 98226. Phone (360) 734-6771. For other information, contact the Mount Baker Ranger District, 2105 State Route 20, Sedro-Woolley, WA 98284. Phone (360) 856-5700.

HEATHER MEADOWS

[Fig. 22(2)] When the snow melts off in the spring, Heather Meadows becomes one of the few places in the Cascade Mountains where visitors can approach the majestic beauty of a high-country meadowland from the comfort of a car. Still, there are trails to be walked, including short, self-guided, interpretative trails, longer trails to lakes, ridges and viewpoints, and the meadows are the starting places for several trails into the adjacent Mount Baker Wilderness (*see* Mount Baker Wilderness, page 128).

Before Europeans arrived, the meadows were visited during the summer by Native Americans, who were attracted by blueberry bushes and abundant game. The highway was built to Austin Pass in 1926 and the large Mount Baker Lodge hotel was built soon after that. The hotel attracted guests from many parts of the world until it burned down four years later. Today the road has been extended about 1 mile to Artist Point, and the meadows still attract many thousands of visitors each summer.

A warming hut built by the Civilian Conservation Corps in 1940 has been converted to the Heather Meadows Visitor Center. It is wheelchair accessible, and has picnic tables nearby, as well as magnificent views.

The meadows lie on ancient andesite lava that solidified into hexagonal columns after erupting from Mount Baker. The predominant trees in the meadow are mountain hemlock, subalpine fir, and Pacific fir. They grow mostly on mounds and ridges where the snow melts away earliest.

Perhaps the most common plants in the meadows are heathers, which blanket their red, white and yellow flowers over the fields. Other common plants include sitka mountain ash, a shrub that grows from 3 to 12 feet tall and has large white flowers that turn into bright red berries. Smaller plants include blueberry bushes, and sedge.

Among the mammals that may be seen from the meadows are mountain goats, black bears, porcupines, hoary marmots, and pikas. Many birds frequent the area including water ouzels, also known as dippers; red-tailed hawk, raven, Steller's jay, and the gray jay, which is probably better known as the camp robber because of its habit of pilfering people's food.

Among the trails are the:

Picture Lake Trail, which leads to Picture Lake, reputedly one of the most photographed mountain scenes in North America. The lake is a tarn, which lies in a depression carved out of the solid rock by ancient glaciers. The glaciers also helped expose the columnar lava walls in the Heather Meadow area. The 0.5-mile Picture Lake Trail approaches the lake without actually reaching it, thus protecting the delicate ecology of the shore.

The trail is accessible by wheelchair, and offers a view of a flowered meadow in the foreground with, on a clear day, Mount Shuksan and its glaciers reflecting in the quiet water of the lake.

Bagley Lakes Trail is a 1.5-mile route on the east shore of Bagley Lake, and meets the Chain Lakes and Wild Goose trails.

The 2-mile **Wild Goose Trail** leads through most of the meadows, providing access to other trails and the Austin Pass Picnic Area.

Artist Ridge Trail has interpretive signs about the area's geology, plants, animals, and history, as it courses 1 mile through heather and berry plants between Mount Baker and Mount Shuksan. Part of the trail is accessible to wheelchairs.

Chain Lakes Trail is a 9-mile loop into the Mount Baker Wilderness. It passes lava walls, Mazama Lake, Iceberg Lake, Hayes Lake, and Bagley Lakes, gaining about 900 feet.

Directions: From Interstate Highway 5 take exit 255 just north of Bellingham, and go east on State Route 542 for 56 miles.

Activities: Hiking.

Facilities: Short scenic trails, interpretive trails, visitor center.

Dates: Seasonal, summer.

Fees: Trailhead fees may be charged.

Closest town: Glacier, 24 miles.

For more information: Mount Baker Ranger District, 2105 State Route 20, Sedro-Woolley, WA 98284. Phone (360) 856-5700.

Darrington Ranger District

[Fig. 26] The 570,000-acre Darrington Ranger District extends through the north-central section of the Mount Baker-Snoqualmie National Forest. The district has 10 campgrounds with individual campsites. The Verlot, Turlo, and Gold Basin campgrounds have piped water. The Verlot Campground has flush toilets. The others all have pit or vault toilets and water is available only from streams. There also are six group

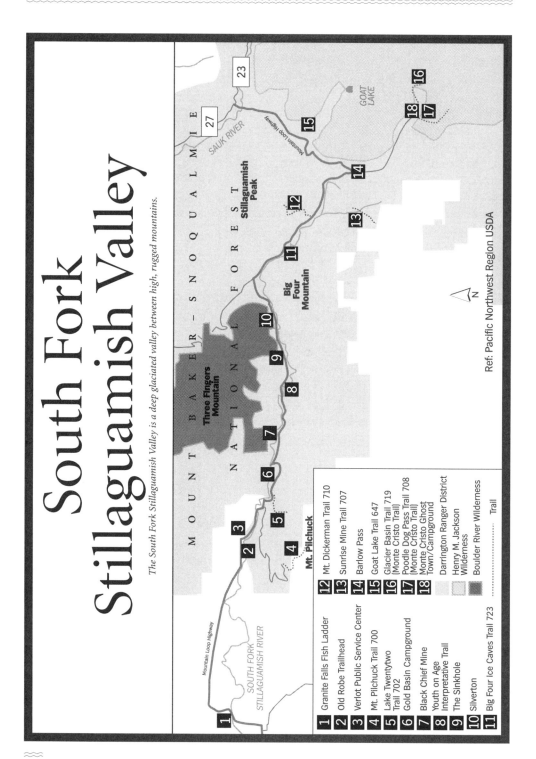

South Fork Stillaguamish Valley

The South Fork Stillaguamish Valley is a deep glaciated valley between high, rugged mountains.

MOUNT BAKER – SNOQUALMIE NATIONAL FOREST

Stillaguamish Peak

Big Four Mountain

Three Fingers Mountain

Mt. Pilchuck

GOAT LAKE

SAUK RIVER

Mountain Loop Highway

SOUTH FORK STILLAGUAMISH RIVER

Mountain Loop Highway

Ref: Pacific Northwest Region USDA

1. Granite Falls Fish Ladder
2. Old Robe Trailhead
3. Verlot Public Service Center
4. Mt. Pilchuck Trail 700
5. Lake Twentytwo Trail 702
6. Gold Basin Campground
7. Black Chief Mine
8. Youth on Age Interpretative Trail
9. The Sinkhole
10. Silverton
11. Big Four Ice Caves Trail 723
12. Mt. Dickerman Trail 710
13. Sunrise Mine Trail 707
14. Barlow Pass
15. Goat Lake Trail 647
16. Glacier Basin Trail 719 [Monte Cristo Trail]
17. Poodle Dog Pass Trail 708 [Monte Cristo Trail]
18. Monte Cristo Ghost Town/Campground

Darrington Ranger District

Henry M. Jackson Wilderness

Boulder River Wilderness

Trail

campgrounds that can accommodate organizations with large numbers of people. Campsites at all of the group campgrounds and three of the campgrounds with individual sites can be reserved. For reservations, phone (800) 280-2267.

The district is crisscrossed by more than 50 trails open to hikers only, and a dozen open to both hikers and livestock such as horses, mules, and, in recent years, llamas. There also are well over 40 roads, some paved, that lead to deep forest and high-country places. By far the most popular is Snohomish County Road 92 which usually is called the Mountain Loop Highway, although it bears little resemblance to a modern highway. The Forest Service has added the road to its list of scenic byways because of the wild beauty of the land it crosses. It is a 50 mile route between Granite Falls and Darrington that loops deep into the mountains, passing rivers, lakes, old-growth and second growth forests, trails, campgrounds, numerous historic sites, and magnificent mountain scenery.

Both ends of the road began as railroads. On the Granite Falls end, the Everett Monte Cristo Railroad was built in the 1890s to supply the mining-boom town Monte Cristo, now deserted, and other communities along the right of way. On the Darrington end, the road originally was a logging railway built by the Sauk River Lumber Company to bring logs from the Sauk River Watershed to mills in Everett and elsewhere.

By the mid-1900s the railroads had died, and the rights of way had been converted to roads by loggers and the Civilian Conservation Corps. They extended the ends to meet at Barlow Pass, which separates the Sauk and the South Fork Stillaguamish river drainages. That made the road part of a loop that begins and ends on State Route 9 and goes through the deep mountains.

Directions: The Darrington Ranger Station is central to the district. It is located at 1405 Emmens Street, Darrington, WA 98241, Phone (360) 436-1155.

Activities: Camping, hiking, mountain climbing, mountain biking, hunting, fishing, snowmobiling, cross-country skiing, snowshoeing.

Facilities: Campgrounds, visitor centers, historical exhibits, environmental exhibits.

Dates: Open year-round

Fees: Fees are charged at all of the district's campgrounds. Trailhead fees may be charged.

Closest towns: Darrington is 2 miles from the northern part of the ranger district. Granite Falls is 10 miles from the southern part.

For more information: Darrington Ranger Station, 1405 Emmens Street. Phone (360) 436-1155. Or the Outdoor Recreation Information Center, 222 Yale Avenue North, Seattle, WA 98109-5429. Phone (206) 470-4060.

South Fork Stillaguamish Valley

[Fig. 26] This deep, glaciated valley between high, rugged mountains is the site of a paved, 30-mile portion of the Mountain Loop Highway. The other 20 miles are in the Sauk River valley and are, for the most part, a one-lane gravel road with turnouts so oncoming cars can pass each other. The route has been called a highway since the 1930s after the logging and mining railroads died out. People from many parts of Western Washington promoted the interconnected valleys as a scenic tourist attraction. They envisioned a broad, paved, loop route through the forested mountains where people could develop summer cabins, hotels and other resort facilities. The dream of intense development quickly evaporated, but after the roads were connected at Barlow Pass, the route became popular, especially the portion in the North Fork of the Stillaguamish Valley after the county paved that portion to the standards of a secondary road. Though many people continue to refer to it as the Mountain Loop Highway, others, more realistically call it the Mountain Loop Byway.

The forest on both sides of the so-called highway was extensively clear-cut during the century since settlers, miners and loggers began to arrive, but most of the people have long since left and the forest has largely regrown into an impressive second-growth forest, and the Mountain Loop Highway passes through much marvelous country, and goes past campgrounds, trails, rivers, lakes and historic sites.

The history began with a hunt for gold that reached a peak after 1889, when prospectors thought they had found bonanzas at the headwaters of the Sauk, and other places scattered through the nearby mountains. There was gold there, but it was imbedded in the solid rock of the mountains and expensive to retrieve. The lure of gold, however, was strong enough to attract big capitalists, including John D. Rockefeller. Elaborate efforts to wrest the gold from the rock withered when it was found that the heaviest concentrations of ore were near the surface, and the deeper the mines went, the more scarce the metal became. The boom died after a decade or so and, for the most part, people deserted the area to look for better opportunities. Even today, however, a few hopefuls continue to work old claims on a small scale.

The gold rush had a profound effect on Snohomish County, all the way to Everett on Puget Sound. Before the gold rush died, the Rockefeller interests and others looked on the newly founded city of Everett as the center of what they thought would be an immense source of mineral wealth. That contributed heavily to the early development of the city, which eventually became the county seat and a major economic center in the Puget Sound area.

Before the gold bubble burst, the North Fork of the Stillaguamish Valley was the site of small scale logging, and related lumber and shingle mills sprang up along the banks of the river. Small operators found ingenious ways to harness energy, sometimes from the rivers and streams but also with steam, and used it to convert the forest into lumber. Their lifeblood was the railroad which brought in the supplies they needed and carried to market the lumber they produced. The mills were associated with small villages that consisted of a few houses where the mill workers lived and, sometimes, a small store where they purchased necessities.

As the mines died out, the railroad owners found it difficult to continue operations and trains became sporadic. That, plus the diminishing supply of logs near the mills, gradually forced the mills to shut down until, by midcentury, there were none left. Logging became mechanized and trucks carried logs from the high country to huge new mills in Everett and elsewhere in the Puget Sound Basin.

Most of that kind of logging also has stopped, and the valley has become a quiet place where beauty and serenity is replacing industry. The residents of the valley, many of whom commute to cities for work, live primarily in the lower end, between Granite Falls and the Verlot Visitor Center, about 11 miles above Granite Falls. Beyond that, residences become progressively fewer. A few scattered houses, mostly used as summer cabins at and near the site of the former mining town of Silverton 22 miles from Granite Falls, mark the current end of settlement and, beyond that, the valley is largely devoted to nature and recreation.

Directions: Go east from Granite Falls on the Mountain Loop Highway (also known as Snohomish County Road 92 and as the Mountain Loop Scenic Byway). That road leads through the North Fork Stillaguamish Valley, ending at Barlow Pass, where it meets the Sauk Valley Road (Forest Road 20) that goes toward Darrington.

Activities: Camping, hiking, mountain climbing, mountain biking, hunting, fishing, snowmobiling, cross-country skiing, and snowshoeing.

Facilities: Campgrounds, a public service center, historical exhibits, environmental exhibits.

Dates: Open year-round

Fees: Fees are charged at all of the district's campgrounds. Trailhead fees may be charged.

Closest town: Granite Falls, 10 miles.

For more information: From spring through fall, Verlot Public Service Center, 33515 Mountain Loop Highway, Granite Falls, WA, 98252. Phone, (360) 691-7791. Or, year-round, Darrington Ranger Station, 1405 Emmens Street. Phone (360) 436-1155.

GRANITE FALLS FISH LADDER

[Fig. 26(1)] This aid to fish habitat demonstrates a great deal about the power of a mountain stream and the nature of the fish that live there. It can be reached by a short, steep, gravel trail that goes several hundred yards from the Mountain Loop Highway down into the canyon of the South Fork of the Stillaguamish River.

Here several steps of the fish ladder may be seen. The ladder was built in 1954 to help steelhead and salmon negotiate the barrier of the Granite Falls waterfalls that gave the town of Granite Falls its name. There actually are two falls of about 10 to 15 feet high and a long stretch of cascading, white water that had been a natural impediment to the fish trying to get up to their spawning grounds.

When the fish are running, usually from July to September, and when the water is clear, the fish may be visible by looking down on them through the steel grates of a walkway. The fish still must leap out of the water to reach the concrete steps of the ladder but the barrier collects the water in relatively quiet pools that make it easier to go from step to step.

There also are good views of the river as it rushes through the narrow valley.

Directions: The fish ladder is on the west side of the Mountain Loop Highway, 1.7 miles north of Granite Falls.

Dates: Open year-round.

Fees: None.

For more information: State Department of Fish and Wildlife Regional Office, 16018 Mill Creek Boulevard, Mill Creek WA 98012. Phone, (425) 775-1311.

OLD ROBE TRAIL

[Fig. 26(2)] In the summer of 1892, when the Everett Monte Cristo Railroad was building its tracks up the South Fork of the Stillaguamish River, it came to formidable obstacles when it reached a place 11 miles east of Granite Falls where the river rushed through a narrow gap in the solid rock walls of a canyon. The river, forced between the walls, became a rushing torrent of white water that threatened to sweep away anything that touched it. The only way through was to build a bridge to cross from the south side of the river to the north, then to blast tunnels through three huge outcrops of rock.

Forcing a passage through the obstructions was a tremendous job, but maintaining the tracks afterward was even more difficult. The New York engineers, who designed the railroad for the Monte Cristo mine developers, were not used to the extremes of rain and snow of the west slopes of the Cascades and when local people warned them of the devastating floods that happened frequently, they responded that the Stillaguamish was no more than a trout stream compared with rivers where they had built railroads. They designed the railroad to a low elevation that would be above the kind of floods they were used to. Unfortunately, the local engineers proved to be right. Frequently in the spring and fall deluges of rain combined with melting snow to bring torrents of water cascading down from the mountains. Floods along the right of way were devastating to the railroad but nowhere more than at tunnels Four, Five and Six, where the right of way bypassed the gap.

After a time, the mistake doomed the railroad and, in turn, the mines, because the expense of rebuilding the tracks and the delayed service was more than the railroad could bear. Eventually it simply stopped operating, but not before it made massive attempts to prevent the floods from destroying the tracks. Even today, visitors to Old Robe can see the railroad ties imbedded in concrete in a vain attempt to protect the tracks from being washed away in the next flood.

Adding to the problems of the floods, the rock walls of the canyon proved to be unstable, and from time to time collapsed, burying the tracks under deep piles of huge rocks, causing more work for the maintenance crews, more delays for the trains, and more problems for the mines that depended on the trains. One tunnel has collapsed, but the others are still there, along with the cemented ties of the ill fated railroad and the right of way that was blasted from the cliffs above the river.

A few feet upstream from the tunnels, T. K. Robe founded, in 1891, the community of Robe around a shake mill he built beside the river. The community never grew beyond a few houses, a railroad station, and a store before it, too, was destroyed by floods. The site of the village has been washed away, but until recently, relics were still being found in what once was the garbage dump and other places near the town site. A 781-ace county park includes the tunnels and the site of the village.

A short, steep trail from the Mountain Loop Highway now leads visitors to what the county park department calls The Robe Canyon Historic Park. There is little to see of the town, but the railroads' struggles to defeat the floods are obvious from the structures that survive, and the roaring river combines with the second growth forest beside the river to make this a major attraction. Neither the railroad bed nor the tunnels are safe, and visitors should be careful where they walk, and avoid going inside the tunnels.

Directions: The trailhead is on the south side of the mountain Loop Highway, 10 miles from Granite Falls.

Activities: Hiking, picnicking.

Facilities: None.

Dates: Open year-round.

Fees: None.

For more information: Snohomish County Parks Department, 2828 Rockefeller Avenue, Everett, WA 98201. Phone, (425) 339-1208.

Trail: 0.75 mile.

Elevation: 230 feet elevation gain.

Degree of difficulty: Easy.

VERLOT PUBLIC SERVICE CENTER

[Fig. 26(3)] This is a complex of Forest Service buildings that once were the ranger station of the Monte Cristo Ranger District. The main building is on the National Register of Historic Places. That structure was built during the Great Depression of the 1930s by young men of the Civilian Conservation Corps. It was used as the Monte Cristo Ranger Station until the Monte Cristo District was incorporated into the Darrington Ranger District as part of the reorganization that followed the creation of the North Cascades National Park in 1968.

The building is used now primarily as a public service center where visitors may get information, literature, and Forest Service permits. Some of the former CCC men who built the structure in their youth have returned as elderly veterans to refurbish it and convert one room into a museum of the CCCs.

There are two campgrounds across the highway from the service center. The Verlot Campground has 26 campsites, piped water and flush toilets, and the Turlo Campground has 19 campsites, piped water and vault toilets.

Directions: The Public Service Center building is on the north side of the Mountain Loop Highway, 11 miles from Granite Falls.

Dates: Open seasonally, spring through fall.

Fees: Fees are charged for camping in the campgrounds.

For more information: From spring through fall, Verlot Public Service Center, 33515 Mountain Loop Highway, Granite Falls, WA 98252. Phone, (360) 691-7791. Or, year-round, Darrington Ranger Station, 1405 Emmens Street. Phone (360) 436-1155.

▨ MOUNT PILCHUCK TRAIL 700

[Fig. 26(4)] This 2-mile trail goes through an old-growth forest of mostly stately western hemlock (*Tsuga heterophylla*), then passes a long, glacier-polished rock slab, and climbs a series of switchbacks to piles of car-sized boulders at the top of the mountain. Balanced on top of the rocks is a fire lookout that has not been used for finding fires for many decades, but has been carefully maintained by the Mountaineers Club, which has decorated the inside with historic photographs of the lookout. The lookout was originally established in 1918.

One of the people who worked in the lookout in the 1940s was a man named Hap Annen who grew up on the east side of Everett where Mount Pilchuck is a dominant geographic feature. As a young child, he could see the mountain from the windows of his home and he acquired a lifetime love for it and the surrounding countryside. When he grew up he operated an auto shop in Everett, but during several summers in the 1940s, he left the shop to serve in the lookout on Mount Pilchuck. Eager to share the beauty of the mountain, he painted yellow markings on the long slab of glacier-polished rock that was a confusing part of the hike when he was there. The markings still exist but the trail has been relocated, so they no longer are a good guide to the top.

The parking lot at the bottom of the trail was once the base for a moderately large downhill ski area, but snowfall was so light during a series of winters during the 1970s that it closed. Now, the area is a poorly maintained, 1,893-acre state park. A rudimentary campground and some picnic tables are located just at the bottom of the trail. The trail wanders between state park and Forest Service land.

The trail recently was rerouted and rebuilt to avoid sections that had become worn and difficult by decades of heavy use. It now is a good trail but, perhaps because the mountain is often foggy, a surprising number of people stray from the trail, become lost, and must be rescued by Search and Rescue volunteers.

The view from the top is full circle and magnificent. Pilchuck is the end of a spur that juts out from the western edge of the Cascades. At 5,340 feet in elevation, it is not especially high, but its far-west orientation makes it a dominant feature from the coast, which may, at least partly, explain its popularity. It also explains the variety of the view. To the north, east, and south, the view is a magnificent horizon of peaks near and far. Across the valley to the north is Mount Three Fingers in the Boulder River Wilderness (*see* Mount Three Fingers-Goat Flat Trail 641, page 133). To the south, massive Mount Rainier pokes its head above the clouds in the far distance. To the east, considerably closer than Rainier and just as imposing, is Glacier Peak.

Between those giants is a sawtooth horizon of uncountable peaks and valleys that add to the awesome Cascade Mountain view, but what makes the scenery here unusual is the view to the west, where, with no mountains in the way, one can see the farms and cities of the Puget Sound lowlands, and, beyond that on a clear day, the sound and the distant peaks of the Olympic Mountains between the sound and the Pacific Ocean. Most hikers make this a day hike but the few who stay overnight are treated to the lights of the cities far below, along the Puget Sound lowlands. The road from the Mountain Loop Highway to the parking lot is a popular cross-country ski route during the winter.

WESTERN HEMLOCK
(*Tsuga heterophylla*)
This hemlock has long cones, flat needles that are dark green above and whitish below, and is found on cool, moist slopes.

Directions: Take the Mountain Loop Highway 12 miles from Granite Falls, turn right onto the Mount Pilchuck Road (Forest Road 42), and go 7 miles to the parking lot and trailhead.

Facilities: There are rudimentary campsites and a pit toilet at the trailhead.

Dates: Seasonal, summer.

Fees: A trailhead fee may be charged.

For more information: From spring through fall, Verlot Public Service Center, 33515 Mountain Loop Highway, Granite Falls, WA 98252. Phone, (360) 691-7791. Or, year-round, Darrington Ranger Station, 1405 Emmens Street. Phone (360) 436-1155.

Trail: 2 miles, one-way.

Elevation: 2,400 feet elevation gain.

Degree of difficulty: Moderate.

🎒 LAKE TWENTYTWO TRAIL 702

[Fig. 26(5)] This is a nice trail through the 790-acre Lake 22 Research Natural Area to a delightful lake nestled under a shoulder of Mount Pilchuck. The research area was set aside by the Forest Service in 1947 as one of two in the South Fork Stillaguamish Valley to preserve its natural, forest ecosystems for research. It was here in 1974 that the nest of a marbled murrelet (*Brachyramphus marmoratus)* was found for the first time. This attractive, robin sized bird lives most of its life near the sea, where it subsists on fish, but it flies many miles inland to nest on the depressions in moss-covered, horizontal limbs of old-growth conifer trees. Since the murrelet leaves few signs at its nesting site and the nests are so far from where the bird usually lives, scientists had not found one until eggs were found in the natural area. The bird is listed as a threatened species on the West Coast.

The trail begins with an easy, level stroll from the parking lot for about 0.5 mile, then it starts steeply upward through the old-growth forest. It closely follows Twentytwo Creek for a mile or so, and gives good views of some roaring waterfalls along the way. Eventually it breaks out of the forest and enters an open area, where the tread becomes rocky and difficult. It curves around under some high, rocky cliffs until it reaches a wooded area where the lake lies, sparkling under the cliffs that border it.

Many years ago there were some buildings of a short-lived YMCA camp here, but they are long gone, and there is no sign that the lake has ever been anything but a pristine jewel.

Directions: The trailhead is on the south side of the Mountain Loop Highway, 12.7 miles from Granite Falls.

Dates: Seasonal, summer.

Fees: A trailhead fee may be charged.

For more information: From spring through fall, Verlot Public Service Center, 33515 Mountain Loop Highway, Granite Falls, WA 98252. Phone, (360) 691-7791. Or, year-round, Darrington Ranger Station, 1405 Emmens Street. Phone (360) 436-1155

Trail: 2.7 miles, one-way.

Elevation: 1,500 feet elevation gain.

Degree of difficulty: Easy.

GOLD BASIN CAMPGROUND

[Fig. 26(6)] This 96-campsite campground, on the banks of the South Fork of the

GREAT BLUE HERON
(Ardea herodias)
Often spotted standing or stalking in water, this heron catches fish by using its bill, like pincers. It grows to 4 feet tall and has a wingspan of 6 feet.

Stillaguamish River, is on land that was originally homesteaded by the Hemple and Rohde families in the late 1800s. It became the site of the Gold Basin Lumber and Shingle Company, which in 1910 included a town of about 75 people, and had a store, a post office, and a school.

Extensive gold mining took place in the basin across the river from the campground, and it is still possible to pan tiny flakes of gold from the sand on the river bank.

Across the road from the campground, the old Gold Basin Lumber and Shingle Company's mill pond still exists and the Forest Service has developed a short, wheelchair accessible, self guided, interpretative area which tells the story of the mill. The Forest Service also has refurbished the pond to provide a safe haven for young salmon. The pond also is frequented by bats, wood ducks, and great blue heron.

Directions: The campground is on the north side of the Mountain Loop Highway 13.4 miles from Granite Falls.

Activities: Camping, hiking, hunting, fishing.

Facilities: Piped water, vault toilets, amphitheater for ranger talks, millpond interpretative trail.

Dates: Seasonal, summer.

Fees: A camping fee is charged.

For more information: From spring through fall, Verlot Public Service Center, 33515 Mountain Loop Highway, Granite Falls, WA 98252. Phone, (360) 691-7791. Or, year-round, Darrington Ranger Station, 1405 Emmens Street. Phone (360) 436-1155.

BLACK CHIEF MINE

[Fig. 26(7)] The portal of this mine is at the end of a trail that extends a few dozen feet off the north side of the Mountain Loop Road. The mine was dug in the 1880s by miners who used steel hand drills and hammers to drill out holes they then filled with explosives to loosen the hard rock. The mine ends about 20 feet from the portal, but it is doubtful that it produced much gold.

The mine is near the western edge of the 64-acre Long Creek Research Natural Area, a 640-acre area of virgin forest that was set aside by the Forest Service at the same time as the Lake Twentytwo Research Area (*see* Lake Twentytwo Trail 702, page 161). The research forest provides grounds for research on low-level hemlock and western redcedar, and the unstable glacial deposits in the soil provide for geologic studies.

Directions: The mine and the research natural area are on the north side of the Mountain Loop Highway, 18.2 miles from Granite Falls.

Dates: Open year-round

Fees: None.

For more information: From spring through fall, Verlot Public Service Center, 33515 Mountain Loop Highway, Granite Falls, WA 98252. Phone, (360) 691-7791. Or, year-round, Darrington Ranger Station, 1405 Emmens Street. Phone (360) 436-1155.

YOUTH ON AGE INTERPRETATIVE TRAIL

[Fig. 26(8)] This short, paved, wheelchair accessible trail wanders in a 0.3 mile loop through huge Douglas fir, and sitka spruce trees, and low-level piggy backplants that thrive on fallen logs. The *Youth on Age* brochure that explains the ecosystem is available at the Verlot Public Service Center (see Verlot Public Service Center, page 159).

Directions: The trailhead is on the south side of the Mountain Loop Highway, 18.7 miles from Granite Falls.

Dates: Open year-round.

Fees: A trailhead fee may be charged.

Facilities: Restrooms at the trailhead, and interpretative signs along the trail.

For more information: From spring through fall, Verlot Public Service Center, 33515 Mountain Loop Highway, Granite Falls, WA 98252. Phone (360) 691-7791. Or, year-round, Darrington Ranger Station, 1405 Emmens Street. Phone (360) 436-1155.

Trail: 0.3 mile.

Elevation: No elevation gain.

Degree of difficulty: Easy.

THE SINKHOLE

[Fig. 26(9)] This aberration of nature still affects travel after more than a century of attempts to eliminate it. The sinkhole is a deposit of slippery glacial clay, about 50 yards wide, that slides slowly down the foot of Liberty Mountain toward the South Fork Stillaguamish River, taking along whatever is on top of it. When the railroad was built in 1892 the tracks were laid over the top. But the clay kept sliding the tracks toward the river, a few feet away, and the railroad eventually built a trestle in the river to get around it.

After the railroad closed down, the county eventually took over the right of way, and developed the current road. It has made elaborate attempts to control the sliding mud, but despite everything it does, the clay keeps sliding. Now the road bears a stop sign at each side of the sinkhole and drivers are warned to go cautiously over the long, rough dip that marks where the surface has gone inexorably into the river. The pilings of the old railroad trestle still stand in the river beside the Sinkhole, silently testifying to nature's tenacity.

Directions: The sinkhole lies directly across the Mountain Loop Highway, 19.1 miles from Granite Falls.

For more information: Snohomish County Courthouse, 3000 Rockefeller Avenue, Everett, WA 98201. Phone (425) 388-3411.

SILVERTON

[Fig. 26(10)] A few houses beside the road here, mostly used as summer cabins, are all that is left of the mining town of Silverton, which, in 1897, had a population of 3,000. There are many vestiges of the mining days in the vicinity, including the site of a 9,000-

foot-cable tramway that brought ore to the railroad from the 45-mine on the other side of the high ridge between the Stillaguamish Valley and the Sultan Basin. One mile beyond Silverton the county stops plowing the road in the wintertime, making possible numerous winter activities, including cross-country skiing, sledding, snowman making, snowmobiling, and snowshoeing.

Directions: Silverton is on both sides of the Mountain Loop Highway, 22.5 miles from Granite Falls.

LABRADOR TEA
(Ledum groenlandicum)
Growing up to three feet tall, this is an evergreen with white blooms.

🏵 BIG FOUR ICE CAVES TRAIL 723

[Fig. 26(11)] This is a short and easy trail from the remnants of a large, luxurious resort to the ice caves at the foot of massive, rugged 6,135-foot Big Four Mountain, which some say was named for four tall brothers who once homesteaded here, while others say it was named because a rock formation on its east side shows a large figure four, and still others say it was named because it has four major peaks.

Regardless of the derivation of the name, the ice caves are a fascinating, if dangerous, phenomenon. They are formed in massive fields of ice, which result from avalanches that smash down from cliffs on the mountainside during the winter, forming interwoven, fan-shaped piles that seem to lean back on the bottom of the cliffs that spawned them. In the summertime, melting snow on the mountainside forms numerous waterfalls between the cliffs and the snow piles. The water forces its way under the ice, melting out caves which become huge by the end of the summer.

The ceiling of the caves turns an eerie blue when the sun shines on them and that adds to the temptation to enter them, but the ice is unstable and the roof can collapse at any moment. This has caused death and injury to people who ignored the warning signs and ventured inside the caves, or who climbed onto the ice above and fell through to the rocky floor when the ice collapsed beneath them.

The trailhead is a picnic ground where the huge inn of the resort stood before it burned in 1949. Nothing is left but a massive, stone fireplace that once graced the lobby, and some sidewalks that once led to the nine-hole golf course, the tennis courts, and the artificial lake. Picnic tables now occupy what once was the lawn.

The short, easy trail goes down the former railroad right of way, then along the old concrete walkway, past a beaver pond and through a delightful forest of Douglas fir, hemlock, and cedar trees. A long foot bridge crosses the rocky South Fork of the Stillaguamish River, providing magnificent views of the countryside. The trail is said to be the most popular in the Mount Baker-Snoqualmie National Forest, and can be crowded on a sunny, summer weekend.

Directions: A side road to one parking lot at the former resort forks off the south side of the Mountain Loop Highway 25.5 miles from Granite Falls. A few hundred feet farther on the highway is the entrance to a second parking lot that was recently opened.

Facilities: Picnic tables, interpretative signs, and vault toilets at the trailhead.

Dates: Seasonal, summer.

Fees: A trailhead fee may be charged.

For more information: From spring through fall, Verlot Public Service Center, 33515 Mountain Loop Highway, Granite Falls, WA 98252. Phone (360) 691-7791. Or, year-round, Darrington Ranger Station, 1405 Emmens Street. Phone (360) 436-1155.

Trail: 1 mile.

Elevation: 200 feet elevation gain.

Degree of difficulty: Easy.

MOUNT DICKERMAN TRAIL 710

[Fig. 26(12)] This steep trail begins with 2 miles of steep switchbacks in a typical western Cascades forest of Douglas firs, which merge into Alaska cedar, and subalpine pine as the trail rises to the high country.

After 2 miles, the trail makes a sharp turn to the left at a pleasant waterfall, then makes a turn to the right and passes a small lake hidden behind a stand of trees. There are campsites at the lake. The trail levels a bit past the lake and emerges into a 0.5 mile-long patch of blueberry bushes. When the berries ripen, they live up to their Latin name of *Vaccinium deliciosum*, and that often slows hikers considerably. A little later in the season, the blueberry leaves turn a brilliant red that paints the entire mountainside when the sun shines on them.

From there, the trail passes through meadows, leads through some switchbacks and ends at a broad meadow on the top. The snowy slopes of Glacier Peak loom 15 miles to the northeast. To the west, Mount Three Finger points rocky digits to the sky, and the entire horizon shows the jagged, rock of innumerable peaks, named and unnamed.

Directions: The trailhead is at a small parking lot directly beside the Mountain Loop Highway 27.7 miles from Granite Falls.

Dates: Seasonal, summer.

Fees: A parking fee may be charged.

For more information: From spring through fall, Verlot Public Service Center, 33515 Mountain Loop Highway, Granite Falls, WA 98252. Phone (360) 691-7791. Or, year-round, Darrington Ranger Station, 1405 Emmens Street. Phone (360) 436-1155.

Trail: 4.25 miles, one-way.

Elevation: 3,900 feet elevation gain.

Degree of difficulty: Difficult.

SUNRISE MINE TRAIL 707

[Fig. 26(13)] This trail begins at a viewpoint where the Sunrise Mine Road ends. The viewpoint provides wide views of the mountains and the valley. The viewpoint also is the trailhead for the trail that begins with a rough tread composed of rocks and roots and goes steeply up, crossing several rushing streams in the first 0.5 mile, including one with a hair-raising log bridge. But that is just the beginning of the travail. The route is an exceedingly steep miners' trail that was created with the miners' characteristic disregard for grade. The trail is not especially long. It is especially steep and rough.

The first 0.5 mile is in forest that has struggled to survive in the thin, rocky soil. The view clears after that, going past exposed, jagged rock spires and through fields of ferns in a series of steep switchbacks. That leads to a narrow gully with an old mine shaft gouged into the hard rock at the entrance.

The trail goes on steeply up the 1-mile-long gully toward Headlee Pass at the far end. The pass is a narrow gap in the cliff which is difficult and unsafe to maneuver and doesn't really lead to anything worthwhile.

During the winter, deep avalanches cover sections of the trail in places where there are sheer drops next to the route. The snow does not melt away until late in the summer, and some remnants may last all year. That adds to the danger, and it is strongly recommended that hikers wait until the last of the snow is gone before they venture onto the trail.

Directions: The Sunrise Mine Road (Forest Road 4065) meets the south side of the Mountain Loop Road, 28.1 miles from Granite Falls. The Sunrise Mine Trailhead is at the far end of the viewpoint, where the Sunrise Mine Road ends, 2.3 miles from the Mountain Loop Highway.

Dates: Seasonal, summer.

Fees: A trailhead fee may be charged.

For more information: From spring through fall, Verlot Public Service Center, 33515 Mountain Loop Highway, Granite Falls, WA 98252. Phone (360) 691-7791. Or, year-round, Darrington Ranger Station, 1405 Emmens Street. Phone (360) 436-1155.

Trail: 2.5 miles one-way.

Elevation: 2,500 feet elevation gain.

Degree of difficulty: Difficult.

BARLOW PASS

[Fig. 26(14)] This low pass between the valleys of the South Fork of the Stillagua-mish River and the Sauk River is named

QUEEN ANNE'S LACE
(Daucus carota)
Growing to 5 feet tall, the plant's flowers are creamy white with a single dark flower in the center.

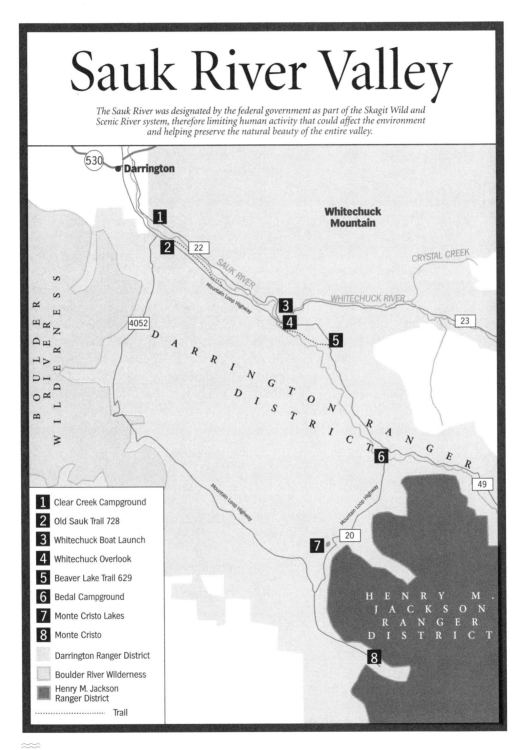

Sauk River Valley

The Sauk River was designated by the federal government as part of the Skagit Wild and Scenic River system, therefore limiting human activity that could affect the environment and helping preserve the natural beauty of the entire valley.

530 • Darrington

Whitechuck Mountain

CRYSTAL CREEK

1

2 22

SAUK RIVER

Mountain Loop Highway

WHITECHUCK RIVER

BOULDER RIVER WILDERNESS

4052

3

4

5

23

D A R R I N G T O N   R A N G E R   D I S T R I C T

6

49

Mountain Loop Highway

Mountain Loop Highway

7 20

1 Clear Creek Campground

2 Old Sauk Trail 728

3 Whitechuck Boat Launch

4 Whitechuck Overlook

5 Beaver Lake Trail 629

6 Bedal Campground

7 Monte Cristo Lakes

8 Monte Cristo

Darrington Ranger District

Boulder River Wilderness

Henry M. Jackson Ranger District

.... Trail

H E N R Y   M.
J A C K S O N
R A N G E R
D I S T R I C T

8

after J. P. Barlow, a surveyor who discovered it in 1891 while he was looking for a route for the Everett Monte Cristo Railway. The original plan had been for the railroad to follow what had first been a trail, then a wagon road down the Sauk River from Monte Cristo to the Skagit River, where steamboats could carry supplies. But that route was nearly 50 miles long and Barlow's discovery led to a decision to adopt a new, shorter, easier, and cheaper route over the pass and down the South Fork of the Stillaguamish.

Early in the twentieth century the pass was the location of a Forest Service guard station and a storehouse of the Penn Mining Company, which was working a mine on the other side of the mountain from Monte Cristo (*see* Goat Lake Trail 647, page 143). This also is the trailhead for the hike to the site of Monte Cristo which has become a ghost town amidst a regrown forest where the buildings once stood (*see* Monte Cristo Ghost Town, page 173).

The pass also is the location of a portion of the railroad right of way that was blasted out of the solid rock of the side of Dickerman Mountain. A short trail following the right of way has interpretative signs with photos that depict the route as it was at the turn of the twentieth century. The trail goes through patches of ferns, shrubs, and small trees where the trains once ran, but there are open spaces that give good views of the valley.

The Sauk River Valley

[Fig. 27] This valley is the other end of what has become the Mountain Loop Highway (also known as the Mountain Loop Scenic Byway). The Sauk River is a tributary of the Skagit River, and a large section of the valley, beginning at the confluence with Elliott Creek (*see* Goat Lake Trail 647, page 143), was designated by the federal government as part of the Skagit Wild and Scenic River system. That designation limits human activity that could affect the environment in and near the river, and helps preserve the natural beauty of the entire valley.

The 8-mile stretch of the road from Darrington to the confluence with the White-chuck River is paved and relatively straight. From there it goes 12 miles to the South Fork of the Stillaguamish River at Barlow Pass over a twisting, one-lane gravel roadway with turnouts where oncoming cars can pass each other. It is a beautiful valley with a fascinating history but the road requires cautious driving.

Directions: The Sauk Valley section of the Mountain Loop Highway is also known as Forest Road 20. To reach it, take the Mountain Loop Highway from Darrington for 2.5 miles to the national forest boundary.

Activities: Camping, hiking, mountain climbing, mountain biking, hunting, fishing, snowmobiling, cross-country skiing, snowshoeing, and white water boating.

Facilities: Campgrounds, trails, boat launch, scenic overlook.

Dates: Open year-round.

Fees: Camping fees are charged and a trailhead fee may be charged.

Closest town: Darrington, 2.5 miles from the national forest border.

A hike along the Sauk River reveals a forest rich in old-growth trees, mosses, and lichens.

Fees: Camping fees are charged.

For more information: Darrington Ranger Station, 1405 Emmens Street. Phone (360) 436-1155. Or the Outdoor Recreation Information Center, 222 Yale Avenue North, Seattle, WA 98109-5429. Phone (206) 470-4060.

CLEAR CREEK CAMPGROUND

[Fig. 27(1)] This pleasant campground has 10 sites for tents or trailers and features a fish-habitat program in a side channel of the Sauk River, which attracts spawning salmon which, in turn, attract bald eagles that feast on the spawned-out carcasses of the fish during the winter.

Directions: The entrance to the campground is on the Mountain Loop Highway 0.5 mile inside the national forest border.

Activities: Camping, hunting, fishing,. hiking, mountain biking, cross-country skiing, snowshoeing, snowmobiling.

Facilities: Pit toilets, fire pits, picnic tables.

Dates: Seasonal, summer.

OLD SAUK TRAIL 728

[Fig. 27(2)] This pleasant, level trail along the bank of the Sauk River leads through old-growth forest of large conifer and, especially, of alder which, like others of their *Alnus* species, absorb nitrogen from the air and store it in nodules on their roots. The nitrogen enters the soil from the nodules and also through leaves, which fall to the ground in the autumn and release the nitrogen into the soil, where it becomes fertilizer for other plants.

The trail begins and ends at the Mountain Loop Highway, and it leads through a floodplain, in the deep forest between the Sauk River and the Mountain Loop Highway, always within a stone's throw of each. The route is a green maze with the trunks of the trees and fallen logs covered in deep-green moss and the branches dripping with chartreuse lichen. The canopy is so thick that little sunlight penetrates to the ground, and the atmosphere seems to take on a hint of the thick green colors of the forest.

Near the south end of the trail, Murphy Creek, a traditional spawning area for salmon and steelhead, empties into the Sauk and man-made fish-habitat structures may be seen from the trail.

Directions: The northern trailhead is on the Mountain Loop Highway 0.8 mile inside the national forest border. The southern trailhead is on the Mountain Loop Highway, 4.3 miles inside the national forest boundary.

Dates: Seasonal, summer.

Fees: A trailhead fee may be charged.

Trail: 3.5 miles. 1 way.

Degree of difficulty: Easy.

WHITECHUCK BOAT LAUNCH

[Fig. 27(3)] This facility provides entry into the wild waters of the Sauk River for boating and rafting. These waters, however, include restricted passages and a series of long, difficult rapids, and should be attempted only by persons with the necessary experience, knowledge and equipment. The boat launch is at the confluence of the Sauk and Whitechuck rivers, and the heavily silted waters that the Whitechuck carries from the glaciers of Glacier Peak mingle with the clear, green water of the Sauk, changing the appearance of the Sauk.

Directions: The boat launch entrance is 6.3 miles inside the national forest boundary on the Mountain Loop Highway.

Facilities: Restrooms, interpretative signs.

WHITECHUCK OVERLOOK

[Fig. 27(4)] This overlook is a good place to get a rare, wide view of the Sauk Valley, including mountain goats, which sometimes can be seen on the rocky sides of White-chuck Mountain across the valley. The overlook is in a small clear-cut near the river. The replanted forest was thinned in 1985 and 1992 and the remaining Douglas fir are nearing maturity.

Directions: The entry to the overlook is on the north side of the Mountain Loop Highway, 6.6 miles inside the national forest boundary.

Facilities: Restrooms, picnic tables.

Dates: Seasonal, summer.

BEAVER LAKE TRAIL 629

[Fig. 27(5)] This 3.2 mile trail was neatly divided in two by an immense, impassable landslide, and now it is two trails that end within a few hundred feet of each other. The trail follows an almost completely level section of the railroad of the Sauk River Lumber Company that logged much of the Sauk River lowlands above Darrington in the early 1900s.

WOOD DUCK
(Aix sponsa)

The north half of the trail passes some immense beaver ponds that may have existed when the railroad was still running. The ponds are a good demonstration of the engineering ability of the beavers, which used sticks and twigs to dam a creek and create what amounts to a small lake.

The south half of the trail passes impressive remnants of moss-covered train trestles. Near the trailhead is an immense western redcedar that measures 48 feet in circumference. This *Thuja plicata* once had a Forest Service ranger station at its base. In 1916 the tree served as a fire lookout for the ranger who climbed it on spikes pounded into the bark to look for smoke. The ranger, the ranger station, and the spikes are gone, but the gigantic tree is as impressive as ever.

Directions: The trailhead at the north end of the trail is on the Mountain Loop Highway, 6 miles inside the national forest boundary. The trailhead on the south end is on the highway, 8.6 miles inside the boundary.

Dates: Seasonal, summer.

Fees: A trailhead fee may be charged.

Trail: Both segments of the trail are about 1.5 miles long.

BEDAL CAMPGROUND

[Fig. 27(6)] This drive-in campground deep in the mountains has 22 campsites, including five suitable for trailers. There are wheelchair-accessible vault toilets and a picnic shelter. The campground is named after the Bedal family, whose members homesteaded here during the gold mining era. Nearby, a Mr. Morehouse established a trading post and a post office called Orient at the turn of the twentieth century. The homesteaders left after the mines petered out, and the land reverted to the government. The Civilian Conservation Corps built the campground during the 1930s.

This is part of the forest that was clear-cut by the Sauk River Lumber Company in the 1930s, but second-growth conifers give the rustic campground the taste of wilderness. Heavy precipitation makes the Sauk Valley ideal for ferns, which grow lushly here. Fossils found near the campground bear the imprint of ferns from the time of the dinosaurs.

Directions: The entrance to the campground is on the Mountain Loop Highway, 13.6 miles inside the national forest border. Note: the Sauk River forks at Bedal Campground and the Mountain Loop Highway follows the south fork.

Facilities: Picnic shelter, fire pits, wheelchair accessible, vault toilets.

Dates: Seasonal, summer.

Fees: Camping fees are charged.

MONTE CRISTO LAKES

[Fig. 27(7)] Three shallow lakes, called collectively the Monte Cristo Lakes, are the result of glacial moraines that dammed the Sauk River during the Ice Age that ended some 16,000 years ago. Tailings from the old mines at Monte Cristo are gradually washing down the Sauk River, and filling the lakes with silt to the point that they are becoming wetlands and meadows.

The lakes were a favorite place for Indians of the Sauk Tribe to camp while they hunted elk during the summer, and the quiet water still attracts fishermen seeking cutthroat, rainbow, Dolly Varden, and bull trout, as well as coho salmon and steelhead.

The lakes are 1.7 miles from Barlow Pass where the Sauk River portion of the Mountain Loop Highway meets the headwaters of the South Fork of the Stillaguamish Valley, and where the road is paved.

Directions: The lakes are on both sides of the Mountain Loop Highway, 18 miles inside the forest boundary.

Activities: Fishing, hunting.

Dates: Seasonal summer and fall.

🐍 MONTE CRISTO GHOST TOWN

Rattlesnake

The only poisonous snake native to Washington's Cascades is the western rattlesnake (*Crotalus viridis oreganus*). Its venom can be lethal to children and small animals but usually is only very painful to adults. It is about 16 inches to 5 feet long and heavily built. It is found on the lower elevations of the dry, east side of the Cascades, some say always below 4,000 feet in elevation, but there are no guarantees of that. They hunt from dusk to dawn often in rocky places. They flee from humans rather than fight but, again, there are no guarantees.

[Fig. 26(18), Fig. 27(8)] At Barlow Pass, where the Sauk and South Fork Monte Cristo portions of the Mountain Loop Highway meet, a spur route goes 4 miles to the south to the ghost town of Monte Cristo at the headwaters of the South Fork of the Sauk River (*see* Monte Cristo Ghost Town Trails, page 144). This route originally was the right of way for the Everett Monte Cristo Railway. After the railroad went out of business, the tracks were removed and it became an extension of County Road 92. Eventually a series of landslides damaged the road so badly that the county put up a gate at the pass. It gives keys only to owners of property beyond the gate, who must agree not to hold the county legally responsible for accidents due to the unsafe roadway.

For everyone else the road, maintained sporadically by property owners, is a 4-mile hike or bike ride (*see* Monte Cristo Ghost Town Trails, page 144). The hike follows the old railroad right of way through largely second-growth forest, and some open places with good views of nearby mountains. Bridges across the Sauk River are sometimes washed out during the same kind of floods that doomed the railroad. It may be months before the property owners can repair them.

There are rustic campgrounds along the old road and another at the entrance to the ghost town. They offer little beyond toilets and fire rings.

The trail to Monte Cristo goes past magnificent stands of trees beside an attractive stream. Except for a few short spots, it is level. It attracts many hikers and mountain bikers say it may be the most popular mountain-bike route in Washington. Once miners were active along the trail and several historic sites along the way are marked with interpretive signs.

Skykomish Ranger District

Skykomish Ranger District encompasses 425,000 acres in the middle of the Mount Baker-Snoqualmie National Forest's five ranger districts, and is divided by US Highway 2.

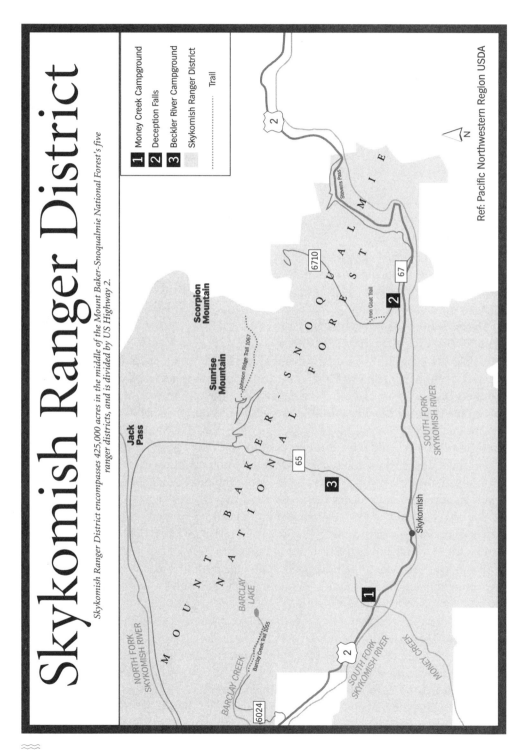

1 Money Creek Campground
2 Deception Falls
3 Beckler River Campground

Skykomish Ranger District

.... Trail

Ref: Pacific Northwestern Region USDA

Directions: The Monte Cristo Ghost Town trailhead is at Barlow Pass, 30 miles from Granite Falls on the Mountain Loop Highway.

Activities: Hiking, camping, hunting, and fishing.

Dates: Seasonal, summer.

Fees: A trailhead fee may be charged.

For more information: From spring through fall, Verlot Public Service Center, 33515 Mountain Loop Highway, Granite Falls, WA 98252. Phone (360) 691-7791. Or, year-round, Darrington Ranger Station, 1405 Emmens Street. Phone (360) 436-1155.

Trail: 4 miles, one-way.

Elevation: 432 feet elevation gain.

Skykomish Ranger District

[Fig. 28] The 425,000-acre Skykomish Ranger District is the middle of the Mount Baker-Snoqualmie National Forest's five ranger districts, and is divided by US Highway 2.

Highway 2 leads to many of the district's attractions, and travels within less than a mile of both the Henry M. Jackson Wilderness and the Alpine Lakes Wilderness. Aside from containing a major highway, the Skykomish District is very similar to the rest of the Mount Baker-Snoqualmie National Forest. The lowland forest is largely Douglas fir, western hemlock, and western redcedar. In the higher elevations, those trees tend to be supplanted by mountain hemlock, subalpine fir, and Pacific silver fir. A large assortment of wildlife includes deer, which often may be seen browsing in open areas. Black bears are seen less often. There are a few cougars but, being cougars, they usually take great pains to avoid detection.

US Highway 2 has been known locally as the Stevens Pass Highway since before the national roadway was built. The highway begins in Everett and heads toward the Midwest, but the first 66 miles lead toward Stevens Pass, and the eastern 16 miles of that segment have been declared a scenic byway, meeting the Wenatchee National Forest's 30-mile portion of the byway at Stevens Pass.

The US Highway 2 route to Stevens Pass is a major attraction in itself. It begins in the sea-level, urban setting of Everett and passes through ever more rural country. It goes through farmlands, lowland forests, mountain foothills, midlevel foothills, and, finally, the high country of the pass, 4,062 feet in elevation, passing through both old-growth and second-growth forest. The route parallels the right of way of the Burlington Northern Railroad, which originally was called the Great Northern Railroad. Part of the highway is located on old railroad grades that were built in the 1890s and abandoned by the railroad when it opened tunnels to bypass some of the original route.

There are many attractions along the way for people with a wide range of interests.

Directions: The Skykomish Ranger Station is central to the district. It is on the north side of US Highway 2, 2 miles east of Skykomish.

Activities: Camping, hiking, mountain climbing, mountain biking, hunting, fishing, snowmobiling, cross-country skiing, downhill skiing, snowshoeing.

Facilities: Campgrounds, downhill ski area, groomed cross-country ski area.

Dates: Open year-round.

Fees: Fees are charged for downhill skiing, groomed cross-country ski trails, camping, and a trailhead parking fee may be charged.

For more information: Skykomish Ranger Station, 74920 NE Stevens Pass Highway, Post Office Box 305, Skykomish, WA, 98288. Phone (360) 677-2414, or The Outdoor Recreation Information Center, 222 Yale Avenue North, Seattle, WA 98109-5429. Phone (206) 470-4060.

JOHNSON RIDGE TRAIL 1067

[Fig. 28] This is not an easy trail for either people on foot or on mountain bikes, but the views are very nice, and it is used so seldom that some parts are overgrown and difficult to find.

The route from the trailhead follows the very upward contours of Johnson Ridge, passing through meadows that display bouquets of flowers, beginning early in the spring with yellow glacier lilies and white avalanche lilies poking their heads through the last few inches of snow cover. The flowering species change through the rest of the season until the snow returns in the autumn. Among the late bloomers are red, orange, or yellow Indian paintbrush and blue or purple lupine. Lupine is a legume that fixes nitrogen in the meadow soil, enriching it for the many other plants in the meadow.

The trail parallels the top of Sunrise Mountain, elevation 5,050 feet, then goes down the other side of the mountain and back up Scorpion Mountain, elevation 5,500 feet, where it ends. An off-trail scramble of a few hundred feet goes to the lush meadow at the peak, where there are panoramic views in every direction.

Directions: On US Highway 2 about 0.2 mile east of Skykomish, turn north onto the Beckler River Road, Forest Road 65. Drive approximately 7 miles, then turn right onto Forest Road 6520. Go about 5.6 miles, turn right onto Forest Road 6526, and go about 1.5 miles to the trailhead.

Dates: Seasonal, summer.

Fees: A trailhead fee may be charged.

Trail: 4 miles one-way for hikers, can be extended to 12 miles for mountain bikers who elect to ride on the road to the trailhead.

Elevation: 2,300 feet from the trailhead, 4,700 feet from Forest Road 6520.

Degree of difficulty: Strenuous.

MONEY CREEK CAMPGROUND-JACK PASS LOOP ROAD

[Fig. 28(1)] Money Creek is not a place to go to escape from civilization. It is within sound of busy US Highway 2 and the whistles of the Burlington Northern Railroad. Some campers here are simply travelers who stop for the night, then strike camp and leave the next morning. Still, for those who don't object to the noise, it is a nice place to spend a few days.

The campground has 23 tent-or-trailer sites, 3 picnic sites, piped water, vault toilets, and fire pits. Camping fees are charged. The campground is central to many attractions, including fishing in the South Fork of the Skykomish River just outside of many of the 24 campsites. Swimming is also possible, but only for those people who don't mind extremely cold water.

Just 3.5 miles east on the highway is the village of Skykomish, the last settlement on US 2 west of Stevens Pass, and an interesting place to spend a few hours exploring turn-of-the-century, railroad-town architecture.

About 0.2 mile east of Skykomish, the Beckler River Road, Forest Road 65, goes north from US Highway 2 for about 13 miles to Jack Pass, passing the Beckler River Campground [Fig. 28(3)], which is more isolated than the Money Creek Campground. It has 27 campsites for either tents or trailers, some of them wheelchair accessible, as well as vault toilets, drinking water, and a picnic area. A camping fee is charged.

From Jack Pass, Forest Road 65 goes approximately 19 miles south, running beside the North Fork of the Skykomish River, back to US Highway 2. It goes through some isolated areas which support forests that vary in type from lowland to high country. It passes Garland Mineral Springs, once the site of a popular mountain resort, several trailheads, some mining relics, and innumerable fishing spots along the river. This is a popular area for deer hunters in the proper season, and there are good views of the mountains.

Three miles west of Jack Pass is San Juan Campground, which has 9 tent or trailer campsites, vault toilets and fire pits. A camping fee is charged. Two miles west of San Juan Campground is the larger, more sophisticated Troublesome Creek Campground with 24 tent-or-trailer campsites and 6 walk-in campsites where it is necessary to carry equipment a few feet to the site. There are five picnic sites, vault toilets, water from a hand pump, and fires pits. A camping fee is charged.

Near the end of Forest Road 65 is Index, another quaint village, and just outside of Index is the formidable Index Climbing Wall, a solid-rock cliff popular with rock climbers. About 0.5 mile from Index, Forest Road joins US Highway 2, and 10 miles east on the highway is the Money Creek Campground where the trip began.

Directions: Money Creek Campground is 3.5 miles west of Skykomish on US Highway 2.

Activities: Camping, fishing, hunting, exploring quaint villages and backcountry.

Facilities: Picnic area, vault toilets, drinking water, fire rings.

Dates: Seasonal, summer.

Fees: There is a camping fee.

Closest town: Skykomish, 3.5 miles.

For more information: Skykomish Ranger Station, 74920 NE Stevens Pass Highway, Post Office Box 305, Skykomish, WA, 98288. Phone (360) 677-2414, or The Outdoor Recreation Information Center, 222 Yale Avenue North, Seattle, WA 98109-5429. Phone (206) 470-4060.

🪨 BARCLAY CREEK TRAIL 1055

[Fig. 28] This trail passes through some forest stands and clear-cut forests, paralleling Barclay Creek for about 1.5 miles to long, narrow Barclay Lake, where there are campsites and good views of Baring Mountain, 6,125 feet high with bare, perpendicular walls. Some of Baring Mountain's climbing routes are considered a major challenge, even by the most skilled climbers.

The trail to the lake is level and makes for a good hike in early spring or late fall. Because it's relatively low in elevation, snow comes late and leaves early. There may be some muddy places and the route undulates somewhat, but it is essentially level.

A faint side trail goes beyond Barclay Lake through steep, rocky terrain, gaining 1,466 feet in elevation in less than 2 miles, going through deep forest, and ending at Eagle Lake.

Directions: On US Highway 2, about 6 miles east of Index, turn north on the County Road called 635 Place NE, which becomes Forest Road 6024. Drive approximately 4.5 miles to the trailhead at the end of that road.

Activities: Hiking, camping, hunting, and fishing.

Dates: Seasonal, summer.

Fees: A trailhead fee may be charged.

Trail: Approximately 2.25 miles to the far end of Barclay Lake.

Elevation: 225 feet elevation gain.

Degree of difficulty: Easy.

🪨 IRON GOAT TRAIL

[Fig. 28] This is a long-abandoned section of the Great Northern Railroad that volunteers, working with the Forest Service, have transformed into a trail that tells the fascinating story of the men who built and operated the railroad under seemingly impossible conditions. It also is a quiet place of awesome beauty where the steel and steam of the railroad once reigned.

The trail is the two ends of a section of track that went into a tunnel, made a 170 degree turn, and came out at a different level. It was an ingenious way to reduce the grade of the tracks, so the train could negotiate the mountain slopes. Ernie Spencer, an early engineer on the trains noted, "I could look down and spit on the tail of my own train."

This part of the railroad was built in 1893 and abandoned in 1929, when the railroad was rerouted through a new tunnel. The bridges to the old tunnel collapsed long ago, so it is no longer accessible. The right of way on both ends became overgrown, but the Forest Service volunteers cleared a narrow trail, where the tracks once were, to make a trail that passes through the beauty of the new growth. Interpretative signs tell the history of the men, many of them Japanese immigrants, who suffered the hardships of weather, long work hours, and primitive living conditions of railroad construction more than a century ago. Huge old construction timbers mark where the hillside was shored up to prevent avalanches.

The trail is composed of two, parallel, 3-mile segments, one on each end of the tunnel. Two cross trails, called Corea and Martin Creek by the old railroad men, make it easy to get from one to the other. A little more than a mile of the lower trail is leveled and graveled for wheelchairs. The route passes through new growth of alder, hemlock, and cedar trees, while the understory is green with moss, shrubs, and huge ferns. Some of the ferns are more than 6 feet tall. Several viewpoints along the way give wide views of the valley of the South Fork of the Skykomish River.

Brochures describing the historic trail are available at the Skykomish District Ranger Station, 1 mile east of Skykomish on US Highway 2.

Directions: Go 9 miles east of Skykomish on US Highway 2 and turn north onto the Old Stevens Pass Highway, Forest Road 67, then go 1.7 miles and take the fork to the right onto Forest Road 6710. The trailhead is 1.5 miles from the fork.

Facilities: There are vault toilets at the trailhead.

Dates: Seasonal, summer.

Fees: A trailhead fee may be charged.

Trail: Two segments, each 3 miles long, one-way.

Elevation: 100 feet elevation gain.

Degree of difficulty: Easy.

DECEPTION FALLS

[Fig. 28(2)] This is a glorified, day-use, picnic area beside US Highway 2 that has paved parking, vault toilets, and sheltered picnic tables. It also has a 0.2 mile trail to Deception Falls, where Deception Creek falls 60 feet in thundering, white froth, an awesome vista. Even more interesting is the 0.5-mile trail that leads to Lower Falls. Although not as big as Deception Falls, it has deep, blue-green pools above and below the white cascades, and provides another awesome site just a short distance from the parking lot.

The longer trail also courses through old-growth forest of tall Douglas fir trees approximately 280 years old. Studies show that the Douglas firs succeeded a 600-year-old cedar forest that was destroyed by fire. Mosses and lichens decorate the branches above the trail. A rare white pine (*Pinus monticola*) stands

The day-use picnic area at Deception Falls.

beside the trail, one of the survivors of the white pine blister rush that has decimated the species. The disease was brought to this country in a shipment of seedlings from France in 1909. Foresters hope that either natural or scientifically engineered resistance can be bred into the species, and bring it back from near extinction.

A few feet beyond the white pine is a new forest mixed with huge stumps of trees that were clear-cut in the 1890s. The stumps still bear the gouges the loggers cut out to hold the springboards they stood on to work their saws and axes, several feet above ground level. Several old logs and stumps along the trail bear nurse trees, that have taken root on the old wood.

Directions: 8 miles east of Skykomish on US Highway 2.

Activities: Hiking, picnicking.

Facilities: Restrooms, picnic tables, interpretative trails.

Dates: Seasonal, summer.

Closest town: Skykomish, 8 miles.

For more information: Skykomish Ranger Station, 74920 NE Stevens Pass Highway, Post Office Box 305, Skykomish, WA, 98288. Phone (360) 677-2414, or The Outdoor Recreation Information Center, 222 Yale Avenue North, Seattle, WA 98109-5429. Phone (206) 470-4060.

Trail: 0.5 mile and O.2 mile.

Degree of difficulty: Easy.

STEVENS PASS

[Fig. 28] At 4,060 feet, this is the high point of US Highway 2 in Washington. During the summer there is little of interest here, except that the Pacific Crest Trail crosses the highway at the summit. The section of the trail to the north of the highway follows the roadbed where the Great Northern's first tracks crossed the pass. It is a pleasant, level hike of about 1 mile, with views of the valley below. It once was popular for cross-country skiing, but it is avalanche prone and after a series of accidents, it has become much less used in the winter.

The south side of the pass, however, is the site of the extensive and popular Stevens Pass Ski Area.

With 1,800 feet vertical drop, the top elevation is 5,700 feet. There are 10 lifts, with a combined capacity of 15,210 persons an hour. The lifts serve 37 runs on 1,125 acres open to both skis and snowboards. About 11 percent of the runs are classified for beginning skiers, 54 percent for intermediate skiers, and 35 percent for advanced skiers. The slopes go between stands of attractive, high-country mountain hemlock, and subalpine and Pacific fir. The ski area rents snow tubes to be used on a groomed, snow-tube run, served by a rope tow.

The average snowfall at the pass is 415 inches. There is night skiing, a retail shop, and three day lodges that serve food and drink in four restaurants, as well as rent and repair skis, and provide child care. There is no lodging at the pass.

The ski area provides groomed cross-country skiing on the Mill Creek Road, just off US Highway 2, 5 miles east of the pass in the Wenatchee National Forest. The main route is rated easiest and goes about 4 miles to the bottom of one of the ski area's downhill runs. Several branches along the way are graded for intermediate and advanced skiers.

Parking, food, ski passes, and rentals are available at the base of the main route.

Directions: The pass is 15 miles east of Skykomish on US Highway 2.

Activities: Hiking, downhill, and cross-country skiing.

Facilities: The downhill area has 37 runs, 10 chair lifts, a rope tow, and 3 day lodges with 4 restaurants, ski rentals, ski repair, a shop, and a ski school. The cross-country area has a small day lodge, a restaurant, and ski rental.

Dates: Hiking in summer. Skiing in winter.

Fees: There are fees for lift passes, cross-country skiing and services at the ski area during the winter. A trailhead fee may be charged during the summer.

Closest town: Skykomish, 15 miles.

For more information: Stevens Pass, PO Box 98, Skykomish, WA 98288. Phone (360) 973-2441. For snow conditions, phone (425)352-4400.

North Bend Ranger District

This is the most heavily visited ranger district in the Mount Baker-Snoqualmie National Forest, mainly because it is bisected by Interstate Highway 90, which gives it a direct connection to the more than 530,000 people who live in Seattle, 30 miles away. Additionally, thousands of people on the freeway cross through the district on their way to or from somewhere else. The 343,000-acre district certainly will be one of the most beautiful places on their trip, no matter where they are going. The highway starts in Seattle at about sea level, and rises through suburban communities, farms, and forests to Snoqualmie Pass, elevation 3,060 feet, where four major ski areas have been consolidated into a single venture.

Local communities, businesses, individuals, the Forest Service and other state and federal agencies have banded together to form the Mountains to Sound Greenway agency that is enhancing the natural beauty of the valley of the South Fork of the Snoqualmie River, where the freeway is located. And many of the attractions of the area are outside the national forest boundary but are part of the outdoor attractions of the general area.

Directions: Interstate Highway 90 crosses the ranger district border about 30 miles east of Seattle. The ranger station is in the city of North Bend at 42404 SE North Bend Way, North Bend WA 98042.

Activities: In and near the ranger district borders, there are hiking, camping, mountain biking, swimming, boating, mountain climbing, horseback riding, downhill skiing, cross-country skiing,

Facilities: Trails, campgrounds, parks, ski areas, visitor centers.

Dates: Open year-round.

Fees: Fees are charged for camping and downhill skiing, and some services. A trailhead fee may be charged.

Closest town: North Bend, 10 miles from the district boundary.

For more information: North Bend Ranger Station, 42404 SE North Bend Way, North Bend, WA 98042. Phone, (425) 888-1421

THE SUMMIT AT SNOQUALMIE SKI AREA

This popular ski area is on Snoqualmie Pass [Fig. 25(2)], elevation 3,010 feet, which, in the space of 150 years, has gone from an Indian trail to a modern transportation route featuring railroads and Interstate Highway 90. The super highway makes it easy and quick to travel the 60 miles from Seattle. Perhaps for that reason, it attracts large numbers of skiers.

The pass has four different downhill ski areas, which once were separate operations. They now have been combined under a single ownership, which is improving the already popular facilities that attract a total of some 500,000 people a year. Each of the four areas has its own facilities, its own character, and its own clientele. Lodging is available at the pass.

PHOEBUS PARNASSIAN

(Parnassius phoebus)

Flying in colder temperatures than many other butterflies, the phoebus is identified by gray markings and red spots on the white male and transparent female.

Three of the areas are connected by trails, and the fourth, Alpental At The Summit, is connected to the others by a shuttle-bus on weekends and holidays. At other times it is necessary to drive between that area and the others. One lift ticket is accepted at all four areas.

There are also some 50 kilometers of groomed, cross-country ski facilities, and a snow-play area with groomed chutes for sliding on inner tubes and plastic equipment. Details of the 6 areas follow:

ALPENTAL AT THE SUMMIT. With runs frequented by expert skiers, this area has a 3,200-foot base, a 2,200 foot vertical rise, and four lifts. It features Snoqualmie Pass's most challenging runs. There are sheer faces, steep chutes, and cliffs. Two day lodges offer restaurants, a bar—open on weekends— lockers, sports shop, repairs and lessons.

SUMMIT WEST. This is a place of gentle slopes and slow chairlifts as well as some more challenging runs. It has a 900 vertical foot rise and a base of 3,000 feet elevation. There are five lifts, including two quad chairs. It has two day lodges, with several restaurants, and a bar. Ski and snowboard schools operate here, and beginners can get packages that include equipment rental and lessons. Two day lodges have restaurants, a bar and grill, and rentals.

SUMMIT CENTRAL. There is terrain here for everyone from beginning skier to advanced, but much of it is for intermediate skiers. The base is at 2,860 feet elevation, and the vertical rise is 1,040 feet. There are eight lifts and lighting for night skiing. A day lodge has a restaurant, day care for children, rentals, and ski/snowboard schools. During the summer, the Summit Central Ski Area operates its Silver Fir Chair lift to take hikers and mountain bike riders and their bikes to a 35-mile network of high-country trails. The bike trails range in difficulty from beginner, to intermediate, to advanced, and expert.

SUMMIT EAST. This is the smallest and least crowded of the four downhill ski areas. Open on weekends only, it has two lifts. The base is at 2,620 feet elevation, and the vertical rise is 1,080 feet. There are a day lodge and restaurant, runs for skiers and snowboarders, night skiing, and schools. Rentals are available.

SUMMIT NORDIC CENTER. This operation has a 5-kilometer lower-trail system, and a 45 kilometer upper trail system which is accessed by taking a chair lift. Base elevation is 2,280 feet, and there are 178 trails of varying difficulty. Volunteers guide skiers during weekends. There is a small day lodge, with a cafe. Rentals and lessons are available. There is night skiing on Tuesdays and Saturdays.

SUMMIT TUBING CENTER. This is a snow-tube area for kids large and small. It is served by rope tows with special handles. Customers can bring their own tubes or plastic sliding equipment; wood, metal, and movable parts are banned. There is an air pump to fill inner tubes. Seven groomed runs are available, and there is a day lodge with a snack bar.

Directions: From Seattle, take I-90 approximately 50 miles to Snoqualmie Pass. Take Exit 52 for West Summit, and Alpental At The Summit downhill areas, Exit 53 for East Summit downhill area, cross-country skiing, and tubing, or Exit 54 for the Summit East downhill area.

GIANT RED PAINTBRUSH (Castilleja miniata) This flower produces red bracts atop straight stems from May until September.

Activities: Downhill, and cross-country skiing, snow-play, hiking, and mountain biking.

Facilities: Lifts, lodges, restaurants, rentals, schools, ski shops, and repairs.

Dates: Seasonal, winter for skiing, summer for hiking, and mountain biking.

Fees: There are fees for lift tickets and services.

Closest town: North Bend, 25 miles.

For more information: For a snow report, phone (206) 236-1600. For other information, Snoqualmie Pass, WA 98068. Phone (206) 236-7277.

MOUNT SI TRAIL

[Fig. 25(1)] This trail is on a 4,167-foot mountain that is a spur extending out from the western edge of the Cascades Range. The mountain dominates the view of travelers on I-90. Even though it is 7 miles outside the eastern border of the national forest, it is a popular mountain, that gets upwards of 30,000 hikers a year.

Mount Si is part of the state Department of Natural Resources' Mount Si Natural Resources Conservation Area. Despite the abundance of human visitors, there is a variety of wildlife on the mountain, including elk, mountain goat, bear, coyote, and cougar. Peregrine falcons (*Falco peregrinus*), an endangered species, successfully nest on the mountain's cliffs.

The hike is a strenuous, steep, 4-mile climb on a tread that is partly rocky, and goes through some attractive stands of typical western Cascade Mountain forests. The trail switches back endlessly around the glacier-carved, south face of Mount Si and ends on a shoulder at 3,900 feet elevation. Here, the views are wide and long of the Snoqualmie Valley below, and of the graceful curves of I-90. A monolithic rock juts 267 feet above, inviting people to climb it, but the view up there is not much better and the crumbling rock makes it unsafe.

Directions: Take I-90 to exit 32, 436 Avenue Southeast. Go 0.5 mile to North Bend Way and turn west. Go 0.25 mile, and turn north on Mount Si Road. Go 2.5 miles to the trailhead parking lot.

BROAD-TAILED HUMMINGBIRD
(Selasphorus platycercus)
These tiny birds (3 inches long) can fly backward or straight up and down, as well as hover and drink nectar without actually landing on a flower.

Facilities: There is a picnic area at the trailhead.

Dates: Open year-round

For more information: State Department of Natural Resources, South Puget Sound Region, PO Box 68, 950 Farman Street North, Enumclaw, WA 98022-0068. Phone (360) 825-1631.

Trail: 4 miles.

Elevation: 3,200 feet elevation gain.

Degree of difficulty: Moderate.

PAINTED TURTLE
(Chrysemys picta)
North America's most wide-ranging turtle, the painted turtle has a smooth, black-to-olive carapace with red bars along the edge.

🏵 LAKE EASTON STATE PARK

[Fig. 25(4)] This is a large, full-service park beside a pleasant lake used for boating, fishing and swimming. Access is quick and easy from I-90 and the entrance goes through the little community of Easton. Its quaint business district, with its wooden buildings, is reminiscent of the early twentieth century.

The 196-acre park has 2,000 feet on the banks of Yakima River and 24,000 feet of shoreline on Lake Easton. There are 90 tent-and-trailer campsites nestled in a mature forest of mixed fir and pine.

Lake Easton State Park also is the headquarters for the Iron Horse State Park, and trails connect the two parks.

Directions: Take Exit 70 from I-90, and go east for about 1 mile on the frontage road on the south side of the freeway.

Activities: Camping, hiking, swimming, fishing, boating, picnicking, bicycling, snowshoeing, cross-country skiing, snowmobiling.

Facilities: Boat ramps, boat rentals, restrooms, water, picnic tables.

Dates: Year round.

Fees: Fees are charged for camping, and boat rentals.

Closest town: Easton, just outside the campground.

For more information: Lake Easton State Park, PO Box 26, Easton, WA 98925. Phone (509) 656-2230.

🏵 IRON HORSE STATE PARK

[Fig. 25(3)] This state park, about 100 feet wide and 102 miles long, is divided into relatively short segments, beginning in the Mount Baker-Snoqualmie National Forest and stretching from the west side of the Cascade Mountains across the summit to the east side, and the Wenatchee National Forest, then on toward the Columbia River.

The park was created in 1981 after the Chicago, Milwaukee, St. Paul, and Pacific

Railroad went out of business, and the Washington State Parks and Recreation Commission acquired much of the right of way. Some sections of the right of way, however, are still in private hands, and some of the old bridges and tunnels are gone or unsafe, so the trail is interrupted many times. Hikers who want to go from one section to another must go to nearby I-90 and drive to the next trailhead.

The segment of the trail in the Cascade Mountains goes its intermittent way from the foothills at Rattlesnake Lake near North Bend on the west side of the Cascades to the foothills at the town of Easton, on the east side.

The long, narrow park parallels the 1-90 corridor, but it wanders far enough away from the highway to be in deep forest and high mountains much of the way. The segments are used in the summer almost entirely as a trail for hiking, horseback riding, horse-pulled wagons and mountain biking. In the winter they are given over to snowshoeing, cross-country skiing, horse-drawn sleighs and dog sledding. All of the route is easy, with the grade a maximum 2 percent, engineered for early twentieth century steam engines.

Along the way, the route passes deep forests, ranging from west-side Douglas fir, to high-country subalpine fir, to east-side pine. There are open lakes, and rivers. The trail skirts the summit at Snoqualmie Ski Area on Snoqualmie Pass. It offers wide views of mountain peaks, and access to high-country meadows. Across the valley in the fall, the trees turn brilliant colors. Deer, bear, hawks and songbirds are among the wildlife that may be seen here. Those bridges and tunnels that are usable are vivid reminders of the railroad that pioneered the trail.

Directions: Access to the Cascades Mountains segments of the trail may be gained from I-90 exits 32, 38, 42, 47, 54, 62, and 71, all on the south side of the freeway. Those trailheads at exits 54 and 62 have designated Sno-Park parking lots that are cleared of snow during the winter.

Dates: Year round.

MULE DEER
(Odocoileus hemionus)
Named for its large, mulelike ears, this deer is unlike the white-tailed deer in its avoidance of areas of human activity.

Fees: There are fees for state Sno-Park permits that are required during the winter for parking at trailheads. Sno-park permits may be purchased at state parks, Forest Service, and commercial outlets throughout the state. A trailhead fee may be charged at trailheads on National Forest land.

Closest town: North Bend, 7 miles, on the west side of the mountains and Easton, 0.3 miles on the east side.

For more information: Lake Easton State Park, PO Box 26, Easton, WA 98925. Phone (509) 656-2230.

Trail: 32 miles in short sections.

Elevation: From Rattlesnake Lake to Snoqualmie Pass, 2,100 feet. From Easton to Snoqualmie Pass, 700 feet.

Degree of difficulty: Easy.

CRYSTAL MOUNTAIN SKI RESORT

[Fig. 25(5)] This major ski area is within the Mount Baker-Snoqualmie National Forest's 163,000-acre White River Ranger District. The district is at the southern extreme of the forest, bordering the Mount Rainier National Park (*see* Mount Rainier National Park, page 227). The ski area is at the end of the road that skirts the northeastern corner of the national park and lies deep in the Cascades highcountry between the park and the Norse Peak Wilderness (*see* Norse Peak Wilderness, page 199).

With a base at 4,400 feet elevation, the ski area has a vertical rise of 3,100 feet to a top elevation of 7,002 feet. There are 5 lifts with a capacity of 15,600 skiers per hour. The 2,300 skiable acres include 50 named runs, 20 percent rated for beginners, 37 percent for intermediate, and 43 percent for advanced skiers. The longest run is 3.5 miles. The average snowfall is 310 inches per year, and there is night skiing.

During the summer, the ski area operates a lift that takes mountain-bike riders and their bikes to a maze of trails in the high country.

There are three hotels and a multitude of restaurants, including one at the 6,800 foot level on the mountain. There are several bars. The ski area offers ski-and-snowboard schools and rental shops, nursery and day care, and the resort has a Kids Club for youngsters from 4 to 11, which includes lift tickets, a lesson, and supervision.

Directions: From Enumclaw go southeast on State Route 410 about 33 miles. Turn left onto Forest Road 7190 and go about 6 miles to the end of the road.

Activities: Skiing.

Facilities: Lifts, lodging, restaurants and bars, instruction, rentals.

Dates: Seasonal, winter.

Fees: There are fees for lift tickets and services.

Closest town: Enumclaw, approximately 40 miles.

For more information: Crystal Mountain Resort, 33914 Crystal Mountain Boulevard, Crystal, WA 98022. Phone (360) 663-2265, for snow report, (888) 754-6199.

Wenatchee National Forest

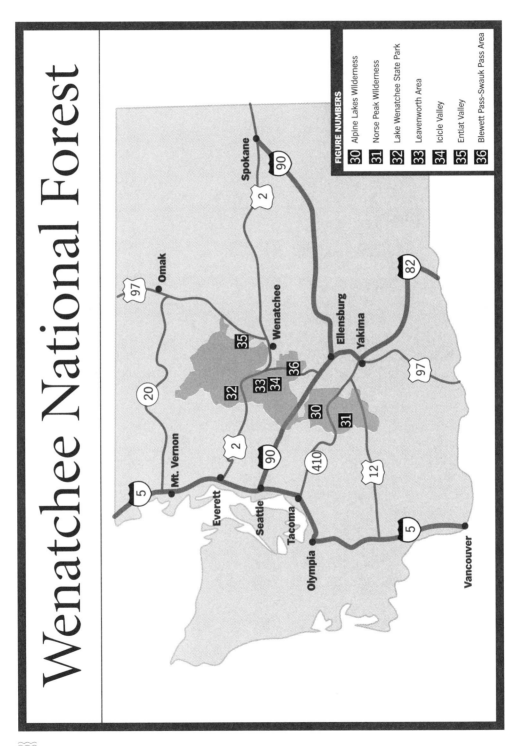

FIGURE NUMBERS

30 Alpine Lakes Wilderness
31 Norse Peak Wilderness
32 Lake Wenatchee State Park
33 Leavenworth Area
34 Icicle Valley
35 Entiat Valley
36 Blewett Pass-Swauk Pass Area

Wenatchee National Forest

🍁

With 2.2 million acres, the Wenatchee National Forest is the largest of the national forests in Washington's Cascade Mountains. It consists of six ranger districts that extend along 135 miles of the east side of the Cascade Range near the center of the state. Its location results in a typically dry, eastern Cascades climate, and the vegetation and wildlife that thrive under those conditions. Like other places on the east side of the Cascades, some parts of the forest are comparatively dry, with as little as 10 inches of rain falling a year.

As in other parts of Eastern Washington, the population is relatively sparse, but the Wenatchee National Forest is easily accessible from the population centers of Western Washington, and is connected to them by major highways such as Interstate 90, US Highways 2 and 12, and State Route 410. That results in the forest being heavily used by people seeking outdoor recreation. And, as in other parts of the Cascades' eastern slopes,

[*Above:* Gold panning on Peshastin Creek near Blewett Pass]

outdoor recreation has become an important part of the area's economy.

The attractions begin with three highways, which the federal government has designated as being among the Northwest scenic byways because of the magnificent mountain scenery they pass. Added to that is the I-90 corridor, which governmental agencies have designated as the Mountains to Sound Greenway in an effort to preserve the scenery there. Those highways reach beyond the Wenatchee National Forest boundaries into its neighboring tracts, the Mount Baker-Snoqualmie and the Gifford Pinchot national forests, and the Mount Rainier National Park. Altogether, these four highways within the Wenatchee National Forest include more than 200 miles of magnificent forest and mountain scenery, all of which can be enjoyed from the comfort of a car on a modern highway.

The three scenic byways coursing through the forest are State Routes 2, and 410, and US Highway 12. They all pass through magnificent scenery, but Highway 410 was declared an All American Highway in 1998 by the U.S. Department of Transportation because of its scenic value and because it follows the historic trail of pioneers in Western Washington during the early 1800s. The present highway's route was called the Naches Pass Trail, and was a branch of the famous Oregon Trail. It was taken by pioneer wagon trains that were going to Puget Sound rather than to Oregon in 1853 and 1854. Before the wagon trains, it had been used by Native Americans and Hudson's Bay Company employees.

Charles Wilkes, the commander of an American Navy expedition that explored the American Northwest Coast, sent an exploration party over this route in 1841 while he was surveying Puget Sound. Author Theodore Winthrop crossed the mountains by this route in 1853 and wrote a book titled *By Canoe and Saddle* about it. His book became a classic and has been in almost continuous printings ever since. And Army Captain George McClellan, who later became the commanding general of Union Army forces in the Civil War, and who ran for President against Abraham Lincoln in 1864, traveled this route while surveying Naches Pass for a railroad route. Better routes across the mountains were discovered and by the late 1850s the Naches Pass Trail was largely abandoned

From where it meets US Highway 12, 4 miles west of Naches, Washington, State Route 410 follows the Naches River for about 20 miles, then curves sharply to the left to parallel the American River. Near that curve, Forest Road 1900 branches off to the north of the highway and leads to Jeep Road 684 which goes to Naches Pass, where the pioneers found it extremely difficult to negotiate the steep terrain. The double-tread, dirt road still gives a taste of the difficulties the pioneers faced in getting their wagons over the route. Maps and directions to the jeep trail can be obtained from the Naches Ranger Station, 10061 US Highway 12, Naches, WA 98937. Phone (509) 653-2205.

In addition to the major routes, the Wenatchee National Forest has some 5,000 miles of secondary roads, 151 campgrounds, and 2,600 miles of trails, including 150 miles of the Pacific Crest Trail. Forty-five percent of the trails are within wilderness areas.

Activities in the forest take place year-round and range from pacific pursuits, such as admiring the flowers of a meadow, to athletic activities such as downhill skiing. They also include hiking, horseback riding, camping, mountain biking, whitewater rafting, mountain climbing, boating, fishing, hunting, cross-country skiing, and snowmobiling.

Seven declared wildernesses, with a total of well over 600,000 acres, are either within the Wenatchee National Forest or adjacent to it. The forest also manages some wilderness lands outside its boundaries. Management policies are the same throughout each wilderness, regardless of which forests share them.

Some of the Wenatchee National Forest land is in the high country, above tree line, and consists largely of ice and rock. Most of the rest is covered in the lower elevations by the typical open ponderosa pine forest of the Cascades' east side. At 1,500 feet, Douglas fir becomes more noticeable and above 2,500-feet there are grand fir, white pine, western larch, subalpine fir, mountain hemlock and Engelmann spruce. Wildlife includes mule deer, elk, moose, black bear, beaver, mountain goat, hoary marmot, bobcat, mountain lion, western rattlesnake, and porcupine. Birds include northern spotted owl, eagle, hummingbird, great blue heron, and red-tailed hawk.

There are hundreds of streams and lakes in the forest with native and planted fish, including brook, Eastern brook, bull, rainbow, cutthroat, and golden trout, whitefish, salmon, and steelhead.

The Wenatchee National Forest was part of the original Washington's Birthday Reserves created by President Grover Cleveland on February 22, 1891 in commemoration of George Washington's birthday. Since then, it has been divided, changed, realigned, and renamed many times. Much of it remains, however, the same unspoiled place of immense natural beauty that it was when President Cleveland created it.

Directions: The Wenatchee National Forest is on the east side of the Cascades Mountains. Take I-90 about 50 miles east from Seattle over Snoqualmie Pass, or US Highway 2 about 60 miles east from Everett over Stevens Pass, or US Highway 12 east from I-5 over White Pass. The Wenatchee National Forest is on the east side of the passes.

For more information: Wenatchee National Forest, 215 Melody Lane, Wenatchee, WA 98801-5993. Phone (509) 662-4335.

NORTH AMERICAN PORCUPINE

(Erethizon dorsatum)
When threatened, the porcupine strikes with its tail, leaving some of its 30,000 barbed quills embedded in its enemy; the quills are actually modified hairs loosely attached to the porcupine's skin.

Alpine Lakes Wilderness

The wilderness encompasses a rugged area of rocky, high mountains separated by forested low valleys.

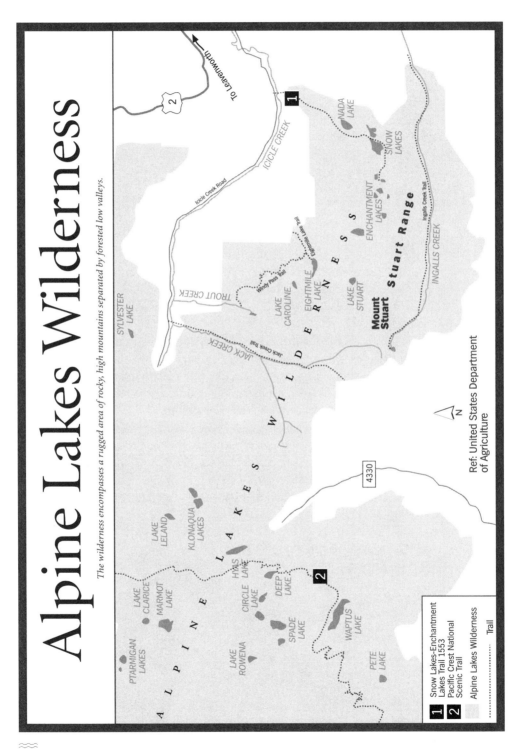

Ref: United States Department of Agriculture

	Snow Lakes-Enchantment Lakes Trail 1553
1	
2	Pacific Crest National Scenic Trail
	Alpine Lakes Wilderness
....	Trail

Wilderness Areas in the Wenatchee National Forest

ALPINE LAKES WILDERNESS

[Fig. 30] This 393,000-acre wilderness was created in the high country of the Wenatchee and Mount Baker-Snoqualmie national forests by Congress in 1976. The proposal to create the wilderness was strongly opposed by people interested in nonhiking recreation such as horseback riding and biking, as well as the timber industry, so Congress also designated the 547,000-acre area around the wilderness as a multiple-use area where the use of the land is less restricted, but where land management must be coordinated with the wilderness programs to ensure the land remains untrammeled by man.

The wilderness encompasses a rugged area of rocky, high mountains separated by forested low valleys. The highest peak is Mount Stuart at 9,400 feet elevation. Some of the valleys on the west side of the area are at about 1,000-feet. The wilderness mountains are primarily characterized by fractured granitic rock, but also include formations of sedimentary and metamorphic rock, as well as intrusive igneous formations of basalt, andesite, and rhyolite. Over the millenniums, glaciers have carved many of the valleys into the U shape typical of glaciated mountain areas. The glaciers also carved hundreds of cirques, typical concave bowls gouged into the bottoms of valleys that fill with water to become lakes. When the glaciers retreated, they often left moraines of the rock and sand they had carried down from the high country. Some of those moraines dammed the valleys, creating more lakes. The result is more than 700 natural lakes that cover 6,000 acres of land. Another 3.3 square miles of the land is covered by snow fields and glaciers.

The rain shadow created by the mountains results in wide variations in the weather. The west side gets an average of about 150 inches a year of precipitation in the high country, while some places on the east side average only about 15 inches.

GLACIER LILY

(Erythronium grandiflorum)
Found in mountain meadows, streambanks and woods near melting snow, this lily's yellow, upswept tepals arise from a leafless stalk.

Timberline in the wilderness is at about 6,000 feet in elevation, and above that the landscape is formed of rugged rock peaks, dwarfed stands of subalpine fir, mountain hemlock, and Engelmann spruce. In the upper elevations, a few whitebark pine and alpine larch struggle against the harsh conditions. Between the tree stands are meadows that exhibit colorful flowers, such as columbine, lupine, and glacier lilies. The glacier lilies here, as *Erythronium grandiflorum* in other places, are early signs of spring as they poke their tough, leathery, green leaves and delicate, yellow flowers through the last few inches of the winter's snow.

The weather in the high country is extreme. Some places retain winter snow through most of the summer. Soil is thin and fragile and in many sites, the surface consists mostly of bare, gray rock. The snow-capped peaks combine with the magnificent forests of the lower elevations and the easy access from heavily populated areas to attract more than 100,000 adventurous visitors a year. That many people make it difficult to maintain the wilderness in its untrammeled condition. The Forest Service has responded with an array of advice and regulations that fill pages of a tabloid-size publication it issues periodically, and which are likely to change from year to year. Among the more stringent regulations is a requirement that visitors obtain special permits to enter the Enchantment Lakes Basin of the Alpine Lakes Wilderness during the summer months. In addition to providing the wilderness managers with a count of the people who visit specific places, the number of permits is limited as a convenient way to reduce the number of visitors and to direct them away from parts of the wilderness that are too heavily used.

The number of people and livestock in a party that visits the wilderness is limited to 12 in most parts of the wilderness, but reduced to 8 in the Enchantment Lakes area. In addition to reducing wear on the wilderness environment, the permit system makes it less likely that visitors will encounter each other. Other regulations, such as a ban on dogs and fires may apply. Check with the ranger station for specifics.

Overnight visitors to the Eightmile-Caroline, Stuart, Colchuck, Enchantment Lakes, and Snow Lakes areas must obtain an overnight permit from the Leavenworth Ranger Station. The number of permits is limited each day. The Forest Service issues reservations in advance for 75 percent of the permits. The other 25 percent of the permits issued at the ranger station on a first-come, first-served basis on the day the visitors intend to enter the wilderness. A fee is charged for overnight permits. Day-use permits are self issued at the trailhead and are free. Permits and detailed information may be obtained from the Leavenworth Ranger Station, 600 Sherbourne, Leavenworth, WA. 98826. Phone (509) 548-6977.

Directions: The southern border of the wilderness roughly parallels I-90 in the vicinity of Snoqualmie Pass. The most direct route to the wilderness from 1-90 is to hike the Pacific Crest Trail on the north side of the pass about 1 mile to the wilderness border. The northern border of the wilderness roughly parallels US Highway 2. The most direct route to the wilderness from US 2 is a 0.5-mile hike on Surprise Creek Trail 1060 from the village of Scenic. To reach the trailhead, turn right off US 2 onto a dirt road just west of the railroad underpass.

Activities: Hiking, camping, fishing, hunting.

Dates: Open summer only.

Fees: Fees are charged for overnight camping in the Eightmile-Caroline, Stuart, Colchuck, Enchantment, and Snow Lakes areas of the wilderness. A trailhead fee may be charged for persons who do not stay overnight and issue free day-use permits to themselves at the trailhead.

Closest town: On I-90, Cle Elum 30 miles. On US 2, Skykomish, 8 miles.

For more information: Leavenworth Ranger Station, 600 Sherbourne, Leavenworth, WA 98826. Phone (509) 548-6977 or Skykomish Ranger District, 74920 Northeast Stevens Pass Highway, Skykomish, WA 98288. Phone (360) 677-2414.

EIGHTMILE LAKE-WINDY PASS TRAILS 1552 AND 1554

[Fig. 30] This is a nice hike in the Alpine Lakes Wilderness, but it gains more than 0.5 mile in elevation, and it is not an easy hike, especially on a hot, dry, eastern Cascades, summer day. The trail skirts the western edge of the area hit hard by the devastating Hatchery Creek Fire, one of a series of fires that burned huge areas of forest in Eastern Washington in 1994. The blaze engulfed the forest between Eightmile and Caroline lakes, consuming nearly everything in its path. Nature's healing powers went to work, even as the last embers died out, and the recovery is now well begun, although it will take many years to complete. The hike also courses past sparkling lakes, old-growth forest, and flowered meadows, making the route worth the effort. The long views from the 7,200-foot summit of Windy Pass are the crowning glory of the hike.

The route follows the Eightmile Lake Trail 1552 for about 3 miles to Little Eightmile Lake. Trail 1552 goes on for another 0.5 mile to the much larger Eightmile Lake. There are campsites at both Eightmile lakes. The Windy Pass Trail 1554 meets the Eightmile Lake Trail 1552 at Little Eightmile Lake and goes steeply up for what seems like an eternity of switchbacks, through typical eastern Cascades pine forest, which gradually gives way to open meadows and views of the immense peaks of the Stuart Range near the eastern edge of the Wenatchee National Forest. The trail enters the wilderness along the way.

MINK

(Mustela vison)

Like other members of the weasel family, which includes the skunk, the mink emits a pungent odor when provoked.

The trail reaches Lake Caroline about 2.5 miles from Little Eightmile Lake. Little Caroline Lake is about a 0.5 mile farther. The mosquitoes at the Caroline Lakes can be vicious when time and conditions are right for them. A forest fire burned at the Caroline Lakes in the 1960s. The gaunt, gray snags of the dead trees remain as a reminder of that fire.

There are campsites at both Caroline Lakes but the best ones are at Little Caroline. Windy Pass is 2 miles beyond Little Caroline Lake on a trail that goes through larch-covered meadows. The elevation gain from the lakes is a little more than 1,000 feet to the pass at 7,200 feet elevation.

The trail goes on from the pass for about 2 miles to the Trout Creek Trail 1555, which goes down parallel to Trout Creek for about 2 miles then turns left and goes over the pass to Jack Creek Trail 1558. This trail goes about 3 miles to the Icicle Creek Road, some 7 miles above the Eightmile Creek Road.

Directions: On the west end of Leavenworth, just east of where US Highway 2 leaves Tumwater Canyon, take the Icicle Road that follows Icicle Creek and becomes Forest Road 76. Follow that road approximately 8.5 miles, then turn left onto the Eightmile Creek Road, Forest Road 7601. Go 3 miles to the trailhead.

Dates: Open summer only.

Fees: Fees are charged for overnight camping in the wilderness during the summer. A trailhead fee may be charged.

Closest town: Leavenworth, 11.5 miles.

For more information: Leavenworth Ranger Station, 600 Sherbourne, Leavenworth, WA 98826. Phone (509) 548-6977.

Trail: 7.5 miles to Windy Pass.

Elevation: 1,200 foot elevation gain to Little Eightmile Lake, 3,900 feet elevation gain to Windy Pass.

Degree of difficulty: Strenuous.

SNOW LAKES-ENCHANTMENT LAKES TRAIL 1553

[Fig. 30 (1)] This is a difficult trail that is heavily used despite the restrictions designed to reduce the numbers of people, and despite the difficulty of the trail. The trail just to the Lower Enchantment Lakes gains more than 1 mile in elevation.

The end of the trail is the Enchantment Lakes, an eerie landscape of bare, glacier-scoured, gray rock, where only a few sparse living things survive the harsh conditions. The name Enchantment was given to the area by A. H. Sylvester, a U.S. Geological Survey topographer who was the first to record a visit here. He noted that he was enchanted, and the name stuck after he became the supervisor of the Wenatchee National Forest in 1908.

The route to that eerie land is filled with forests and lakes. The trip is a wonderful experience for those with the strength to make it.

The trail begins at the Icicle Creek Road, crosses a bridge over Icicle Creek, and begins a long siege of mildly steep switchbacks. It reaches Nada Lake after 5.5 miles. There are campsites and fish here. After another 1.25 miles the route crosses between the Snow Lakes, which offer numerous campsites but often are ice covered until late in the season.

The Snow Lakes are a good place for inexperienced hikers to turn around.

The trail curves around the back side of the Upper Snow Lake, and then becomes steeper, working its laborious way through the alpine forest toward the open country of the Enchantment Lakes. It reaches the first lake, Lake Viviane, at 6,800 feet elevation, about 10 miles from the trailhead. The route goes on from here, through the lower Enchantment Basin at about 7,000 feet, and to the upper Enchantment Basin at about 7,500 feet. There are more than a dozen small lakes gouged into the gaunt, gray, glacier-polished rock of the mountains. The lakes have mythologic names, such as Talisman, Gnome, Leprechaun, and Rune. The surrounding mountains have similarly elegant names, such as The Temple, Little Annapurna, and Prusik Peak.

The upper Enchantment Basin, especially, has a melancholy, desolate atmosphere that is, at the same time, both gloomy and attractive, with sparse, stunted vegetation showing the effects of the desperate struggle against bare rock, and long, harsh winters.

It is, indeed, an enchanting place, well worth the effort of the long, difficult trail.

Directions: On the west end of Leavenworth, just east of where US Highway 2 leaves Tumwater Canyon, take the Icicle Road that follows Icicle Creek and which becomes Forest Road 76. Approximately 4 miles from US 2, turn left into the Snow Lakes Trailhead.

Activities: Hiking, camping, fishing, hunting.

Dates: Open summer only. The Enchantment Basin often doesn't open until late July or early August.

Fees: Fees are charged for overnight camping in the wilderness during the summer. A trailhead fee may be charged.

Closest town: Leavenworth, 4 miles.

For more information: Leavenworth Ranger Station, 600 Sherbourne, Leavenworth, WA 98826. Phone (509)48-6977.

Trail: 6.75 miles to Snow Lakes, one-way. 10 miles to lower Enchantment Lakes, one-way.

Elevation: 4,100 feet elevation gain to Snow Lakes. 5,400 feet to Lower Enchantment Lakes.

Difficulty: Strenuous.

PIPSISSEWA
(Chimaphila umbellata)
The Cree Indians named this plant "pipsisikwev," meaning "it breaks into small pieces" because of their belief in its ability to break down kidney stones and gallstones.

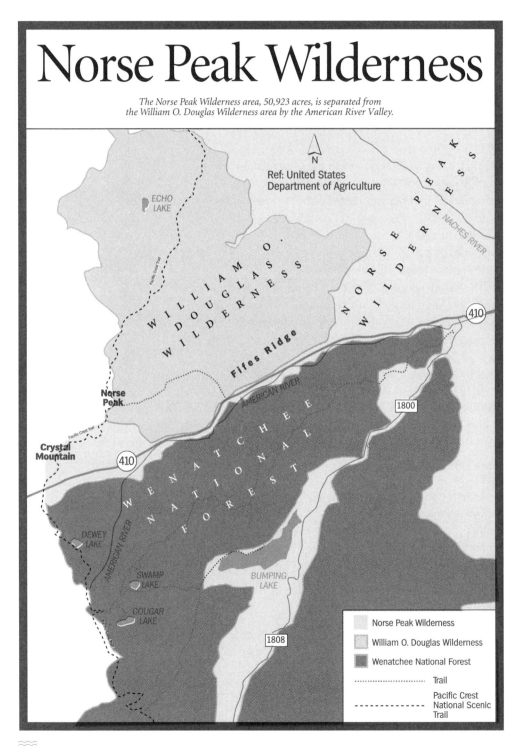

Norse Peak Wilderness

The Norse Peak Wilderness area, 50,923 acres, is separated from
the William O. Douglas Wilderness area by the American River Valley.

N

Ref: United States
Department of Agriculture

ECHO
LAKE

NORSE PEAK WILDERNESS

NACHES RIVER

WILLIAM O. DOUGLAS WILDERNESS

Pacific Crest Trail

Fifes Ridge

410

Norse
Peak

AMERICAN RIVER

1800

Pacific Crest Trail

Crystal
Mountain

410

WENATCHEE NATIONAL FOREST

AMERICAN RIVER

DEWEY
LAKE

SWAMP
LAKE

BUMPING
LAKE

COUGAR
LAKE

1808

Norse Peak Wilderness

William O. Douglas Wilderness

Wenatchee National Forest

.... Trail

- - - - - - - - - - - Pacific Crest
National Scenic
Trail

NORSE PEAK WILDERNESS

[Fig. 31] This relatively small, 50,923-acre wilderness straddles the Cascade Crest between Naches and Chinook passes with Norse Peak, 6,850 feet elevation, as the highest peak on its western border. The elevation of the low valleys is about 3,200 feet. The Norse Peak Wilderness is slightly northeast of the Mount Rainier National Park and, on the south, separated from the William O. Douglas Wilderness by the American River valley. The topography is steep, high, and, in the high elevations, rocky. There are 52 miles of trail in the wilderness.

Prospectors panned for placer gold here from 1885 to 1920, and there still are some historic remains of those efforts within the wilderness.

The diverse forest here includes Douglas fir, true fir, ponderosa pine, white pine, lodgepole pine, mountain hemlock, western hemlock, western redcedar, Alaska cedar, and Engelmann spruce. Wildlife includes both mule and black-tailed deer, elk, cougar, fisher, wolverine, mountain goat, and black bear. Lakes and streams have a variety of fish, including cutthroat, Eastern brook, and rainbow trout. Blue grouse, ruffed grouse, and spruce grouse populate the wilderness.

Crow and Morse creeks contain placer gold and are popular with hobby miners.

Directions: To access the edge of the wilderness take State Route 410 approximately 33 miles southeast from Enumclaw. Turn east on the Crystal Mountain Road, Forest Road 7190, and go about 4.2 miles. Or take State Route 410, 20 miles southeast from Enumclaw and turn left onto the Greenwater Road, Forest Road 70. Drive 8.5 miles, turn right onto Forest Road 7033, and go about 0.25 mile. Or take State Route 410, 35 miles northwest from Naches to a 7-mile stretch where the highway parallels the southern wilderness border and where several trailheads give access to it.

Activities: Hiking, hunting, fishing.

Dates: Open summers only.

Fees: A trailhead fee may be charged.

Closest town: Naches, approximately 31 miles.

For more information: Naches Ranger Station, 10061 US Highway 12, Naches, WA 98937. Phone (509) 653-2205.

WILLIAM O. DOUGLAS WILDERNESS

[Fig. 31] This 166,000-acre wilderness is administered by the Wenatchee National Forest even though it is technically in the Mount Baker-Snoqualmie National Forest. The wilderness bears the name of the late U.S. Supreme Court Justice William O. Douglas who grew up in nearby Yakima and maintained a cabin at Goose Prairie, adjacent to the wilderness, for many years. His book, *Of Men and Mountains,* describes the area and how its wild beauty influenced him.

The wilderness is adjacent to the eastern border of Mount Rainier National Park. The Pacific Crest National Scenic Trail courses through a 27-mile stretch of the wilderness high country, and many other trails also lead into the interior.

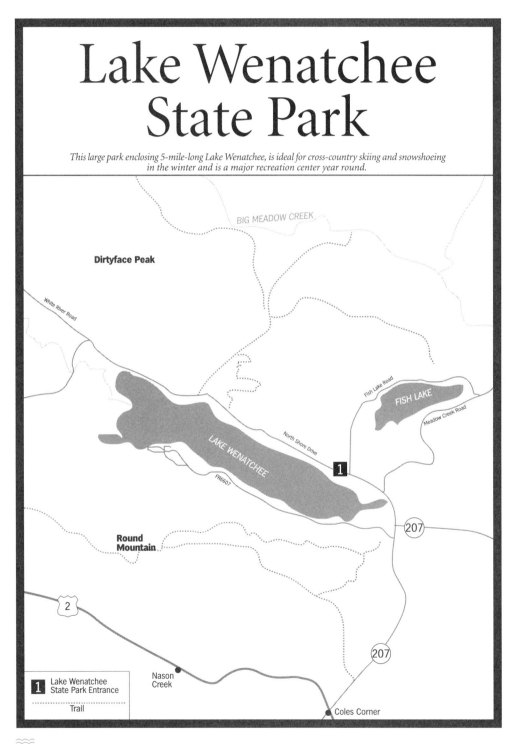

Lake Wenatchee State Park

This large park enclosing 5-mile-long Lake Wenatchee, is ideal for cross-country skiing and snowshoeing in the winter and is a major recreation center year round.

BIG MEADOW CREEK

Dirtyface Peak

White River Road

Fish Lake Road

FISH LAKE

Meadow Creek Road

North Shore Drive

LAKE WENATCHEE

FR6607

1

207

Round Mountain

2

207

Nason Creek

1 Lake Wenatchee State Park Entrance

.... Trail

Coles Corner

The topography of the wilderness ranges from 3,000 to 7,000 feet in elevation. High country lakes surrounded by sub alpine forest characterize the western section of the wilderness, while the bare ridges, and exposed basalt plateaus of the eastern slopes tend to have midelevation pine forest.

Directions: To access one of the trails to the wilderness, drive 66 miles southeast of Enumclaw on State Route 410. Turn south on Bumping Lake Road, Forest Road 18 and go to Bumping Lake. Turn onto Forest Road 394, drive 2 miles to the end of the road, and hike 3 miles on Trail 971 to the edge of the wilderness.

Activities: Hiking, camping, hunting, fishing.

Dates: Seasonal, summer.

Fees: A trailhead fee may be charged.

Closest town: Enumclaw, 68 miles.

For more information: Naches Ranger Station, 10061 Highway 12, Naches, WA 98937. Phone (509) 653-2205.

Lake Wenatchee State Park

[Fig. 32] This is a large park, at the head of a large lake, surrounded by large mountains. The lake is approximately 5 miles long and 1 mile wide, and has been a campsite since before Europeans arrived here. Indians from the east side of the Cascades used it as a stopover on their way to trade with tribes on the west side.

In 1890, John Stevens sought a route the Great Northern Railway could use to cross the Cascades. After searching several places without finding a practical crossing, he went up the Wenatchee River and noticed a stream coming from the direction of the mountains (now called Nason Creek) and emptying into the Wenatchee River near Lake Wenatchee. Later, while exploring the crest of the mountains, he noticed the headwaters of a creek that ran to the east, and guessed that it was Nason Creek and that the creek would be the shortest route from Lake Wenatchee to Puget Sound. In a note he made later, Stevens wrote, "I immediately sent Mr. Haskell to Wenatchee Lake, and to the Creek I have described with orders to follow it clear up to every one of its heads..." Mr. Haskell, C.F.B. Haskell, an engineer on Steven's staff, followed the creek to the end and blazed a tree at the pass with the words, "Stevens Pass". That became the route for the railroad, now called the Burlington Northern Santa Fe, and, later, for US Highway 2, which led to the area becoming one of the major outdoor recreation areas of the Cascades.

Lake Wenatchee is a major part of that recreation area. It is surrounded by the U.S. Forest Service's Lake Wenatchee Ranger District and has numerous streams, lakes, and trails for short hikes within the park and longer ones on nearby national forest land. But the state park is a central attraction to the lake.

During the winter the park becomes a winter playground. Park staff members groom 30 kilometers of cross-country skiing trails over park, national forest, and private land.

Leavenworth Area

Leavenworth buildings sport the exposed timbers, bright murals, and flower boxes typical of a Bavarian mountain village.

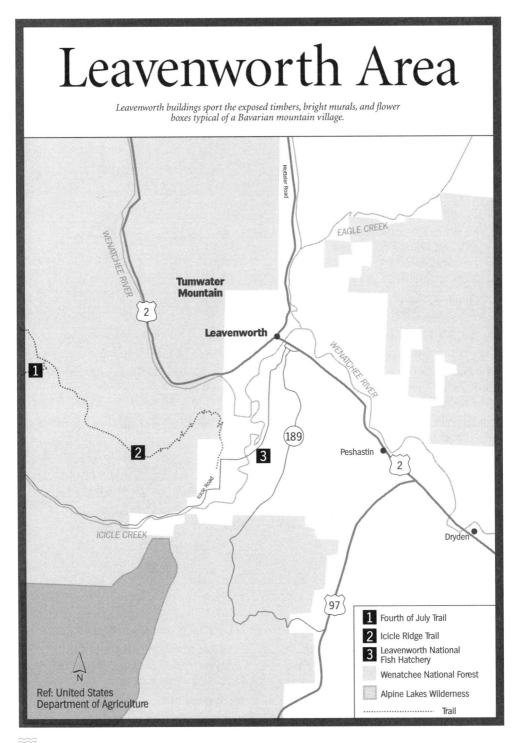

1 Fourth of July Trail
2 Icicle Ridge Trail
3 Leavenworth National Fish Hatchery
  Wenatchee National Forest
  Alpine Lakes Wilderness
.... Trail

Ref: United States Department of Agriculture

There also are opportunities for snowshoeing in and near the park grounds. The lakefront bathhouse is kept open as a restroom and warming hut during the winter.

Directions: 16 miles northwest of Leavenworth on US Highway 2, at Coles Corner, turn north onto State Route 207, and go 3 miles to the main park entrance on the left.

Activities: Camping, picnicking, boating, canoeing, hiking, horseback riding, cross-country skiing, snowshoeing. Fishing, hunting, and snowmobiling are available in the adjacent national forest.

Facilities: 197 campsites for either tents or self-contained recreational vehicles, 2 primitive campsites for tents only, piped water, flush toilets, a trailer dump station, a store, bathhouse, showers, fire grills, a boat launch, equestrian facilities, picnic facilities, children's playground, and a sandy beach. Some of the facilities are wheelchair accessible.

Dates: Open year-round.

Fees: Fees are charged for campsites, reservations, and some services.

Closest town: Leavenworth, 19 miles.

For more information: Washington State Parks Information Center. 7150 Clearwater Lane, Olympia, WA 98504-2650. Phone (800) 233-0321. For recorded information, phone Lake Wenatchee State Park at (509) 763-3101. To make a reservation for a campsite, phone Reservations Northwest at (800) 452-5687.

The Leavenworth Bavarian Village

[Fig. 33] In this mountain town with a population of about 1,800, the roaring, white Wenatchee River flows out of the mouth of deep, narrow Tumwater Canyon into a broad valley. When it was incorporated in 1906, its economy depended on the Great Northern Railway, timber, and fruit orchards. But in the 1920s the railroad moved to a better route, and the timber business began a long decline. By the 1950s many of the businesses had closed. The town, working with the University of Washington, developed a plan to adopt a Bavarian theme in keeping with the towering mountains that were reminiscent of the European Alps. First a few stores were renovated on the lines of the Alpine architecture of the Bavarian mountains. Slowly, the rest of the town's business district was renovated and the community depended less on a Cascades logging and agriculture economy and more on the new tourist theme, with local structures sporting the exposed timbers, bright murals, and flower boxes typical of a Bavarian mountain village. Business boomed, and new hotels, restaurants and shops sprang up to cater to the visitors.

The community adds to the attraction by holding art shows, folk music and dancing exhibitions, chamber music programs, accordion competitions, craft fairs, and other events that have expanded over the decades until there nearly always is something going on. Festivals and special events take place year-round, and include an Autumn Leaf Festival and a Christmas Lighting Festival. People come from far places to take part in the festivities.

Despite the theme attractions, Leavenworth continues to be essentially an American town in the high Cascade Mountains with numerous year-round outdoor attractions and hotels and restaurants to provide a base to enjoy them. During the winter, the Leavenworth Winter Sports Club grooms and maintains more than 20 kilometers of cross-country ski tracks and skating lanes in or near the town.

The Leavenworth Golf Course Ski Trail is a large groomed network with 10 kilometers of trails on the Leavenworth Golf Course. It is on the Icicle Road, approximately 0.5 mile south of US Highway 2. The golf course trail connects with a trail to the Waterfront Park in downtown Leavenworth.

The Ski Hill Trail is a 5-kilometer-loop cross-country course, with 3 kilometers lighted for night skiing. It is located on Ski Hill Drive, which meets the north side of US Highway 2, two blocks east of Icicle Road. Turn north on Ski Hill Drive and follow the signs to the Leavenworth Ski Hill area.

The Icicle River Trail is an 8-kilometer trail that winds through a forested area beside the Icicle River. Tickets for the Leavenworth Winter Sports Club's groomed ski trails can be obtained from booths at the trailheads.

For more information about cross-country skiing in the Leavenworth area contact the Leavenworth Ranger Station, 600 Sherbourne, Leavenworth, WA 98826. Phone (509) 548-6977. Or, the Leavenworth Winter Sports Club, phone (509) 548-5115.

Directions: Leavenworth straddles US Highway 2 about 100 miles east of Everett.

Activities: Mountain-related entertainment, arts, and crafts with a Bavarian theme, as well as winter and summer sports activities.

Facilities: Complete facilities are available, including lodging, food, and shops that sell and rent outdoor equipment.

Dates: Open year-round.

Fees: There are the usual fees for food, lodging, and shopping, but much of the entertainment is free.

For more information: Leavenworth Chamber of Commerce, PO Box 327, Leavenworth, WA 98826. Phone (509) 548-5807.

LEAVENWORTH NATIONAL FISH HATCHERY

[Fig. 33(3)] Each year this establishment raises millions of salmon and steelhead, which are released into the Icicle River from whence they go to the Wenatchee River, down to the Columbia River, and out to the Pacific Ocean, where they mature and, years later, return up some 500 miles of river and past seven dams to the hatchery.

The 170-acre hatchery complex provides tours, classroom educational programs, teacher workshops, and interpretative nature trails, and sponsors Kids' Fishing Days events. Additionally, the hatchery and the Wenatchee National Forest jointly sponsor a four-day Wenatchee River Salmon Festival each fall to celebrate the return of the salmon to the river. The celebration is held on the hatchery grounds. The first two days are attended largely by school classes from throughout the region. Saturday and Sunday are open for everyone. The programs are staged by 56 public and private organizations, including 12 Indian reservations. They combine education, entertainment, and science to demonstrate the complexity of nature and how salmon play a significant part in the culture of the Pacific Northwest.

The hatchery is open to visitors year-round, daily except Christmas. From May to August adult salmon, weighing as much as 30 pounds, can be seen in the hatchery and the river.

Directions: The hatchery is located at 12790 Fish Hatchery Road. Go 1.5 miles south of US Highway 2 on Icicle Road and turn left onto Fish Hatchery Road.

Activities: Fish and wildlife viewing, fishing, horseback riding, picnicking, hiking, and cross-country skiing.

Facilities: Viewing and fishing areas, trails, picnic area, and a natural-resource gift store.

Dates: Open year-round.

Fees: None.

Closest town: Leavenworth, 2 miles.

For more information: Leavenworth National Fish Hatchery, 12790 Fish Hatchery Road, PO Box 549, Leavenworth, WA 98826. Phone (509) 548-7641.

ICICLE ROAD

[Fig. 34] This long, dead-end forest road goes through typical eastern Cascades pine forest, and parallels the pleasant Icicle Creek, which, during the spring, has wild stretches that provide rafting thrills. It leads to an array of recreation activities, including camping, hiking, mountain biking, fishing, and hunting, but the road itself is also a nice place to take a pleasant afternoon ride. Black bear, deer, coyote, porcupine, and cougars are among the native residents.

The road is in the valley between some of the Cascades' magnificent mountains and, even without leaving the car, there are awesome views of forested slopes and high peaks. Part of the forest was destroyed in the Hatchery Creek Fire of 1994, leaving some of the mountains completely burned off from the valley bottom to the peak. The dead snags of the former forest point to the sky, while the small plants that are the pioneers of the next stage of forest succession grow at their feet.

The road leads to trailheads for several high-country trails, including to the Alpine Lakes Wilderness trails (*see* Snow Lakes-Enchantment Lakes Trail 1553, page 196, and Eightmile Lake-Windy Pass Trails 1552 and 1554, page 195).

The Icicle Road also leads to the Icicle Gorge Loop Trail 1596, a much easier, short, level trail that takes only a few hours to hike but wends its way through some magnificent scenery. The 3.5-mile loop trail begins at a trailhead 0.5 mile west of the Chatter Creek Campground, approximately 16.5 miles from US Highway 2.

Much of the trail is in deep ponderosa pine forest, but there are places where it closes in on the high bank above Icicle Creek, providing a good look both to the creek below and the mountains above. Signs along the way explain the history and natural processes of the forest.

At the Rock Island Campground, the trail crosses a bridge over Icicle Creek and goes to the Chatter Creek Campground on the other side of Icicle Creek, then returns to the

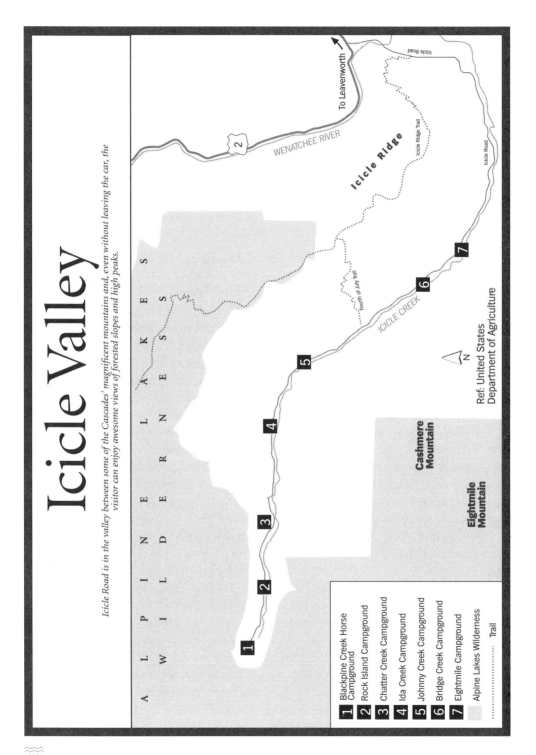

Icicle Valley

Icicle Road is in the valley between some of the Cascades' magnificent mountains and, even without leaving the car, the visitor can enjoy awesome views of forested slopes and high peaks.

A L P I N E L A K E S
W I L D E R N E S S

To Leavenworth

Icicle Road

WENATCHEE RIVER

Icicle Ridge

Icicle Ridge Trail

Fourth of July Trail

ICICLE CREEK

Icicle Road

N

Ref: United States
Department of Agriculture

Cashmere Mountain

Eightmile Mountain

1 Blackpine Creek Horse Campground
2 Rock Island Campground
3 Chatter Creek Campground
4 Ida Creek Campground
5 Johnny Creek Campground
6 Bridge Creek Campground
7 Eightmile Campground
Alpine Lakes Wilderness
.... Trail

trailhead. The route on both sides of the creek is pleasant and level with only slight variations in elevation. During the winter the snowplows stop at the Bridge Creek Campground and the Icicle Road beyond that becomes a popular snow play area, including especially for cross-country skiing and snowmobiling.

Directions: Turn south off US Highway 2 onto Icicle Creek Road at the west end of Leavenworth, near the mouth of Tumwater Canyon.

Facilities: Campgrounds and trailheads.

Activities: Hiking, biking, cross-country skiing, snowmobiling, snow play, camping, hunting, fishing.

Dates: Open year-round.

Fees: There are fees at campgrounds and a trailhead fee may be charged.

Closest town: Leavenworth.

For more information: Leavenworth Ranger District, 600 Sherbourne Street, Leavenworth WA 98826. Phone (509) 782-1413.

CAMPING IN THE ICICLE VALLEY

There are seven campgrounds scattered along the Icicle Road with a total of 170 campsites for tents or recreation vehicles. Fees are charged for camping in all of them during the summer camping season. All of them have garbage service, and wells with hand pumps for water.

EIGHTMILE CAMPGROUND. [Fig. 34(7)] 8 miles from Leavenworth at 1,800 feet elevation, 45 campsites, 40 capable of taking recreation vehicles more than 20 feet long. There are handicap-accessible vault toilets.

BRIDGE CREEK CAMPGROUND. [Fig. 34(6)] 9.4 miles from Leavenworth at elevation 1,900 feet, 6 campsites, with none capable of accommodating recreation vehicles more than 19 feet long. There are vault toilets.

JOHNNY CREEK. [Fig. 34(5)] 12.4 miles from Leavenworth at 2,300 feet elevation, 65 campsites, 56 of them capable of accommodating recreation vehicles more than 20 feet long. There are handicap-accessible vault toilets.

IDA CREEK CAMPGROUND. [Fig. 34(4)] 14.2 miles from Leavenworth at 2,500 feet elevation, 10 campsites, 5 of them capable of accommodating recreation vehicles more than 20 feet long. There are handicap-accessible vault toilets.

CHATTER CREEK CAMPGROUND. [Fig. 34(3)] 16.1 miles from Leavenworth at 2,800 feet elevation, 12 campsites, with none capable of accommodating recreation vehicles more than 22 feet long. Small group shelter with fireplace. There are vault toilets.

ROCK ISLAND CAMPGROUND. [Fig. 34(2)] 17.7 miles from Leavenworth at 2,900 feet elevation, 22 campsites, with none capable of accommodating recreation vehicles more than 22 feet long. There are handicap-accessible vault toilets.

BLACKPINE CREEK HORSE CAMPGROUND. [Fig. 34(1)] 19.2 miles from Leavenworth at 3,000 feet, 10 campsites, with none capable of accommodating recreation vehicles more than 22 feet long. This campground has an unloading ramp and vault toilets.

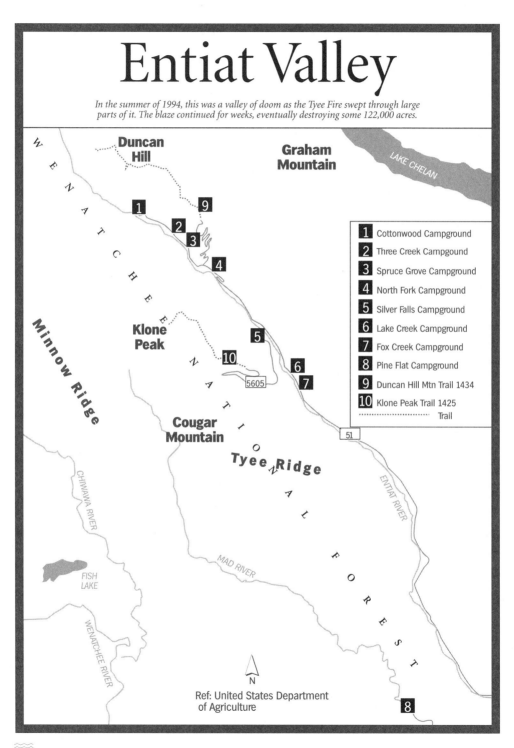

Entiat Valley

In the summer of 1994, this was a valley of doom as the Tyee Fire swept through large parts of it. The blaze continued for weeks, eventually destroying some 122,000 acres.

Duncan Hill

Graham Mountain

LAKE CHELAN

WENATCHEE

Minnow Ridge

Klone Peak

1 Cottonwood Campground
2 Three Creek Campgound
3 Spruce Grove Campground
4 North Fork Campground
5 Silver Falls Campground
6 Lake Creek Campground
7 Fox Creek Campground
8 Pine Flat Campground
9 Duncan Hill Mtn Trail 1434
10 Klone Peak Trail 1425
.... Trail

Cougar Mountain

Tyee Ridge

NATIONAL FOREST

CHIWAWA RIVER

ENTIAT RIVER

FISH LAKE

MAD RIVER

WENATCHEE RIVER

N

Ref: United States Department of Agriculture

🔲 MOUNTAIN BIKING IN THE ICICLE VALLEY

Trails open to mountain bikes are limited to the loop formed by the steep and difficult Icicle Ridge Trail 1570 and Fourth of July Creek Trail 1579. Biking experts warn that while these trails run through beautiful landscape and magnificent wide views, they are grueling, dangerous trails that require excellent riding skills. About 5 miles of the Fourth of July Trail must be negotiated by walking rather than riding.

ICICLE RIDGE/FOURTH OF JULY BIKING, HIKING TRAILS 1570 AND 1579

[Fig. 34] The loop begins and ends at the Icicle Ridge Road so one strategy is to park a car at either trailhead. Another is to park at one trailhead and ride the bike on the road between. Either way, the trail almost immediately becomes steep, rough, and rocky.

Those who start on the Fourth of July Trail will reach the Icicle Ridge Trail after a little more than 5.3 miles. The Icicle Ridge Trail to the northwest goes 1 mile or so to the border of the Alpine Lakes Wilderness. Bikes are banned in the wilderness so that is as far as one can go on a bike, although hikers who have wilderness permits can go on for many miles and choose between an assortment of branch trails.

The Icicle Ridge Trail to the southeast follows the ridge for 0.3 mile to the high point of the trail at 6,830 feet elevation, then begins a mostly downhill, 9-mile route that courses through meadows, forests, and logged areas. Some of the forests are the dead remainders of the 1994 fires. The trail in some of the meadows and burned areas is difficult to find. Eventually, at 18.8 miles, the trail begins a series of switchbacks, where the ride becomes easier as it heads toward the trailhead.

Directions: The Fourth of July trailhead is basically a wide spot in the Icicle Creek Road approximately 9.5 miles from US Highway 2. For the Icicle Ridge trailhead, go 1.4 miles from US Highway 2 on the Icicle Road. Jog right then left on the Icicle Ridge trailhead road. Go a short distance to the trailhead parking lot on the right.

Activities: Mountain biking, hiking and camping.

Dates: Open summer only.

Fees: A trailhead fee may be charged.

Closest town: Leavenworth, 9.5 miles.

For more information: Leavenworth Ranger Station, 600 Sherbourne, Leavenworth, WA 98826. Phone (509) 548-6977.

Trail: 22.7 steep, rough miles.

Elevation: 5,590 foot elevation gain.

Degree of difficulty: Strenuous.

Entiat Valley

[Fig. 35] In the summer of 1994, this was a valley of doom as the Tyee Fire swept through large parts of it, leaving vast clouds of ugly, thick smoke, and huge swaths of gaunt, black forest in its wake. The blaze continued for weeks, eventually destroying some

122,000 acres in and far beyond the Entiat Valley, and leaving a good place to see both the devastation of a major forest fire and the natural healing process that began restoring the valley even as the embers were cooling.

The valley, part of the U.S. Forest Service's Entiat Ranger District, now is a mosaic of burned forest interspersed with stands of Douglas fir, ponderosa and lodgepole pine in the lower valley, and cedar and spruce in the upper valley.

The Entiat River begins at the Entiat Glacier on the side of Maude Mountain, deep in the Cascades. It flows some 45 miles through the dry valley and empties into the Columbia River at the town of Entiat. US Highway 97 crosses the mouth of the valley. The valley is interesting because of what it says about forest fires and because it offers opportunities to see portions of the forest that escaped the fire. It is a beautiful place, with many things to attract a visitor's interest. There are rainbow trout in the river and mule deer, black bear, coyote, and cougar are among the wildlife. There may be a few rattlesnakes anywhere in the drainage, more in some places than in others.

🏕 CAMPING IN THE ENTIAT VALLEY

There are seven Forest Service campgrounds on the Entiat River and one on the Mad River, a tributary of the Entiat River. The campgrounds have a total of 100 campsites. Only 7 of the campsites are specifically rated as suitable for trailers, although a few others are vaguely listed as possible for trailers. Fees are charged at all campsites. The campgrounds on the Entiat Road, Forest Road 5100, are the following:

FOX CREEK CAMPGROUND. [Fig. 35(7)] 27 miles from US Highway 97, elevation 2,100 feet. 16 campsites. Water is supplied by a hand-pump well, and garbage service is provided. Activities include fishing, hiking, mountain biking, picnicking, and camping.

LAKE CREEK CAMPGROUND. [Fig. 35(6)] 28 miles from US Highway 97, 2,200 feet elevation. 18 campsites. Water is supplied by 2 hand-pump wells, and garbage service is provided. Activities include fishing, hiking, picnicking, and camping.

SILVER FALLS CAMPGROUND. [Fig. 35(5)] 30.4 miles from US Highway 97, elevation 2,400 feet. 31 campsites, 4 trailer units, 1 group camping site capable of accommodating as many as 50 persons. A deposit is required for reservations at the group camp. The reservations are available at the ranger station in Entiat. Water is supplied by 2 hand-pump wells, and garbage service is provided. Activities include fishing, hiking, picnicking, and camping.

NORTH FORK CAMPGROUND. [Fig. 35(4)] 33.5 miles from US Highway 97, elevation 2,500 feet. 8 tent sites, and 1 unit for trailers 22 feet long, or less. Water is supplied by a hand-pump well. Garbage service is provided. Activities include fishing, mountain biking, and camping.

SPRUCE GROVE CAMPGROUND. [Fig. 35(3)] 35 miles from US Highway 97, elevation 2,900 feet. 2 tent sites. No water, and no garbage service. Activities include fishing and camping.

THREE CREEK CAMPGROUND. [Fig. 35(2)] 35.7 miles from US Highway 97, elevation 2,900 feet. 3 campsites. No garbage service or water. Activities include fishing, hiking, and camping.

COTTONWOOD CAMPGROUND. [Fig. 35(1)] 38 miles from US Highway 97, elevation 3,100 feet. 25 campsites, 2 trailer sites. Water is supplied from 2 hand-pump wells. Garbage service is provided. Activities include fishing, mountain biking, hiking, and camping.

PINE FLAT CAMPGROUND. [Fig. 35(8)] 3 miles up the Mad River Road 5700, which intersects with the Entiat River Road, 8 miles from US Highway 97. Elevation 1,600 feet. 7 campsites, 1 group camping site capable of accommodating as many as 50 persons. A deposit is required for reservations at the group camp, available at the ranger station. No water and no garbage collection. Activities include fishing, hiking, and camping.

WINTER ACTIVITIES IN THE ENTIAT VALLEY

In the winter the snowplows keep the roads open in the lower section of the valley where there are homes. Beyond the plowed area, snow clogs the roads, stopping wheeled vehicles, and making a perfect place for snowmobiles that come by the thousands to trails groomed for them.

The trailhead is on the Mad River Road, which connects to the Entiat River Road about 10 miles from US Highway 97 at the mouth of the Entiat Valley. The trailhead is a Sno-Park and requires a Sno-Park pass, available at government and commercial outlets throughout the state.

The Forest Service grooms around 175 miles, leading in many directions along the Mad River and other roads. The Entiat Valley trails extend to Lake Wenatchee, 15 miles away in the Lake Wenatchee Ranger District, where they connect with another network of trails. Some of the trails are loops, beginning and ending in the same place. Others simply go far into the snow-covered fields and end, requiring a return by the same route.

The burned, denuded forest is largely open ground now, making a perfect place for snowmobiles to reach territory with long views. One popular destination is the Sugarloaf Fire Lookout on Sugarloaf Peak, about 6 miles from the trailhead as the crow flies. The peak, at 5,814 feet elevation, overlooks the landscape for many miles, from the wheat fields on the other side of the Columbia River, 15 miles to the east, to Lake Wenatchee and its neighbor, Fish Lake, 15 miles to the northwest. It was just this view that

BELTED KINGFISHER
(Ceryle alcyon)
Identified by its blue-gray breast band (an additional chestnut band is on the female), the kingfisher can be seen near water where it swoops close to the surface before plunging in after its prey.

caused the Forest Service to establish a fire lookout here sometime around the early 1920s, making it one of the first such lookouts. Originally there was just a tent to live in. A building was erected after a road was extended to the lookout in 1924. The building was replaced by another structure about 1986 and the road was improved. The view was so enticing that Sugarloaf became a popular place on summer weekends, much to the chagrin of the lookout people who were ordered to dress in full uniform, including ties, to greet the visitors.

The lookout is not only still standing, but is also one of the last to still be used to spot fires during the summer. Winter storms, however, pretty much bury the lookout until it becomes just a mound in the snow. But the views remain, winter and summer, and still attract numerous people. The advent of the snowmobile has extended the season for visiting the mountain through the winter, and it is, perhaps, the most popular destination for snowmobiles in the national forest.

Other trails form a maze and lead to many of the more beautiful places of the Entiat Valley, and the number of people who come here astonishes even the Forest Service people who developed the system. They estimate that on a sunny, midwinter, weekend day there may be as many as 2,000 people in the far recesses of the valley.

One reason for grooming the trails is to allow the ranger district's wildlife staff to direct people away from places where the machines might disturb some animals. The trails are groomed 12 to 16 feet wide, providing two lanes of packed snow that make for easy riding, and the vast majority of winter visitors stay on the trails.

Although the trails are designed primarily for snowmobiles, they also are used to some extent by cross-country skiers and snowshoe hikers.

Directions: The trailhead is 1.5 miles up the Mad River Road 5700, which intersects with the Entiat River Road, 8 miles from US Highway 97.

Activities: Snowmobiling, cross-country skiing, snowshoe hiking.

Facilities: The trailhead is a state Sno-Park, kept open by snowplows.

Dates: Open winter.

Fees: A fee is charged for Sno-Park permits, available at government and commercial outlets throughout the state. Snowmobile Sno-Park permits are included in the annual snowmobile license fee.

Closest town: Entiat, 9.5 miles.

For more information: Entiat Ranger Station, 2108 Entiat Way, PO Box 476, Entiat, WA 98822. Phone (509) 784-1511.

Trail: The trail network totals an estimated 150 miles. Approximately half of them are within the Entiat Valley.

Elevation: Sugarloaf Mountain, 5,814 feet elevation, is the highest peak on the trail network.

🪨 DUNCAN HILL MOUNTAIN TRAIL 1434

[Fig. 35(9)] This is a hike to a long-gone fire lookout where the views are magnificent. It is not used very much, which provides the solitude some hikers seek in the backcountry.

Since the trailhead is at 5,200 feet in elevation, much of the climbing work is done in a car, but the hike gains a grueling 0.5 mile in elevation to the summit. The trail parallels the Duncan Ridge, gaining altitude as it goes. Hikers will find water and good campsites in a meadowlike place some 3.5 miles from the trailhead, near the headwaters of Duncan Creek.

About 3 miles beyond the meadow the trail passes within 0.5 mile of the peak of Duncan Hill Mountain. A side trail goes up the slope to the summit, elevation 7,819 feet, and the long views once enjoyed on a summer-long basis by the lookouts. Included in that view is a long segment of the Entiat Valley, Seven Fingered Jack Mountain, Mount Maude, where the Entiat River begins, and, in the far distance, the glistening white cover of Glacier Peak, one of the Washington Cascades' gigantic dormant volcanoes. The lookout tower was removed from Duncan Hill in 1969 after aircraft took over the fire-spotting function. There is, however, a solar-powered radio relay here.

It is possible to make this a longer hike by going back down the side trail from the summit and turning right on the main trail. That route goes past fields of rock scree and is so seldom used that it sometimes is hard to find. At about 7.75 miles from the trailhead the trail meets the Anthem Creek Trail 1435, which goes through prime deer country on a long series of switch-backs down 3.5 miles and some 2,400 feet to the Entiat River Trail 1400. The left leg of that junction goes 2.5 miles in a southeasterly direction to a trailhead at the end of the Entiat Road. That trailhead is about 11 miles from the Duncan Ridge Trailhead, but hikers who left a second car here, or arranged to be met, can catch a ride to their starting point.

Directions: From US Highway 97 Alternate at Entiat, drive about 33 miles on the Entiat River Road, and turn right on Forest Road 5608. Go about 6 miles on that road, turn left and go a short distance to the trailhead. Or go 38 miles from US Highway 97 to the Entiat River Trail 1400 trailhead at the end of the Entiat River Road, just past the Cottonwood Campground. Hike about 2.5 miles on the Entiat River Trail then turn right onto the Anthem Creek Trail 1435, climb 2,400 feet in 6 miles to the junction with the Duncan Ridge Trail 1434, which leads to Duncan Hill.

Activities: Hiking, camping.

Dates: Open summer.

Fees: A trailhead fee may be charged.

Closest town: Entiat, approximately 40 miles.

For more information: Entiat Ranger Station, 2108 Entiat Way, PO Box 476, Entiat, WA 98822. Phone (509) 784-1511.

Trail: On Duncan Hill Trail 1434 to Duncan Hill, 7 miles, one-way. An extended hike by Anthem Creek Trail 1435 and Entiat River Trail 1400 to the end of the Entiat River Road is about 15.5 miles, one-way.

Elevation: 3,000 foot elevation gain.

Degree of difficulty: Strenuous.

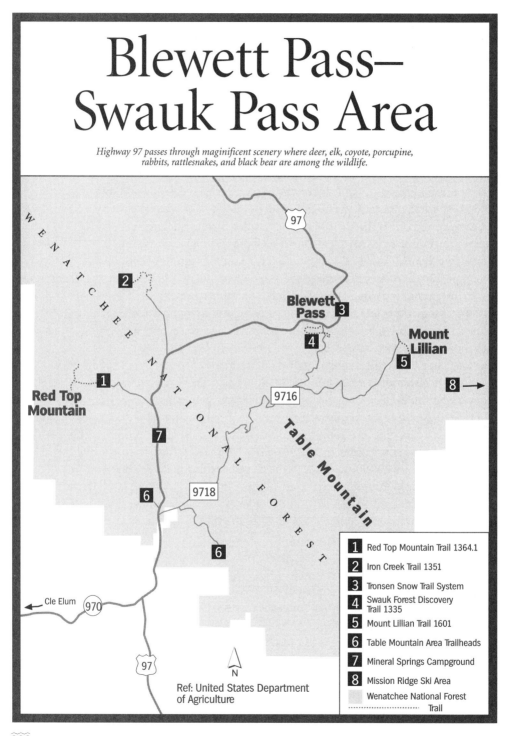

Blewett Pass–Swauk Pass Area

Highway 97 passes through maginificent scenery where deer, elk, coyote, porcupine, rabbits, rattlesnakes, and black bear are among the wildlife.

WENATCHEE NATIONAL FOREST

97

Blewett Pass

Mount Lillian

Red Top Mountain

9716

Table Mountain

Cle Elum 970

97

N

Ref: United States Department of Agriculture

1	Red Top Mountain Trail 1364.1
2	Iron Creek Trail 1351
3	Tronsen Snow Trail System
4	Swauk Forest Discovery Trail 1335
5	Mount Lillian Trail 1601
6	Table Mountain Area Trailheads
7	Mineral Springs Campground
8	Mission Ridge Ski Area
	Wenatchee National Forest
	Trail

❧ KLONE PEAK TRAIL 1425

[Fig. 35(10)] This is a trail for hikers that also is called a mountain biker's dream. It is well graded and just moderately steep. It also is popular for trail bikes. The route goes past a series of lesser peaks with good views of the countryside, and then reaches Klone Peak, at 6,820 feet elevation, where the views are best.

The trail undulates over a series of lesser peaks, losing a total of about 500 feet elevation along the way but ultimately gaining 2,900 feet to the site of a fire lookout that was removed in the mid-1960s. Only the foundation remains.

The view from the top includes the mosaic of burned forest next to stands of living trees in the Entiat Valley. Beyond that is the white top of Glacier Peak and, in the fall, the wilderness hillsides, covered by the glistening gold of larch trees about to shed their summer foliage.

As the trail nears the summit of Klone Peak, it intersects with trails that lead to a maze of routes to other destinations. One of them is the Klone Meadow Trail 1426, which drops into the Mad River drainage and goes about 2 miles past the Klone Meadow and the Marble Meadow. There, it joins the Mad River Trail 1409, which leads to the Mad River Road system and back to Entiat.

Directions: From US Highway 97 Alternate, in Entiat, go 30.8 miles northwest on the Entiat River Road and turn left on Forest Road 5605. Follow Forest Road 5605 for 7 miles to the trailhead at the end of the road.

Dates: Open summer, fall.

Fees: A trailhead fee may be charged.

Closest town: Entiat, 37.8 miles.

For more information: Entiat Ranger Station, 2108 Entiat Way, PO Box 476, Entiat, WA 98822. Phone (509) 784-1511.

Trail: 7.5 miles one-way.

Elevation: 2,900 foot elevation gain.

Degree of difficulty: Moderate.

Blewett Pass-Swauk Pass

[Fig. 36] While most state highways in the Washington Cascades go in an east-west direction, crossing between the east and west side of the range, an unusual 35-mile section of US Highway 97 goes lengthwise through the range in a north-south direction, between Ellensburg on I-90 to near Peshastin on US Highway 2, thus forming a connection between those two major east-west highways.

Highway 97 passes through magnificent scenery where deer, elk, coyote, porcupine, rabbits, rattlesnakes, and black bear are among the wildlife. Many birds frequent the area, including golden eagles, hawks, ravens, turkey vultures, grouse, jays, and owls. There are numerous recreation possibilities here, in an area where gold seekers have hunted for wealth from the early days, even until now.

The road originally crossed the divide between the Yakima and Wenatchee rivers by going over Blewett Pass, elevation 4,102 feet, and was known widely as the Blewett Pass Road. Later, the route was moved a short distance to the lower and easier Swauk Pass but the old name stuck to the new location. The original road still exists under the name Forest Road 7320, but it still is often referred to as the Old Blewett Pass Highway, leading to considerable confusion. The pass is on the border between the national forest's Leavenworth Ranger District to the north and the Cle Elum Ranger District to the south.

Once, there were several small towns of miners in the Blewett Pass-Swauk Pass vicinity. One was Blewett, located 12.2 miles south of US Highway 2 on Peshastin Creek, directly beside the current right of way of US Highway 97. The tiny village sprang up at the narrow bottom of Peshastin Valley after gold was discovered on the creek in 1860.

By 1874, prospectors had washed out all of the easy "placer" gold from the sand and gravel and began digging thousands of feet of mine tunnels into the hard rock of the nearby mountains to get at veins of ore imbedded in the rock. In 1879 investors built a 41-mile wagon road to Cle Elum to bring in workers and equipment and to take out ore. The town grew until, eventually, it had a school, a three-story hotel, boarding houses, stores, a saloon, a telegraph station, and frame and log houses.

By 1898 there was a second road. This one went 13 miles to Peshastin and a stagecoach made the trip three times a week. A post office was established in 1893 under the name of Warner. But the name was changed a few months later to Blewett, after Edward Blewett, a wealthy Seattle investor who owned many of the mining claims near the village.

Today, nothing is left of the village that once was home to an estimated 200 to 300 people, except a small, flat place beside the creek, surrounded by a thick forest of pine and fir trees. A sign beside the road designates the site of the village.

PIKA
(Ochotona princeps)
Although this small mammal looks like a rodent with ratlike head and body, it is actually related to the rabbit. The vocal pika communicates with nasal bleats and is known for its ventriloquist talents as well.

The last surviving village of those that sprouted along what is now US Highway 97 during the gold rush is Liberty, located 2.5 miles east on a short county road called, simply, the Liberty Road. It meets Highway 97 approximately 4.5 miles north of the intersection of US Highway 97 and State Route 970.

A designated National Historic District, the little community consists of a cluster of weather-worn buildings beside the road. There are some old mines nearby, and old mining equipment lies sprinkled by the roadside.

People are still panning nearby creeks

for tiny bits of color, which is what they call the diminutive flakes of yellow in the bottom of their gold pans, and there are active mineral claims in the nearby hills. No one has found the "mother lode" where the gold flakes come from, so the dream of digging immense wealth from the mountains lives on, more than a century after it started.

Liberty was established in 1880 as Williams Creek. In 1897 it was renamed Meaghersville. In 1912 the post office was moved from a dying village on Swauk Creek called Liberty, and Meaghersville became Liberty because of postal requirements.

Much of the land near the village is privately owned, so strangers must be careful to avoid trespassing. Liberty, however, is a charming, old-American community consisting of a handful of weathered houses, a false-front store building, and scattered old mining machines left over from better days. It is a fascinating place tucked away in the midst of forested mountains, and it reminds visitors of America as it was long ago.

There are two campgrounds on US Highway 97 in the Blewett Pass area, with a total of 35 campsites for tents and trailers. Fees are charged for camping in both of them:

BLACK-BILLED COMMON MAGPIE
(Pika pika)
The magpie's black and white pattern, which is seen while it is in flight, contrasts with its long, metallic green tail.

Swauk Campground, 22 miles north of Ellensburg, has 23 units for tents or trailers. There are 34 picnic sites, a shelter, drinking water, and toilets. There are hiking trails nearby.

Mineral Springs Campground, [Fig. 36(7)] 18 miles north of Ellensburg, has eight tent or trailer campsites and one group site for up to 50 people and 10 vehicles. The group site can be reserved through the National Recreation Reservation Service, phone (877)-444-6777. The campground has drinking water, picnic tables, and toilets. There are hiking trails and fishing nearby. A camping fee is charged.

A good time to visit the Blewett Pass Highway is during the brief period in late October or early November when the larch and the deciduous trees turn bright yellow, tan, and chartreuse, contrasting starkly with the deep green of the evergreen pine and fir and painting an immensely colorful mountain scene.

Directions:s The Blewett Pass Section of US Highway 97 runs between US Highway 2, 1 mile east of Peshastin, and State Route 970, 10 miles east of Cle Elum.

Facilities: Hiking, horse and cross-country skiing trails, campgrounds.

Activities: Hiking, camping, horseback riding, all-terrain vehicle operation, cross-country skiing.

Dates: Open year-round.

Fees: There are camping fees and a trailhead fee may be charged.

Closest town: Peshastin, 1 mile, on the north end and Cle Elum, 10 miles, on the south end.

For more information: Leavenworth Ranger Station, 600 Sherbourne, Leavenworth, WA 98826. Phone (509) 548-6977. Or Cle Elum Ranger Station, 803 West Second Street, Cle Elum, WA 98892. Phone (509) 674-4411.

INGALLS CREEK TRAIL 1215

[Fig. 30] This trail parallels Ingalls Creek, which is not very wide but stretches 16 miles into the Alpine Lake Wilderness. The trail passes the immense granite bulk of Mount Stuart and the Stuart Range as it goes toward a maze of connecting trails on the other side of Stuart Pass. There are several side trails that are less used and offer opportunities for solitude.

The route follows the creek, going gently upward for the first 6 miles, passing stands of high-country forest interspersed, depending on the season, with fields of Indian paintbrush, glacier lily, trillium, and queen's cup. Several campsites are scattered along the way. Falls Creek, 6 miles from the trailhead, is a good place for day hikers to turn around, especially since the trail ahead may be closed by snow during the early months of the season.

For those who go farther, the trail continues past several campsites, going higher above Ingalls Creek and becoming steeper about 10 miles from the trailhead. It becomes even more steep at about 13 miles, until it reaches Stuart Pass at 6,400 feet, where it meets the Jack Creek Trail 1558. That trail goes 10 miles to the Icicle Road (*see* Icicle Road, page 205).

Directions: Approximately 1 mile east of Peshastin, turn south onto US Highway 97 from US Highway 2. Go about 7 miles and turn right onto the Ingalls Creek Road 39. Drive around 1 mile to the trailhead at the end of the road.

Activities: Hiking, camping.

Dates: Open summer.

Fees: A trailhead fee may be charged.

Closest town: Peshastin, about 9 miles.

For more information: Leavenworth Ranger Station, 600 Sherbourne, Leavenworth, WA 98826. Phone (509) 548-6977.

Trail: 16 miles to Struart Pass.

Elevation: 1,200 foot elevation gain.

Degree of difficulty: Moderate.

MOUNT LILLIAN TRAIL 1601

[Fig. 36(5)] This is a short hike that goes through lodgepole pine forest, across meadows along ridgetops, and past outcrops of sandstone. It goes over Mount Lillian, 6,100 feet elevation, but it is not an especially steep trail. It is open for hikers, horses, pedaled mountain bikes, and motorized trail bikes.

The trail begins in a backcountry campground with a few facilities but no drinking water. The trailhead is in the north end of the campground, and the route follows the boundary between Chelan and Kittitas counties, paralleling Forest Road 9712 for approximately 1 mile. Here it crosses Four-Wheel-Drive Trail 312, and turns east for about 1 mile to the top of Mount Lillian. It goes 0.5 mile past the peak where it meets Forest Road 9712. Hikers can walk the forest road about 3 miles to the campground where they left their car. Or they can walk 1,000 feet east on the road and take the Howard Creek Trail 1372, approximately 0.75 mile to the Old Ellensburg Trail 1373. Go 2 miles on that trail back to the vicinity of the campground. Or, hikers can turn around and return by the trail over Mount Lillian.

Directions: Drive 10 miles from Cle Elum on State Route 970, which turns into US Highway 97. Go north on Highway 97 for about 13 miles and turn south on Forest Road 9716. Take that road approximately 3.8 miles, and turn east on Forest Road 9712. Go about 5 miles on that road to the campground at Haney Meadows. The trailhead is in the meadow.

Activities: Hiking, camping.

Dates: Open summer.

Fees: A trailhead fee may be charged.

Closest town: Cle Elum, 24 miles.

For more information: Cle Elum Ranger Station, 803 West Second, Cle Elum, WA 98922. Phone (509) 674-4411.

Trail: 2.5 miles to Mount Lillian summit.

Elevation: 540 foot elevation gain.

Degree of difficulty: Easy.

🌲 IRON CREEK TRAIL 1351

[Fig. 36(2)] This is a short hike to a high-country ridge of flowered meadows and long views. It begins with a steep climb on a rocky trail and goes 1 mile to a pass where it meets two other trails.

The trail straight ahead goes down Bear Creek. The other trail is the Teanaway Ridge Trail that goes along the ridge in both directions. Going left on the Teanaway Ridge Trail leads downward, but the trail to the right takes

PRONGHORN
(Antilocapra americana)
Sometimes called an antelope, the pronghorn is North America's swiftest mammal, with speed of 40 miles per hour and 20-foot leaps.

hikers upward along the narrow ridge for 2 miles to a high point and views that stretch across the alpine forests and meadows. The view includes glacier-covered Mount Rainier in the distance and the granite bulk of Mount Stuart in the foreground. The trail goes beyond the high point and it is possible to extend the hike to other trails, but for a day hike this is a good place to turn around.

Directions: Drive 10 miles east from Cle Elum on State Route 970 and turn left onto US Highway 97. Go 8 miles on that road, and turn left onto the Iron Creek Road, Forest Road 9714. Go 3.5 miles to the trailhead at the end of the road.

Dates: Open summer.

Fees: There may be a trailhead fee.

Closest town: Cle Elum, 21 miles.

For more information: Cle Elum Ranger Station, 803 West Second, Cle Elum, WA 98922. Phone (509) 674-4411.

Trail: 3 miles, one-way to the high point on Teanaway Ridge Trail.

Elevation: 1,900 foot elevation gain.

Degree of difficulty: Easy.

SWAUK FOREST DISCOVERY TRAIL 1335

[Fig. 36(4)] This loop trail is a combination of a pleasant walk in the woods and an education in the nature and management of a high-country forest. The trail begins and ends near the south side of US Highway 97 at Blewett Pass and winds past stands of trees that are common in the eastern Cascades Mountains high-country forest, including grand fir, western larch, western white pine, ponderosa pine, Douglas fir, Lodgepole pine, Engelmann spruce, and willow.

The trail is 2.5 miles long, undulates with slight ups and downs, and is rocky in some places. At the 2-mile point there is a shortcut, turnoff trail that avoids the steepest part. It goes through different forest types. At the high point, 4,700 feet, there are good views of the surrounding mountains. In the fall this area is a migration route for many raptors, and the trail is a good vantage point for watching hawks.

Twenty-five interpretive signs along the way describe the forest, its trees, its nature, and its management. A 32-page brochure, available at the trailhead or at the ranger station in Cle Elum, adds to that information, explaining the forest ecology, foresters' management techniques, and how the forces of nature and man interact in the forest. There are close-up views of the forest microcosm and longer views of the forests on nearby mountains and ridges.

Directions: This trail is on the border between the Leavenworth Ranger District to the north and the Cle Elum Ranger District to the south. From the north, approximately 1 mile east of Peshastin, turn south onto US Highway 97 from US Highway 2. Go about 19 miles to the summit of Blewett Pass, and turn south onto Forest Road 9716. Go through the Tronsen Sno-Park parking lot, and drive about 0.4 mile to the trailhead. From the south, drive 10 miles east from Cle Elum on State Route 970, which turns into US

Highway 97. Go 13 miles on US 97, turn south onto Forest Road 9716. Go through the Tronsen Sno-Park parking lot and drive about 0.4 mile to the trailhead.

Facilities: Restrooms at the trailhead, interpretive signs, and benches along the trail.

Dates: Open summer and fall.

Fees: A trailhead fee may be charged.

Closest towns: North, Peshastin, 20 miles. South, Cle Elum, 24 miles.

For more information: Cle Elum Ranger Station, 803 West Second, Cle Elum, WA 98922. Phone (509) 674-4411. Or, Leavenworth Ranger Station, 600 Sherbourne, Leavenworth, WA 98826. Phone (509) 548- 6977.

Trail: 2.5 miles.

Elevation: 500 foot elevation gain.

Degree of difficulty: Easy.

RED TOP MOUNTAIN TRAIL 1364.1

[Fig. 36(1)] This is a short trail to a fire lookout that was renovated in 1996. The lookout is staffed by volunteers in the summer and provides a wide view of the forests and mountains in every direction. The route follows an old road for about 2 miles then branches near the top. The left branch goes steeply to the lookout site, elevation 5,360 feet. There are agate fields nearby, and raptors such as hawks and golden eagles frequent the area. A forest fire burned some of the forest in the early 1900s but there are still old-growth trees in the vicinity.

RED-TAILED HAWK
(Buteo jamaicensis)

Directions: Take State Route 970 east 10 miles from Cle Elum, where it turns into US Highway 97. Then go about 7 miles north to Forest Road 9738, on the left. Follow

GRAY JAY
(Perisoreus canadensis)

Road 9738 west to Forest Road 9702, and follow Road 9702 about 0.3 mile to the trailhead.

Activities: Hiking, viewing raptors.

Facilities: There are toilets and three fire pits at the trailhead.

Dates: Open summer.

Fees: A trailhead fee may be charged.

Closest town: Cle Elum, 22 miles.

For more information: Cle Elum Ranger District, 803 West Second, Cle Elum, WA 98922. Phone (509) 674-4411.

Trail: 2.3 miles, one-way to the lookout.

Elevation: 480-foot elevation gain.

Degree of difficulty: Easy.

TABLE MOUNTAIN AREA

[Fig. 36] This forested area of old mines on and near Table Mountain has a maze of trails that are open for off-road vehicles, such as four-wheel-drive vehicles and motorized trail bikes, as well as pedaled mountain bikes, horses, and hikers. It has about 48 miles of roads designated for four-wheel-drive vehicles and another 48 miles for motorized trail bikes. Both types of vehicles must meet the legal standards for off-road vehicles. The four-wheel-drive trails are approximately 5 to 6 feet wide and may also be used with other types of equipment. The trail-bike trails are about 2 feet wide and vehicles with more than two wheels are banned. Both types of trail also are also used by horses and mountain bikes, as well as hikers. Maps of the approved routes are available at the Cle Elum Ranger Station.

The roads are very rough, steep, and narrow. In some places they run beside steep slopes. They are not suitable for ordinary road vehicles. The Forest Service has designated the specific routes that cross terrain where environmental damage will be minimal. The roads are closed from October 15 until June 15 partly to allow for the big-game hunting season and partly to avoid erosion during the heavy-precipitation and snow-melt periods.

The trails begin from the four-by-four camping area near Liberty, in an unofficial, unimproved area at the intersection of the Liberty Road with Forest Road 9726, where off-road vehicle enthusiasts often meet. The trails are marked by posts, bearing the trail number.

There are five, four-wheel-drive vehicle routes, totaling 12 miles, on the west side of US Highway 97. On the east side, there are more than two dozen four-wheel-drive vehicle routes totaling 36 miles, and an additional 48 miles of trail for trail bikes. The trails twist around obstacles and uneven terrain until they look like strands of spaghetti on the map.

Some roads in the area are closed throughout the year. Roads where motorized vehicles are permitted are marked with green diamonds, and signs designate the type of vehicles allowed.

The routes are a maze of winding, twisting, irregular ways through the forest. They were chosen because of the challenge they present to drivers. They often interconnect with more developed forest roads, which the Forest Service designates as improved dirt roads, and which are somewhat easier to negotiate.

The possibility of becoming stuck, or of a mechanical breakdown, is an inherent part of the four-wheel-drive experience.

The geology of the area varies from sandstone to basalt, and there are both agates and plant fossils in the vicinity. Douglas fir, ponderosa pine, and grand fir are among the tree species. Elk and deer abound in the area.

The routes go through typical eastern Cascades forest and into the high areas to long views of the mountains. Lion Rock, on Table Mountain, elevation of about 6,300 feet, is adjacent to the trail. It was once the site of a fire lookout and commands long views in all directions.

Directions: Take State Route 970 east 10 miles from Cle Elum, where it turns into US Highway 97. Then go about 3 miles east. Forest Road 9700116, on the west side of the highway, and 970026, on the east side, lead to the off-road vehicle routes.

Activities: Off-road vehicle riding, trail bike riding, mountain biking, horseback riding, and hiking.

Dates: Open June 15 to October 15.

Fees: A trailhead fee may be charged.

Closest town: Cle Elum, 13 miles.

For more information: Cle Elum Ranger Station, 803 West Second, Cle Elum, WA 98922. Phone (509) 674-4411.

Trail: 48 miles for trail biking, mountain biking, horseback riding, and hiking, and an additional 48 miles which may be used for those activities and for four-wheel-drive vehicles.

Elevation: Approximately 3,700 foot elevation gain from Blewett Pass to the high spot, about 1 mile east of Lion Rock on Table Mountain.

Degree of difficulty: Strenuous.

TRONSEN SNOW TRAIL SYSTEM

[Fig. 36(3)] This is a 5-mile network of ungroomed cross-country ski trails that begin at the summit of US Highway 97 on Blewett Pass and go upward on both sides of the highway.

The system follows snake-like routes on forest roads and trails that cross each other at frequent intervals, allowing skiers to go from one trail to another throughout the day. The trails vary in difficulty from easy to strenuous.

PONDEROSA PINE
(Pinus ponderosa)
Also called the western yellow pine, this tree grows to 180 feet tall with needles up to 7 inches long.

The trail on the north side of US Highway 97 is about 1.5 miles long plus a 0.25-mile loop, and is graded easiest for its whole length. It is a good place for beginners to get used to skiing.

Unlike many other cross-country ski trails, no machines groom these into smooth tracks during the small hours of the morning. The trails often are marked out by the skis of early arrivals so skiers who follow have an increasingly flat and obvious trail, until the next snow storm, when the process begins anew.

There are five trailheads to the network, but the main one, with by far the most parking space, is at the Blewett Pass summit on both sides of US Highway 97. The others are on US Highway 97 within 1.5 miles to the north of the pass, the lowest at about 3,900 feet elevation. The main trailhead is a Sno-Park and requires a Sno-Park pass, available at governmental offices and commercial outlets throughout the state. The other trailheads are too small to accommodate more than a handful of vehicles and do not require Sno-Park passes.

Most of the trails are in forest, but some pass through open areas with views that include the rugged peaks of the Stuart Range Mountains, some 20 miles to the northwest. The trails are marked by blue diamonds on the trees, and usually there are maps where the trails intersect, showing the location of the intersection and how to get to the other trails.

The cross-country trail from the main trailhead is shared with snowmobiles for about 300 yards, then branches off to a ski-only route.

Directions: This system is on the border between the Leavenworth Ranger District to the north and the Cle Elum Ranger District to the south. From the north, approximately 1 mile east of Peshastin, turn south onto US Highway 97 from US Highway 2. Go about 19 miles to the summit of Blewett Pass, and the Tronsen Sno-Park parking lot. From the south, drive 10 miles east from Cle Elum on State Route 970, which turns into US Highway 97. Go 13 miles on US 97 to the summit of Blewett Pass and the Tronsen Sno-Park parking lot. There also are trailheads with limited parking north of Blewett Pass on US Highway 97.

Activities: Cross-country skiing.

Facilities: Sno-Park parking.

Dates: Open winter.

Fees: Fees are charged for Sno-Park passes, available at government and commercial outlets throughout the state.

Closest town: Peshastin, 19 miles.

For more information: Leavenworth Ranger Station, 600 Sherbourne, Leavenworth, WA 98826. Phone (509) 548-6977

Trail: 5 miles.

Elevation: 900 foot elevation gain.

Blaze: Blue diamonds on trees.

Mission Ridge Ski Area

[Fig. 36(8)] This major ski area is on the far eastern slopes of the Cascades, near where the Columbia River brushes against the base of the mountains. Frigid air rolls down the Columbia Basin from the far north, resulting in the ski area's reputation for ideal, powder snow.

The base elevation is 4,570 feet and the high spot is 6,770 feet, a vertical drop of 2,200 feet. There are 2,100 skiable acres, and there is an average snowfall of 170 feet. Six lifts take skiers to an assortment of 33 trails, 60 percent of them rated for intermediate skiers, 30 percent for advanced, and 10 percent for beginners. The slopes are open to both downhill skiing and snowboards.

The ski area opened a 3-mile, groomed cross-country ski and snowshoe track in 1998, and planned to extend it in later seasons. The snowshoe-cross-country facility is 4 miles from the downhill ski area on the Mission Ridge Road. It also has a tow for a groomed inner tube area, and a lodge with food, drink, and restrooms.

Directions: From Wenatchee go south on Wenatchee Avenue, and turn right on Crawford Avenue. Go two blocks on Crawford Avenue, and turn left on Mission Street which becomes Squilchuck Road in about 0.5 mile. Go approximately 8 miles to Squilchuck State Park, and turn right onto Mission Ridge Road. Go about 4 miles to the ski area.

Activities: Downhill and cross-country skiing, snowboarding, snowshoeing, inner-tubing.

Facilities: Hampton Lodge and restaurant. A separate Border Cafe at the base and Midway Cafe on the slopes, equipment rentals, a ski school for both children and adults, and child care facilities.

Dates: Open winter.

Fees: There are fees for lift tickets, rentals, and services.

Closest town: Wenatchee, 9 miles.

For more information: Mission Ridge Ski Area, PO Box 1668, Wenatchee, WA 98807. Phone (509) 663-6543. For snow reports, phone (800) 347-1693.

STRIPED SKUNK
(Mephitis mephitis)
Look for the striped skunk's white facial stripe, neck patch, and V on its back.

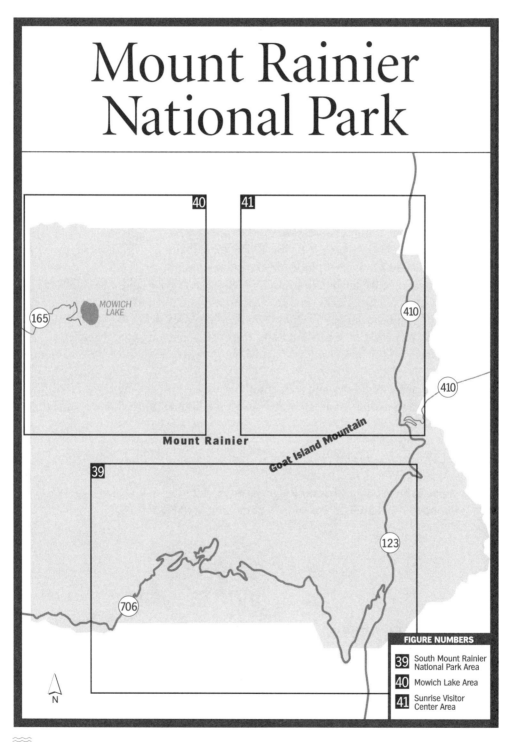

Mount Rainier
National Park

MOWICH LAKE

165

410

410

Mount Rainier

Goat Island Mountain

39

123

706

FIGURE NUMBERS

39 South Mount Rainier National Park Area

40 Mowich Lake Area

41 Sunrise Visitor Center Area

N

Mount Rainier National Park

T he ice, rock, forest, and meadow of Mount Rainier were established as the nation's fifth national park on March 2, 1899. A century later the 378-square mile park attracts some 2 million visitors a year. It is easy to see why.

Mount Rainier is the commanding geographical fact of Washington's Puget Sound Region. It overshadows the region with its ancient, white enormity. Its perpetual white cap reigns in cold, brooding beauty, neither knowing nor caring about the puny civilization at its feet.

It is a constant presence to anyone who lives in the region. Many can see it from the windows of their homes. To visitors it may come as a surprise as they gain the top of a hill or come around a curve in a highway to find it suddenly confronting them from scores of miles away.

People are attracted to its beauty as it sits, white, silent, and immovable in the

[*Above:* At 14,410 feet high, Mount Rainier is by far the highest of Washington's mountains]

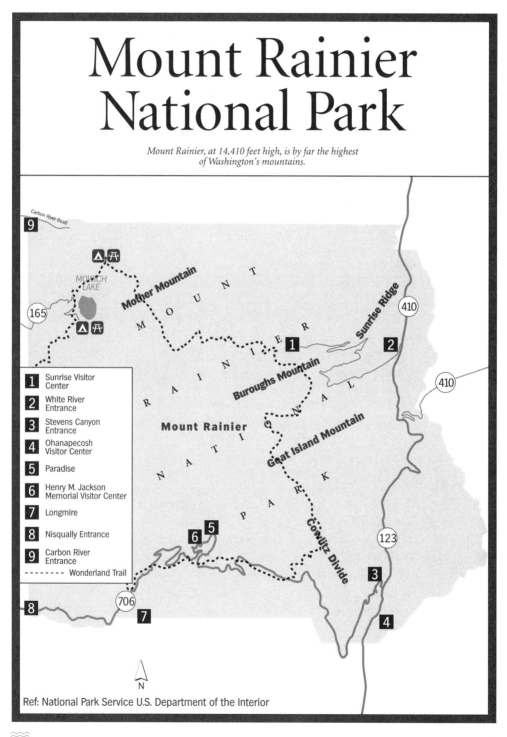

Mount Rainier National Park

Mount Rainier, at 14,410 feet high, is by far the highest of Washington's mountains.

Carbon River Road

MOWICH LAKE

Mother Mountain

M O U N T

Sunrise Ridge

410

Buroughs Mountain

410

R A I N I E R

Mount Rainier

N A T I O

Goat Island Mountain

N A T I

N A L

P A R K

Cowlitz Divide

123

1 Sunrise Visitor Center

2 White River Entrance

3 Stevens Canyon Entrance

4 Ohanapecosh Visitor Center

5 Paradise

6 Henry M. Jackson Memorial Visitor Center

7 Longmire

8 Nisqually Entrance

9 Carbon River Entrance

- - - - - - - - Wonderland Trail

165

706

N

Ref: National Park Service U.S. Department of the Interior

distance. But it is menacing, too; its size alone testifying to the massive powers that created it and continue to mold it. Mount Rainier is 14,410 feet high, by far the highest of Washington's mountains. It is a volcano that, like the state's four other volcanoes, is younger than the smaller, uplifted mountains that surround it. It is twice as high as most of the uplifted mountains and nearly 0.25 mile higher than the next highest volcano, 12,307-foot Mount Adams in the far southern section of the state. And, like the other volcanoes in Washington, it is part of the "ring of fire," a series of volcanoes that circle the Pacific Ocean with fiery volcanoes that result from the tectonic plates drifting against the coastal land masses of the Pacific Ocean.

Rainier was probably built, beginning about 750,000 years ago, when earthquakes began tearing open vents in the earth's surface, and volcanic eruptions spilled out of the vents to begin filling the valleys between the uplifted mountains and spread over the ridges. Later eruptions built layers on top of layers in an endless succession that culminated in the new giant.

Scientists call Mount Rainier a composite or stratovolcano, which means it consists of various kinds of eruptive materials. Some eruptions spewed molten lava from the earth's deep interior. It ran in liquid form over the landscape until it froze into flat, hard rock. Others threw pumice that fell to the surface, slowly accumulating in a cone that would then be covered by an ensuing lava flow. A series of eruptions took place between 1820 and 1894, when, according to newspaper articles and reports by eye witnesses, the mountain may have erupted as many as 14 times, leaving a layer of pumice covering the landscape. In December 1963, millions of cubic yards of volcanic rock fell onto Emmons Glacier on the side of Rainier from Little Tahoma Peak, one of the mountain's minor peaks. It is uncertain whether that incident was caused by an eruption or an explosion of steam that may have resulted from water seeping into the hot innards of the mountain. The falling rocks, some as large as railroad cars, became a rock avalanche, flowed off the end of the glacier, and traveled some 4 miles before stopping.

Eventually, Rainier's peak rose to some 16,000 feet elevation. Then, about 10,000 years ago, the eruptions subsided, while erosion and a series of collapses began reducing the cone at the peak. About 5,800 years ago the summit again collapsed and sent immense amounts of debris down the northeast slopes. A 100-foot-high wall of mud, called the Osceola Mudflow and consisting of snowmelt mixed with silt, sand, volcanic ash, and other debris, flowed down the White River valley, across 125 square miles of landscape to the shores of Puget Sound. Scientists believe the mudflow was nearly 100 feet high and that it contained a 0.5 cubic mile of material. The cities of Puyallup, Kent, Auburn, and Sumner are built on top of it. Other mud flows, larger and smaller, occurred over the years, changing the face of the mountain and inundating its surroundings.

The Kautz Mudflow, although not especially large, is a relatively recent one that occurred on October 2, 1947. It crossed the Nisqually Road 3 miles from the park's Nisqually entrance, one of the most heavily used roads in the park, so the mudflow is easily accessible. It started after heavy rains, augmented by snowmelt, and washed out nearly 1 mile of the lower part of the Kautz Glacier. Morainal debris and chunks of ice dammed a narrow box canyon below the glacier. When the dam broke, huge masses of debris and mud surged down the stream. An estimated 50 million cubic yards of material, including 13-foot boulders, flashed down the mountain side, snapping off trees up to 3 feet in diameter and destroying large areas of forest along the banks. Part of the Nisqually Road was buried under about 10 feet of debris, and the highway bridge that crossed Kautz Creek was destroyed. The road was rebuilt over the top of the debris.

Standing trees on both sides of the creek were hit by stones and sand that wore away the cambium layer of bark, which carries trees' nourishment. That, plus the fact that the roots were smothered by the mud that settled above them, resulted in large numbers of upright trees dying. The dead forest still stands, gray and gaunt, stripped of its foliage, but at its base new vegetation marks where the forest is recovering.

An exhibit beside the road tells the story of the mudflow and its aftermath. The Mirror Lakes-Kautz Creek Trail begins at the exhibit and can be followed through the dead forest for about 1 mile before it forks away from Kautz Creek (*See* Mirror Lake-Kautz Creek Trail, page 255). There are picnic tables at the trailhead.

A recent series of eruptions on Mount Rainier began some 2,000 or more years ago, causing more changes as the mountain grew and diminished until it reached its present size and shape, temporarily until more changes take place.

Mount Rainier is the most heavily glaciated peak in the contiguous United States, with more than 26 officially named glaciers and many that still have not been named. They cover more than 35 square miles, and some are hundreds of feet thick. Six of them radiate from the peak. The others begin on the sides of the mountain. The Emmons Glacier, on the northeastern side, is the largest in the contiguous United States.

The result of the many millenniums of volcanic activity is the massive mountain that dominates the western Washington landscape. But nature's process of building and destroying the mountain has not ended. Glaciers, wind, and rain still combine with gravity to erode the slopes, and U.S. Geographical Survey studies indicate the mountain is still active and will probably erupt again, endangering heavily populated areas of western Washington. A USGS exhibit depicting the continuing geological activity is on display at the Sunrise Visitor Center on the east side of the mountain.

Despite its enormity and immobility the mountain seems to change its appearance as the viewer sees it at different times and from different viewpoints. At midday it seems white and cold. At sunrise and sunset it is bathed in warm colors reflected from the sky. From a long distance it seems to be an immense, white cone on the horizon. From a closer distance, the glaciers take form and the tortured, black rock that separates them becomes obvious. Being on the mountain proper narrows the view to the immediate vicinity—the immense beauty of the flowered meadow, the awesome trees of the old-growth forest, the cold white of the glaciers and snow fields, or the ragged dark rock of the cleavers and ridges.

The mountain is beautiful and deserving of the admiration it gets from people who see it from near or far. It also demands reverence for its testimony to the powers of the earth that formed it, and for the serene old-growth forests that grow on its sides.

The mountain was named by Captain George Vancouver, the British Navy explorer who also named Puget Sound and many of its landmarks when he explored the sound during the summer of 1792. On May 7, he noted in his log that he saw, "a remarkably high, round mountain covered with snow." The following day, he named it "after my friend, Rear Admiral Peter Rainier." That was 13 years before Lewis and Clark reached the Pacific Ocean.

Native American tribes throughout much of Washington could see Mount Rainier and were aware that it existed, and many had legends about it, such as the Chehalis story that Rainier and Mount Saint Helens were females who quarreled over the handsome male Mount Adams

BLUE COLUMBINE
(Aquilegia caerulea)
Colorado's state flower, the blue columbine, has five spurs stretching from the petals to give it a birdlike form and inspiring its name — "columbine" means dove.

and threw hot rocks at each other. Mount Rainier was hit by a rock that knocked her head off. The Nisqually Indians believed that Mount Rainier was a female monster that ate people who came close. The mountain and a The Changer, a fox, had a contest to see which could consume the most people. Mount Rainier died in the contest and The Changer changed the blood that ran down the slopes into the water that still flows in the rivers and creeks.

Only limited artifacts have been found to indicate ancient Indian visits to Mount Rainier but archeologists theorize that such visits may have begun 6,000 to 8,000 years ago.

By the mid-1800s, when Europeans began arriving, only five tribes claimed part of the lower slopes as part of their homeland. They were the Puyallup, Nisqually, Taidnapam, Yakima, and Mukulshoot. They all hunted and gathered food and materials during the summer, where the park is now, but none had permanent villages here. The Yakima may have made the greatest use of the mountain since their lands were on the east side, where the open landscape made it easy for them to roam on their horses. The others, on the west side, where the forest was nearly impenetrable, were more oriented toward canoes and a water-based economy. For the Yakimas the mountain was a source of forest materials, while the others already lived in forests that covered the western lowlands.

Climbing Mount Rainier

Sixty years after Vancouver named Mount Rainier, Americans with a European background were establishing permanent settlements on the shores of Puget Sound and were beginning to take an interest in the immense mountain in their back yard. There is a brief note in the historical records that Robert Bailey, Sidney Ford, Benjamin Shaw, and John Edgar climbed the mountain in 1852 to look for passes to the east side of the mountain. The skimpy record indicates they stopped at about the 14,000-foot level, where they could look down on several of the passes they were searching for. They decided that it was possible to build a road between Puget Sound and the east side of the Cascades and went home without going the final 400 feet to the top. They noted in passing that Mount Rainier is "extremely rugged and difficult of ascent."

There also is a record of two men, whose names are not mentioned, climbing to the summit in June of 1854 to establish survey lines. There are no details except that the climb took six days and that they found the top to be covered in ice with a lake in the center, and, they said, there was "smoke or steam coming out all around." The only record of their climb was given 62 years later by a Yakima Indian named Saluskin who described guiding them part of the way.

August Valentine Kautz, a first lieutenant in the Army at Fort Steilacoom on Puget Sound, persuaded a doctor and four soldiers to attempt a climb in 1857. They gathered a few rudimentary articles of equipment and, with an Indian named Wapowety to guide them to a campsite on the upper slope of the mountain, left the fort on July 8. Most of his companions stopped someplace on the side of the mountain, but Kautz and one soldier made it almost to the summit, then turned back after finding that the water in their canteens had frozen. When they got back to camp, they found that the party was nearly out of food and Wapowety was snow blind and needed to be led off the mountain. They got back to the fort on the 14th day, convinced that it would be a long time before anyone got to the top of Mount Rainier.

That long time was 13 years and one month. In August 1870, Hazard Stevens, the son of the first governor of Washington Territory, Isaac Stevens, Philemon Beecher Van Trump, and an Englishman named Edward Coleman left Yelm, Washington, about 30 miles west of the mountain, with a settler named James Longmire, who had agreed to lead them part way and to help them find an Indian guide. After hiking four days, they hired an Indian named Sluiskin, not to be confused with Saluskin who had guided the 1854 climb.

His job done, Longmire left the party and headed for home. Stevens, Coleman, and Van Trump followed Sluiskin over a difficult route across the Tatoosh Mountain Range. Coleman gave up and left the party. On August 17, at a camp near present-day Paradise, Stevens and Van Trump ignored Sluiskin's warning that they would die if they attempted the climb and started up the mountain, leaving the guide, their coats, and blankets in camp.

They fought their way through bitter cold and wind and reached the crater at the peak during a vicious storm and so late in the day that it would be impossible to get back to camp before dark. With no coats or blankets, there was also little chance they would survive the night in the crater. The situation was desperate until Van Trump smelled sulphur. That led them to a cave melted in the ice by a steam jet from the mountain's interior. They spent a miserable night in the cave. The steam was too hot to bear for more than a few moments at a time, but when they backed away their clothing, soaked by the steam, froze on their backs. They spent the night alternating between too hot and too cold, as well as being nauseated by the sulphur smell.

The next day they made their way back to camp to find Sluiskin preparing to return to civilization to report them dead. After he convinced himself that they were not ghosts, he exclaimed, "*Skookum tilicum, skookum tum tum*," meaning, "strong men, strong hearts." Sluiskin Falls, near Paradise, memorializes the climb (*see* Stevens-Van Trump Memorial Trail, page 247).

The steam vent that saved the lives of Stevens and Van Trump was one of many that occur around the inside of the crater on top of the mountain. The crater is about 0.25 mile across and about 15 to 20 feet below the rim, which marks the top of the mountain. The bottom of the crater is filled with ice and snow, while wind often exposes the black, volcanic rock at the top of the rim. The inside of the rim is heated by steam, which billows from the caves and has been measured at temperatures as high as 180 degrees Fahrenheit. The caves interconnect to form a network that goes down as much as 300 feet into the ice inside the north, east, and south edge of the crater. At the deepest part, the sun is blocked out and it becomes necessary to use flashlights.

The summit crater intersects on its western edge with a slightly older, partial crater. That crater, a few feet below the summit crater, is rimmed with caves on its western edge. About 150 feet below the surface, that crater has a huge grotto that has been measured at about 170 by 130 feet and contains a small lake of melted snow about 15 feet deep and 50 by 20 feet around. The lake temperature hovers around 32 degrees Fahrenheit.

Stevens and Van Trump were the first to leave a record of climbing to the top of Mount Rainier, but their achievement was only the beginning. Many tens of thousands of people have climbed the mountain since they reached the top. The record number of attempts occurred in 1998, when about 10,959 people attempted the climb and 5,401 succeeded in getting to the peak.

It is not unusual for accidents to occur on the mountain. More than 50 people, including professional guides, have died here. Many others have been injured attempting to climb it. One accident alone, on June 21, 1981, resulted in 11 members of a climbing party being killed when they were caught in the collapse of a massive wall of ice above Camp Muir at the 11,000-foot level. Park rangers and professional guides work to rescue people who get in trouble on the mountain, but they are not always successful.

Climbers must register and obtain a permit before leaving and on returning. A fee is charged for the permit to finance the human waste removal system and to help cope with the problems of having so many people on the mountain where facilities are extremely limited.

The climb to the peak from Paradise is 8 miles long, with an elevation gain of 9,000 feet. Climbers attempting the climb must be in good physical condition and have proper training and equipment. A climbing school and guide service operates from the climbing base at Paradise: Rainier Mountaineering, Inc., 535 Dock Street, Suite 209, Tacoma, WA 98402. Phone (206) 627-6242. A guide service based at Sunrise was also operating on a trial basis. More information on that program is available from the Mount Rainier National Park, Tahoma Woods, Star Route, Ashford, WA 98304-9751. Phone (360) 569-2211.

Climbing alone requires advance approval from the superintendent of the national park. It takes as long as two weeks to obtain a permit. Write to Park Superintendent, Mount Rainier National Park, Tahoma Woods, Star Route, Ashford, WA 98304-9751.

People and the Mountain

James Longmire, the settler who helped Stevens and Van Trump get started on their climb to the Mount Rainier peak in 1870, had a farm on a homestead near Yelm. Word spread about his knowledge of the country and his part in the first climb. Other adventurers sought him out as a guide, but he did not climb to the peak himself until 1883, when he was 63 years old. During that trip he camped near some soda and iron springs. Recognizing the economic possibilities, he established a resort there operating the resort in the summer and returning to the farm during the winter. (*see* Trail of the Shadows, page 247). The resort attracted numerous guests, and word about the attractions of the place spread. John Muir, the famous naturalist, came by in 1888 to rent some horses from Longmire. He wrote his wife that he hadn't intended to climb the mountain but he became so enthralled by it that he "got excited and soon was on top."

Longmire and his family operated the resort for many years. His son, Len Longmire, often guided climbers from Camp Muir to the peak for $1. Today's Longmire is a collection of park buildings and an interpretive trail in the national park on the site of his resort.

Muir and Arthur C. Warner, the photographer who accompanied him, published articles and photographs about the mountain, spreading its reputation throughout the country. The records indicate that by 1890, 47 people had attempted to climb the mountain and 28 had succeeded. That year 10 more made the attempt and all 10 succeeded, including Fay Fuller, a Tacoma schoolteacher who became the first woman to reach the summit. She wore a blue, ankle-length flannel bloomer suit, and a blouse with long sleeves, but she was criticized for immodesty.

As the mountain became well known, it also became more and more popular throughout the country, and in 1899, Congress voted to make it the fifth of the nation's national parks, setting it aside to be protected and enjoyed.

Today Mount Rainier National Park consists of 235,612.5 acres of vastly varied terrain, ranging from the moist rain forest of the Carbon River valley, elevation 1,880 feet, to the ice, snow, rock, and steam of the crater at the peak, elevation 14,410 feet. Between the Carbon River valley and the peak are vast acres of glaciers and snow fields, magnificent meadows, old growth forests, lakes, and rivers, all looking much like they did when Captain Vancouver named the mountain in 1792.

About 2 million people visit the park each year. Many of them arrive on sunny, summer weekends and find large crowds taxing the ability of the park staff and facilities to cope with them. But even then the park layout is such that the natural beauty and awe-inspiring vistas can be enjoyed. In less crowded times the experience is even better.

The park has 240 miles of trails, and 147 miles of roads. All of the roads are open during the summer. Only the road from the Nisqually entrance to Paradise is open during the winter, and sometimes even that road may be closed temporarily by heavy snow or avalanches. Many of the other roads become snowshoe, and cross-country ski routes during the winter. Overnight ski and snowshoe trips into the backcountry require a permit from the park office or a ranger.

There is a museum at Longmire, and, during the summer, visitor centers operate daily at Paradise, Ohanapecosh, and Sunrise. The major visitor center at Paradise also operates on weekends in winter. It has displays, motion pictures, food service, and other attractions. The visitor center building at Paradise is round and the top floor offers a panoramic view of Mount Rainier and the entire landscape in every direction. It is named the Henry M. Jackson Visitor Center after the late U.S. Senator from Everett, Washington, who hiked and climbed in the Cascades as a boy and took a strong interest in promoting wilderness and parks here while he was in Congress.

At Longmire and Paradise there are rustic but comfortable hotels hat were built in 1917. They have food service, but the larger one, at Paradise, is closed during the winter. The hotels are booked most summer weekends, and reservations are highly recommended. Reservations and information may be obtained by contacting Mount Rainier Guest Services, Inc., PO Box 108, Ashford, WA 98304. Phone (360) 569-2275.

In addition to the inns at Paradise and Longmire there are numerous inns, motels, and bread-and breakfast accommodations on the roads leading to the major entrances at Nisqually, White River, and Ohanapecosh. For further information, addresses, and phone numbers, consult the Mount Rainier National Park's official Internet home page at www.nps.gov/mora/accom.

Life on Mount Rainier

Below the perpetual, barren glaciers, snow, ice, and rock of the peak, the slopes of Mount Rainier are a place of stark contrasts of weather. The rain shadow effect that governs the weather throughout the Cascades is manifested at Rainier because the peak is so high. The moist air, borne inland from the Pacific Ocean on prevailing westerly winds, is forced upward when it reaches the mountain. The air cools and its moisture condenses as precipitation, a process much like that which occurs throughout the rest of the Cascades. The heaviest snowfalls are between 5,000 and 10,000 feet elevation. Not only does less snow fall above 10,000 feet, but some of that which does fall there is blown away by the strong winds that buffet the high country.

The snow accumulation at the lower levels is immense. During the winter of 1971-1972, 1,122 inches fell at Paradise, a world record. The snow sometimes accumulates so deep at Paradise that people can stand on it at the top of a 23-foot weather tower.

Paradise, at 5,400 feet elevation, is less than half the way up to the peak of Mount Rainier, but it nevertheless is higher than many mountains in the Cascades. The additional elevation of Mount Rainier intensifies the adverse conditions for vegetation. Thus, plants that grow here are uniquely adapted to extreme conditions. Winter often lasts until June in the midlevel meadows. And winter may begin in October, leaving only a few months of growing season for the plants in the meadows.

Even in the summer, conditions can be extreme. Temperatures at ground level can range some 75 degrees Fahrenheit during a day, from 35 degrees at night to 110 Fahrenheit during the day. At the same time, above-ground temperatures may range only from 40 to 70 degrees Fahrenheit. The extremely strong winds that can occur at any time in the high elevations can also be a problem for vegetation, so herbs, grasses, and other plants tend to adapt by growing lower than their cousins in the lower elevations. Some plants between 6,000 and 8,000 feet elevation, such as the moss campion (*Silene acualis*), produce only two or three leaves on stems that grow to less than 1 inch high, while their roots grow deep into the ground, providing an anchor against the mountain's severe winds. Moss campion and similar cushion plants have streamlined shapes to reduce the effects of wind. They also grow matted stems that form a blanket to hold in heat absorbed during the day during the chill of the night. The plant within the blanket may be 20 degrees Fahrenheit warmer than the air above.

Despite the seemingly impossible conditions, Mount Rainier's high-country meadows are magnificently beautiful. Two of the most well known of these natural gardens surround the visitor centers at Paradise and Sunset. Paradise became a popular attraction in the earliest days, long before the national park was established. Located just 7 straight-line miles from Longmire, its beauty was discovered and appreciated almost from the beginning. The name is said to have originated from the first time Longmire's daughter-in-law, Martha, visited the meadow and exclaimed that it was what she imagined Paradise to look like.

Soon after the Longmires established their resort at the Longmire Hot Springs, businessmen began a sort of bed-and-breakfast service in tents they erected in the fields of Paradise. By 1911, there was a rough, muddy road, and President William H. Taft was a passenger in the first car to arrive at Paradise. The mud, however, was too much for the early-twentieth-century car, and it was pulled by horses for the last part of the trip. That occurred three years after the road reached the Nisqually Valley near the snout of the Nisqually Glacier and became famous as the first road in the United States to reach a glacier.

Despite modern development, the National Park Service, somehow, has managed to keep the meadows of Paradise startlingly beautiful. The trail network goes through the meadows to various attractions such as the Glacier Vista, which overlooks the Nisqually Glacier (*see* Panorama Point Trail, page 246).

Wildflowers thrive at Paradise despite the adverse weather in both the winter and summer. Usually they begin to appear about the middle of June, a few weeks later than at Sunrise Visitor Center, on the east side of the mountain, where the winter's snow cover is less deep. As in meadows throughout the high Cascades, the wildflowers begin with avalanche and glacier lilies poking their fragile-looking heads through the last few inches of the melting snow. Soon after that, western anemones and marsh marigolds appear, and by late July some 30 species of flowers may be covering the fields with brilliant color.

All of the flowers of the meadow are beautiful either individually or as a bouquet spread over acres of sloping mountainside. Among the noticeable specimens is the paintbrush, which looks a bit like a brush dipped in brightly colored paint. It gained its Latin name, *Castilleja parviflora*, in honor of Spanish botanist Domingo Castillejo. It is usually a magenta pink or red and grows in bunches throughout the meadows. It is beautiful because of its color, and it is interesting because it isn't the flower that gives it color, but the large, leaflike bracts that grow under the inconspicuous flower.

Another strange beauty of the meadow is beargrass, a member of the Lily family with a Latin name, *Xerophyllum tenax*, that means "dry leaves" and "tough." Beargrass grows taller than other meadow plants on long, spindly stems with large balls of delicate, white flowers on top, reminiscent of a scoop of vanilla ice cream on a long stick.

As elsewhere in the high country, the meadow flowers' season on Mount Rainier that began in June is usually over by September, with only a few, rather bedraggled blooms still valiantly defying the weakening sun and cold nights. By October the snow returns, piling ever more deeply until spring, when the cycle begins anew.

The trees of Mount Rainier's forests are much like those of the rest of the western slopes of Washington's Cascade Mountains, including some 27 species. In the lowlands the trees are predominantly gigantic, old-growth Douglas fir, true fir, western hemlock, and western redcedar. Some of these majestic giants are as many as 500 years old, tower 300 feet high, and measure as much as 8 feet in diameter at the base. These trees are mixed with lesser trees such as Pacific yew (*Taxus brevifolia)*, Pacific dogwood (*Cornus nuttalli*), and vine maple (*Acer circinatum)* in the lowlands, while riverbanks might be lined with red alder, black cottonwood, big leaf maple, and others.

Higher on the mountain slopes, silver fir and noble fir appear, and subalpine fir grows in the meadows.

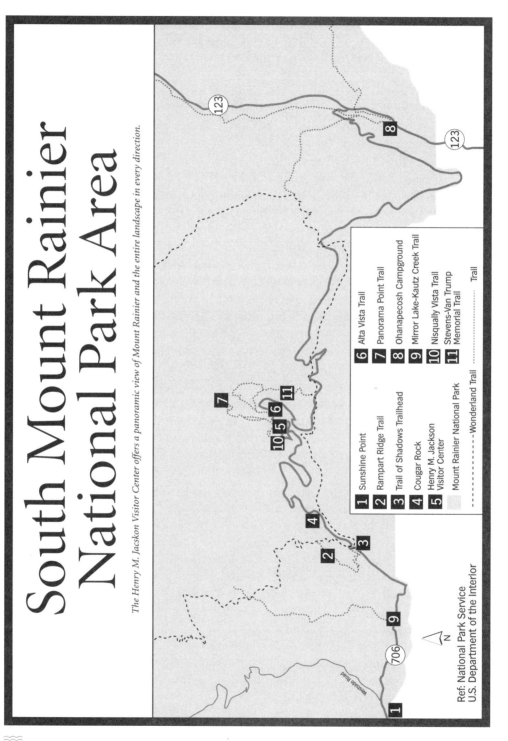

South Mount Rainier National Park Area

The Henry M. Jackson Visitor Center offers a panoramic view of Mount Rainier and the entire landscape in every direction.

1 Sunshine Point
2 Rampart Ridge Trail
3 Trail of Shadows Trailhead
4 Cougar Rock
5 Henry M. Jackson Visitor Center

6 Alta Vista Trail
7 Panorama Point Trail
8 Ohanapecosh Campground
9 Mirror Lake-Kautz Creek Trail
10 Nisqually Vista Trail
11 Stevens-Van Trump Memorial Trail

Mount Rainier National Park

- - - - - Wonderland Trail

.... Trail

Ref: National Park Service
U.S. Department of the Interior

Mammals in the Park

The 54 species of mammals in the park also are sensitive to the immense changes in weather conditions. Some have been found in surprising places. A white footed mouse has been reported scurrying about on the rocks in the rim of the crater where no *Peromyscus leucopus* should be. Packrats (*Neotoma cinerea*) have been seen in the snowy reaches of Camp Muir, elevation 10,188 feet, where there is little but rock and ice to feed on. Those sightings are anomalies, and it is not known how the animals reached those seemingly uninhabitable heights. But even in more hospitable places, the mountain mammals have adapted to the mountain's severe conditions in surprising ways. Heat and occasional drought make it difficult to survive in the alpine areas during the summer, but with snow packed as much as 30 feet deep, temperatures far below freezing, and winds gusting as much as 60 miles an hour, winter confronts wildlife with severe challenges.

Nature has provided the mammals with three major strategies for surviving winter's assaults. Some hibernate. Some migrate to lower elevations, where conditions are less severe. Some adapt their life-style.

Among those that hibernate is the hoary marmot, which stays in its winter den longer than most hibernators. These *Marmota caligata* live their lives close to their dens in talus slopes made up of large boulders where the cat-sized animals can quickly disappear when predators such as red-tailed hawks appear. When the marmot sees danger coming, it emits a sudden, piercing, whistle-like squeal that warns every other marmot for a great distance of the intruder. It is that habit that earns it the nickname of whistler or whistle pig. When the whistle sounds, all the marmots in the neighborhood scurry into the talus rocks. They may, however, soon emerge, climb onto the highest rock, and stand on their hind legs to see whether it is safe to resume basking in the sun or finding enough herbs and grasses to get fat enough to survive a long winter.

About September, when the food supply begins to dwindle, the marmots go into the rocks to curl up in their burrows and go into hibernation, a deep, sleeplike condition where their metabolic level reduces sharply, breathing slows to about one breath a minute, and the heart may beat only four to eight times a minute. Body temperature drops to about that of the surrounding air until it reaches a point near freezing. In the early part of the season, the little animal may occasionally awaken briefly to eliminate waste or eat a little stored food. But in deep winter the hibernation becomes more profound, and the marmot may spend half the year in that condition, then tunnel up through 4 feet of snow to greet the spring.

Black bears in the Cascades, as elsewhere, adopt a shallower and shorter condition that is similar to hibernation. It is interrupted by midwinter rambles more frequently than the marmots' sleep. Regardless of the depth of their winter sleep, the bears are certain to be extremely hungry when they leave the den in the spring, and that tends to put them in a bad temper.

Deer and elk are among the migrating animals of the park. Elk, also known by their

Shawnee Indian name of *wapiti*, and their Latin name of *Cervus elaphus*, are the largest of the park's animals, growing to 7 or 8 feet long. They are tan with a light patch on the rump and have cloven hooves. Each year the males grow huge antlers. The herds in the Cascades are largely descended from Rocky Mountain elk, which were imported when the native Roosevelt elk became nearly extinct.

The elk wander in herds with males in one group, females in another, to the lush meadows of the high country in the summer. In winter they migrate down to the protection of the forest where the wind is broken, the snow less deep, and forage more available. The bulls separate from each other in the fall and divide the female herd into harems. That period is marked by the males bugling, emitting a deep bellow that rises to a whistling sound, which, presumably, the females consider to be a serenade.

Perhaps the most extraordinary of all the adaptations to winter is that of the snowshoe hare. This *Lepus Americanus* changes its fur color from the dark brown of summer to a white that blends with the snow and camouflages the hare from hungry predators.

A major source of the hare's winter food is the succulent shoots of young trees. During the early part of the season, hares eat the lower shoots they can reach easily from the ground. As they consume the lower branches, the snowfall accumulates. With the wide, padded feet that give them their name, the hares are able to snowshoe on top of the snow as it deepens, rising above the ground so they can reach higher branches on the tree. If the snow doesn't accumulate fast enough so they can reach the shoots, they burrow tunnels under the snow and eat whatever food they can find on the ground. That, however, puts them out of reach of predators such as the lynx which is unable to burrow, and reduces the food source for those predators.

White-tailed ptarmigan (*Lagopus leucurus*) is another creature that changes its camouflage from brown to white in the winter. It stays on the snow all winter, digging into it only for shelter and to reach buds of dwarf willows, which are its staple food.

Pikas (*Ochotona princeps*) have evolved still another method for escaping the hazards of winter. Like the marmot, these 6-inch long little furbearers, also known as conies, live among the rocks of talus slopes. Rather than sleep through the winter, they survive by spending the summer storing vegetation, which they harvest from nearby meadows and carry crossways in their mouths to their rocks where they store it in haystacks they eat throughout the winter.

Roads in Mount Rainier National Park

Roads, automobiles, and parking lots are incidental and pretty much confined to the periphery of Mount Rainier National Park. The main road parallels the south and eastern borders of the park and is an extension of three state highways (State Routes 706, 123, and 410). It has various names such as Nisqually-Paradise Road, Stevens Canyon Road, and Mather Memorial Parkway. They interconnect so it is not obvious where one ends and the other begins. They total 59.8 miles and run between the southwest and northeast borders of the park. The Mather Memorial Parkway section was named after Stephen T. Mather, the first director of the National Park Service when the road was built in 1932.

Extensions of the road on the east side go to the Sunrise Visitor Center, and on the south side to Paradise, where the Henry M. Jackson Visitor Center and the Paradise Inn are located. The Nisqually Road passes Longmire, where the Longmire Museum and National Park Inn are located. The only other major roads are the Carbon River Road, which goes 5 miles from the northwest corner of the park to campgrounds and trails; the Mowich Lake Road, which goes 6 miles from the western border of the park to a campground, trails, and Mowich Lake; and the West Side Road, which goes from near the Nisqually Park entrance 13 miles along the park's western boundary to several trailheads. The entire Carbon River Road and all but 3 miles of the West Side Road were closed to vehicles in 1998 after a series of washouts. It was not certain whether or when they would be reopened.

Only the road from the southern boundary to Ohanapecosh and the road from the Nisqually entrance to Paradise are open during the winter, and even they can be temporarily closed by weather conditions. The section of the Nisqually-Paradise Road from Longmire to Paradise is open only during daylight hours during the winter.

The roads all are built to blend into the park's natural surroundings and lead to magnificent views of mountains, meadows, and forests, as well as to major attractions, including dozens of trailheads.

Directions: Among the accesses to the park are the Nisqually entrance, on State Route 706, 6 miles east of Ashford; the White River entrance, 38 miles east of Enumclaw; and the Stevens Canyon Entrance, 10 miles north of Packwood. Longmire is 6 miles from the Nisqually entrance on the main road. Paradise is 12 miles from Longmire on a loop off the same main road. Sunrise is on the White River Road 16 miles from the park's White River entrance.

Activities: Camping, hiking, picnicking, snowshoeing, snowboarding and tubing, cross-country skiing, mountain climbing, nonmotorized boating, fishing, horseback riding, ranger walks and interpretive talks.

Facilities: Campgrounds, trails, museum, visitor centers, hotels, food service, picnic areas, interpretive trails, mountain climbing schools and guide services.

Dates: Open year-round, with limited access in winter.

Fees: A fee is charged to enter the park and there are camping fees.

Closest town: Ashford, 6 miles.

For more information: Mount Rainier National Park, Ashford, WA 98304-9751. Phone (360) 569-2111. Drive-in campsites can be reserved by phoning (800) 365-2267. Backcountry camping reservations can be made by calling the park's main number (360) 569-2211.

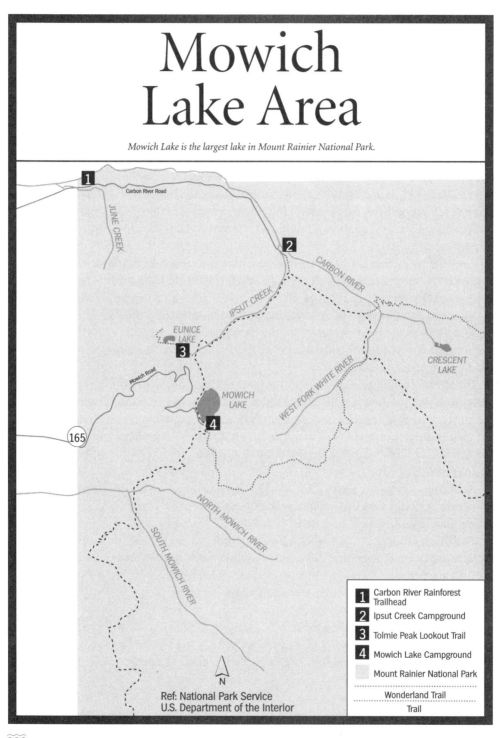

Mowich Lake Area

Mowich Lake is the largest lake in Mount Rainier National Park.

Carbon River Road

JUNE CREEK

CARBON RIVER

IPSUT CREEK

EUNICE LAKE

CRESCENT LAKE

Mowich Road

WEST FORK WHITE RIVER

165

MOWICH LAKE

NORTH MOWICH RIVER

SOUTH MOWICH RIVER

N

Ref: National Park Service
U.S. Department of the Interior

1	Carbon River Rainforest Trailhead
2	Ipsut Creek Campground
3	Tolmie Peak Lookout Trail
4	Mowich Lake Campground
	Mount Rainier National Park
	Wonderland Trail
	Trail

Campgrounds in Mount Rainier National Park

In addition to numerous backcountry, hike-in campgrounds, the national park has six drive-in campgrounds, with a total of 571 designated campsites. The campgrounds are all open through the summer, but only the Sunshine Campground remains open during the winter. Campsites may be occupied by one party for only 14 nights during July and August. Two of the campgrounds have a total of 7 sites capable of accommodating groups with large numbers of people.

Sunshine Point Campground, [Fig. 39(1)] 2,000 feet elevation, is at the southwestern corner of the park, about 0.25 mile from the Nisqually entrance and just off the south side of the Nisqually-Paradise Road. It has 18 campsites, piped water, chemical vault toilets, a trailer dump station, fire grates, and picnic tables. A fee is charged.

Cougar Rock Campground, [Fig. 39(4)] 3,180 feet elevation, is 2.3 miles northeast of Longmire on the Longmire-Paradise Road. There are 200 individual campsites and 5 campsites for groups of from 10 to 24 persons. Camping is available by reservation only during the midsummer season. To reserve a site, contact National Park Reservation Service, Inc., PO Box 1600, Cumberland, MD 21502. Phone (800) 365-2267. During the rest of the season, camping is on a first-come, first-served basis. The campground has piped water, flush toilets, a trailer dump station, fire grates, picnic tables, an amphitheater, and hiking trails. A fee is charged for camping.

Ohanapecosh Campground [Fig. 38(8)] is 11 miles north of Packwood at 1,914 feet elevation, about 1 mile from the park entrance. There are 205 individual campsites. Camping is by reservation only during the midsummer season. To reserve a site, contact National Park Reservation Service, Inc., PO Box 1600, Cumberland, MD 21502. Phone 1-800-365-2267. During the rest of the season camping is on a first-come, first-served basis. The campground has piped water, flush toilets, a trailer dump station, fire grates, picnic tables, an amphitheater, a visitor center, and hiking trails. A fee is charged for camping.

White River Campground [Fig. 41(4)] is in the northeastern part of the park, 5 miles west of the White River entrance on the White River Road. The White River Road is a branch of the Mather Memorial Parkway section of State Route 410. Elevation is 4,400 feet. There are 112 individual campsites, piped water, flush toilets, a trailer dump station, fire grates, picnic tables, and hiking trails. A fee is charged.

Ipsut Creek Campground [Fig. 40(2)] is located 6 miles from the Carbon River entrance, near the end of the Carbon River Road. Elevation is 2,300 feet. There are 29 individual campsites, and 2 sites for groups from 10 to 24 persons. The campground has picnic tables, hiking trails, and pit toilets, but no potable water. There is no fee for camping, but campers must register at the Wilkeson Ranger Station at the park's Carbon River entrance. (Note: In 1988 the road to Ipsut Creek Campground was closed due to undercutting and the campground was accessible only by foot or bicycle. Check with the

Mount Rainier National Park office, Tahoma Woods, Star Route, Ashford, WA 98304-9751, phone 360-569-2211 for updated information.)

Mowich Lake Campground [Fig. 40(4)] is in the northwestern part of the park at the end of State Route 165, 6 miles from the park entrance, at 4,929 feet elevation. There are 30 undesignated, walk-in campsites, chemical-vault toilets, picnic tables, and hiking trails, but no potable water, and fires are not allowed. There is no fee and no registration for camping.

Snow Camping in the Paradise Area

During the winter, group and individual camping on snow in tents, snow caves, and igloos is permitted in the immediate Paradise area. Groups of 12 or more are required to camp within 300 to 600 feet of the restrooms in the upper parking lot and must either use the restrooms or use blue bags to deposit human waste. The bags and information on how to dispose of them may be obtained at the Henry M. Jackson Visitor Center at Paradise or the museum at Longmire.

Groups are limited to 120 persons and all campers must obtain a wilderness permit from either the museum or the Henry M. Jackson Visitor Center. Igloos and snow caves are banned until the snow is at least 8 feet deep. Caves and igloos must be collapsed when they are abandoned to prevent them from forming holes that endanger later campers.

Directions: Group snow camping is permitted in Paradise in the areas designated on park maps as the lower Deadhorse Creek area, below Alta Vista, near Paradise Inn, and on the slope between the upper parking lot and Barn Flats.

Activities: Snow camping.

Facilities: Restrooms and telephones are available in the upper parking lot at Paradise.

Dates: Open winter.

Fees: None.

For more information: The National Park Museum at Longmire can be contacted in person or by phone at (360) 569-2211, extension 3314.

Hiking Trails in Mount Rainier National Park

There are a multitude of trails in the national park, covering more than 240 miles from the lowland forests to the high meadows. By far the longest inside the park is the Wonderland Trail, which winds 93 miles and makes a complete circle around the mountain (*see* Wonderland Trail, page 299).

Many of the trails are under deep snow until midsummer or later, but they are open year round and can be used in the winter for snowshoeing and winter camping.

The Pacific Crest Trail, which parallels the mountain crests from Canada to Mexico, (*see* Pacific Crest Trail, page 295) follows the park's northeastern border, crossing into the park in only a few places, but some trails within the park lead to it. There is a rich variety of trails available throughout the park, some long and difficult, some short and easy. All of the trails go through and to magnificent country.

Permits, available from the visitor centers and ranger stations, are required for overnight camping as well as for all winter use of the backcountry. Camping beside the trails is permitted only in specially designated campgrounds, which usually have marked campsites, toilets, and a nearby source of water. Off-trail camping, at least 1 mile from any road or established trail, is permitted but must be at least 100 yards from lakes, streams, and wetlands. For people hiking in alpine zones above tree line on exposed rock, glaciers, and snow fields, camping is limited to permanent snow or ice, and on bare ground. Among the multitude of inviting trails are the following:

Avalanche Track Growth

Avalanches that flow down the same gullies on the mountainside yearly leave a bare surface of rock at the gully bottom called an avalanche track in the summer. Two tree species have evolved to grow in these rocky tracks. One, at the higher elevations, is the Alaska cedar (*Chamaecyparis nootkatensis*). The other, at lower elevations but sometimes in the same track, is the sitka alder (*Alnus sinuata*). Both bend beneath the onrushing snow of an avalanche that has the power to snap off larger, less supple trees. Both also tend to grow in thick patches, almost like hair, that are difficult for hikers to work their way through.

ALTA VISTA TRAIL

[Fig. 39(6)] This short, paved but steep trail is one of the interconnecting routes that go through the meadow above the Paradise Visitor Center. It passes some of the meadow's flower fields and stands of subalpine fir. The upper third of the trail is a loop that goes to Alta Vista, the high point. At Alta Vista there are views of the meadow and of the mountainous skyline, including Mount Adams in the distance to the south and the glaciers of Mount Rainier nearby to the north.

Directions: The trailhead is just above the Henry M. Jackson Visitor Center.

Facilities: Restrooms and food service are available in the visitor center.

Dates: Open summer.

Fees: None.

For more information: The information desk in the visitor center can provide information and advice about the trail, phone (360) 569-2211, extension 2328.

Trail: 1.5 miles, round trip.

Elevation: 600 foot elevation gain.

Degree of difficulty: Easy.

PANORAMA POINT TRAIL

[Fig. 39(7)] This trail is paved for the first 2 miles then becomes gravel and earth. It is a fairly short and steep route that takes its name from the panoramic view at the summit of the trail. The mountain rises steadily from that point, and the snow fields reach upwards toward the sky while the flowered meadow stretches far below. The view expands down Stevens Canyon to the east and the Nisqually Valley to the west.

The trail joins the Alta Vista Trail for a time, then climbs up a ridge to a looped branch that goes to Glacier Vista. The Glacier Vista branch goes to the Glacier Vista overlook then continues on briefly to rejoin the Panorama Point Trail at a second junction a short distance above the lower junction. At Glacier Vista, the view sweeps along the broken ice of Nisqually Glacier. It would be a shame not to take the short loop that goes there, either on the way up or the way down.

Above the upper Glacier Vista junction, the Panorama Point Trail disappears in the permanent snow on the mountain slopes. This is the unmarked route toward the stone huts of Camp Muir, a jump-off spot for climbers seeking the top of the mountain.

Shortly after the upper junction with the Glacier Vista Trail, the route turns right and proceeds toward Panorama Point. There often are snow patches along the higher part of the trail until late in July.

Directions: The trailhead is near the ranger station across from the Paradise Inn, in the upper parking lot at Paradise.

Facilities: Paradise Inn, near the trailhead, has full facilities.

Dates: Open summer.

Fees: None.

For more information: The ranger station at the trailhead, and the information desk in the nearby Henry M. Jackson Visitor Center can provide information and advice about the trail, phone (360) 569-2211, extension 2328.

Trail: 4 miles, one-way.

Elevation: 1,400 foot elevation gain.

Degree of difficulty: Moderate.

NISQUALLY VISTA TRAIL

[Fig. 39(10)] Perhaps the easiest of the Paradise trails, this short route may also be the prettiest. With the far end forming a loop on itself, in the summer the trail passes meadows with flowers of many colors blooming gloriously, as species succeeds species through the growing season. The dark green of subalpine fir and mountain hemlock stands provides marked contrast to the brightly colored flowers.

Near the trailhead, the route passes a hollowed rock that was formed by one of the ancient lava flows that built Mount Rainier. Beyond that, the trail goes through a meadow with a tiny pond called the Fairy Pool and awesome views of the mountain above.

Then it follows the rim of the Nisqually River canyon and a fenced viewpoint that looks over the broken ice formations of the Nisqually Glacier from top to toe. Heading back on the loop in the far end of the trail, the route winds through an open meadow with the rugged rock peaks of the Tatoosh Range in the background.

Directions: The trailhead is at the west end of the parking lot at the Henry M. Jackson Visitor Center.

Facilities: Restrooms and food service are available in the visitor center.

Dates: Open in summer for hiking and winter for snowshoeing.

Fees: None.

For more information: The information desk in the visitor center can provide information and advice about the trail, phone (360) 569-2211, extension 2328.

Trail: 1.5 miles.

Elevation: 200 foot elevation gain.

Degree of difficulty: Easy.

STEVENS-VAN TRUMP MEMORIAL TRAIL

[Fig. 39(11)] This trail, also called the Skyline Trail, goes past the Sluiskin Falls, a beautiful waterfall named after the Indian who guided Hazard Stevens and Philemon Beecher Van Trump to the base camp from which they made the first successful climb of Mount Rainier in August 1870. It also goes to a memorial plaque on Mazama Ridge at the site of the camp where Sluiskin waited for his companions to return from the peak. From there, the views include a rocky basin and a flowered meadow that lines the Paradise River.

A short distance from the memorial, the trail reaches a junction with the Paradise Glacier Trail, which leads 1 mile over a rocky surface to the snout of the Paradise Glacier. Once, huge caves formed in the end of the glacier, attracting large numbers of people to see the eerie blue light caused by the sun shining through the icy ceiling. The glacier has receded to the point where the ice caves have disappeared, but the jumbled ice and the rocky surface left as the glacier retreated are well worth seeing.

Directions: The trailhead is near the ranger station across from the Paradise Inn, in the upper parking lot at Paradise.

Facilities: Paradise Inn, near the trailhead, has full facilities.

Dates: Open summer.

Fees: None.

For more information: The ranger station at the trailhead and the information desk in the nearby Henry M. Jackson Visitor Center can provide information and advice about the trail, phone (360) 569-2211, extension 2328.

Trail: 3.8 miles, one-way.

Elevation: 600 foot elevation gain.

Degree of difficulty: Moderate.

TRAIL OF THE SHADOWS

[Fig. 39(3)] This is a short, easy hike through the place where, in 1883, James Long-mire discovered a cluster of hot springs and developed the first tourist attraction in what

Stevens and Van Trump

Hazard Stevens and Philemon Beecher Van Trump, who are credited with making the first successful climb of Mount Rainier, both were distinguished individuals. Stevens, the son of Isaac Stevens, the first governor of the Washington Territory, won the Congressional Medal of Honor and, at age 22, became the youngest Union general during the Civil War. Van Trump, who was the secretary of Washington Territorial Governor Marshall F. Moore, returned to climb Rainier four more times, the last time in 1892.

is now the national park. The trail passes a log cabin built by Longmire's son, Elcaine, in 1888. The cabin is 14-by-16 feet and has a door and a window. It was built of cedar logs carefully fitted to make solid walls. It was restored by the Civilian Conservation Corps in 1934 and, later, by the National Park Service, and it is the oldest structure in the park. A little beyond Elcaine's cabin, the trail passes the elaborate rock work at the Soda Springs that was part of the Civilian Conservation Corps development in Longmire. It, too, demonstrates the careful workmanship of the builders.

The trail makes a loop around the marshy meadows of the springs that emit water, ranging from 50 to 85 degrees Fahrenheit, that is not safe to drink. Interpretive signs tell of the historic and natural features along the way. There is a beaver pond; the Iron Mike Mineral Spring, which emits rust-colored water; and a calcium carbonate mound formed by carbon dioxide gas that escapes from the warm water of another spring. Lovely, but poisonous, orange and gold fly amanita mushrooms (*Amanita muscaria*) are native to the area.

Directions: The trail begins across the road from the museum at the National Park Inn parking lot in Longmire.

Facilities: Lodging and food service are available in the National Park Inn. Restrooms are located in the parking lot.

Dates: Open year-round.

Fees: None.

For more information: A hiker information center is located at the parking lot, or the National Park Museum in the parking lot can be contacted in person or by phone at (360) 569-2211, extension 3314.

Trail: 0.75 mile.

Elevation: 80 foot elevation gain.

Degree of difficulty: Easy. The trail is wheelchair accessible to Elcaine Longmire's old cabin, about 0.25 mile.

EMMONS GLACIER MORAINE TRAIL

[Fig. 41(5)] This trail is a study in contrasts as it goes from lush stands of old-growth fir and hemlock to the barren rock and sparse vegetation in the till left by the receding Emmons Glacier.

The trail begins in the forest along a fork of the White River then goes about 1 mile to a fork. The right fork goes to Glacier Basin. The left fork drops down to the river and a bridge. Across the river, the trail climbs past the moraine where there are wide views of the ice and rock of the mountain.

In another 1 mile or so, the trail ends at the snout of the gigantic Emmons Glacier, where there are views of the tortured ice that flows from the mountain peak where the glacier begins.

Directions: The trailhead is at the end of Loop D in the White River Campground in the northeastern section of the park.

Facilities: There are restrooms in the campground.

Dates: Open summer.

Fees: None.

For more information: The ranger station in the campground. Or contact Mount Rainier National Park headquarters, Tahoma Woods, Star Route, Ashford, WA 98304-9751. Phone (360) 569-2211.

Trail: 3 miles, one-way.

Elevation: 880 foot elevation gain.

Degree of difficulty: Easy.

SHADOW LAKE TRAIL

[Fig. 41(3)] This is a short, level hike that goes through forest and meadow, to a pretty, high-country lake. There are campsites on the Wonderland Trail about 1 mile west of the lake. Overnight permits, required for all overnight stays in the national park backcountry, are available at the Wilderness Information Center in the White River Campground. They must be obtained in person within one day of when the hike is to begin.

The route begins in subalpine meadows, often inhabited by deer and other wildlife. There are good views of Mount Rainier. A short distance from the trailhead, there is a junction with the Wonderland Trail, which leads to the subalpine forest stands at the mouth of Shadow Lake.

Directions: The trailhead is at the southeastern corner of the parking lot at the Sunrise Visitor Center.

Facilities: Restrooms and food service are available in the visitor center.

Dates: Open summer.

Fees: None.

For more information: The information desk at the visitor center can provide information and advice about the trail. Or contact Mount Rainier National Park head-quarters, Tahoma Woods, Star Route, Ashford, WA 98304-9751. Phone (360) 569-2211.

Trail: 1 mile, one-way.

Elevation: 200 foot elevation gain.

Degree of difficulty: Easy.

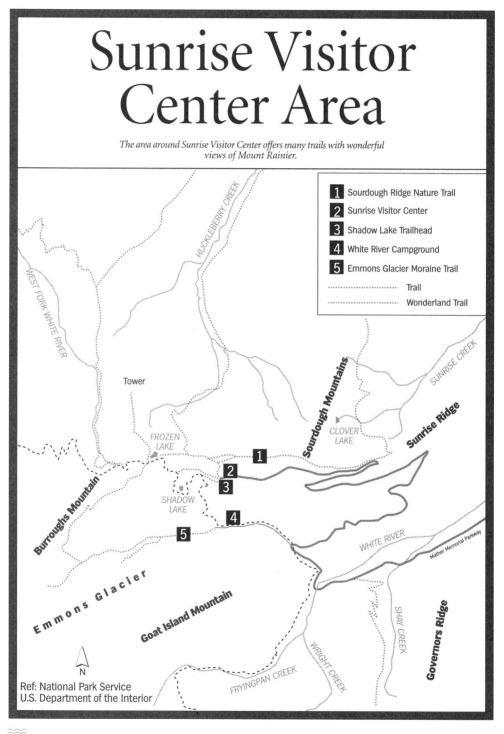

Sunrise Visitor Center Area

The area around Sunrise Visitor Center offers many trails with wonderful views of Mount Rainier.

1 Sourdough Ridge Nature Trail
2 Sunrise Visitor Center
3 Shadow Lake Trailhead
4 White River Campground
5 Emmons Glacier Moraine Trail

·········· Trail
·········· Wonderland Trail

HUCKLEBERRY CREEK

WEST FORK WHITE RIVER

Tower

SOURDOUGH MOUNTAINS

SUNRISE CREEK

Sunrise Ridge

FROZEN LAKE

CLOVER LAKE

Burroughs Mountain

SHADOW LAKE

WHITE RIVER

Mather Memorial Parkway

Emmons Glacier

Goat Island Mountain

SHAY CREEK

Governors Ridge

N

Ref: National Park Service
U.S. Department of the Interior

FRYINGPAN CREEK

WRIGHT CREEK

▨ SOURDOUGH RIDGE NATURE TRAIL

[Fig. 41(1)] This is a triangular loop that never gets very far from the Sunrise Lodge but offers fine close-up views of the Yakima Park Meadows and awesome wide views of Mount Rainier's icy slopes. An interpretative booklet available at the trailhead or in the Sunrise Visitor Center gives a description of the natural features along the way.

The trail begins at the Sunrise Visitor Center parking lot and passes near the picnic area, which provides a nice spot for a sandwich and a cool drink when the hike is finished. It goes upward from the parking lot through the Yakima Park Meadows toward Antler Peak. Near the foot of the mountain there is a junction with the Sourdough Ridge Trail, and the nature trail turns left to follow that trail for a short distance, to where the views of Mount Rainier are at their best. Along the way, watch for the various species of Jacob's ladder (*Polemonium* spp), a leafy plant with delicate little flowers that bloom in bunches on the stalk. These plants tend to grow around the edge of stands of trees in the alpine meadows and are very attractive. But, visitors are advised not to pick them, partly because the law requires hikers to leave meadow flowers intact for the next visitors to enjoy, and partly because the leaves of most *Polemoniums* smell a little like skunks.

At a broad saddle, the nature trail splits to the left from the Sourdough Ridge Trail and goes back down, past the picnic area, to the parking lot.

Directions: The trailhead is at the northwestern corner of the Sunrise Visitor Center parking lot.

Facilities: Restrooms, and food service are available in the visitor center.

Dates: Open summer.

FORGET-ME-NOT
(*Myosotis scorpioides*)

Fees: None.

For more information: The information desk at the visitor center can provide information and advice about the trail. Or contact Mount Rainier National Park headquarters, Tahoma Woods, Star Route, Ashford, WA 98304-9751. Phone (360) 569-2211.

Trail: 1.5 miles, one-way.

Elevation: 400 foot elevation gain.

Degree of difficulty: Easy.

CARBON RIVER RAINFOREST TRAIL

[Fig. 40(1)] This is a short, almost completely level, loop trail past the ancient trees of a rare inland temperate rainforest. Temperate rain forests usually occur near an ocean where they get the maximum effect of moist ocean winds rising as they meet rising land formations. The elevation causes the clouds to cool. As they do, the moisture condenses and falls as copious amounts of rain, creating a forest that is an awesome experience.

The huge old cedar and fir trees are covered with green lichen and moss, while the ground at their feet is laden with ferns and other moisture-loving greenery. There is so much green growth that the forest takes on a greenish ambience.

The trail begins where the Carbon Creek Road enters the northwestern corner of the park. A few feet beyond the trailhead, the trail forks. Since it is a loop trail it makes little difference which fork hikers take.

There are bridges over June Creek just beyond the fork on both legs of the trail. Going counterclockwise, the ground is soggy and the trail has been reinforced with cedar puncheon (split-cedar rails laid side by side to form a relatively dry walkway above the marshy ground).

After a short walk the trail reaches a less soggy area, makes a sharp left turn, goes over another bridge, then turns back toward the trailhead, always passing between the giant trees of the rainforest.

Directions: The trailhead is across the road from the ranger station at the Carbon River entrance in the northwestern corner of the park.

Facilities: There are toilets near the trailhead.

Dates: Open summer.

Fees: None.

For more information: The ranger station across the road from the trailhead can provide information and advice about the trail. Or contact Mount Rainier National Park headquarters, Tahoma Woods, Star Route, Ashford, WA 98304-9751. Phone (360) 569-2211.

Trail: 0.3 mile.

Degree of difficulty: Easy.

TOLMIE PEAK LOOKOUT TRAIL

[Fig. 40(3)] This trail provides long views and a walk beside two very attractive lakes, as well as scenes of old-growth forests and subalpine meadows. The biggest reward for hikers is the view of the mountain landscape in and beyond the park's northwest corner from the fire lookout on Tolmie Peak at the end of the trail.

The mountain is named after Dr. William Fraser Tolmie, a young Scottish physician at the Hudson Bay Company's Fort Nisqually on Puget Sound. He and five Indian guides left the fort on August 29, 1833 to search for plants with medicinal qualities. In the process he became the first European to enter what is now the park. The

Red Alder (*Alnus rubra*)

This close relative of the birch tree is among the early trees of the forest cycle that begins with a fire or other catastrophe, destroying the old forest. The cycle continues through a long succession of new plants and ends with the old forest being replaced. Red alders grow well in poor soil beside streams or other moisture sources. The trees' roots host bacteria in nodules that convert nitrogen from the air and deposit it in the soil, where it becomes a fertilizer for other plants. Native Americans used red alder as a source of red dye they used to make their nets invisible to fish. They also used it to smoke salmon, a practice still used today. Long considered a weed tree by loggers in the Pacific Northwest, it now is recognized as a hardwood that makes handsome furniture.

peak was named in the belief that it was the peak he climbed on September 2, as the climax of his hike. Later research led to the belief that he actually was in another part of the park but his name stuck on the original mountain.

The lookout, perched on the very tip of the peak at 5,930 feet elevation, was built in 1935 by a Seattle contractor after young men of the Civilian Conservation Corps built the trail and bridges to the site. Before that, the peak had been used to spot fires by people who lived in tents. The structure is used now primarily as a base for backcountry rangers.

The trail begins at the Mowich Campground and winds over a short segment of the Wonderland Trail through a forest of Douglas fir and hemlock beside Mowich Lake, the largest lake in the national park. Mount Rainier, in all its icy glory, is clearly visible across the lake.

From the lake, the route goes over a ridge and past a cliff of columnar andesite to a junction with the Tolmie Creek Trail. The right fork goes a short distance to Ipsut Pass, where there are views of the Ipsut Creek Canyon and the Carbon River valley.

The left fork from the junction leaves the Wonderland Trail and goes first down, then up through the forest to a side trail that goes a short distance to Eunice Lake, a sparkling mountain beauty. The trail curves around the lake and climbs a bluff where there are striking views of Mount Rainier and its glaciers reflected in the dark waters of the lake.

Beyond the lake, the trail leaves the forest and enters subalpine meadows, then goes up the final slope to Tolmie Peak and its lookout.

Directions: The trailhead is on the north side of the parking area of the Mowich Lake Campground, at the end of State Route 165, 5 miles east of the park boundary.

Activities: Hiking, fishing.

Facilities: There are chemical-vault toilets and picnic tables in the Mowich Lake Campground.

Dates: Open summer.

For more information: Mount Rainier National Park headquarters, Tahoma Woods, Star Route, Ashford, WA 98304-9751. Phone (360) 569-2211.

Trail: 4 miles, one-way.

Elevation: 425 foot elevation gain.

Degree of difficulty: Moderate.

RAMPART RIDGE TRAIL

[Fig. 39(2)] This is a loop hike that goes through deep forest with some open spaces where there are long views. The hike begins on the Trail of the Shadows (*see* Trail of the Shadows, page 247) then, after about 800 feet, going clockwise around the loop, the route takes a fork to the left onto the Rampart Ridge Trail.

The trail goes up a long series of switchbacks for about 2 miles to where there are good views of tree-covered Tumtum Peak, elevation 4,678 feet, which some say looks like a pyramid with a rounded top, and others say it resembles an elephant's head. Either way it is a pleasant sight of a not very big, but nevertheless, beautiful mountain.

Then the trail edges along a cliff, where there is a view of the Nisqually Valley stretching from Longmire to Paradise. The route from here levels off for 1 mile through alpine forest, with glimpses of Mount Rainier. There are junctions with two other trails along the way. Take the right fork in both places. The last leg heads back down toward Longmire in the valley below. The trail crosses the road at the bottom and returns to the parking lot at Longmire.

Directions: The hike begins in Longmire at the Trail of the Shadows trailhead, across the road from the museum at the National Park Inn parking lot. It follows that trail in a clockwise direction for some 800 feet, then branches to the left onto the Rampart Ridge Trail.

Facilities: Lodging and food service are available in the National Park Inn. Restrooms are located in the parking lot.

Dates: Open summer.

Fees: None.

For more information: A hiker information center is located at the parking lot, or the National Park Museum in the parking lot can be contacted in person or by phone at (360) 569-2211, extension 3314.

Trail: 4.5-mile loop.

Elevation: 1,800 foot elevation gain.

Degree of difficulty: Moderate.

▓ MIRROR LAKE-KAUTZ CREEK TRAIL

[Fig. 39(9)] This trail begins in the forest of dead trees left by the Kautz Mudflow in October 1947, and provides a good illustration of the kind of desolation even a relatively minor flood of mixed silt, sand, volcanic ash, and other debris can create when a sudden flow of water is released high on a mountain such as Mount Rainier. It also demonstrates the healing power of nature with a new, young forest that has sprouted amidst the devastation.

The trail is one of several that go to Indian Henry's Hunting Ground, an immensely beautiful park-like area in the high country of Mount Rainier. One of its many awesome scenes is of the mountain reflected in Mirror Lake, a tiny lake that reflects the mountain's southwest face. Countless photographs have been taken of the scene, including one by Asahel Curtis, the famed outdoor photographer of the early twentieth century. That photograph was used on a postage stamp issued in 1934.

The subalpine park is named after an Indian named Satolick, whose English name was Henry. He apparently hunted mountain goats here in the late nineteenth century.

The trail goes over the mudflow and through the reincarnating dead forest without gaining much altitude. Then, it crosses Kautz Creek into dense forest, where it begins to climb, gently at first, then more steeply up a series of switchbacks. After the fourth mile the trail becomes a tad less steep as it goes into meadows with long views to the west and south. Eventually, Mount Rainier comes into view as a backdrop to the many wildflowers of the meadows.

Above Indian Henry's Hunting Ground, toward Pyramid Peak, Tahoma Glacier comes into view and there is the constant sound of rock and ice falling from the glacier.

Directions: The trailhead is across the Nisqually-Longmire Road from the parking lot of the Kautz Creek Picnic Area nature exhibit, about 3 miles from the park's Nisqually entrance.

Facilities: There are picnic tables and chemical toilets at the nature exhibit.

Dates: Open summer.

Fees: None.

For more information: Mount Rainier National Park headquarters, Tahoma Woods, Star Route, Ashford, WA 98304-9751. Phone (360) 569-2211.

Trail: 5.5 miles, one-way.

Elevation: 2,300 foot elevation gain.

Degree of difficulty: Moderate.

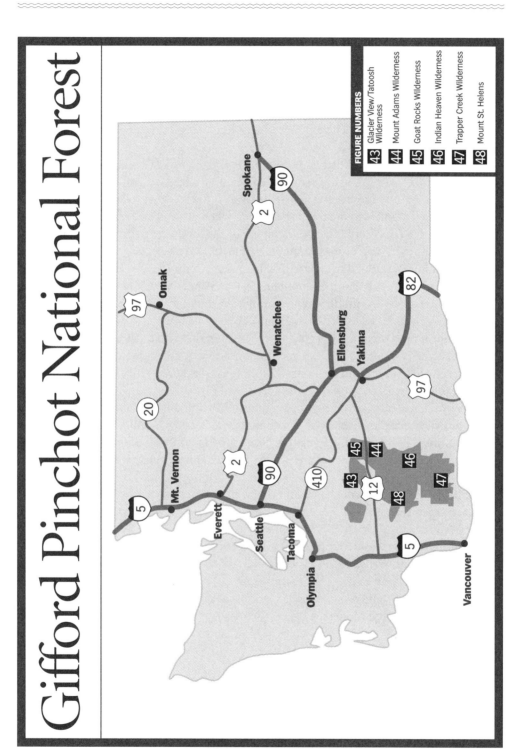

Gifford Pinchot National Forest

Gifford Pinchot
National Forest

T he Gifford Pinchot National Forest gained world notoriety in the spring of 1980
when its second largest mountain exploded in a cataclysm of destruction.

Until that momentous eruption of Mount St. Helens (*see* Mount St. Helens
National Volcanic Monument, page 281), the GP, as it is known to the Forest Service, had
been little different from the other awesomely rugged and immensely beautiful places in
the Cascade Mountains. After that eruption, it was the center of international attention as
the site of one of the major eruptions in world history.

The GP is the southernmost of the national forests in Washington's Cascades and
most of its mountains are comparatively puny. The Cascades in the northern extremes of
the state average about 8,000 feet in elevation, while in the southern extremes they
average about 3,500. Still, the Gifford Pinchot has two large volcanoes. One of them,
Mount Adams, is the second highest mountain in the state at 12,276 feet in elevation. The

[*Above:* The Mount St. Helens ash and steam eruption plume] other, Mount St. Helens, is 0.25 mile lower than it was before the major 1980 eruption, but at 8,363 feet in elevation, it still is higher than most peaks in the state.

The national forest consists of 1,372,000 acres between the Mount Rainier National Park and the state border at the Columbia River. It has seven wildernesses. Five of them are entirely within the GP borders, while the William O. Douglas and Goat Rocks wildernesses are shared with the Wenatchee National Forest. There also are unique attractions such as the Dark Divide Roadless Area, the immense meadows and berry fields on Silver Mountain, caves that penetrate into the earth's dark interior (*see* Ape Cave, page 290), and numerous lakes. But by far the most unusual and popular attraction is the Mount St. Helens National Volcanic Monument that was established by Congress in 1982 for research, education, and recreation in part of the area affected when the volcano erupted two years earlier (*see* Mount St. Helens National Volcanic Monument, page 281).

The Gifford Pinchot National Forest is part of the area that was established as the Pacific Forest Reserve in 1893. It became the Columbia National Forest in 1908, and was renamed the Gifford Pinchot in 1949 in honor of the active conservationist who became the first chief of the U.S. Forest Service.

Archeological studies indicate that the area that now is the national forest was used some 10,000 years ago by Native Americans who hunted in the meadows left when the most recent glaciers receded as the climate warmed. Later, the native people developed ways to manage the land by methods such as using fire to clear forest areas so they would produce blueberry bushes and fodder for game animals.

George Vancouver, the British Navy captain who explored the northwest American coast, named Mount St. Helens in 1792, but the larger Mount Adams is so deep in the Cascades that he missed it. Europeans did not penetrate into what is now the Gifford Pinchot National Forest until 1825, some 20 years after Lewis and Clark had returned to St. Louis, when the Hudson's Bay Company established Fort Vancouver on the north bank of the Columbia some 20 miles from the southwestern corner of the national forest's border. Hudson's Bay trappers and traders made the early records of the forest while they sought beaver and other fur-bearing animals.

During the 1890s, miners and loggers came to the forest, followed by homesteaders who farmed the valleys and ranchers who grazed sheep and cattle in the meadows. From 1932 until 1942, young men of the Civilian Conservation Corps built trails, roads, and other facilities until the United States entered World War II and the CCC was disbanded.

Like other national forests, the Gifford Pinchot once condoned harvesting the forests as well as providing recreational opportunities and other uses. In recent years it has drastically reduced the harvesting function and now concentrates more heavily on recreation and conservation programs. The annual harvest during the 1980s, for instance, was in the neighborhood of 300 to 400 million board feet. In a normal year during the 1990s that was reduced to about 52 million. By the mid-1990s, the forest was planting five trees for each tree it was harvesting.

Douglas fir and Pacific silver fir are major species in the national forest, but there also are many other species, including mountain hemlock, alpine fir, lodgepole pine, white-bark pine, noble fir, and Engelmann spruce.

As part of its emphasis on science and conservation, the Gifford Pinchot National Forest works with the Forest Service's Pacific Northwest Research Station at the University of Washington to operate the Wind River Canopy Crane, which allows scientists to conduct what they call three-dimensional studies of the old-growth forest. The program is built around a crane that extends 250 feet above the forest floor. The crane is equipped with a gondola that can carry as many as seven people to the upper story of the old-growth Douglas fir and western hemlock trees in the Thorton T. Munger Research Natural Area. The crane swings in a radius of 280 feet, allowing researchers to travel over and through a circle of forest that is 560 feet wide, nearly 6 acres. It gives scientists easy access to the high parts of the forest. The crane was established in the forest in 1995 and scores of researchers from numerous institutions have conducted dozens of experiments with it. Research is overseen by a national scientific committee, while a local committee supervises operations. The trees are as much as 220 feet tall. Most of them are Douglas fir and western hemlock but the forest also includes Pacific yew, Pacific dogwood, western white pine, Pacific silver fir, redcedar, and grand fir. Some are as many as 500 years old.

The crane is fenced off, but tours are conducted on the forest floor for groups. To arrange a tour, phone (509) 427-3344 several weeks in advance. The crane has used in studies into such questions as the role of lichens and fungi on the uppermost parts of trees, volatile gas measurements, how the trees respond to pollutants, how trees absorb green house gasses, and even the difference between how much rain reaches the top story as compared with the amount that reaches the ground.

The forest is crisscrossed by about 4,100 miles of road, including 450 that are paved. Because of the decrease in harvest and to protect wildlife habitat, enhance water quality, control erosion, and improve recreation programs, the forest has begun a program of eliminating some existing roads and had permanently closed some 100 miles by the late 1990s.

The national forest has many species of wildlife, including black tailed deer, black bear, Roosevelt elk, beaver, grouse, mountain goat, coyote, bobcat, and the snowshoe hare, which makes up a major portion of the bobcat's diet. Some 280 varieties of birds have been identified in the forest, among them woodpeckers, warblers, red-tailed hawk, golden and bald eagles, peregrine falcon, osprey, and goshawk.

The forest includes a noble fir that is world record size. It is growing in a large stand of noble firs near the headwaters of Yellowjacket Creek, south of Randle. The record tree is more than 200 feet tall and more than 6 feet in diameter. Nearby noble firs are almost as large as the champion.

In the forest there are 1,100 miles of hiking trails, ranging from easy to very difficult. Most of them are in the higher elevation forest and alpine areas. Some 300 miles of the

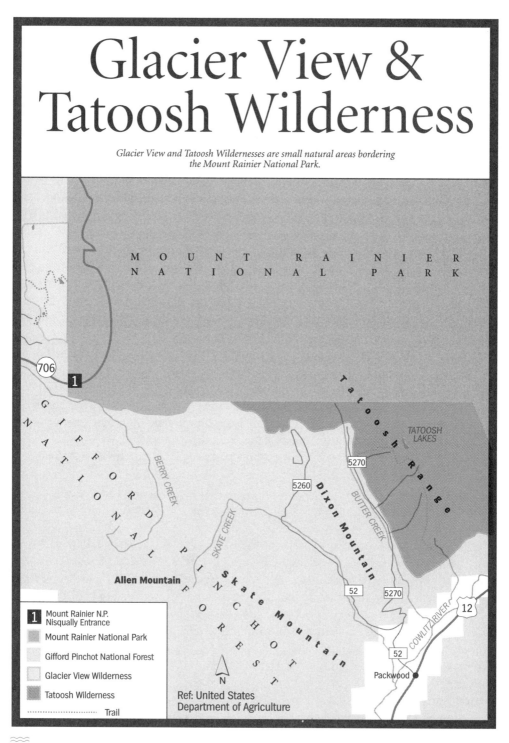

Glacier View & Tatoosh Wilderness

Glacier View and Tatoosh Wildernesses are small natural areas bordering the Mount Rainier National Park.

MOUNT RAINIER NATIONAL PARK

706

1

GIFFORD

NATIONAL

PINCHOT

FOREST

BERRY CREEK

SKATE CREEK

Allen Mountain

Skate Mountain

Dixon Mountain

BUTTER CREEK

Tatoosh Range

TATOOSH LAKES

5270

5260

52

5270

52

COWLITZ RIVER

12

Packwood

N

Legend:

1 Mount Rainier N.P. Nisqually Entrance

Mount Rainier National Park

Gifford Pinchot National Forest

Glacier View Wilderness

Tatoosh Wilderness

.... Trail

Ref: United States Department of Agriculture

trails are in Congressionally declared wilderness areas, and about 150 miles are barrier-free to allow use by persons in wheelchairs or with limited physical abilities. Many of the trails are open to mountain bikes. They range from easy to challenging. Some 190 miles of the trails are open to motorized use. Nine horse camps are scattered through the national forest. They have facilities for both people and livestock, and are adjacent to trails where livestock are allowed. Fees are charged in some. At others, donations are accepted to help defray development and maintenance costs.

There are more than 100 lakes in the forest and 1,360 miles of streams run through it. The lakes and streams contain more than 20 species of fish, including chinook and coho salmon, steelhead, and rainbow, brown, cutthroat, bull, and Eastern brook trout. Ninety percent of the streams have self-sustaining fish populations. The rest are supplemented with hatchery fish.

The forest has more than 60 campgrounds and many picnic areas accessible by road as well as innumerable dispersed camping areas along the trails.

Directions: The Gifford Pinchot National Forest is more than 70 miles long and as much as 40 miles wide. One way to enter the southern portion is to take State Route 14, which follows the north bank of the Columbia River to about 9 miles west of White Salmon. Turn north onto County Road 18 and go about 7 miles to the forest border. A route to the northern part is along US Highway 12 to about 3 miles east of Packwood where the highway enters the national forest. The forest can be accessed at several places along the highway.

Activities: Hiking, camping, picnicking, mountain climbing, hunting, swimming, rafting, caving, horseback riding, mountain bike (pedals) riding, trail bike (motorized) riding, cross-country skiing, snowshoeing, snowmobiling.

Facilities: Trails, campgrounds, horse camps, groomed winter trails.

For more information: Gifford Pinchot National Forests Headquarters, 10600 NE 51st Circle, Vancouver, WA, 98682. Phone (360) 891-5001.

Wilderness Areas in the Gifford Pinchot National Forest

GLACIER VIEW WILDERNESS

[Fig. 43] With just 3,080 acres, this is the smallest of the wildernesses in the Washington Cascades. Congress established it along with other wildernesses in 1984. It is about 4 miles long and 1.5 miles wide and is adjacent to the western border of Mount Rainier National Park near the park's Nisqually entrance. It offers majestic views of Mount Rainier.

Directions: Take State Route 706 approximately 3.5 miles east from Ashford and turn

WESTERN TANAGER
(Piranga ludoviciana)
The male tanager is bright yellow with a red head and black upper back, wings and tail; the female is greenish above and yellowish below.

north onto the Copper Creek Road (Forest Road 59). Go about 2.5 miles and turn right (east) onto Forest Road 5920 and go about 1 mile to the Trail 249 Trailhead at the end of the road. The trail crosses into the wilderness at about 0.5 mile from the trailhead.

Activities: Hiking, mountain climbing.

Facilities: None.

Fees: A trailhead fee may be charged.

Closest town: Ashford, 7 miles.

For more information: Packwood Work/Information Center, 13068 US Highway 12, Packwood, WA 98361. Phone (360) 494-0600.

TATOOSH WILDERNESS

[Fig. 43] This relatively small, 15,800 acre wilderness hangs down from the southern border of the Mount Rainier National Park, and is about 9 miles long and 5 miles wide. It is steep and rugged country with the highest point being on Tatoosh Ridge at 6,310 feet in elevation.

A trail that crosses the wilderness in a north and south direction has a branch that leads to the summit of Tatoosh Ridge, where the Forest Service built a fire lookout in the 1920s, rebuilt it in 1932, and removed it in the 1960s when aircraft took over much of the fire spotting work in the mountains. The lookout became famous after a book titled *Tatoosh* by Martha Hardy, a Seattle schoolteacher, was published by the Macmillan Company in 1946. She was the lookout there during the summer of 1943.

The book told of her experiences as the lookout, and it featured characters from the Forest Service and the wildlife, including Impie, a golden mantled ground squirrel she befriended. The lookout structure is gone now, but there still is a population of

Spermophilus lateratus, which may be descendents of Impie. The book became a bestseller and was reprinted in 1980 by The Mountaineers Books.

The terminals of the trail are at Forest Roads 5290 and 5270, but hiking the entire route requires either having a car at both ends or hiking it both ways. The trailhead on Forest Road 5270 is some 1,000 feet higher than the other trailhead. The trail in some places is thin and difficult to find. At the top, the trail parallels Tatoosh Ridge through high-country meadows. At the site of the old lookout, Mount Rainier dominates the view to the north while Mount St. Helens, Mount Adams, and the Cowlitz Valley are part of the view to the south. Another branch leads to the twin Tatoosh Lakes where Mount Rainier peeks between the shoulders of the basin that forms the lakes.

In the lower elevations the wilderness is covered by a typical Douglas fir forest, which gives way in the high country to mountain hemlock and Alaska cedar.

Directions: To reach the southern trailhead, drive to Packwood on US Highway 12 and turn left on Skate Creek Road (Forest Road 52). Cross the Cowlitz River and drive a short distance to Forest Road 5290. Stay on that road to the trailhead where the road ends at the edge of the wilderness. For the northern trailhead, turn off US Highway 12 on the Skate Creek Road (Forest Road 52) in Packwood. Cross the Cowlitz River and go about 4 miles. Turn right onto Forest Road 5270. Go approximately 6 miles to the trailhead on the right.

Activities: Hiking, hunting, fishing, mountain climbing.

Facilities: None.

Dates: Open summer.

Fees: A trailhead fee may be charged.

Closest town: Packwood, 11 miles.

For more information: Packwood Work/Information Center, 13068 US Highway 12, Packwood, WA 98361. Phone (360) 494-0600.

Trail: 6 miles, one-way.

Elevation: 3,600-foot elevation gain.

Degree of difficulty: Strenuous.

ENGELMANN SPRUCE
(Picea engelmannii)
This spruce grows up to 120 feet tall and is identified by four-sided blue-green needles and cones with wavy edges on the scales.

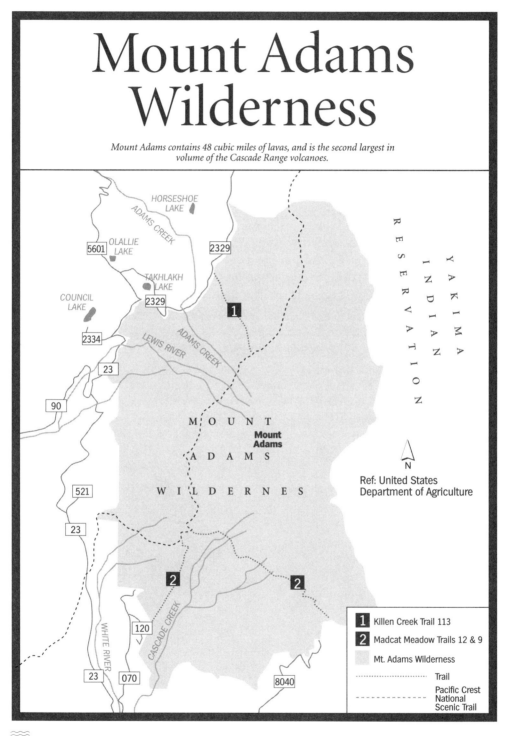

Mount Adams Wilderness

Mount Adams contains 48 cubic miles of lavas, and is the second largest in volume of the Cascade Range volcanoes.

HORSESHOE LAKE

ADAMS CREEK

OLALLIE LAKE

5601

2329

TAKHLAKH LAKE

2329

COUNCIL LAKE

2334

LEWIS RIVER

ADAMS CREEK

23

90

1

M O U N T

Mount Adams

A D A M S

W I L D E R N E S

521

23

2

2

120

CASCADE CREEK

WHITE RIVER

23

070

8040

Y A K I M A   I N D I A N   R E S E R V A T I O N

N

Ref: United States Department of Agriculture

1 Killen Creek Trail 113

2 Madcat Meadow Trails 12 & 9

Mt. Adams Wilderness

.... Trail

- - - - - Pacific Crest National Scenic Trail

▓ MOUNT ADAMS WILDERNESS

[Fig. 44] This 47,270-acre wilderness features the snow-clad heights of Mount Adams and the fascinating wild lands that surround it. Congress created the wilderness with 36,356 acres when it adopted the original 1964 National Wilderness Act and expanded it to the current 47,270 acres in the Wilderness Act of l984. At 12,276 feet in elevation, Mount Adams is the second highest mountain in Washington.

Mount Adams is deep in the Cascade range and not readily seen from the lowlands. Some Indians called the mountain *Pa-toe*. Others called it *Klickitat*. According to Indian legend, Mount Adams and Mount Hood were warriors who were in love with the lovely (before the 1980 eruptions) maiden of Mount St. Helens. They fought over her, and in the fierce battle, huge rocks were thrown, fire destroyed the forest, and the land was devastated. The three mountains are still here to commemorate the disastrous battle, although the beautiful maiden of St. Helens had a disaster of her own in 1980.

It wasn't until the 1850s that Europeans got around to putting their own name on Mount Adams. And when they did it was through a mistake in geography. A program to rename the Cascades volcanoes after United States presidents began in the middle of the nineteenth century, and a geographer who intended to name Mount Hood in northern Oregon after John Adams, the second president, mistakenly put the name on *Pa-toe*, where it remains today. Adams is the only volcano in Washington to be named after an American president.

The first European to report seeing Mount Adams was William Clark of the Lewis and Clark Expedition. On October l9, 1805 he climbed a hill near the confluence of the Snake and Columbia rivers and saw what he said "must be one of the Mountains laid down by Vancouver," the British Navy captain who had explored the American West Coast 13 years earlier. Clark thought it was Mount St. Helens. He apparently never learned that it was Mount Adams.

Mount Adams contains 48 cubic miles of andesite and dacite lavas, and is the second largest in volume of the Cascade Range volcanoes, behind Mount Shasta in California. The lava field that forms its base covers an area of more than 480 square miles. It was created by andesitic volcanic flows that began about 520,000 years ago and that covered a field of olivine basalt. The basalt had flowed from a fissure zone that opened up about 940,000 years ago. Shifting eruptions built successive peaks for Adams and lesser nearby mountains until Adams's present craters were formed about 15,000 years ago. Young vents continued to produce small flows around the base of Adams until about 3,000 years ago.

The first recorded climb of Adams was in the summer of 1854, when a party of three or four men reached the summit. In modern times more than 5,000 people climb it each year. There are numerous climbing routes on Mount Adams. Some are for experienced technical climbers only. All require climbers to be equipped with at least an ice ax and crampons. The south route is the easiest. It goes over the Lunch Counter and the False Summit, which appears from below to be the goal. Upon arriving there it becomes obvious there still is a climb of some 600 feet to get to the top.

The south route is considered a nontechnical climb because the slope is comparatively gentle and unobstructed. Nevertheless, it takes six to eight hours going up and four to six hours going down. A trail goes part way up the route, but eventually it disappears in the snow and gravel. There are camping spots along the way, mostly identified by piles of rocks climbers have stacked up to break the nearly constant and quite strong wind. One of the popular camping spots is the Lunch Counter, where many climbers stop for a sandwich or for an overnight stay. It is a relatively flat place above Crescent Glacier and is above 8,600 feet in elevation. Spending the night at that high elevation helps climbers' bodies adjust to the altitude, in preparation for the hard work of climbing the last 3,600 feet. Before starting their trip, climbers should register at the ranger stations in Randle or Trout Lake.

Mount Adams has a dozen glaciers radiating in all directions from the peak. The largest, about 2 square miles, is Adams Glacier on the northwest flank of the mountain. The lower slopes of the mountain are blanketed with forests of Douglas fir, true fir, western redcedar, Alaska cedar, mountain hemlock, whitebark pine, lodgepole pine, Engelmann spruce, and other species common in the Cascades. Deep-rooted pines tend to grow on the dry east side of the mountain, where it extends out of the national forest and onto the huge Yakima Indian Reservation.

Among the numerous flowers strewn through the wilderness are beargrass, false-hellebore, avalanche lily, white marsh marigold, gentian, mountain daisy, partridge foot, and lupine. Blueberries and other berries have been attracting people to the mountain since the Native Americans arrived some 10,000 years ago.

Wildlife in the wilderness is much like that in the rest of the Gifford Pinchot National Forest and includes elk, blacktail deer, mountain goat, black bears, squirrels, pika, hoary marmots, coyotes, and pine marten (*Martes americana*). Among the many bird species are the red-tailed hawk; gray jay; blue, ruffed, and spruce grouse; and, in the high country, white-tailed ptarmigan.

The peak of Mount Adams extends far above the highest of its neighbors, and in good weather it provides a view for many miles in all directions. For that reason the Forest Service built the highest fire lookout in the nation here in 1921. Bur the snow was too heavy and the clouds often blocked visibility so it was closed in 1924. By that time more than 1,800 pounds of supplies had been carried up the high slopes to the lookout building in backpacks. Five years later, the Glacier Mining Company began mining sulphur at the summit, using the old Forest Service lookout structure as the mine building. The company built a trail for horses and mules, and as many as 168 pack trains a year carried supplies to the miners. The operation hit a peak from 1932 to 1936 and the company's claim expired in 1959. The building is still on the peak, usually buried year-round under many feet of snow.

Directions: There are many ways to enter the wilderness. For one, travel for about 1 mile north from Trout Lake on Forest Road 17 and turn left onto Forest Road 23. Follow that road about 8 miles and turn right onto Forest Road 8031. Then go about 0.4 mile and turn left onto Forest Road 070. Go about 3 miles and turn right onto Forest Road 120. Go about 0.5 mile to the trailhead on the left side of the road. Hike around 0.4 mile to the wilderness border.

Activities: Hiking, hunting, fishing, mountain climbing.

Facilities: None.

Dates: Open summer.

Fees: A trailhead fee maybe charged.

Closest town: Trout Lake, 13 miles.

For more information: Mount Adams Ranger Station, 2455 State Route 141, Trout Lake, WA 98650-9724. Phone (509) 395-3400. Or Cowlitz Valley Ranger Station, 10024 US Highway 12, PO Box 670, Randle, WA 98377. Phone (360) 497-1100.

KILLEN CREEK TRAIL 113

[Fig. 44(1)] This trail goes to a pleasant meadow near the snout of the immense, 2-square-mile Adams Glacier. The meadow, at about 6,800 feet elevation (halfway up the mountain), provides tremendous views of Mount Adams and the jumbled, crevasse-riddled ice of the Adams Glacier, which flows 1 vertical mile down the side of the mountain. In the distance, Mount Rainier and Mount St. Helens, and the ridges that were denuded by the blast of St. Helens's major eruption in 1980 spike the landscape.

All this is experienced amidst the green grasses, fresh flowers, and stunted brush of the meadow. There are tiny creeks, ponds, and trickling waterfalls from the melting glaciers and snow fields of the mountain. Moraines and lava flows testify to the history of this land.

Fires are banned, but there are stoves-only campsites to be found where they will not harm the vegetation. In the evening the sunset colors the sky, and at night the sky glows from the lights of Western Washington's cities. In addition to providing awesome beauty, this is a jumping-off place for people who climb the mountain. People who are not equipped and trained for that activity should not be deceived by the easy appearance of the mountain. It is a dangerous place.

The trail parallels Killen Creek but never gets within much less than 0.5 mile of the stream. The route begins in a forest of pine. It crosses the Pacific Crest National Scenic Trail, then rises to the large meadow, which exhibits avalanche lilies as the snow melts away. Soon after that, marsh marigolds and shooting stars raise their lovely heads, followed by summer beauties such as the brightly colored Indian paintbrush, cinquefoil, and phlox. Clusters of heather provide a dark green hue as well as their tiny purple flowers. No wonder this place attracts large numbers of visitors.

Directions: Drive south from Randle on State Route 131 for 1 mile and turn left onto Forest Road 23. Go 31 miles and turn north onto Forest Road 2329. Go 6 miles to the trailhead.

Activities: Hiking, camping, mountain climbing.

Facilities: None.

Dates: Open summer.

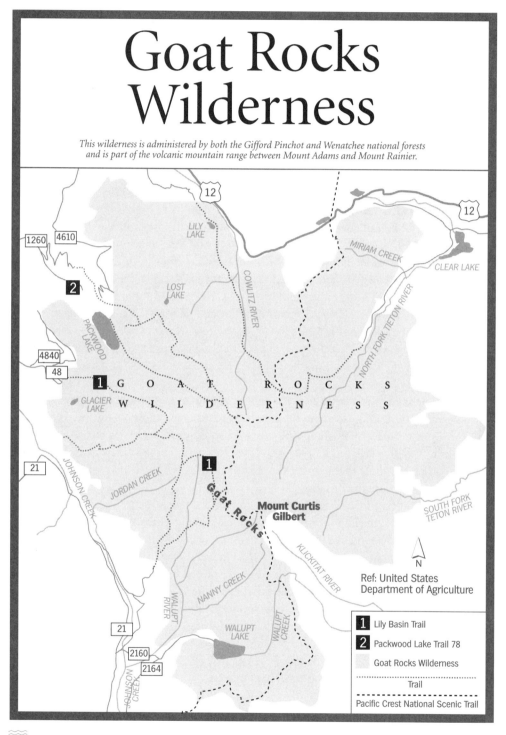

Goat Rocks Wilderness

This wilderness is administered by both the Gifford Pinchot and Wenatchee national forests and is part of the volcanic mountain range between Mount Adams and Mount Rainier.

12

12

LILY LAKE

1260 4610

MIRIAM CREEK

CLEAR LAKE

2

LOST LAKE

COWLITZ RIVER

NORTH FORK TIETON RIVER

PACKWOOD LAKE

4840

48

1 G O A T   R O C K S

GLACIER LAKE

W I L D E R N E S S

21

JOHNSON CREEK

JORDAN CREEK

1

Goat Rocks

Mount Curtis Gilbert

SOUTH FORK TETON RIVER

KLICKITAT RIVER

N

Ref: United States Department of Agriculture

NANNY CREEK

WALUPT RIVER

WALUPT CREEK

21

WALUPT LAKE

2160

2164

JOHNSON CREEK

1	Lily Basin Trail
2	Packwood Lake Trail 78
	Goat Rocks Wilderness
....	Trail
– – –	Pacific Crest National Scenic Trail

Fees: A trailhead fee may be charged.

Closest town: Randle, 32 miles.

For more information: Mount Adams Ranger Station, 2455 Highway 141, Trout Lake, WA 98650. Phone (509) 395-3400.

Trail: 4 miles, one-way.

Elevation: 2,300-foot elevation gain.

Degree of difficulty: Moderate.

MADCAT MEADOW TRAILS 12 AND 9

[Fig. 44(2)] This is a hike that features forests, meadows, glaciers, and moraines formed by glaciers that retreated long ago.

The trailhead to Trail 12 is in a clear-cut just outside the Mount Adams Wilderness border. After entering the wilderness, the route leads into a forest and climbs the long, straight, crest of Stagman Ridge. In another mile or so the trail begins to twist and turn to accommodate the land contours until it meets the Pacific Crest National Scenic Trail about 4.3 miles from the trailhead.

The route goes to the right (east) at the intersection and follows the Crest Trail for 0.5 mile to where the Crest Trail takes a sharp left turn. The Madcat Meadow route joins the Round the Mountain Trail 9, and goes straight ahead. A little more than 1 mile from there, the route leaves the Round the Mountain Trail and branches to the right (south), leading about 0.5 mile above Madcat Meadow and ending at Lookingglass Lake. Camping must be at least 100 feet from the lake.

Directions: Go about 1 mile north from Trout Lake on Forest Road 17 and turn left onto Forest Road 23. Follow that road about 8 miles and turn right onto Forest Road 8031. Then go about 0.4 mile and turn left onto Forest Road 070. Go about 3 miles and turn right onto Forest Road 120. Go about 0.5 mile to the trailhead on the left side of the road.

Activities: Hiking, camping.

Facilities: None.

Dates: Open summer.

Fees: A trailhead fee may be charged.

Closest town: Trout Lake, 13 miles.

For more information: Mount Adams Ranger Station, 2455 State Route 141, Trout Lake, WA 98650-9724. Phone (509) 395-3400.

Trail: 4.5 miles, one-way.

Elevation: 1,400 foot-elevation gain.

Degree of difficulty: Moderate.

GOAT ROCKS WILDERNESS

[Fig. 45] This 105,600-acre wilderness is administered by both the Gifford Pinchot and Wenatchee national forests and is in the volcanic mountain range between Mount Adams and Mount Rainier. The wilderness takes its name from the Goat Rocks, remnants of a large volcano that became extinct some 2 million years ago. The original peak, about

12,000 feet in elevation, has eroded into a multitude of lesser ridges, spires, and peaks that reach to about 8,000 feet in elevation. The highest is Mount Curtis Gilbert at about 8,002 feet in elevation. The valleys are about 2,200 feet in elevation.

The oldest rocks in this part of the Cascades date back about 140 million years. They were formed in the ocean off the North American coast by major basalt lava flows combined with volcanic sediments. Tectonic plate movement brought them to their present position. They were uplifted, folded, and fractured beginning about 17 million years ago. Beginning about 3.8 million years ago, fresh magma began intruding through the older rocks in activity that included andesite extrusions from vents in the vicinity of the present Gilbert and Johnson peaks. That began the construction of the Goat Rocks volcano. Sporadic volcanic activity occurred in what now is the wilderness until about 300,000 years ago. The result of the 140 million years of volcanic activity is a massive area of rock exposed in a rugged series of peaks, spires, ridges, and cliffs that appear in a seemingly endless panorama. This is a place where living things struggle to gain a foothold amidst hard rock and extreme conditions.

The Forest Service and its parent agency, the U.S. Department of Agriculture, recognized the unique values of the area early on and designated about 44,500 acres of the area as the Goat Rocks Primitive Area on February 13, 1931. Four years later, the Forest Service expanded the primitive area to 72,440 acres, and in 1940 the chief of the Forest Service increased the area to 82,680 acres. When Congress adopted the Wilderness Act on September 3, 1964, it created the Goat Rocks area as a designated wilderness. In 1984, Congress expanded the wilderness to its present 105,802 acres.

As in other wildernesses, the Forest Service manages the land to preserve its natural condition, and, as the Wilderness Act directs, to leave it "untrammeled by man." The Forest Service has established regulations to maintain that condition, including limiting visitors to a maximum combined party size of 12 people and livestock. Numerous other regulations prohibit mechanical and motorized devices, and restrict camping and other activities. Detailed regulations are available from the Cowlitz Valley and Naches ranger stations.

The "goat" part of the name Goat Rocks comes from bands of mountain goats that live here. The landscape varies from subalpine to subalpine parkland, with flowered meadows and stunted trees. The Pacific Crest National Scenic Trail runs through the central portion of the wilderness. In addition to the mountain goats, wildlife includes elk, marmots, black bear, and deer. Visitors are required to register by filling out a form at the trailhead as they enter the wilderness, but officials have announced that they are considering requiring people to report to the ranger station to obtain a permit.

Directions: There are numerous trails into the wilderness. Perhaps the easiest approach is to drive 0.7 mile east of White Pass on US Highway 12 to the Leech Lake Campground. The trailhead and parking lot for the Pacific Crest National Scenic Trail is across the highway from the campground. The trail switchbacks parallel the wilderness border before entering it about 2 miles from the trailhead.

Activities: Hiking, hunting, fishing, mountain climbing.

Facilities: None.

Dates: Open summer.

Fees: A trailhead fee may be charged.

Closest town: Packwood, 21 miles.

For more information: Packwood Work/Information Center (Gifford Pinchot National Forest) 13068 US Highway 12, Packwood, WA 98361. Phone (360) 494-0600. Or Naches Ranger Station (Wenatchee National Forest) 10061 US Highway 12, Naches, WA 98937. Phone (509) 653- 2205.

LILY BASIN TRAIL

[Fig. 45(1)] This high-country trail provides magnificent views of the large Packwood Lake (*see* Packwood Lake Trail 78, page 277) far below and Mount Rainier high above.

The trail begins in forest, some of which was burned in an old forest fire. It enters the Goat Rocks Wilderness after 0.5 mile and gains 1,400 feet in elevation in the first 4 miles, then becomes relatively level in meadows of heather and flowers. This is the high point of the hike, where the view includes Packwood Lake, nearly directly below, and, in the distance, the sparkling white glaciers of Mount Rainier, a startlingly beautiful scene.

This is a good place for day hikers to turn around, but the trail continues for about 2.5 miles to Heart Lake on a ridge that juts out from 7,487-foot Johnson Peak. Along the way, the route curls around Lily Basin and passes an intersection with the Angry Mountain Trail. Then it drops steeply down to the lake and some campsites. There are nice views of Mount Adams along the way.

Directions: About 2 miles west of Packwood on US Highway 12, turn south onto Forest Road 48. Go about 10 miles to the trailhead on the right side of the road.

Activities: Hiking, camping, hunting, fishing, mountain climbing.

Facilities: None.

Dates: Open summer.

Fees: There may be a trailhead fee.

Closest town: Packwood, 12 miles.

For more information: Packwood Work/ Information Center (Gifford Pinchot National Forest) 13068 US Highway 12, Packwood, WA 98361. Phone (360) 494-0600.

Trail: 7.5 miles to Heart Lake, 4 miles to Packwood Lake and Mount Rainier view. Both one-way.

Elevation: 1,700-foot elevation gain to Heart Lake, 1,400-foot elevation gain to Packwood Lake and Mount Rainier view.

Degree of difficulty: Moderate.

QUAKING ASPEN
(*Populus tremuloides*)
Like other poplar trees, this is a pioneer tree that can be found in logged or burned-over areas.

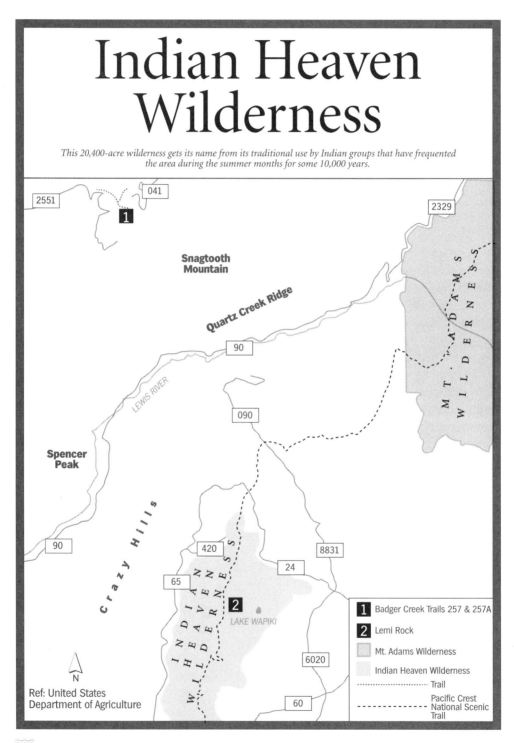

Indian Heaven Wilderness

This 20,400-acre wilderness gets its name from its traditional use by Indian groups that have frequented the area during the summer months for some 10,000 years.

2551   041   1   2329

Snagtooth Mountain

Quartz Creek Ridge

90

LEWIS RIVER

090

Spencer Peak

MT. ADAMS WILDERNESS

Crazy Hills

90   420   8831
65   24
   INDIAN HEAVEN WILDERNESS
   2   LAKE WAPIKI

6020

N

Ref: United States
Department of Agriculture

60

1 Badger Creek Trails 257 & 257A
2 Lemi Rock
   Mt. Adams Wilderness
   Indian Heaven Wilderness
············· Trail
- - - - - - Pacific Crest
         National Scenic
         Trail

INDIAN HEAVEN WILDERNESS

[Fig. 46] This 20,400-acre wilderness takes its name from its traditional use by Indian groups that have frequented the area during the summer months for some 10,000 years. Historical records indicate that from 1902 until the 1920s, local tribes, including the Wishram, Wasco, Yakima, Klickitat, Cascade, and Umatilla, would meet in an area in the northern part of the wilderness called the Sawtooth Berry Fields with tribes from as far away as Montana and Wyoming. They gathered blueberries, played games, traded, processed food, and took part in festivities. A series of fires in the late 1800s and early 1900s cleaned the fields, allowing vast numbers of blueberry bushes to grow and produce immense numbers of berries. The Indians preserved the berries by drying them on mounds of earth next to large fires. Some of the fires escaped, spreading through the fields and helping keep them clear enough to grow more berry bushes.

Near the southern border of the wilderness, remnants of what is called the Indian Racetrack can still be seen. Historical records from the 1850s indicate the racetrack was where people of the various tribes conducted horse races, riding skillfully and with reckless abandon, using hair ropes tied under the horses' jaws for bridles and stuffed pads with wooden stirrups for a saddle. They often bet everything they had, including their clothing, on the outcome of a race. Much of the racetrack now is overgrown by trees but originally the rut was 2,000 feet long.

In 1932, during a council with the Yakima Indians, Forest Service representatives designated part of the Sawtooth Berry Fields just outside the northeast corner of the wilderness to the exclusive use of local Indians. Signs in the fields designate those areas where the berry harvest is reserved. The rest of the area, specifically west of Forest Road 24, is open to everyone, but portions of the berry field are inside the wilderness border and pickers there may pick only the berries they can consume before leaving the wilderness.

The wilderness was designated by Congress in the Washington Wilderness Act adopted in 1984. It is located on a high plateau and has 42 miles of trails that course through open meadows and forested areas. Among the trails is a portion of the Pacific Crest National Scenic Trail that leads through the middle of the wilderness from the northern border to the southern border.

There are some 150 lakes in the wilderness, many of them stocked with fish. Interesting volcanic formations include Lemi Rock, which at 5,927 feet in elevation is the highest point in the wilderness. The rock is just west of Lake Wapiki in the east-central portion of the wilderness. The lake is at the end of Trail 34A. The rock provides majestic views of the lake and a horizon full of peaks of Cascade Mountains. The wilderness is especially attractive in the fall when the vegetation turns colors and the worst of the mosquito season is over.

Directions: Take State Route 141 west from Trout Lake for about 4 miles to where it becomes Forest Road 24. At an intersection of Forest Road 24 some 7.5 miles from Trout Lake, take a sharp right turn, staying on Forest Road 24. Go another 15 miles to the Cultus Creek Campground. Trailheads for Trails 33 and 108 are within the campground.

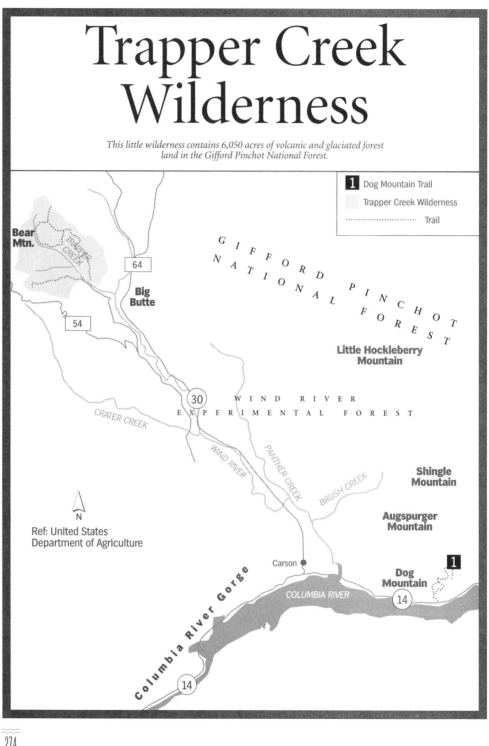

Trapper Creek Wilderness

This little wilderness contains 6,050 acres of volcanic and glaciated forest land in the Gifford Pinchot National Forest.

1 Dog Mountain Trail

Trapper Creek Wilderness

·········· Trail

Bear Mtn.

TRAPPER CREEK

64

Big Butte

54

G I F F O R D   P I N C H O T   N A T I O N A L   F O R E S T

Little Hockleberry Mountain

30

W I N D   R I V E R   E X P E R I M E N T A L   F O R E S T

CRATER CREEK

WIND RIVER

PANTHER CREEK

BRUSH CREEK

Shingle Mountain

Augspurger Mountain

N

Ref: United States Department of Agriculture

Carson

Dog Mountain

1

COLUMBIA RIVER

14

Columbia River Gorge

14

Either will lead a short distance to the wilderness border.

Activities: Hiking, camping, hunting, fishing.

Facilities: None.

Dates: Open summer.

Fees: A trailhead fee may be charged.

Closest town: Trout Lake, 22 miles.

For more information: Mount Adams Ranger Station, 2455 State route 141, Trout Lake, WA 98650-9724. Phone (509) 395-3400.

TRAPPER CREEK WILDERNESS

[Fig. 47] This little wilderness contains only 6,050 acres of volcanic and glaciated forest land in the Gifford Pinchot National Forest's Mount Adams Ranger District. It offers a diverse Douglas fir habitat with old growth on the lower reaches and second growth at the higher elevations.

Rushing whitewater streams and waterfalls cascade down the steep slopes of the mountains and there are numerous blueberry fields. Observation Peak, at 4,207 feet in elevation, was once the site of a fire lookout built in 1917. The vast vista here includes four volcanoes: Mount Rainier, Mount St. Helens, Mount Adams, and Mount Hood.

Only four trails in the wilderness are at least partly maintained by the national forest staff and meet Forest Service standards for elevation gain, tread, and other features, but there are numerous other trails built and maintained by the Mazama Club, a mountaineering group based in Portland, Oregon. The Mazama Trails are classed as primitive and tend to be steep and rough.

Wildlife in the wilderness include Roosevelt elk, black-tailed deer, and black bear. The barred owl (*Strix variana*) emits a strange rhythmic hoot that sounds like a dog howling at the moon, and the pine marten (*Martes americana*) lives among the trees of the remote wilderness and is rarely seen by humans. The pileated woodpecker (*Dryocopus pileatus*) occupies deep forest where there is an ample number of standing dead trees. The goshawk (*Accipiter gentilia*) also is found primarily deep in the wilderness forests.

Directions: From Carson, go north 15 miles on the Wind River Highway to Government Mineral Springs. Cross the Wind River, go 0.2 mile, and turn right on Forest Road 5401. Go 0.4 mile to the Trail 192 trailhead and hike about 1 mile to the wilderness boundary.

Activities: Hiking, camping, hunting, horseback riding.

Facilities: None.

Dates: Open summer.

Fees: A trailhead fee may be charged.

Closest town: Carson, 16 miles.

For more information: Wind River Work/Information Center, 1262 Hemlock Road, Carson, WA 98610-9725. Phone (509) 427-3200.

Trails in the Gifford Pinchot National Forest

🏞 BADGER CREEK TRAIL 257 AND 257A

[Fig. 46(1)] This is a short hike to the site of a former fire lookout that was built in 1926 and removed in 1960 after aircraft took over the responsibility for spotting forest fires. The peak, at 5,664 feet in elevation, looks out over some 700 square miles of the Gifford Pinchot National Forest's Dark Divide area, which includes a large roadless area.

The geology of the area goes back to between 24 and 26 million years ago and consists of thick layers of extruded lava flows, lava fragments, and sandstone made up of volcanic material. On top of that are younger formations that resulted from a series of eruptions that ended about 19 million years ago. Over the eons since then, some of the older formations have been intruded by magma that solidified into rock that is harder than the host rock. When the softer rock eroded, it left peaks and ridges of the newer material. That process continued until about 650,000 years ago, and since then the area has been molded by major earthquakes that resulted in landslides.

The trail is open to about every type of trail travel from hiking to mountain bikes (pedaled), trail bikes (motorized), and both saddle and pack livestock. The road to the trailhead is affected by all that use and can become very rough by the end of the season, especially for passenger cars.

The beginning of the hike is on Trail 257 and courses through mountain hemlock mixed with blueberry bushes, then goes under a high cliff and through large pieces of rock that have fallen from the cliff. The tread consists of ash from the 1980 eruptions of Mount St. Helens. The route climbs steeply into improving views of the countryside until it reaches a ridgetop. A short hike on the ridge leads to a downhill grade and the intersection with Trail 257A. The route follows the left fork, which goes steeply up about 0.5 mile to Badger Peak and the view that once was enjoyed by the people who staffed the lookout. On a clear day it includes four major volcanoes, Rainier, Adams, and St. Helens in Washington, and Hood in Oregon.

Directions: From Randle, go 1 mile south on Forest Road 131 which merges onto Forest Road 25. Go south for 21.8 miles, then turn east on Forest Road 28 and go 2.8 miles to the junction with Forest Road 2816. Turn south and go 4.6 miles to the trailhead at the end of the road.

Activities: Hiking, camping, mountain biking, trail biking, and horseback riding.
Facilities: None.
Dates: Open summer.
Fees: A trailhead fee may be charged.
Closest town: Randle, 28 miles.
For more information: Cowlitz Valley Ranger Station, 10024 US Highway 12, PO

Olive-sided Flycatcher (*Contopus borealis*)

These little birds spend the summer in the forest. They perch in trees and dart out to catch passing medium-sized flying insects one at a time. They grow to about 6 inches and are olive gray with a whitish throat and breast. Their song, *pip-whee-beer*, has been interpreted as "THREE cheers" or "FREE beer."

Box 670, Randle, WA 98377. Phone (360) 497-1100.

Trail: 1.3 miles, one-way.

Elevation: 785 foot elevation gain.

Degree of difficulty: Moderate.

▒ PACKWOOD LAKE TRAIL 78

[Fig. 45(2)] This is an easy trail to a delightful 462-acre lake. The lake is touched on three sides by the attractive mountains of the Goat Rocks Wilderness, but it is not actually part of the wilderness.

The view includes Johnson Peak, which rises to 7,487 feet in elevation, high above the southeastern shore (*See* Lily Basin Trail, page 271). Fishing is good in the spring.

The trail begins at the end of the road several miles from the lake and courses through deep forest with occasional glimpses of the mountains of the Goat Rocks Wilderness, including Johnson Peak. The trail reaches the lake in about 4.5 miles, undulating a little, but essentially level. It is a popular trail to a popular place, and those who seek to be alone in the woods should probably go somewhere else, especially on warm, sunny weekends. For those who don't mind seeing people this can be a pleasant hike.

There is a trail along the northeastern side of the lake and beyond to an intersection with the Pacific Crest National Scenic Trail. But forking left where the main trail (Trail 78) meets the north end of the lake takes hikers across the outlet and past some campsites to a fork about 4.6 miles from the trailhead. The left fork follows Trail 78 up into the mountains about 2.2 miles to Mosquito Lake. It is possible to continue on a network of other trails that loop back to Packwood Lake. That loop totals about 15 miles in addition to the distance from the trailhead to the lake and is at least an overnight hike.

OLIVE-SIDED
FLYCATCHER
(Contopus borealis)
The flycatcher's call is pip-whee-beer or, when alarmed, pip-pip-pip-pip.

Directions: From Packwood, drive east on Forest Road 1260 for 6 miles to the trailhead.

Activities: Hiking, camping, fishing.

Facilities: None.

Dates: Open summer.

Fees: A trailhead fee may be charged.

Closest town: Packwood, 6 miles.

For more information: Packwood Work/Information Center, 13068 US Highway 12, Packwood, WA 98361. Phone (360) 494-0600.

Trail: 4 miles to Packwood Lake, 7 miles to Mosquito Lake.

Elevation: 165 foot elevation gain to Packwood Lake. 2,200-foot elevation gain to Mosquito Lake.

Degree of difficulty: Easy.

DOG MOUNTAIN TRAIL 147

[Fig. 47(1)] At the extreme southern end of both Washington State and the Gifford Pinchot National Forest, a scant mile from the banks of the Columbia River, Dog Mountain gives long views from its peak, 2,948 feet in elevation, and on a hand-dug shelf 500 feet below the peak is the site of a fire lookout that once kept tab on forests of two states. The original lookout building was erected in 1931 and replaced in 1952. It was dismantled when aircraft took over the fire-spotting duty in the 1960s. Because it was only partway up Dog Mountain, the lookout was called Puppy.

The Columbia River comes down from Canada and heads south, paralleling the eastern foothills of the Cascade Mountains. It continues that way the entire width of Washington State until it finds a place where it can get past the volcanic rock of the mountains and flow westward toward the Pacific Ocean some 100 miles away.

The cleft in the mountains is called the Columbia River Gorge. It is the result of the river eroding the volcanic material from the mountains faster than the uplifting mountains could replace it. Although the top of Dog Mountain, for instance, is nearly 3,000 feet in elevation, the river at its foot is less than 200 feet above sea level.

In the earliest historical times it was in this area that explorers ran into cascading whitewater that interrupted their attempts to navigate the river, and they tagged the area with the name The Cascades. The name eventually transferred to the mountains that rise on either side of the river, and spread both north and south until the entire range became known as the Cascade Mountains.

This 80-mile stretch of the river has been designated by Congress as the Columbia River Gorge National Scenic Area and is administered by the Forest Service to protect and enhance the natural, scenic, cultural, economic, and recreational resources of the area. Strong, steady winds on the wide, quiet river make it an ideal place for wind-surfing, and the river often is spotted with colorful sails whisking across the water at amazing speeds.

Dog Mountain provides a good overview of the scenery as well as a pleasant hike. Watch for rattlesnakes and poison oak. From the trailhead, the route goes up steeply

Western Redcedar (*Thuja plicata*)

This slow-growing giant often lives more than 1,000 years and may reach more than 30 feet around. It likes ground that is too wet for other large trees, and thick stands grow in such locations. Individuals, however, may grow in other locations. Western redcedars' need for moisture makes it much more common on the wet, western side of the Cascades. On the dry, eastern side, they are likely to be found only in places where moisture seeps through the soil on a year-round basis. Their wood is aromatic and strongly resists rotting. The tree's long grain makes it easy to split into straight boards, which Native Americans used to build permanent lodges. The soft wood was also easy to carve into large dugout canoes, which were the major means of transportation.

through switchbacks that gain 700 feet in elevation in the first 0.5 mile. The trail passes windswept trees and meadows along the way. A fork in the trail makes a loop hike possible. Both forks go 2.5 miles but the northern one is steeper. Near the far end of the loop, the route passes the place where, in 1931, muscular men shoveled out the hillside to make a shelf, at 2,500 feet in elevation, for the Puppy Lookout. The lookout was rebuilt in 1952 and removed during the 1960s. The view from here is almost entirely of the river below and the forest covering the side of the comparatively low mountains that line both sides of the river. The only sign of a major mountain is the tip of Mount Hood, across the Columbia in Oregon.

The trail goes on for 1 mile from the lookout site, reaching toward the top of the mountain. The route goes north from the lookout site, meanders around the peak, then heads south and climbs to the top where more of Mount Hood can be seen.

Directions: The trailhead is in a parking lot that can be reached by driving east from Stevenson for 9 miles on State Route 14, which runs along the north bank of the Columbia River.

Activities: Hiking.

Facilities: None.

Dates: Open summer.

Fees: A trailhead fee may be charged.

Closest town: Stevenson, 9 miles.

For more information: Wind River Work/Information Center, 1262 Hemlock Road, Carson, WA 98610-9725. Phone (509) 427-3200. Or The Columbia River Gorge National Scenic Area office, 902 Wasco Avenue, Suite 200, Hood River, WA 97031. Phone (541) 386-2333.

Trail: 3 miles, one-way.

Elevation: 2,650-foot elevation gain.

Degree of difficulty: Moderate.

Mount St. Helens

The Mount St. Helens National Volcanic Monument is managed to allow the natural recovery of the area and to provide for the scientific study of the mountain's processes.

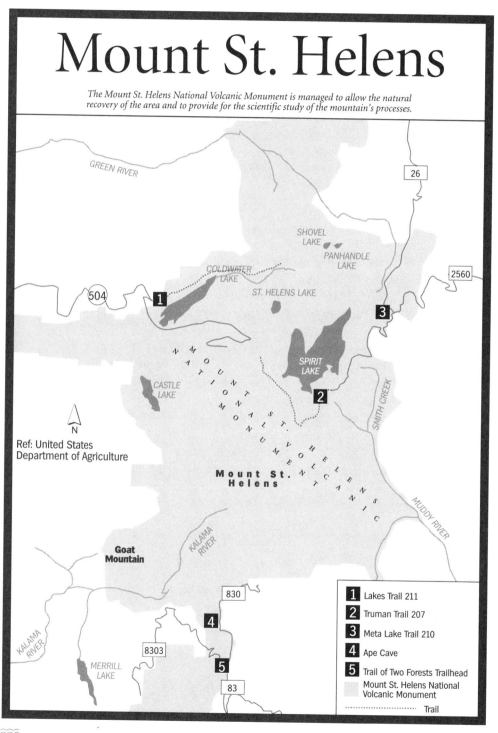

Ref: United States
Department of Agriculture

1	Lakes Trail 211
2	Truman Trail 207
3	Meta Lake Trail 210
4	Ape Cave
5	Trail of Two Forests Trailhead
	Mount St. Helens National Volcanic Monument
	·········· Trail

Mount St. Helens National Volcanic Monument

The scientists were right when they warned that Mount St. Helens was a catastrophe in the making. But even they didn't know how devastating the catastrophe would be. The warnings were hard to accept. Mountains seemed to be the ultimate in permanence: solid, unchanging, unyielding, and unmoving. Science and history told of immense eruptions of other mountains, but that seemed unreal.

People could look at the solid mass of the Cascades running through the middle of Washington and believe they could never change. That seemed especially true of Mount St. Helens, a symmetrical, white-capped beauty that attracted people as a place to relax and enjoy the splendor. The mountain's image, reflected in the quiet, blue water of Spirit Lake at its foot, was a perfect picture of permanent, serene, peaceful beauty.

But there were ancient stories about violent activities of Cascade Peaks. The Indian legend about Mount Hood and Mount Adams throwing fire and stone at each other as they fought over the beautiful maiden, Mount St. Helens, had all the earmarks of a story based in fact. And, soon after Europeans began coming to the area, they produced paintings of the mountains in eruption.

More to the point, scientists were saying that the Cascades had a violent past and would probably have violence in their future. Possibly the most prescient of the scientific predictions was made in 1978 when geologists Dwight Crandell and Donal Mullineaux of the U.S. Geological Survey reported in their study that Mount St. Helens could erupt at any time. They had found evidence that the mountain had erupted violently 23 times during the past 4,500 years. The most recent eruption had been only about 123 years earlier. The media duly noted the report, but most people promptly forgot it.

Then, on March 20, 1980, the seismic monitors at the University of Washington in Seattle, 100 miles north of the mountain, registered an earthquake with a magnitude of 4.0 on the Richter Scale directly under Mount St. Helens. That was the strongest earthquake in the southern part of Washington's Cascades during the seven years the monitors had been operating. Neither the media nor the people of Washington took much notice. But instead of diminishing as expected, the number of earthquakes became more frequent over the next few days until, by March 24, the monitors were recording about 60 a day, many of them strong. Ominously, they seemed to be rising toward the earth's surface.

The next day the Forest Service closed the mountain above timberline. Two days later steam and black ash shot out of the snow near the summit, rising 7,000 feet above the peak. A line of cracks, running 3,000 feet long near the north side of the summit indicated the mountain was beginning to slump. On March 27, the Forest Service evacuated its ranger station on the south side of the mountain. The media and the people took notice.

Above, Mount St. Helens stood 9,677 feet tall before the major 1980 eruption. Below, the eruption that left it 0.25 mile shorter. The volcano now stands at 8,363 feet.

Many of them flocked to the mountain to see what was happening. State officials established a "red zone" where people, including property owners, were not allowed.

The indications that the mountain might be about to erupt continued and some people evaded the roadblocks to get a close-up view. Property owners who had been evacuated clamored to be allowed to return to get their belongings. Harry Truman, the 83-year-old operator of a resort on Spirit Lake, directly below the mountain, refused to leave and gained worldwide notoriety. On May 17 officials allowed a caravan of 20 property owners to enter the restricted zone for 4 hours to obtain their belongings. A second convoy was scheduled for the next day.

The complacency ended abruptly on that next day, May 18, two hours before the second convoy was scheduled to start up the road. The immense forces inside the mountain had raised a bulge on the north flank. It grew as much as 5 feet a day until it was 450 feet higher than normal. At

8:32 a.m., a 5.1 magnitude earthquake beneath the mountain shook the bulge loose and precipitated the greatest earth slide in recorded history. The entire north side of the mountain slid into the valley below at more than 100 miles an hour. The force was so great that the mass of material rose up the wall of the valley on the opposite side, smashing everything in its way, and carrying the water of Spirit Lake as much as 800 feet up the opposite slopes with it.

When the landslide subsided, the water of the lake rushed back down the valley wall, carrying downed logs that filled large sections of the lake. But it was not the same Spirit Lake. The earth slide filled the basin, raising the surface of the lake some 180 feet and leaving the lake much larger across than it had been.

The jumbled rocks of the avalanche flowed down the North Fork of the Toutle River for 14 miles. When they stopped they had filled the valley with debris from the mountain averaging 150 feet deep. In some places it was as much as 500 feet deep.

As the mass of earth slid away from the top and side of the mountain, it released the extreme forces inside. On the north slope, a lateral explosion blew out a horizontal blast. The hot gas, rock, and ash in the blast rammed across the land north of the mountain at a speed of about 670 miles an hour. The temperature of the gas within the blast was about 600 degrees Fahrenheit.

For 6 miles from the new crater, all exposed life was obliterated, leaving only a desolate, gray, moonlike desert. The huge trees of the forest were pulverized or carried away. Beyond the blast area, in what is called the blowdown area, the explosive force slowed enough that the trees in some 86,000 acres of forest were simply uprooted or snapped off their trunks, leaving the entire forest of trees as much as 500 years old and 7 feet in diameter lying in ranks, like the hair on a dog's back.

Beyond the blowdown zone, about 14 to 17 miles from the crater, was the scorch zone where the explosive force had lost the power to uproot the forest but the super hot winds, estimated at 480 degrees Fahrenheit, killed them by scorching, leaving them standing dead, gray, and gaunt, like tombstones in a barren graveyard.

Shortly after the lateral blast, pyroclastic flows made up of a mixture of hot gas, pumice, and ash, superheated to more than 1,200 degrees Fahrenheit, flashed down the slope of what was left of the north side of the volcano at speeds of up to 100 miles an hour. They deposited layers of pumice and ash as much as 60 feet thick and formed a fan-shaped deposit at the front of the crater. It is called the Pumice Plain. Wind and water have been eroding the soft, loose material ever since, producing still more changes in the landscape.

As the lateral explosion blasted the earth for 16 miles on the north side of the mountain, a vertical vent shot a column of ash in a mushroom cloud upward 15 miles over the crater. The mountain continued to spew the huge column of material for nine hours. High in the sky, prevailing winds blew it eastward at 60 miles an hour, blanketing parts of four states with thick layers of gray ash that covered fields and cities. The black cloud blocked out the sun, making a vast area as dark as midnight. Residues of the ash were detected in eastern parts of the United States three day later. Some particles entered the jet stream and circled the world, returning to the West Coast two weeks later.

The rock at the edge of the newly formed crater, estimated at 700 to 1,000 degrees Fahrenheit, collapsed when the vertical ash column shot up. The collapse released water that had been trapped inside the volcano, and at the same time melted huge glaciers and snow fields on the sides of the mountain. That released immense floods of mud, called lahars, to the west, south, and east. The biggest of the lahars, on the North Fork of the Toutle River, also picked up water from Spirit Lake.

The floods were so huge that they carried boulders as much as 20 feet in diameter. Traveling as fast as 30 miles an hour, they flowed down the North and South forks of the Toutle River on the west side of the mountain. The flood carried millions of tons of debris, smashing bridges, ruining businesses, destroying some 300 homes, and ripping huge trees out of the ground. Silt flowed down the Cowlitz River and into the Columbia River some 70 miles away, clogging both streams as it settled in the river beds. Thirty-one seagoing vessels in ports along the Columbia were stranded until the river could be dredged.

According to the official count, 57 persons were killed in the eruption, but the toll may actually have been more than that. Harry Truman, who had refused to be evacuated from his resort on Spirit Lake, was one of the dead, buried 300 feet under the debris of the avalanche. A ridge near the lake has been named Harrys Ridge. It looks down on Spirit Lake, where he is buried with the resort he owned and loved.

Another victim was David Johnston, a geologist who had been assigned to a station on a ridge where a laser beam was being used to monitor the bulge that was growing on the side of the mountain. His camp was 6 miles from the crater. He had only time to shout into his radio, "Vancouver, Vancouver, this is it." Then he, his monitoring equipment, his jeep, and his 22-foot trailer were overwhelmed by the blast. No trace was ever found. They named the ridge where he died Johnston Ridge and built a visitor center there. It is not far from Harrys Ridge.

When the eruption was over, the top 1,313 feet of Mount St. Helens was gone.

There was shock and confusion throughout the state and the world after the eruption. It was so much larger and more destructive than people had expected that it took time to understand what had happened and what to do next. The desolation seemed complete and absolute. Rescue crews hunting for survivors in the devastated area saw nothing but dead trees, barren rock, and dust stretched across the horizon; there were no plants, no animals, and seemingly no hope for recovery for many years in a land that had been a lush green forest of trees, lakes and streams.

The only glimmer of good news in those early days was that the mountain had erupted in an advanced part of the world, convenient to scientists and their instruments, so the event and its aftermath could be studied closely, giving new insights into the processes that bring about volcanic eruptions and methods for predicting them.

Then, surprisingly, within a few days the desolated area began to show signs of life. In some places buried roots of plants sprouted through the blanket of pumice and ash. Scientists found insects blown in by the wind. The same winds brought the seeds of plants. Birds brought in more seeds. Perhaps best of all, some burrowing animals that were underground during the eruption emerged from their shelters. Fish and other aquatic life forms were found unharmed in frozen lakes. Soon, pioneering plants began growing in moist ground near ponds that formed on the surface. Among them was fireweed.

The eruption of Mount St. Helens devastated this log camp on the South Fork Toutle River.

The tiny, light seed of fireweed *(Epilobium angustifolium)* have tufts of long hairs that catch the wind and carry the seeds for long distances. Winds brought them into the devastated area, just as they carry them into forests that have been denuded by fire, disease, or harvest. But the pioneer plants need light and warmth, and as seeds of new plants arrive, perhaps in the dung of birds or caught in the fur of animals, they thrive on the organic material left when the pioneers die out with the seasons. Soon the newcomers crowd out the pioneers and a new succession of plants has begun. At the same time, wildlife drift into the recovering area to take advantage of the new plant life.

And the debris of the eruption contributes to the recovery. When Spirit Lake was sloshed 800 feet up the opposite slope by the original avalanche, it washed back down into the valley, carrying thousands of logs felled by the avalanche. They still float on the surface in a huge mat that is pushed back and forth by the wind. The vegetable matter in the decaying wood provides nourishment for the fish and other creatures in the lake.

Twenty years after the eruption all of the species that lived here before the eruption have returned to the blast zone, even large animals such as elk, which roam in herds within the area.

And the mountain has begun to recover, too. The terrific blast left it a hollowed shell. Seen from the north, what once was the deep inside of the magnificent mountain is a gaping crater stretching a mile wide with sheer walls 2,000 feet deep on three sides and an open chasm on the fourth side.

But almost immediately after the blast, a series of 17 smaller eruptions began, continuing until 1986, and extruding thick, black lava. They left a dome on the crater floor that grew to about 600 feet high and 2,900 feet wide, filling part of the crater. The eruptions stopped then, but they could begin again at any time, pushing up more material to fill the void left in the crater by the major 1980 eruption.

In 1982 Congress established an 110,000-acre area, including the remnants of the mountain and much of the surrounding area, as the Mount St. Helens National Volcanic

Monument. The area is managed by the Gifford Pinchot National Forest to allow the natural recovery of the area and to provide for the scientific study of the mountain's processes. More than 500 individual research studies have been conducted here by scientists from around the world.

The monument also has been developed as both an educational and recreational area for the public. A popular part of the monument is State Route 504, also called the Spirit Lake Memorial Highway, which leads 52 miles from Interstate Highway 5 to Johnston Ridge where the Forest Service and U.S. Geological Survey have an elaborate observatory that gives an up-close view of the mountain, its crater, and the pumice plain at its foot.

In addition to the observatory, the highway passes four elaborate visitor stations. The Forest Service's Mount St. Helens Visitor Center; The Coldwater Visitor Center; The Hoffstadt Bluff Visitor Center, sponsored by Cowlitz County and Washington State; and the Forest Learning Center, sponsored by the state, the Rocky Mountain Elk Foundation, and The Weyerhaeuser Company, which owns much of the land in the area. Weyerhaeuser harvested and replanted much of its forest that was blown down by the eruption. The healthy, vigorous new forest is an added attraction to the highway. The observatory and the visitor stations have educational exhibits, educational talks, and theater presentations telling the story of the mountain, its eruptions, and its recovery. Food service, restrooms, gift shops, and other amenities are available.

There are 200 miles of trails in the monument. Some course through old-growth and second-growth forests, and meadows with long views far beyond the border of the monument. Those are very similar to the trails in other parts of the Cascades. But the unique trails in the monument are those that lead through the pumice plains, downed forest, and standing dead forest that resulted from the major 1980 eruption. Many of the trails are interconnected so it is possible to wander through several fascinating places on a single hike.

East of the mountain, Forest Road 99 leads to Windy Ridge where there is an even closer view of the crater than those at the visitor centers, but this view is from a different angle. Windy Ridge also has close views from above of Spirit Lake and of huge logs that were partly buried in the eruption.

The crater is closed to the public but the south side of the mountain is open to climbers who wish to go to the rim above the crater. The view of the crater from the rim directly above it is, perhaps, the most graphic display of the tremendous force that hollowed out the entire mountain. Climbing permits are required year-round above 4,000 feet in elevation. They are free and an unlimited number is available during the winter, although Sno-Park permits are required for parking at the trailhead during the winter. During the summer the climbing permits are limited to 100 persons per day, and a fee is charged. Some permits are available on a first come, first served basis. Others may be reserved. Contact the monument headquarters. The climb is difficult and dangerous and climbers should be in good physical condition and have the necessary equipment and training.

Directions: There are several roads to the Mount St. Helens National Volcanic Monument. The most popular, and probably the most interesting, is the Spirit Lake Memorial Highway (State Route 504). Turn east off Interstate Highway 5 onto State Route 504 at Exit 49 near Castle Rock. The highway goes 52 miles, past many attractions and ends at the Johnston Ridge Observatory Center, 5 miles from the crater. The Forest Service's Mount St. Helens Visitor Center is 5 miles from I-5 on State Route 504. Maps, information, advice, and permits to visit certain attractions in the monument are available there.

Activities: Hiking, camping, hunting, fishing, mountain climbing, driving tours, horseback riding, caving, cross-country skiing.

Facilities: Full-service visitor centers, trails, viewpoints, boat docks.

Dates: Open year-round.

Fees: A fee is charged for a permit to enter many of the monument's features. The permits are available at visitor centers and other locations where they are required.

Closest town: Castle Rock, 6 miles.

For more information: Mount St. Helens National Volcanic Monument Headquarters, 42218 Yale Bridge Road, Amboy, WA 98601. Phone (360) 247-3900. For recorded general information, (360) 247-3961. For recorded climbing information, phone (360) 247-3961.

▓ TRUMAN TRAIL 207

[Fig. 48(2)] This trail begins on a closed extension of Forest Road 99, which goes to the Windy Ridge Viewpoint that looks down on Spirit Lake and the huge raft of logs that was washed into the lake during the eruption. The hot, dry, dusty trail crosses areas of pyroclastic flow and the debris deposits of the avalanche that began the eruption. It takes visitors to the heart of the new landscape left by that cataclysmic event, and to the new plant life that is regaining a foothold in the devastated area. There are good views of the new dome the mountain has built in the middle of the new crater. The trail ends at a junction with Harrys Ridge Trail 208, which goes 1 easy mile to the Harrys Ridge Viewpoint, where the debris avalanche of the major eruption scoured the forest surface down to bedrock. That trail has a direct view into the Mount St. Helens Crater. It adds 1 mile and a 200-foot elevation gain to the one-way hike.

The trail begins on a section of the closed road and goes downward, then leads onto the pumice plane where it is identified by wooden posts. The route is through a restricted area where visitors are allowed to travel only on approved trails. Leaving the trail may interfere with natural features and scientific studies.

Directions: The trailhead is in the parking lot of the Windy Ridge Viewpoint at the end of Forest Road 99, 16.4 miles from the junction with Forest Road 25, which parallels the eastern border of the monument.

Activities: Hiking.

Facilities: There are restrooms at the trailhead.

Dates: Open summer.

Fees: A trailhead fee may be charged.

Closest town: Randle, 30 miles.

For more information: Mount St. Helens National Volcanic Monument Headquarters, 42218 Yale Bridge Road, Amboy, WA 98601. Phone (360)247-3900. For recorded information, phone (360) 247-3903.

Trail: 6.5 miles, one-way.

Elevation: 600 foot elevation gain.

Degree of difficult: Easy.

🏵 META LAKE TRAIL 210

[Fig. 48(3)] This short, easy trail is paved and barrier-free for wheelchairs and goes into the blast zone 8.5 miles from the volcano. At the time of the major eruption the little lake was sheltered behind a neighboring ridge and under a deep blanket of snow and ice so living things in and around it survived.

Now the lake has a good population of Eastern brook trout, salamanders, and frogs. Swarms of tadpoles collect at the shore in July. The lake is edged by small trees and other plants.

The trailhead is in the Miner's Car Parking Lot, where the blast mangled the car of a miner who worked in the area. The car is on display behind a protective fence.

Directions: The trailhead is in the Miner's Car Parking Lot, on Forest Road 99, 8.9 miles from the junction with Forest Road 25, which parallels the eastern border of the monument.

Activities: Hiking on foot or wheelchair.

Facilities: None.

Dates: Seasonal, summer.

Fees: A trailhead fee may be charged.

Closest town: Randle, 30 miles.

For more information: Mount St. Helens National Volcanic Monument Headquarters, 42218 Yale Bridge Road, Amboy, WA 98601. Phone (360) 247-3900. For recorded information phone (360) 247-3903.

Trail: 0.25 mile.

Elevation: Level.

Degree of difficulty: Easy.

🏵 LAKES TRAIL 211

[Fig. 48(1)] The mudflow that flashed down the Toutle River when Mount St. Helens erupted contained both liquid mud and large, intact pieces of the mountain called hummocks. The mud slide was so thick and so deep that it dammed the mouths of some of the Toutle's tributaries, including Coldwater Creek. The creek waters collected behind that dam and formed one of the new lakes that was born of the eruption. The lake is 200 feet above the level of the valley floor before the eruption. This trail follows the lake shoreline.

The lake is 5 miles long and as much as 0.5 mile wide. When it formed, it seemed to be a barren mud hole in a barren landscape, but nature's healing process is making it a place of vigorous, young life. Cottonwood and alder trees have sprouted on the beaches, and in the gulches of little tributary streams there are fields of flowers, Mixed with the new life are the trunks of dead trees uprooted by the blast.

Nature's process of building the shoreline is still in progress as the forces of erosion continue to wear the deposit of new material along the edge of the lake, leveling it to a shelf that has become a beach. The Coldwater Ridge Visitor Center overlooks the lake from a bluff 600 feet above the southwest corner.

There are fish in the lake, and deer, elk, and many varieties of birds can be seen from the trail. There are views of Mount St. Helens and other mountains along the way. A wooden walkway at the boat launch leads out over the lake and through a marsh area. It is barrier-free and suitable for persons in wheelchairs or with other types of disabilities. It has interpretive signs telling the story of the lake. Beyond the wooden walkway, the trail goes about 2 miles past the end of the lake to connect with the Coldwater Trail 230.

Directions: The 0.5-mile Elk Bench Trail 210 trailhead is at the Coldwater Ridge Visitor Center and takes hikers on a steep, 600 foot descent to the lake. The Elk Bench Trail connects to the Lakes Trail 211 a short distance northeast of the Lakes Trail 211 trailhead. That trailhead can be reached by turning left onto the Spirit Lake Memorial Highway from the Coldwater Ridge Visitor Center parking lot, driving 2.2 miles, and turning left on the access to the Coldwater Lake Boat Launch. The trailhead is reached from the parking lot. Accessing the trail this way eliminates the steep trail between the lake and the visitor center.

Activities: Hiking, boating, fishing.

Facilities: Facilities at the Coldwater Ridge Visitor Center include restrooms, food service, interpretive displays, a theater, a book store, a gift shop and information. The trailhead at the boat launch includes toilets.

Dates: Open year-round.

Fees: A trailhead fee may be charged. A fee is charged for entry to the visitor center.

Closest town: Castle Rock, 44 miles.

For more information: Mount St. Helens National Volcanic Monument Headquarters, 42218 Yale Bridge Road, Amboy, WA 98601. Phone (360) 247-3900. For recorded information, , phone (360) 247-3903.

Trail: 3 miles to end of lake, 5 miles to Coldwater Trail 230 junction.

Elevation: 620-foot elevation gain from boat launch to Coldwater Creek.

Degree of difficulty: Easy.

COMMON JUNIPER
(Juniperus communis)
Also called dwarf juniper, this produces blue berries that are used in flavoring gin.

☙ TRAIL OF TWO FORESTS

[Fig. 48(5)] This short, level loop trail goes through an area affected by another eruption of Mount St. Helens, 1,900 years ago. The eruption poured molten basaltic lava through an ancient forest. The lava flowed around the standing trees, cooled , and hardened. When the wooden material rotted away, it left the imprint of the trees. Eventually, the ancient forest was replaced by a new one of lodgepole pine, but the impressions of the old trees still remain, usually as vertical shafts in the hard rock. The shafts are as much as 12 feet deep and 5 feet in diameter.

Two of the old tree trunks had fallen when the lava engulfed them. When the logs rotted away they left a connecting, 50-foot tunnel about 3 feet in diameter. It is just wide enough to crawl through, although it is a good idea to have a flashlight and some kind of head protection, such as a hard hat.

The trail is a barrier-free boardwalk and has interpretive signs to explain the story of the two forests.

Directions: Starting from Cougar, go 6.8 miles east on State Route 503, which becomes Forest Road 90, and turn left onto Forest Road 83. Go 2 miles on Forest Road 83, turn left onto Forest Road 8303, and go 0.2 mile to the trailhead.

Activities: Interpretive hike.

Facilities: A barrier-free boardwalk suitable for wheelchairs. There are toilets and picnic tables.

Dates: Open summer.

Fees: A trailhead fee may be charged.

Closest town: Cougar, 9 miles.

For more information: Mount St. Helens National Volcanic Monument Headquarters, 42218 Yale Bridge Road, Amboy, WA 98601. Phone (360) 247-3900. For recorded information (360) 247-3903.

Trail: 0.14 mile.

Elevation: Level.

Degree of difficulty: Easy.

☙ APE CAVE TRAIL 239

[Fig. 48(4)] This is two trails, one underground and the other on the surface above. The Ape Cave got its name because it was first explored by a local youth group called the Mount St. Helens Apes.

The cave was discovered in 1947 by Lawrence Johnson, a local logger who was working in the area. Ape Cave is recognized as the third longest lava tube in the continental United States at 2.5 miles long. The tube was formed during an eruption of fluid lava, called pahoehoe, nearly 2,000 years ago. The cave was created when the exposed surface of the flowing lava cooled and solidified, becoming the roof. After the roof formed, the liquid lava below continued to flow through the tube, perhaps for many months, enlarging and deepening its channel by melting the floor beneath it, a process called thermal erosion. When the eruption ended, the lava remaining in the tube drained away, leaving Ape Cave. Since the cave was formed, three separate mudflows entered the lower cave entrance, flooding to the end of the cave and leaving the floor covered with sand. The most recent of these mudflows was about 350 years ago.

The main entrance to the cave is on a stairway in an opening left when a portion of the roof collapsed near the middle of the 12,810-foot-long cave. The entry marks the division between two distinct parts of the cave. The lower cave, 0.8 mile long, is wide with a smooth floor of sand. It is a relatively easy walk through interesting geologic formations, including what is called the Lava Ball, a block of solidified lava wedged between protruding ledges of the walls.

The upper cave is 1.25 miles long and is much more difficult because it twists and turns and leads over large piles of rock, as well as an 8-foot lava fall. The far end of the upper cave has an entrance and stairway leading to the Ape Cave Trail 239 and a hike on the surface through the forest back to the main entrance.

The temperature in the cave averages 42 degrees Fahrenheit so warm clothing is advised. In the lower cave it is necessary to take two sources of light, such as a flashlight and a lantern. Lanterns can be rented at the Ape Cave headquarters in the parking lot during the summer. In the upper cave, headlights are advised to leave hands free for climbing over rocks.

Tours led by Forest Service guides may be arranged at the headquarters building during the summer.

Directions: Starting from Cougar, go 6.8 miles east on State Route 503, which becomes Forest Road 90, and turn left onto Forest Road 83. Go 2 miles on Forest Road 83, turn left onto Forest Road 8303, and go 1 mile to the trailhead.

Activities: Cave exploration.

Facilities: Toilets, lantern rentals, and guides are available at the parking lot during the summer.

Dates: Open year-round.

Fees: Fees are charged during the summer.

Closest town: Cougar, 10 miles.

For more information: Ape Cave Headquarters in the parking lot, or Mount St. Helens National Volcanic Monument Headquarters, 42218 Yale Bridge Road, Amboy, WA 98601. Phone (360) 247-3900. For recorded information, phone (360) 247-3903.

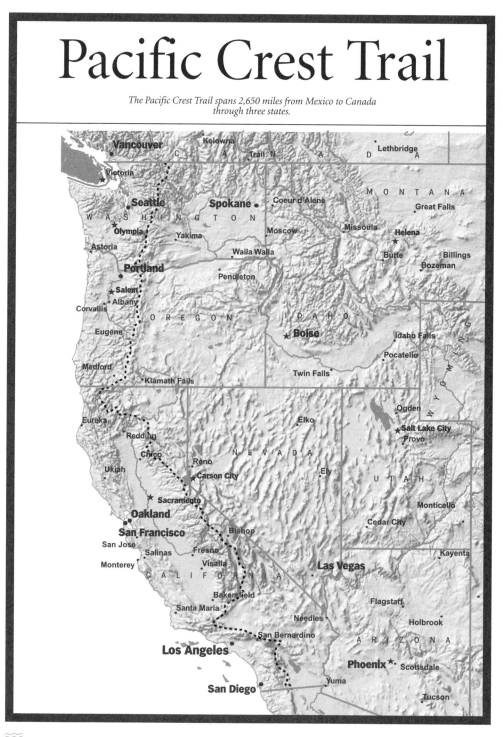

Pacific Crest Trail

The Pacific Crest Trail spans 2,650 miles from Mexico to Canada through three states.

Long Trails

There are thousands of miles of trails in Washington's Cascade Mountains and many of them are interconnecting. That makes it possible for hikers to go many miles and many days on a seemingly infinite number of routes without retracing their steps. Hikers are only limited by the amount of food they can carry before returning to civilization for more supplies.

Some routes, however, stand out as unique and select because of their length, the scenery they pass through, and their isolation from the modern world.

These trails are similar in many ways. They go through high-country forests and meadows, past peaks and snow fields. They tend to be so high that they are closed by snow long before and long after lower trails are open and dry.

But perhaps the most striking similarity is the experience they offer of being in raw, isolated country where people are scarce and where hikers depend on their own resources

[*Above:* Independence Pass inside the Mount St. Helens National Volcanic Monument]

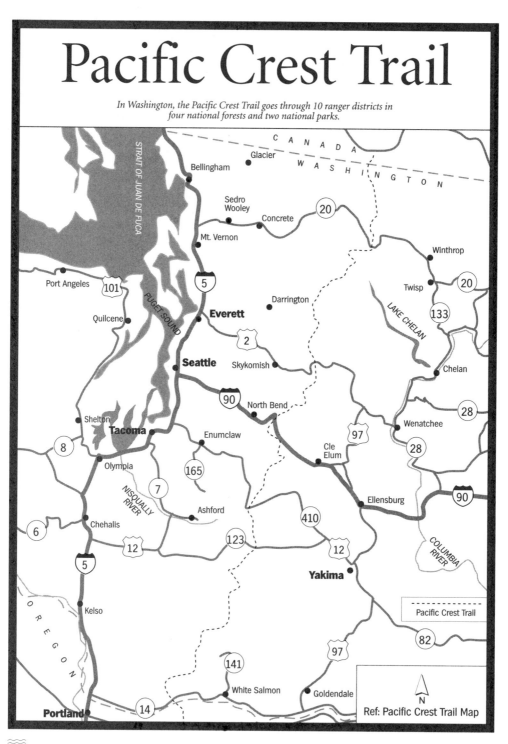

Pacific Crest Trail

In Washington, the Pacific Crest Trail goes through 10 ranger districts in four national forests and two national parks.

for coping with the environment, using only what they brought with them to survive far from the comforts and convenience of the civilized world.

Pacific Crest Scenic Trail 2000

[Fig. 49, Fig. 50] For many people, this is one of the truly classic trails, rivaled by only a few others such as the Appalachian Trail that extends over 2,150 miles of the Appalachian Mountains between Maine and Georgia. The Pacific Crest Trail reaches 2,665 miles from Canada to Mexico, roughly paralleling the crest of the Cascades. About 510 miles of the trail are in Washington.

The earliest recorded suggestion for the trail is in Joseph T. Hazard's book *Pacific Crest Trails*. He reported that during a conversation in 1926, Miss Catherine Montgomery told him she had a dream of "a high trail winding down the heights of our Western mountains..." Hazard, a hiking enthusiast, promoted the idea among outdoor groups and the idea caught on. Two years later Fred W. Cleator, recreation supervisor for the U.S. Forest Service Region Six (Washington and Oregon) proposed developing a trail through the Cascades high country from Canada to the Columbia River. Then he extended the proposal to take the trail through Oregon's high Cascades. In 1932 Clinton Clarke of the Mountain League of Pasadena, California, proposed that youth groups, hiking and outdoor groups be formed to extend a trail the entire width of the country from Canada to Mexico. He and Warren Rogers lobbied for the trail and succeeded in getting parts of it after Rogers and different YMCA groups spent the summers from 1935 through 1938 exploring 2,000 miles of the route. Volunteer groups and the Forest Service became involved in developing the trail and it sporadically took shape through the decades. Congress designated the route as a national scenic trail in 1968, giving added impetus to its development and maintenance. It was dedicated in 1993.

The trail still is a work in progress in California but it is largely completed in Washington and Oregon. Much of the route courses over previously existing trails developed by the Forest Service, miners, or, in some cases, by Indians. Other parts were built specifically as part of the Pacific Crest Trail. Most of the route is on public land, but in some places where public land is not available, it crosses private lands. Regardless of where and how the trail was built, it is still possible to walk across all of Washington, Oregon, and California through some of the most magnificent land on earth.

Much of the route is in high country and covers rugged, even dangerous territory. People who hike here should be experienced, well equipped, and in good physical condition.

Only a handful of people hike the full 2,600 miles of the trail. That trip is likely to take about 5 to 6 months for hikers averaging about 20 miles a day. People who attempt it all in one season probably should start in the southern end where spring arrives a little earlier. Then they can hope to get to the northern end after last winter's snow has melted away and before next winter's snow begins.

Hiking the full length of the trail in Washington is more practical and is attempted a little more frequently. But the great majority of people are content with hiking small segments of the trail as day hikes or overnight for one or more days. Those who live nearby can easily hike several parts in a season and over a series of seasons cover most or all of the trail in the state. Those from other parts of the country, of course, would have to make a series of visits to Washington to follow that program. Those who hike the full length must plan to return to civilization from time to time to replenish their supplies, perhaps by leaving a car at the highway trailheads or having someone meet them there.

The trail in Washington goes through 10 ranger districts in four national forests, and two national parks, including 8 wilderness areas as well as stretches of private and state land. Each of the jurisdictions makes its own regulations, although some special provisions are made for people traveling the Pacific Crest Trail; backcountry permits, for instance, are not required for hiking the trail as long as hikers stay within 200 feet of it. The regulations in each jurisdiction, however, change from time to time and it is advisable to contact the authorities before starting a hike.

The national forests crossed by the trail in Washington are the Gifford Pinchot, the Wenatchee, the Mount Baker Snoqualmie, and the Okanogan. The national parks are the Mount Rainier and North Cascades.

The trail in Washington passes through a vast array of landscapes, covering the full gamut from the deep forests in the lowlands to the rock and ice of the alpine meadows. The average elevation of the trail in Washington is about 4,550 feet, but the low point is the southernmost trailhead at State Highway 14, where the elevation is 180 feet, and the high point is 7,126 feet in the Pasayten Wilderness near the northern end. The climb is not steady, however. The trail hits 7,080 in the Goat Rocks Wilderness and goes down to 3,060 at Snoqualmie Pass.

The trail not only undulates but meanders, so that a hike may be partly in the wet and mild climate of the western side of the Cascades and partly in the hot and dry atmosphere of the east side. The trail also passes numerous kinds of rock ranging from igneous, to sedimentary, to metamorphic, much of it glaciated. It passes peaks, valleys, lakes, streams, forests, meadows, clear-cuts, and ski areas, complete with lifts and condos. Most of the trail is in virgin country but some of the land has been denuded by fire or harvest so that the landscape is dead and bare. Other denuded areas are in various stages of regrowth, with vegetation ranging from tiny saplings to near-mature second growth.

Much of the trail is in highcountry, where mountain hemlock thrives. In the lower elevations these trees give way to the western hemlock and Douglas fir of the western side of the mountains and the pine forests of the eastern side. Meadow plants along the way may include Indian paintbrush, glacier lily, avalanche lily, western anemone, phlox, and the prolific fireweed.

Wildlife includes deer, black bear, coyotes, cougar, snowshoe hare, mountain goat, golden mantled ground squirrel, marmot, pika, and robins, and an unwary hiker may lose his lunch sandwich to a gray jay, also known as the camp robber. Rattlesnakes and vast hordes of mosquitoes may also be encountered along the way.

Directions: Throughout its entire length, many feeder trails lead to the Pacific Crest Trail, but the easiest accesses to the trail in Washington are from the state's six east-west highways, all of which intersect with the trail. Perhaps the easiest of all is on State Route 14, which parallels the north bank of the Columbia River. The trailhead here is off the highway near the west end of the Bridge of the Gods, east of Vancouver, Washington. The other highway accesses are at White Pass on US Highway 12, Chinook Pass on State Route 410, Snoqualmie Pass on Interstate Highway 90, Stevens Pass on US Highway 2, and Rainy Pass on State Route 20. Access to and from the Canadian end of the trail is over the 7-mile Windy Joe Trail (actually a rough service road that is closed to private vehicles). The trailhead is near the visitor center in Manning Park in British Columbia. The trail leads to Monument 78, one of the monuments that mark the border between Canada and the United States. The hitch to this access is that the border here is not manned by border guards so it is required by both U.S. and Canadian Customs that hikers contact a customs office before making the crossing.

Activities: Hiking, camping, hunting, fishing.

Facilities: The trail has few facilities, but various services and merchandise are available near the trail on the highways that intersect it.

Dates: Open summer.

Fees: Trailhead fees may be charged.

For more information: For an overall view, contact the Pacific Crest Trail Association, 5325 Elkhorn Boulevard, Sacramento, CA 95842. Phone (888) 728-7245. For specific trail information, depending on the portion involved, the trail is managed by various jurisdictions. The contacts for the national park segments are the Mount Rainier National Park, Star Route, Ashford, WA 98304. Phone (206) 569-2211. The North Cascades National Park, Lake Chelan National Recreation Area, PO Box 549, Chelan, WA 98816. Phone (509) 682-2549. The national forest contacts are

MOUNTAIN LION
(Felix concolor)
This solitary and nocturnal animal stalks its prey from trees or high rocks before pouncing; it is one of the few cat species without spots or stripes.

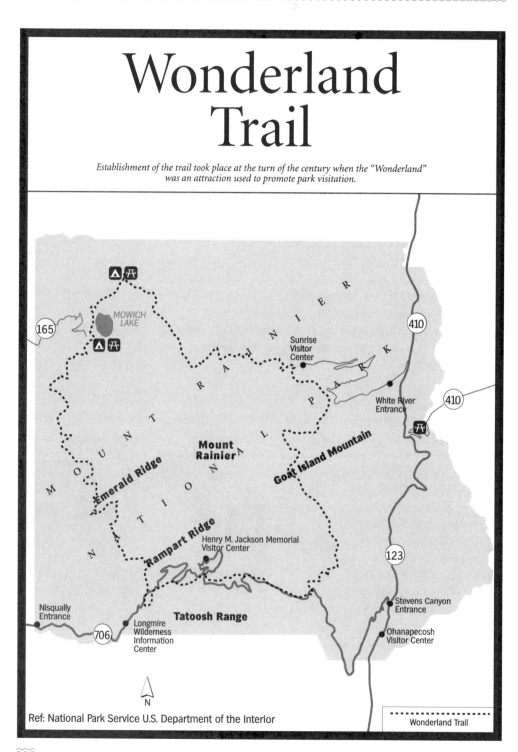

Wonderland Trail

Establishment of the trail took place at the turn of the century when the "Wonderland" was an attraction used to promote park visitation.

165

MOWICH LAKE

Sunrise Visitor Center

410

White River Entrance

410

MOUNT RAINIER NATIONAL PARK

Mount Rainier

Emerald Ridge

Goat Island Mountain

Rampart Ridge

Henry M. Jackson Memorial Visitor Center

123

Nisqually Entrance

Tatoosh Range

Stevens Canyon Entrance

706

Longmire Wilderness Information Center

Ohanapecosh Visitor Center

N

Ref: National Park Service U.S. Department of the Interior

Wonderland Trail

as follows: in the Gifford Pinchot National Forest, the Mount Adams Ranger Station, Trout Lake, WA 98650. Phone (509) 395-2501. Gifford Pinchot National Forest, Packwood Ranger Station, Packwood, WA 98361. Phone (360) 494-5515. Wenatchee National Forest, Naches Ranger Station, 630 US Highway 12, Naches, WA 98937. Phone (509) 653-2205. Wenatchee National Forest, Cle Elum Ranger Station, Cle Elum, WA 98922. Phone (509) 674-4411. Wenatchee National Forest, Lake Wenatchee Ranger Station, Lake Wenatchee Rural Delivery, Star Route, Box 109, Leavenworth, WA 98826. Phone (509) 763-3103. Mt. Baker-Snoqualmie National Forest, Darrington Ranger Station, Darrington, WA, 98241, phone (360) 436-1155. Mount Baker- Snoqualmie National Forest, Skykomish Ranger Station, Skykomish, WA, 98288. Phone (360) 677-2414. Mount Baker-Snoqualmie National Forest, North Bend Ranger Station, 42404 Southeast North Bend Way, North Bend, WA 98045. Phone (425) 888-1421. Mount Baker-Snoqualmie National Forest, White River Ranger Station, 857 Roosevelt Avenue East, Enumclaw, WA 98022. Phone (360) 825-6585. Okanogan National Forest, Winthrop Ranger Station, Winthrop, WA 98865. Phone (509) 996-2266.

Trail: 510 miles, one-way in Washington State.

Elevation: 6,950 feet elevation gain.

Degree of difficulty: Strenuous.

Wonderland Trail

[Fig. 51] This is a 93-mile trail that entirely encircles Mount Rainier, the centerpiece of the Mount Rainier National Park. The trail leads to magnificent high-country views ranging from the towering, old-growth forest of the valleys, to flowered meadows of the mid-levels, to barren rock and ice of the highest parts of Mount Rainier. The landscape is dominated by Rainier, which towers over the trail, cold and regal in its majestic beauty.

In the early twentieth century the trail was proposed as a road by Major Hiram Chittenden of the Army Corps of Engineers. He envisioned a route similar to the road he had built to loop around Yellowstone National Park. The preliminary surveys were completed before the proposal for a road was dropped, and the trail was built in 1915 following much of Chittenden's original route. It has become a major feature of the park, and it both challenges and enthralls even people who walk it only a short distance during a day hike.

WHITE-TAILED PTARMIGAN
(Lagopus leucurus)

BEAVER
(Castor canadensis)

It is possible to complete the loop in a week by averaging some 14 miles a day but that is an athletic exercise, which leaves little time to enjoy the scenery. Ten days to two weeks is recommended to get the full benefit of the magnificent landscape. Some people simply take a series of short hikes on the trail, covering it all over a period of years.

Those who do the entire trail at once must either weight themselves with a large amount of food that can be a real burden during the first few days or make arrangements to resupply themselves. One method for resupply is to leave caches of supplies at park stations where they can be stored until they are picked up. Caches may be dropped off in person or they may be delivered by U.S. Mail or UPS, allowing two weeks for delivery. The stations at Longmire, Mowich Lake, and Sunrise are near the Wonderland Trail. There also are stations at Ohanapecosh and White River, which are distant from the trail and require a side trip. Caches must be in rodent-proof containers and may not include fuel. In addition to the shipping label, packages must be marked with the name of the person they are for, the name of the station where the cache will be picked up, and the date on which it will be picked up. To obtain specific requirements of each station phone Longmire, (360)569-2211 ext. 3317 or ext. 3314; Mowich Lake, (360) 829-5127; Ohanapecosh, (360) 569-2211 ext. 2353; Sunrise and White River (360) 663-2425 or (360) 663-2272.

Four of the places where the trail meets a road are at or near drive-in campgrounds or visitor centers where there are at least a few comforts of civilization. Aside from those drive-in campgrounds, camping along the trail is allowed only at 20 designated campsites, and permits for specific trailside camping must be obtained in advance. Forty percent of the permits may be obtained free no more than 24 hours before the start of the trip. The other 60 percent may be reserved for a fee up to 60 days in advance. During the height of the hiking season there are times when campsites are full and no more permits are issued. Off-trail, cross-country hiking also is allowed under certain conditions. Check with a park office for specifics.

The trail includes many up-hill and down-hill miles, so that a hike over the full length will include a cumulative elevation gain of about 20,000 feet, some of it more than a little steep. There also are some level places. Some of the route parallels roads, but most of it is far into the wilderness where the landscape is much like it was in Columbus's time, with only the trail itself to testify that people have been here before.

The landscape is magnificent. The trail passes the snouts of the Carbon, Tahoma, and Winthrop glaciers, all of them some 4 miles long. Sylvia and Martha waterfalls crash down the slope, and lakes shimmer in the summer sun. In the distance the immense volcanic rock of Willis Wall stretches some 4,000 feet high at the head of the Carbon Glacier. An ice cap hundreds of feet thick overhangs Willis Wall. From time to time an immense piece of the ice breaks loose and crashes down the rock face of the wall. Those avalanches are among the largest of Mount Rainier.

Indian Henry's Hunting Ground is one of the many high-country meadows where a succession of flowers bloom. By mid-July some 40 species bloom in the high country. Among the beauties to be seen along the trail are Valerian (*Valeriana sitchensis),* phlox *(Phlox diffusa*), marsh marigold (*Caltha leptosepala*), and bistort (*polygonum bistortoides).*

There is a large variety of wildlife here, including black bear, mountain goat, deer, marmot, coyote, chipmunk, pika, and harmless garter and rubber boa snakes.

Directions: Among the best accesses to the Wonderland Trail are the places where it crosses roads or passes campgrounds. Longmire is a good place to begin a Wonderland hike, so are Mowich Lake Campground and White River Campground.

Activities: Hiking, camping.

Facilities: Visitor centers and drive-in campgrounds are available sporadically along the trail.

Dates: Open summer.

Fees: There are fees for entry to the national park and for campsite reservations.

Closest town: Ashford, 6 miles from the Nisqually entrance to the park.

For more information: Mount Rainier National Park, Ashford, WA 98304-9751. Phone 360-569-2111.

Trail: 93 miles, one-way.

Elevation: 4,200 foot elevation gain from the low point at Ipsut Creek (2,500 feet) to the high point at Skyscraper Pass (6,700 feet).

Degree of difficulty: Strenuous.

Chelan Summit Trails 1258 and 1259

This is a high-country trail that climbs to the crest of the mountains on the north side of Lake Chelan. It is so high and so deep in the mountains that only rarely does it offer a glimpse of the lake. Once this area had a significant number of big horn sheep (*Ovis canadensis*), but about the turn of the twentieth century shepherds moved in with domestic sheep, which, biologists believe, carried diseases that were fatal to their wild cousins. Eventually the natives died out. In 1999, the Forest Service and other agencies bought up the perpetual domestic-sheep grazing permit of the shepherds and began a program of transplanting big horns from other places. If the reintroduction is successful, hikers here may be able to get a glimpse of the magnificent animals in their natural habitat, perhaps even witness their spring mating ritual when the rams butt the immense horns on their foreheads into each other with a bang that may be heard a mile away. That is how they decide which gets to mate with the ewes and the next spring the ewe will bear a single lamb on a high, narrow, protected ledge far in the backcountry.

The trail is purely a mountain route and is closed to motorized vehicles. The route begins at the Summer Blossom trailhead and follows Trail 1258 paralleling the crest of the Sawtooth-Chelan Ridge north of Lake Chelan for several miles, then it veers a little to the south of the ridge and intersects with Trail 1259. A right turn at the junction onto Trail 1259 leads into the Lake Chelan-Sawtooth Wilderness (*see* Lake Chelan-Sawtooth Wilderness, page 89) and then into the Lake Chelan National Recreation Area of the North Cascade National Park Complex (*see* Lake Chelan National Recreation Area, page 57).

The route continues to parallel the south side of the Lake Chelan-Sawtooth Crest undulating so that hikers are going either up or down much of the way, but the trail rarely gets below 5,500 feet and goes as high as 7,400 feet. The crest is in the rain shadow of the Cascade Mountain crest, so less snow falls here and it melts away earlier in the season than in other places of the backcountry. Here, hikers will find some subalpine forests but much of the hike is in meadows and there are numerous good campsites along the way. Stands of larch trees turn bright golden in the fall.

The route passes under many large peaks, including Switchback Peak, 8,321 foot elevation; Courtney Peak, 8,392 feet; and Star Peak, 8,690 feet. Much of the route is over rolling land that was carved smooth by the glaciers of the last Ice Age.

The trail intersects with the steep and rough Prince Creek Trail 1255 and the Fish Creek Trail 1248, which go down to Lake Chelan, allowing hikers to catch the excursion boats on the lake to shorten the hike (*see* Lake Chelan National Recreation Area, page 57).

The high-country hike begins to end at a saddle between War Creek Pass and Purple Pass, where hikers get their first good view of Lake Chelan and a choice of how to end the trip. They can turn right and hike 8 miles over War Creek Pass and down the War Creek Trail 408 to the War Creek Campground on the Twisp Road (Forest Road 44). There they can meet someone to drive them back to civilization. Or, they can turn left and go over Purple Pass and 8 miles down the Purple Creek Trail, where some really huge rattlesnakes live, to Stehekin Landing and the terminal of the excursion boats, which can take them back to the city of Chelan.

Directions: To reach the north trailhead, take State Route 150 northwest from Chelan for 2 miles, and bear right on Boyd Road, following the Echo Valley Ski Area signs to Cooper Gulch. Pass the ski area and take the left fork onto Forest Road 8020. Go 7 uphill miles to Cooper Mountain. Continue northwest on Forest Road 8020 along a ridge for approximately 20 miles to the Summer Mountain Trailhead and the beginning of Trail 1258. To start on the north end from the War Creek Trailhead, go 14 miles west of Twisp on Forest Road 44, (the northern Twisp River Road), pass the War Creek Campground, cross the bridge over the Twisp River, jog 0.5 mile north on Forest Road 4430, turn west on Forest Road 100 and drive to the trailhead at the end of the road. To start on the north end from the Purple Creek Trailhead, take an excursion boat from Chelan to Stehekin

Landing and find the Purple Creek Trailhead behind the landing.

Activities: Hiking, camping.

Facilities: There are full facilities at Stehekin Landing for those who begin or end their hike there. The other trailheads have no facilities.

Dates: Open summer.

Fees: A trailhead fee may be charged.

Closest town: From the Safety Harbor Creek trailhead, Manson, 40 miles; from War Creek trailhead, Twisp, 14.5 miles. Purple Creek trailhead is at Stehekin Landing.

For more information: Chelan Ranger Station, 428 Woodin Avenue, Rt. 2, Box 680, Chelan, WA 98816. Phone (509) 682-2576. Or Methow Valley Ranger District, 502 Glover, Twisp, WA 98856. Phone (509) 997-2131.

Trail: 38 miles, one-way.

Elevation: 3,000 foot elevation gain.

Degree of difficulty: Strenuous.

SEGO LILY
(Calochortus nuttallii)
This lily is the state flower of Utah, designated as such because of their edible bulbs' role in keeping pioneer Mormons from starving.

Mt. Adams Round The Mountain Trails 183, 9, 2000, and 114

This is really four, separate interconnecting trails, including a stretch of the Pacific Crest National Scenic Trail 2000. The route leads hikers through the high country around the south, west, and north sides of Mount Adams. It omits the east side of the mountain because that is part of the Yakama Indian Reservation. That area is so dangerous that the tribe does not issue hiking permits for the full circuit of the mountain.

The route begins on Trail 183 and goes about 1 mile to the wilderness boundary. A short distance beyond the boundary, Trail 183 intersects with Trail 9, where the Round the Mountain hike begins. Turning right and walking about 2 miles on Trail 9 takes hikers to the boundary between the national forest and the Yakama Indian Reservation. To the left of where Trails 183 and 9 intersect, Trail 9 undulates along the southern flank of Mount Adams through subalpine forest and meadows. There are occasional long views as well as access to moraines and glaciers. At about 5 miles from Trail 183, the route reaches Horseshoe Meadow where it joins the Pacific Crest Trail 2000. At a high point near that junction there is a viewpoint that looks out over a wide range of peaks, including Mount Hood.

The route follows the Pacific Crest Trail for about 6 miles along the western and northwestern flanks of Mount Adams, passing attractions like Sheep Lake and the Mutton Creek Lava Flow. About 6 miles from the junction of Trail 183 and the Pacific Crest Trail is a junction where the Crest Trail passes the Killen Creek Trail 113 to the west and the High Camp Trail 10 to the east (*see* Killen Creek Trail 113, page 267). A 1-mile side trip on Trail 10 goes to the meadowland near the snout of the immense, crevasse-riddled Adams Glacier. A little northeast of the junction with Trail 10, the route forks to the right off the Pacific Crest Trail and onto Trail 114. It goes through a pleasant meadow called Foggy Flat, then climbs steeply toward the lava fields of Lava Glacier and another boundary of the Yakama Indian Reservation.

Along the way, the trail passes old-growth and subalpine forest, alpine meadows, lakes, glaciers, moraines, and lava fields. All of the trail is more than 1 mile in elevation, high enough so there are good views of distant mountains, including four volcanoes: Mount Hood, Mount Adams, Mount St. Helens, and Mount Rainier. A deposit of gritty, gray ash from the 1980 eruption of Mount St. Helens landed on Mount Adams and tends to get into hikers' gear. Plastic bags to protect food and other sensitive material from the ash might be a good idea. Water from the creeks tends to be muddy and should be allowed to settle before being boiled or otherwise treated.

The main attractions are the close-up views of Mount Adams with its tumbling glaciers flowing down from the 12,276 foot summit. Huge moraines mark the path of the glaciers as they retreated in times past. Some of the trail goes through country so high and rocky that the trail is difficult to find and is marked by cairns of rock piled up along the way. The weather at this elevation can be severe. Glacier-fed streams may be running high enough that crossing them is dangerous. Prudent hikers should consider turning back at that point.

Directions: Drive north from Trout Lake on the county road called the Mount Adams Recreation Highway, which also is Forest Road 17, for about 1.5 miles, then branch off onto Forest Road 80. About 5 miles from Trout Lake, veer right onto Forest Road 8040. Go about 7 miles to the Morrison Creek Horse Campground and turn right onto Forest Road 500. Go about 3 miles to the Cold Springs Campground and the trailhead.

Activities: Hiking, camping, horseback riding.

Facilities: None.

Dates: Open summer.

Fees: A trailhead fee may be charged.

Closest town: Trout Lake, 16 miles.

For more information: Mount Adams Ranger Station, 2455 Highway 141, Trout Lake, WA 98650. Phone (509) 395-3400.

Trail: 25 miles, one-way.

Elevation: 2,150 foot elevation gain.

Degree of difficulty: Strenuous.

Appendixes

A. Books and References

Agents of Chaos by Stephen L. Harris, Mountain Press Publishing Company, Missoula, MT, 1990.

Ape Cave by William R. Halliday, ABC Printing & Publishing, Vancouver, WA, 1983.

A Complete Guide to Mount St. Helens National Volcanic Monument, by Klindt Vielbig, The Mountaineers, 1997.

A Sierra Club Naturalist's Guide, The Pacific Northwest, by Stephen Whitney, Sierra Club Books, San Francisco, CA,1989.

A Visitors Guide to Ancient Forests of Washington by the Dittmer Family, The Mountaineers, in association with the Wilderness Society, Seattle, WA,1996.

A Year in Paradise by Floyd Schmoe, The Mountaineers, Seattle, WA, 1979.

Best Easy Day Hikes: North Cascades, by Eric Molvar, Falcon Publishing, Helena, MT, 1998.

Best Short Hikes in Washington's South Cascades and Olympics by E. M. Sterling, The Moutaineers, Seattle, WA, 1995.

Cascade-Olympic Natural History by Daniel Mathews, Raven Editions/Portland Audubon Society, Portland, OR, 1988.

Cascadia by Bates McKee, McGraw-Hill Book Company, New York, NY, 1972.

Exploring Mount Rainier by Ruth Kirk, University of Washington Press, Seattle, WA, 1969.

Geological Survey Professional Paper 1249, United States Government Printing Office, Washington, DC, 1984.

Hiking the North Cascades, by Dr. Fred T. Darvill, Jr. Stackpole Books, Mechanicsburg, PA, 1998.

Hiking Washington by Ron Adkison, Falcon Press, Helena, MT, 1993.

Island In The Sky, Pioneering Accounts of Mt. Rainier, 1833-1894 by Pat Schullery, The Mountaineers, Seattle, WA, 1987.

Lookouts by Ira Spring and Byron Fish, The Mountaineers, Seattle, WA 1981.

Mountain Bike Adventures in Washington's North Cascades and Olympics by Tom Kirkendall, The Mountaineers, Seattle, WA 1996.

Mount Rainier: The Story Behind the Scenery by Ray "Skip" Snow, KC Publications, Inc., Las Vegas, NV, 1984.

Mount St. Helens National Volcanic Monument Trail Guide, Northwest Interpretive Association in cooperation with the Gifford Pinchot National Forest.

National Audubon Society Pocket Guide: Familiar Mammals of North America, Alfred A. Knopf, Inc., New York, NY, 1995.

100 Hikes in Washington's Alpine Lakes by Vicky Spring, Ira Spring, and Harvey Manning, The Mountaineers, Seattle, WA, 1993.

100 Hikes in Washington's Glacier Peak Region: The North Cascades by Ira Spring and Harvey Manning, The Mountaineers, Seattle, WA 1996.

100 Hikes in Washington's North Cascades National Park by Ira Spring and Harvey Manning, The Mountaineers, Seattle, WA, 1985.

100 Hikes in Washington's South Cascades and Olympics by Ira Spring and Harvey Manning, The Mountaineers, Seattle, WA, 1992.

Pacific Northwest Hiking, by Ron C. Judd and Dan A. Nelson, Foghorn Press, San Francisco, CA, 1997

Roadside Geology of Washington by David D. Alt and Donald W. Hyndman, Mountain Press Publishing Company, Missoula, MT, 1984.

The Forest by Roger Caras, Holt, Rinehart, and Winston, New York, NY, 1979.

The Northwest Coast: A Natural History by Stewart T. Schultz, Timber Press, Inc., Portland, OR, 1990.

Northwest Trees by Stephen Arno and Ramona P. Hammerly, The Mountaineers, Seattle, WA, 1977.

The Pacific Crest Trail, Volume 2, Oregon & Washington by Jeffery P. Schaffer and Andy Selters, Wilderness Press, Berkeley, CA, 1990.

The Smithsonian Guides to Natural America: The Pacific Northwest by Daniel Jack Chasan, Smithsonian Books, Washington, DC/ Random House, New York, NY, 1995.

Trees: A Guide to Familiar American Trees by Herbert S. Zim and Alexander C. Martin, Golden Press, New York, NY, 1987.

12 Short Hikes: Mount Rainier National Park: Paradise by Jeff Smoot, Chokestone Press, Evergreen, CO, 1997.

12 Short Hikes: Mount Rainier Natonal Park: Sunrise by Jeff Smoot, Chokestone Press, Evergreen, CO, 1997.

Volcanic Eruptions of 1980 at Mount St. Helens: The first 100 Days by Bruce Foxworthy and Mary Hill, Geological Survey Professional Paper 1249, United States Government Printing Office, Washington, DC, 1984.

Washington's South Cascades Volcanic Landscapes by Marge and Ted Mueller, The Mountaineers, Seattle, WA, 1995.

Washington Wildlife Viewing Guide. by Joe La Tourrette, Falcon Press, Helena and Billings, MT, 1992.

Wildflowers of Mount Rainier and the Cascades by Mary Fries, The Mount Rainier Natural History Association and The Mountaineers, Seattle, WA, 1970.

B. Conservation & Outdoor Organizations

Abundant Life Seed Foundation. PO Box 772, 930 Lawrence, Port Townsend, WA 98368. Phone (360) 385-5660. Preserves and propagates seeds of Northwest indigenous plants, as well as nonhybrid vegetables, herbs, and flowers. The foundation also donates seeds, both nationally and internationally, to those in need. Seed distribution is done by mail-order catalog. Publications: *Seed and Book Catalog; Seed Midden.*

Adopt-A-Stream Foundation. 601 128 Street SE, Everett, WA 98208. Phone (425) 316-8592. Promotes stewardship of streams, watersheds and wetlands by local residents. Conducts training workshops, creates environmental curricula, and is developing an education facility. Publications: *Adopting a Stream: A Northwest Handbook; Adopting a Wetland: A Northwest Guide; A Streamkeeper's Field Guide.* Also produced a video featuring Bill Nye, the Science Guy, *The Streamkeeper.*

Chautauqua Northwest. 412 IBM Building, 1200 5th Avenue, Seattle, WA 98101. Phone (206) 223-1378. Teams of retired men and women volunteer to help scientists monitor programs for the state departments of ecology, fisheries, health, natural resources, and wildlife.

Earthstewards Network. PO Box 0697, Bainbridge Island, WA 98110. Phone (206) 842-7986. Uses urban forestry and rain forest reforestation projects to bring conflicting cultural groups together. Publications: *Earthstewards Handbook; Warriors of the Hearth; Earthstewards Newsletter; Essene Book of Meditations and Blessings.*

Federation of Western Outdoor Clubs. 512 Boylston Avenue. E., #106, Seattle, WA 98102. Phone (206) 322-3041. Has 45 affiliated clubs in the western states, Alaska, and British Columbia. Promotes proper use, enjoyment, and protection of America's outdoor resources. Publication: *Outdoors West.*

Greenhouse Action. 2120 N. 140 Street., Seattle, WA 98133. Phone (206) 361-0282. Uses public education and advocacy to promote the reduction of global warming and ozone depletion. Publications: *Warming Trends*

International Bicycle Fund. 4887 Columbia Drive. S., Seattle, WA 98108. Phone (206) 767-0848. Email: intlbike@scn.org. Addresses environmental issues including energy policies, land use, and health through promotion of alternative transportation and sustainable economic development. Publication: *IBF News.*

Issaquah Alps Trails Club. PO Box 351, Issaquah, WA 98027. Phone (206) 328-0480. Its goal is to promote and preserve open space and trails along the I-90 freeway corridor from Lake Washington to the area of the Cascades locally known as the Issaquah Alps. It seeks to perpetuate in the urban area working forests and wildlife habitats by acquiring land and development rights, and through zoning.

Long Live the Kings. 19435-184 Place NE, Woodinville, WA 98072. Phone (425) 788-6023. This non-membership group seeks to rebuild wild salmon populations and enhance their habitat in specific rivers. Publication: *Long Live the Kings Newsletter*

Marine Conservation Biology Institute. 15806 NE 47 Court, Redmond, WA 98052. Phone (425) 883-9014. Email: chorse@u.washington.edu. web site: www.mcbi.org. Promotes new multidisciplinary science of marine biology through workshops, popular and scientific press articles, and other such activities.

The Mountaineers. 300 3 Avenue W., Seattle, WA 98119. Phone (206) 284-6310. Club that organizes outdoor recreational opportunities and training, and works to protect the environment through community outreach, political activities, and education.

Northwest Conservation Act Coalition. 219 1 Avenue. S, Suite 100, Seattle, WA 98104. Phone (206) 621-0094. Email: ncac@nwenergy.org. Web site www.nwenergy.org/ncac. Regional coalition of public interest groups and progressive utilities that serves as a watchdog of the Northwest Conservation Act; works for clean, affordable energy; and advocates for both energy conservation and renewable resources, wild salmon, and low energy costs. Publication: *Northwest Conservation Act Report; Energy Activist; Plugging People into Power: Campaign Update.*

Northwest Ecosystem Alliance. 1421 Cornwall Avenue, Suite 201, Bellingham, WA 98225. Phone (360) 671-9950. Email: nwea@ecosystem.org. Aims to protect and restore Pacific Northwest wildlands. Publications: *Northwest Conservation: News and Priorities; Wild Salmon and Trout Action Plan; Of Wolves and Washington; Cascadia Wild; Protecting an International Ecosystem; Conservation Biology and National Forest Management in the Inland Northwest; A Handbook for Activists.*

Northwest Environment Watch. 1402 3 Avenue. #1127, Seattle, WA 98101. Phone (206) 447-2270. Email: new@northwestwatch.org. Web site: www.northwestwatch.org. Fosters economic and environmental sustainability in the region by providing citizens with intelligence reports on the latest natural and social sciences findings, and providing guidance for citizens to create sustainability. Publications: *State of the Northwest; This Place on Earth; The Car and The City; Stuff; Misplaced Blame.*

Northwest Interpretive Association. 909 1 Avenue, Suite 630, Seattle, WA 98104. Phone (206) 220-4140. Supports education and interpretation on public lands administered by the National Park Service, U.S. Forest Service, and various Pacific Northwest agencies.

Pacific Northwest Trail Association. 1361 Avon Allen Road, Mount Vernon, WA 98273. Phone (360) 424-0407. Promotes the establishment of a continuous horse and foot trail from the Continental Divide to the Pacific Ocean. Publications: *Nor'wester; Pacific Northwest Trail; Blanchard Hill and Chuckanut Mountain Map.*

Rivers Council of Washington. 1731 Westlake Avenue N., Suite 202, Seattle, WA 98109. Phone (206) 283-4988. Email: riverswa@brigadoon.com. Works toward the restoration and preservation of the state's rivers and watersheds by developing local grassroots organizations. Publication: *Washington Rivers.*

Sierra Club. 1516 Melrose Avenue., Seattle, WA 98122. Phone (206) 621-1696. Local chapter of national organization aimed at the preservation and continued expansion of wilderness land.

Trout Unlimited, Washington Council. 2401 Bristol Court, SW, Olympia, WA 98502. Phone (360) 754-2131. Email: kbob@halycon.com. Works to enhance and protect coldwater fisheries in the state, with 31 local chapters. Publication: *Trout and Salmon Leader.*

Washington Bass Chapter Federation. 16569 162nd Place S.E., Renton, WA 98058. Phone (425) 271-6569. Dedicated to the realistic conservation of water resources through pollution control, assisting state and national conservation agencies, and a teaching program.

Washington Environmental Council. 615 2 Avenue, #380, Seattle, WA 98104. Phone (206) 622-8103. Email: greenwec@aol.com. Dedicated to preserving, protecting, and restoring the Pacific Northwest's environment, this organization has over 100 affiliated organizations. Publications: *WEC Voices; Forest Resources News.*

Washington Native Plant Society. PO Box 28690, Seattle, WA 98118. Phone (206) 760-8022. Dedicated to the preservation of state native plants and the habitats they depend on. Works through study and education. Publication: *Douglasia.*

Washington Recreation and Park Association. 350 S. 333 Street, Suite 103, Federal Way, WA 98003. Phone (253) 874-1283. Works to enhance parks, recreation, and leisure activities in the state, and promote public support for parks and recreation. Publication: *Syllabus.*

Washington Trails Association. 1305 4 Avenue, #512, Seattle, WA 98101. Phone (206) 625-1367. Involved in trail planning, management, and maintenance in order to protect and enhance the state's trail systems. Also offers education and information programs.

Washington Wilderness Coalition. 4649 Sunnyside Avenue N., #242, Seattle, WA 98103. Phone (206) 633-1992. Email: wawild@aol.com. Offers outreach, public education and support of grassroots conservation groups in order to preserve the wilderness areas and biodiversity of the region for future generations. Publication: *Washington Wildfire.*

Washington Wildlife and Recreation Coalition. 4001 SW Cloverdale, Seattle, WA 98136. Phone (206) 938-4513. Supports the acquisition of public land through public education, legislation, and research into the need for wildlife and conservation. Publication: *Land News.*

Wildlife Society, Washington Chapter. U.S. Fish and Wildlife Service, 3704 Griffin Lane SE, Suite 102, Olympia, WA 98501. Phone (360) 753-4325. Provides support and training for professional wildlife biologists, as well as a forum for presenting research results and management ideas. Publication: *Wildlife Society Washington Chapter Newsletter.*

YMCA Earth Service Corps. 909 4 Avenue, Seattle, WA 98104. Phone (206) 382-5013. Students work with teachers and Y staff on community environmental projects, including tree plantings and recycling, in order to learn to be effective global citizens. Publication: *Only Green World.*

C. Outfitters and Guides

For current information on outfitters and guides who work in Washington's Cascade Mountains contact the following association:

The Washington Outfitters and Guides Association
110 W. Sixth Avenue, Number 398
Ellensburg, WA 98926
Phone (509) 962-4222 or, toll free, (877) 275-9642.

D. Special Events, Fairs, and Festivals

JANUARY

Columbia River Circuit Rodeo Finals—Finalists in events ranging from bull riding to barrel racing compete to see who's best. Yakima. Phone (509) 454-3663.

Methow Pursuit—Cross-country ski event, awards, prizes, refreshments. Winthrop. Phone (509) 996-3287.

Bavarian Ice Fest—Bavarian Alps village puts on a weekend of fun with dog sled contests and rides, activities for kids, and a fireworks display. Leavenworth. Phone (509) 548-5807.

Kids & Critters Naturefest—Northwest Trek Wildlife Park takes a look at indigenous predators and their prey. Eatonville. Phone (360) 832-7152.

Fire and Ice Winterfest—Get warm cross-country skiing. Then cool off in the Polar Bear Splash. Alternative activities include a chili cook-off, and games. Lake Chelan. Phone (800)424-3526.

Rendezvous Mountain Tour—35K cross-country ski race. Winthrop. Phone (509) 966-3287.

FEBRUARY

Fasching—Dancing in the streets to live music, parties at participating restaurants, and a best costume contest. Leavenworth. Phone (509) 548-5807.

Teddy Roosevelt Trek—Tram tours feature a professional actor entertaining (and educating) as T.R., the country's first conservationist president. Northwest Trek Wildlife Park. Eatonville. Phone (360) 832-7152.

Washington's Birthday Celebration—This traditional celebration also marks the beginning of Indian people's root harvest and includes includes ceremonial dancing, crafts, arts, and foods. Toppenish. Phone (509) 865-2800 or (509) 865-5121.

Race of the Methow—Classic 5K and 10K cross-country ski races. Winthrop. Phone (509) 996-3287.

White Pass Winter Carnival—Fun in the white stuff, with snow sculptures, a costume contest, live music, and wine tastings. White Pass. Phone (509) 453-8731.

MARCH

Speelyi-Mi Indian Arts and Crafts Fair—Featuring traditional, heirloom, and modern native crafts and arts. Toppenish. Phone (509) 865-5121.

APRIL

Ridge to River Relay—Ski, run, bike, canoe, and kayak for glory and fun, this race from ridge to river is aimed at both recreational and serious athletes. Wenatchee. Phone (509) 662-8799.

Festival of the Rain—Along with deciding the "Biggest Drip" around, this festival features a fun run as well as arts, crafts, and food. Stevenson. Phone (800) 989-9178.

MAY

Maifest—Bavarian village of the Cascades welcomes spring with a grand march, Bavarian dances, oompah music, and a plethora of beautiful flowers. Leavenworth. Phone (509) 548-5807.

49er Days—Parade and coronation of the 49er queen tops off the program. Winthrop. Phone (509) 996-2125.

Boneshaker Mountain Bike Races—The name "Boneshaker" says it all about these downhill and cross-country bike races. Prizes and awards to those who make it downhill first—and in one piece. Winthrop. Phone (509) 996-3287.

Baby Shower—The arrival of the season's crop of new baby animals is the focus at Northwest Trek Wildlife Park. The shower includes tours of animal feedings. Eatonville. Phone (360) 832-7152.

Ski to Sea Race—This relay race features eight-member teams racing from Mt. Baker to Bellingham Bay on skis, road bikes, canoes, mountain bikes, and sea kayaks. Pick your favorite sport and watch the fun. Bellingham. Phone (360) 734-1330.

JUNE

Craft Fair—Northwest craftsmen and women exhibit their wares, and demonstrate how they make them. Leavenworth. Phone (509)548-5807.

Yakama Nation Treaty Day— Indians from around the region gather to observe the Yakama Nation treaty with an Indian rodeo and powwow. White Swan. Phone (509) 865-5121.

Kinderfest—A festival for children. Leavenworth. Phone (509) 548-5807.

Deming Logging Show—One of the few such shows left in a region once renowned for its logging activities. Hundreds of loggers challenge each other to see who's the best at spar climbing, cutting events, relay races, and log rolling. Deming. Phone (360) 592-3051.

Women in the Wilderness—Women learn backcountry etiquette and outdoor survival skills—including how to cook with a Dutch oven—at a three-day women's workshop. Cle Elum. Phone (425) 392-6107.

International Folk Dance Performance—Beautifully costumed folk dancers give live performances. Leavenworth. Phone (509) 548-5807.

Wildflower Festival—The home of one of those defunct logging shows, this festival is dedicated to the region's abundant supply of wildflowers. It features slide shows, seminars, educational booths as well as arts, crafts, and food. Darrington. Phone (888) 338-0976.

Timber Bowl Rodeo—Major rodeo events. Darrington. Phone (888) 338-0976.

JULY

Pioneer Days— A logging heritage festival with a hearty pioneer breakfast, a parade, a street fair and dance, a 10K race, and logging events. If you were a fan of the television show *Northern Exposure*, Roslyn was the stand-in for Cicely, Alaska. Cle Elum and Roslyn. Phone (509) 674-5958.

Slug Festival— Celebrate our native banana slug population by attending the one and only Slug Festival. Features slug races, in which you can be a slug jockey! Eatonville. Phone (360) 832-7152.

Birthday Cake Bash—Northwest Trek Wildlife Park's annual Birthday Party features cakes for animals and visitors and hay bale cake for the bison. Eatonville. Phone (360) 832-7152.

Bluegrass Festival—Bluegrass music aimed at the whole family, with camping, food, and crafts. Darrington. Phone (888) 338-0976.

Rhythm and Blues Festival—The oldest rhythm and blues festival in the state, features national and regional acts. The festival also includes nonjuried crafts, food, and wine. Winthrop. Phone (509) 997-2541.

Old-Time Fiddlers—Playin' their hearts out. Arlington. Phone (360) 403-9170.

Columbia Gorge Bluegrass Festival— The best Northwest bluegrass bands perform at concerts and dances. Stevenson. Phone (509) 427-8928.

Klickitat Canyon Days—This timber carnival has a fun run, parade, tournaments, arts, crafts, and food. Klickitat. Phone (509) 369-2322.

Eagle Spirit Celebration—Native Americans join in a song and dance competition. The celebration also includes food, arts, and crafts. White Swan. Phone (509) 865-5121.

AUGUST

Trout Lake Community Fair Days—Music and talent show, as well as a parade, fun run, and various and sundry contests. Trout Lake. Phone (509) 395-2900.

Festival of the River—The Stillaguamish River becomes the center of festivities of local Native American tribes. Arlington. Phone (360) 652-7362.

Northwest Washington Fair—An old-fashioned state fair, featuring produce, animals, home crafts, carnival rides, food, fun, and some great music. Lynden. Phone (360) 354-4111.

Big Foot Daze—Does Big Foot really exist? Catch up on Big Foot lore with discussions addressing issues surrounding the sightings. Or just eat a lot of Big Foot Burgers and listen to the live music. Carson. Phone (509) 427-4441.

SEPTEMBER

Mountain Triathlon—The triathlon features individuals, or two- to three-person teams taking on a 1K lake swim, 15K bike ride, and 8K run on the Sun Mountain Trail System.

Winthrop. Phone (509) 996-3287.

Wenatachee River Salmon Festival—Events and activities are geared toward the whole family at this celebration of the return of the salmon. Leavenworth. Phone (509) 548-5807.

Washington State Autumn Leaf Festival—Although Washington is the Evergreen State, deciduous trees do exist, and come fall, they put on an astonishing and colorful display. Leavenworth is a focal point, and this festival offers a parade, entertainment, including street dancing and oompah music, and food. But the trip there alone is worth it. Leavenworth. Phone (509) 548-5807.

OCTOBER

Washington State Autumn Leaf Festival—*see* above.

White Swan Indian Summer Celebration—Arts, crafts, music, and dancing. White Swan. Phone (509) 865-5121.

Methow Valley Mountain Bike Festival—Enjoy the fall color with rides, bike races, a kids' bike rodeo, and a salmon dinner. Winthrop. Phone (509) 996-3287.

Harvest Moon Festival—Tours of fall's colorful leaves and a crafts fair combine at this festival. Cle Elum. Phone (509) 674-5958.

NOVEMBER

Christkindlmarkt—Booths full of Christmas gift and food items. This event is modeled on the Christmas markets seen throughout Germany. Leavenworth. Phone (509) 548-5807.

Christmas in Cle Elum—The town gets in the holiday spirit with a tree lighting, carols, sleigh rides, a visit from Santa, and a live nativity scene. Cle Elum. Phone (509) 674-5958.

Christmas Tree Lighting Ceremony—Santa does the honors at the annual tree lighting. The day also includes train rides, free candy, and entertainment. Granite Falls. Phone (360) 691-6441.

DECEMBER

Christmas in the Gorge—A Christmas mystery hunt and a nighttime fire truck parade, along with pictures with Santa, caroling, arts and crafts, and food. Stevenson. Phone (800) 989-9178.

Christmas Bazaar and All-Indian Talent Show—Toppenish. Phone (509) 865-5121.

Christmas Lighting—Leavenworth turns on its Christmas tree lights and provides other activities, too, such as sledding in the park, sleigh rides, and caroling. Leavenworth. Phone (509) 548-5807.

Western Christmas Light Parade—Lights adorn everything in this nighttime parade—from wagons drawn by horses and mules to farm equipment, floats, and individual riders. Toppenish. Phone (800) 569-3982.

Ski Rodeo—Cross-country freestyle races. Mazama. Phone (509) 996-3287.

Toppenish Creek New Year's Celebration—Native American song and dance, including contest dancing, and a masquerade parade welcome in the New Year. Toppenish. Phone (509) 865-5121.

G. Glossary

Algae—Plants that grow in water and contain chlorophyll.

Anadromous fish—Fish that hatch in fresh water, migrate to the sea to mature, then return to breed in the freshwater site where they hatched.

Andesite—Usually gray or brown volcanic rock with a high silica content.

Ashfall—Volcanic ash that rains from the cloud of a volcanic eruption.

Ash flow—Hot gas and ash flowing from a volcanic vent.

Archaeology—The scientific study of ancient cultures.

Basalt—A fine-grained, dark, volcanic rock with a heavy content of magnesium and iron.

Bacteria—Unicellular microorganisms that may cause disease in plants or animals.

Chlorophyll—Green matter that is essential to the photosynthesis process of plants.

Cirque—A circular recess caused by glacial erosion on a mountain.

Clear-cut—The practice of harvesting all the trees in a given area at the same time.

Col—A pass between mountain peaks or in a ridge, often caused by cirques forming on both sides of the ridge.

Conifer—Evergreen, cone-bearing trees and shrubs.

Continental ice flow—A glacier that covers a large area of a continent.

Dacite—A usually light-colored volcanic rock with a high silica content.

Deciduous—Plants that lose their leaves on a seasonal basis and are leafless until they grow new leaves.

Ecology—Scientific study of the interrelationship of organisms and their environment.

Environment—The conditions and circumstances that surround organisms or groups of organisms.

Evergreen—Plants with foliage that remains green throughout the year.

Extinct—A plant or animal species that no longer exists or a volcano that no longer is active.

Fauna—Animals of a specific period or region.

Folded—Rock warped or tilted by internal earth forces.

Fumarole—A vent in the earth's surface that allows steam or gas to escape into the atmosphere.

Forest canopy—The upper level of trees in a forest.

Fungi—A simple plant that lacks chlorophyll.

Geography—The science that deals with the topography of the earth's surface.

Geology—The science that deals with the origin of the earth's crust and its rocks.

Glacier—A large body of ice formed of compacted snow that is forced to move by its own weight.

Glaciated valley—A valley carved or changed by glacial action.

Gneiss—A metamorphic rock consisting of light and dark bands.

Granite—Coarse igneous rock made up primarily of feldspar and quartz.

Grass—Any of many plants with jointed stems, seed-like fruit, and slender, sheathing sleeves.

Herb—A flowering plant whose stem does not produce persistent, woody tissue.

Igneous—Rock formed when magma solidifies.

Juan de Fuca Plate—A small segment of the Pacific Ocean tectonic plate that is being subducted under the Pacific Northwest shore.

Lava—Magma that has been erupted onto the surface of the earth.

Lichens—Composite organisms formed by the symbiotic union of fungus and algae growing on trees or rocks.

Magma—Molten rock inside the earth.

Mammals—Warm-blooded, vertebrate animals that nourish their young with milk from the females' mammary glands.

Meadow—An area of land where grasses and other low growing plants predominate.

Metamorphic rock—Rock changed by heat and pressure from the earth's interior or by chemical processes.

Millennia—Periods of 1,000 years.

Moraine—A ridge of fragmented rock left when a glacier recedes.

Mudflow—Rock debris saturated by water flowing downhill as a result of volcanic action.

Nonvascular—Organisms lacking the ability to efficiently circulate-life giving fluids.

Outcrop—Bedrock that protrudes out of the earth.

Peneplain—A surface area reduced by erosion to a near plain.

Plate tectonics—A theory that large slabs of the earth's outer shell float on the molten rock beneath and are in constant motion.

Pollination—The transfer of pollen from an anther to a stigma as part of the reproductive process of flowers.

Prevailing wind—Wind that usually blows from the same direction because of atmospheric conditions.

Pyroclastic flow—An avalanche of hot, incandescent rock fragments mixed with hot gas that flows from an erupting volcano.

Rapids—A fast moving stream caused by a steep descent of the stream bed and often associated with rocks and boulders that impede the flow.

Rush—Grasslike, stiff marsh herbs with hollow or pithy stems and small flowers, used to make baskets. Also various similar plants.

Saprophyte—An organism, usually bacterium or fungus, that derives nourishment directly from dead or decaying matter it grows on.

Sedge—Grasslike plants of the family that has solid stems, leaves that grow in three vertical rows and inconspicuous flowers surrounded by scalelike bract.

Sedimentary rock—Rock formed of sediment of older rock, or the remains of plants or animals.

Shrub—A low, woody plant with multiple stems rising from the base, and lacking a main trunk.

Snow field—A permanent or semipermanent field of snow that lacks the characteristic movement of glaciers.

Species—A classification of organisms that ranks below genus or subgenus. Members of the same species are capable of interbreeding.

Stratovolcano—A volcano made up of layers of fragmented material and lava flows.

Talus—Broken rock that has fallen from a cliff and accumulated at the bottom.

Understory—Plant life growing beneath the dominant trees of the forest.

Vascular—Organisms with vessels that circulate life-giving fluids.

Vent—An opening in the earth surface that emits lava, volcanic ash, or gas.

Index